Jane Brown is the author of seventeen books on varied subjects, including Vita Sackville-West, Gertrude Jekyll, Edwin Lutyens, Henrietta Luxborough and Lancelot 'Capability' Brown, and the critically acclaimed classic *Gardens of a Golden Afternoon* (Penguin, 1985). All of her earlier books inform *Angel Dorothy*. Jane has lectured in the UK and in America, and she enjoyed a Harvard fellowship for her book *Beatrix* (Viking, 1995), a biography of the landscape architect Beatrix Farrand. She has also curated exhibitions and written garden histories for three Cambridge colleges.

ANGEL DOROTHY

How an American Progressive Came to Devon

JANE BROWN

This edition first published in 2017

Unbound
6th Floor Mutual House, 70 Conduit Street, London W1S 2GF

www.unbound.com

Text Design by PDQ

Art Direction by Mark Ecob

A CIP record for this book is available from the British Library

ISBN 978-1-78352-314-6 (trade hbk)
ISBN 978-1-78352-315-3 (ebook)
ISBN 978-1-78352-316-0 (limited edition)

Printed by Clays Ltd, St Ives plc

1 2 3 4 5 6 7 8 9

'I doubt the accuracy of the reporting. Nobody has ever recorded a miracle accurately... How could it have happened that Fate should have placed an immense fortune in the hands of a woman so brave, so true, so beautiful as Dorothy Straight? A real angel.'

—Alvin Johnson in 1952, recalling the founding of *The New Republic* in 1913

In Memoriam
William Knight Elmhirst, 1929–2016

Dear Reader,

The book you are holding came about in a rather different way to most others. It was funded directly by readers through a new website: Unbound. Unbound is the creation of three writers. We started the company because we believed there had to be a better deal for both writers and readers. On the Unbound website, authors share the ideas for the books they want to write directly with readers. If enough of you support the book by pledging for it in advance, we produce a beautifully bound special subscribers' edition and distribute a regular edition and e-book wherever books are sold, in shops and online.

This new way of publishing is actually a very old idea (Samuel Johnson funded his dictionary this way). We're just using the internet to build each writer a network of patrons. Here, at the back of this book, you'll find the names of all the people who made it happen.

Publishing in this way means readers are no longer just passive consumers of the books they buy, and authors are free to write the books they really want. They get a much fairer return too – half the profits their books generate, rather than a tiny percentage of the cover price.

If you're not yet a subscriber, we hope that you'll want to join our publishing revolution and have your name listed in one of our books in the future. To get you started, here is a £5 discount on your first pledge. Just visit unbound.com, make your pledge and type **angel** in the promo code box when you check out.

Thank you for your support,

Dan, Justin and John
Founders, Unbound

CONTENTS

Author's Notes   xv

Introduction   1

One: Gilded Angel   8

Two: 'Dorothy Always Takes the Hard Chair'   19

Three: 'Destiny and Intricate Affairs'   39

Four: Porcelain and Polished Marble   58

Five: 'DWS, the Argosy of Grace'   81

Six: 'All Things Change'   99

Seven: A School 'Such as Has Not Happened Yet'   115

Eight: 'The Yeast in the Leaven', the Arts Come to Devon   129

Nine: 1935, Sitting for Mr Beaton in Her Schiaparelli Hat   147

Ten: Mischa and *The Possessed*   167

Eleven: The Children of Light   187

Twelve: 'The Hasting Day'   215

Thirteen: The Time of Few Flowers   238

Sources and Further Reading   268

Endnotes   274

Acknowledgements   318

List of Images   320

Index of Persons   322

Supporters   330

ANGEL DOROTHY

AUTHOR'S NOTES

The image of the galleon used at the opening of the American chapters is taken from Herbert Croly's 1920 sketch for the masthead of *The New Republic*. The badge of King Richard II – the white hart set on the Red Rose of Lancaster – used at the opening of the English chapters is from a photograph of a ceiling boss found at Dartington Hall in the 1920s. Dorothy's Whitney bloodline was traced back to Edward III by Henry Melville, thus she was descended from King Richard II, though she would never have mentioned this.

Dorothy was an avid diary-keeper. The early diaries and notebooks she brought with her when she came to England in 1925, as well as those she kept until her final year, 1968, are in the Papers of Dorothy Whitney Elmhirst 1914–1968, in the Devon Record Office, see endnotes 228, 230, 243, 276 *et seq*. These small and fragile diaries, the key to her life of activity, have formed the bedrock of this book; in quoting from them I have preserved Dorothy's original writing rather than attempting to correct her.

INTRODUCTION

Dorothy's story is an alternative history of more than half of the twentieth century. It is a feminine, not feminist, history, closely following her own record of her life of incessant activity. Here are some truths, truly 'stranger than fiction', that did not need fictionalising, though my readers may find themselves in scenes reminiscent of Henry James, which the passage of time melds into situations found in the novels of Nancy Mitford.

Dorothy Whitney was born within a whisper of the White House and it was confidently expected that she would live there herself one day; she was an orphan at seventeen, and started to give her energies and her money to help the emigrants crowding into New York's Lower East Side and to other radical and reforming causes. As Dorothy Straight she financed an influential liberal paper of opinion (which was to last for one hundred years), and as she and her husband Willard were political favourites it seemed likely that her destiny would be fulfilled. Many of her admirers thought that she should be the first female president of the United States.

The Great War and Willard Straight's death ended all her hopes. She was left with a remnant belief in the power of education to change society, inspired by the progressive methods of John Dewey, with whom she had campaigned for international disarmament, and also for the defence of Sacco and Vanzetti, which failed.

1

In 1925 she married an Englishman, Leonard Elmhirst, so committing herself to a life spent on two continents; she was to make almost one hundred crossings of the Atlantic by sea and air. In Devon they set up the Dartington Experiment to revive farming and the related rural industries to build a community embracing her progressive school. Dorothy's fortune enabled these enterprises to prosper for more than five years, employing a hundred local people, and sometimes twice that number, until Dartington was organised into a limited company and a charitable trust in the early 1930s.

To enrich community life Dorothy introduced studios for art and design, drama and contemporary dance; to stimulate efforts and Dartington's reputation she 'courted' and supported the potter Bernard Leach, the actors Paul Robeson and Peggy Ashcroft, the painter Ben Nicholson, the sculptor Barbara Hepworth and the composer Benjamin Britten, to name but a few. As the political mood of the 1930s darkened she unhesitatingly found housing and employment for dozens of refugees from Germany. In her war work in America (accompanied by Leonard Elmhirst) and in England (on her own) she was embroiled for months of speaking and travelling in the cause of the 'Special Relationship' between the Allies, on anything but a primrose path.

Dorothy was sixty in 1947; she encouraged the post-war revivals at Dartington, especially of the musical life under Imogen Holst and the establishment of the College of Arts with Peter Cox as principal. She played her part as consort to her now distinguished husband and as a grandmother, and she enjoyed her garden, which gave pleasure to all who found their way there. She was seriously ill in 1955, but 'the warm-hearted Elmhirsts', as they were known, continued their benevolent influences on the social and cultural life of Britain in unnumbered ways. They discreetly and politely declined the honours that were offered. Dorothy died at Dartington in December 1968; Leonard married Dr Susanna Isaacs and they went to live in California, where he died in 1974.

My first visits to Dartington were at that time; beside me now is a copy of *Dartington Hall and its Work*, published in 1976. It is a

2

booklet of few words and many plainly informative black and white photographs of the place and some of the people, of the school, the Tweed Mill, Staverton Joinery and Dartington Glass, of the activities of the College of Arts, outreach to youth clubs and adult education, and to the welfare of the very young and the elderly. The tone is more practical than utopian, and refreshingly welcoming, telling visitors where they are free to wander rather than where they are not; no ticket kiosk barred the approach to the Great Hall nor to Dorothy's beautiful garden. Her memory was fiercely protected by the many Dartingtonians who had known and loved her, and her legacy – her papers and books, her art collection and her home – were all intact and well guarded. She had not wanted her story told, it was said, and in that timeless and enchanted place, there seemed no need.

However, on the other side of the Atlantic things were different, and the Pulitzer Prize-winning author W.A. Swanberg had become fascinated by the youthful Dorothy while he was writing about her father. His book, *Whitney Father, Whitney Heiress*, published by Scribner's in 1980, had a dedication, 'Blessings on Dorothy'. It is a flamboyant society saga of the Gilded Age, the excesses of avarice and ambitions all redeemed by one 'princess'. Swanberg leaves his princess in 1919 as she faces up to her widowhood; perhaps like many of her friends he is dumbfounded at her decision to leave America for England and is unable to follow.

With the benefit of his own experience as part of her extended family at Dartington, and to put the record straight, Michael Young published *The Elmhirsts of Dartington* in 1982. His affection for Dorothy is revealed but the book is dominated by the philosophy of Dartington and the character of Leonard Elmhirst, to whom Young (later Lord Young of Dartington) was ideologically devoted.

In another part of the wood my first two books were also published in 1982, *The Everywhere Landscape* and *Gardens of a Golden Afternoon* (the story of the partnership of Edwin Lutyens and Gertrude Jekyll). I wrote *Vita's Other World* (1985) without discovering that Vita Sackville-West and Dorothy had a lightweight friendship, visiting each other's gardens several times through twenty years. If any thought crossed my mind it was that Sissinghurst was so outrageously famous, while Dartington was very little known, both gardens reflecting the minds of their mistresses. A commission to write about Lanning Roper, the much-loved American gardener who worked in Britain, and who had died in 1983, sent me to stay with his sister-in-law Laura Wood Roper in Washington. Laura, the biographer of Frederic Law Olmsted (of Central Park fame), was a formidable, well-connected and very dear person, who mixed huge whiskey sours; she gave me an American home for whenever I needed it and introduced me to her friends, one of whom was Belinda Straight, Dorothy's former daughter-in-law. The ambience and talk of Laura's home in Georgetown had not changed for twenty-five years or longer, there were echoes from Camelot, and the America of Dorothy's last visits. It was a short walk up the hill to Dumbarton Oaks, the garden masterpiece of Dorothy's older friend Beatrix Farrand, whose English and European travels and her own hard work had established her as a successful landscape architect. I must confess to a 'mystical moment' at the Oaks after hours in the library reading Beatrix's letters when I paused halfway down the stairs and looked out over the snow-covered garden – seeing, or rather feeling, her encouraging presence.

From that moment serendipity took over, expressed by one of Laura's most distinguished friends who had known Beatrix. After quite a severe grilling over my intentions he stood up to leave, saying, 'Well, she's just been sitting here waiting for you, hasn't she?' I paid a return visit to the University of California at Berkeley where Farrand's Reef Point Gardens Collection of drawings and other belongings are held; 'return' because the archive includes Gertrude Jekyll's drawings which were rescued from wartime England on Farrand's behalf, and were part of my research in 1979 for *Gardens of a Golden Afternoon*. Buoyed by the warmth and enthusiasm of American friends and strangers I searched out Beatrix's gardens from Maine to Virginia and back again, and along the way came across Dorothy's places, not only the remnants of her beloved Old Westbury home but the other Long Island and

New England haunts that meant so much to her. These adventures feature in 'How This Book came to be Written' in the early pages of *Beatrix*, which was published in New York in 1995.

Several years later, for *Spirits of Place* in 2001, I was at Dartington for the Ways With Words festival, speaking in the Barn Theatre; it was a sunny morning and we all lingered on the lawn afterwards. I remember being introduced to a group of people, which included William Elmhirst, Dorothy's youngest son, and his wife Heather. Over convivial lunches, literary festival conversations tend to run on well-worn paths:

'What are you working on now?' – followed by, 'Why don't you write about so-and-so?'

Dorothy's name floated across the lunch table towards me – what is a writer if not suggestible? In her garden afterwards almost everyone I met attested to her guardian spirit surviving in that place.

While working on other books my curiosity about Dorothy led me on to gain the permission of the Dartington trustees to research in their archive; William Elmhirst was characteristically kind and generous with his papers and memories, and I was fortunate to gain brief blessings from Michael Straight, James Cornford and Lord Young. At almost every stage I was astounded at the story, Dorothy's story, that was revealed, soon followed by disbelief and not a little fury that my long and detailed book proposal attracted only publishers' rejections. 'No one knows who she is,' they said, 'and now celebrities are all the rage.' It was a catch-22.

Change of tactics. Soon after their arrival in England in the spring of 1925, Dorothy and Leonard had driven to Stratford-upon-Avon, visited Shakespeare's grave and Clifford Chambers and gone on to visit Mary Anderson de Navarro and her American friends at Broadway. The purchase of Dartington was not going well; was Clifford Manor an alternative? Dorothy had been an ardent Shakespeare fan since her schooldays, he was essential to her image of England, and his countryside sprinkled with genial gardening Americans was attractive, in contrast to chilly conservative Devon, where she, quite rightly, feared rebuffs. This diary whim led me to Sarah Hosking's cottage refuge for women writers, which shares an ancient wall, 'O wall, O sweet and lovely wall', with Clifford's churchyard. My 2010 Hosking Houses Trust bursary, and the conviviality and inspiring conversations in Sarah's gift, encouraged me to write about Dorothy by giving her Thisby's cue, 'she is to enter now, and I am to spy her through the wall', and to see her life through the words of Shakespeare's heroines. This *Dorothy*, an essay fronted by Cecil Beaton's 1935 portrait and elegantly designed and set by Libanus Press, was published in 2011.

William Elmhirst wrote that he was 'thrilled to bits' with this *Dorothy* and the 'poetic treatment' of his mother's life, and 'she' was widely circulated and admired. I suppose his verdict released the catch of my nervousness at writing about his mother, to whom he was so devoted and spiritually close. I sat down to write the 'big book', which took me over a year and amounted to a hundred and twenty thousand words. This was read by colleagues and friends and revised, and I went down to Somerset with a copy for William – his response is dated Sunday, 7th April 2013:

> Last night late I finished reading your manuscript, I am not a fast reader so this will indicate how absorbed I have been… Somehow, in describing her life's journey, you become part of it, you lived it through, I suppose, your writer's gifts – but more than that – through your own power of empathy…

> Just by reading it, I feel as though I too relived her life and that a whole part of mine has been cleansed and purified… Surely you have joined her energy with yours in some mysterious way so that the relentless forward movement of the book or the journey never falters. Like her many sea voyages you are there to record every cross current and surge of the ocean as she and you journey on. So please be careful not to sacrifice this quality to please others who never knew her.

INTRODUCTION

William gave me a generous commission to continue working on the manuscript, which went through careful revisions until that happy day in April 2015 when my agent Caradoc King introduced me to Mathew Clayton and his young colleagues at Unbound, who were thrilled at the prospect of publishing *Angel Dorothy*.

Apart from several visits to William's serene house and garden overlooking the Bristol Channel, I knew very little of his present life, beyond the pages of this book, and *Angel Dorothy* filled our conversations. He was born in 1929 but that seemed immaterial; at the end of phone calls he used to say, 'I'm here, always here, if you want to know anything, or I can help,' which was the theme of his undemanding patronage. Then, at some time last year he said he was buying a small house in Jersey, where he spent weeks at a time and seemed very happy. I suppose I noticed that he no longer ended his phone calls with 'I'm here, always here', but perhaps that was because he could be in either place? Then, at the beginning of February 2016, he rang to ask for a copy of the latest manuscript version, the version with Unbound. I packed this off to Jersey; he rang at the end of the month with the surprising news that he was off to India, and we spoke several times over that weekend. He was again rapturous over the manuscript, grateful for it and the emotional release it gave him – 'I have been able to shed a whole lot of baggage that she has been carrying for us' – he felt he spoke for himself and other members of his family. He said that he was happy, and at peace. With his companions he left for India on Monday, 29th February; the next day he was taken ill in Dubai and died. Dorothy's book is dedicated to her beloved youngest son, for it could not have been written without him.

Jane Brown
Elton
23rd April 2016

ONE: GILDED ANGEL

In the long centuries from the Battle of Hastings to the death of King James in 1625, Dorothy's Norman, Welsh and English forebears transformed themselves from warring ruffians into gentle landed knights. Ten years of Charles I's preference for popish plots over parliamentary integrity then persuaded John and Elinor Whitney, with their five sons, to board the little ship *Elizabeth & Ann* in April 1635 for the perilous Atlantic voyage to the New World. They had to begin their climb back to prosperity all over again, but they did well. One of the intermediate eighteenth-century American Whitneys, Eli, pioneered the very assembly-line process – 'while the worker brings his intelligence more and more to the study of a single detail, each day the master casts his eye over a more far-reaching ensemble' – that enabled American entrepreneurs to create the industrial aristocracy into which Dorothy was born.[1] Her mother's family, the Paynes, were firmly entrenched with Rockefeller's Standard Oil, and her father William Collins Whitney oversaw the 'far-reaching ensemble' of the Navy Department in President Cleveland's first administration.

Dorothy was a late and welcome child, named their 'Gift of God', and born on a Washington day of grey cold and winter slush on 23rd January 1887. Her mother Flora hugged her. 'This is better than all,' she told her friends, the 'all' being her successes as a Washington hostess in Dolley Madison's style. In early April the bells rang out for

Dorothy's christening before a congregation of five hundred, which included the president and his cabinet. The flags waved for 'the Navy's Baby Dot', her arrival coinciding with her father giving contracts to the Newport News Shipyard for their first battleship, though the very first hull laid was for an iron tugboat named *Dorothy*.[2]

Dorothy's father, William Collins Whitney   Dorothy's mother, Flora Payne Whitney

Will Whitney, a tall, dark-haired, moustachioed and handsome stripling of forty-six, had been Secretary of the Navy for two years. His money and his marshalling of the New York Democrats had brought Grover Cleveland's success as the twenty-second president, the first Democrat to be elected since the fifteenth president, James Buchanan. The Whitneys had moved from New York to their big house near the White House, 1731 Eye Street at Lafayette Square, where Dorothy was born. Summer came early to that southern city and as soon as she was christened the family moved from the marshy bottom to their farm, Grasslands, four miles out on airy Nevada Avenue. The English diplomat Cecil Spring-Rice, feeling his way in the still rather raw republic, found them there:

The Secretary keeps open house, or rather open cottages, and everyone who goes there has anything to eat, drink or smoke that they can wish. He is a clever lawyer who has married an enormously rich (and fat) lady with whose money he is gaining popularity and influence. They are both perfectly kind, and the reverse of snobbish.[3]

Everyone was déshabillé because of the heat and perhaps Flora was in something tent-like and without her corset and hour-glass curves; she was in her mid-forties and Dorothy had been her sixth confinement. Flora was a proud Clevelander born of two prominent families, the Paynes and the Perrys, with her brother named Oliver Hazard Payne for their mother's family hero, Captain Oliver Hazard Perry, famous for hounding the British Navy from the Great Lakes in the War of 1812. Their riches came from Senator Payne's alliance with John D. Rockefeller, a Clevelander by adoption, whose Standard Oil refineries and petro-chemical works prospered in the city in the 1860s. After serving in the Union Army, Colonel Oliver Payne became treasurer of Standard Oil; he did not marry but lavished his wealth upon his sister, whom he adored.

Flora had always been plump and pretty, with a head of fair curls and a pair of beautiful blue eyes; she seemed to have the Perry spirit, she was wilful and determined – though perhaps too wise and well educated to be spoilt – and she invariably won her way with her powder-blue gaze. The colonel, her brother, claimed to have found her husband, his Yale friend William Collins Whitney, who had been to Harvard Law School and was then a corporate attorney in New York, but Flora was uncertain about marriage. She had been free to finish her education at the Spingler Institute in New York, to study with the Swiss geologist Louis Agassiz and his wife Elizabeth in Boston and then to travel in Europe and discover the delights of Paris. If she epitomised de Tocqueville's American girl of the nineteenth century, the product of democracy and education, a girl who thought for herself, spoke freely and acted independently and had learned to consider the great world 'with a firm and tranquil eye', then she could have read for herself his verdict on the American wife:

> In America the independence of woman is irretrievably lost within the bounds of marriage. If the girl is less constrained there than everywhere else, the wife submits to stricter obligations. The one makes the paternal home a place of freedom and pleasure, the other lives in her husband's dwelling as in a cloister.[4]

The perils of marriage, as well as the guilt of oil-bound riches, bothered her. She had kept Will Whitney waiting and had written to him of her determination to appreciate the good things that life had brought her, 'to enjoy them with senses you are thankful for... [and] I want to live my life cheerily, exultantly and if the trials come to take them not as the necessities of life, but as the chastisements of a great God'.[5] In October 1869 she left her father's house on Euclid Street for the last time to be married in the Old Stone Presbyterian Church in the Public Square of Cleveland. She and Will spent their honeymoon at Niagara. The Payne family had bought and furnished their first home in New York, a brownstone at 74 Park Avenue, which they came to love. Their first child Leonora died, but Harry, Pauline, Payne and Olive Whitney were safely born at two-year intervals during the 1870s.[6] Will Whitney was working too hard for long holidays but Flora had insisted on taking her children summering to Bar Harbor or the Catskills each year. In 1883 she took them to Paris, where they became ill, and Olive, aged five, died.

Flora seemed to recover first, and it was she who encouraged her husband to his new interest in politics, to Grover Cleveland's campaign, and so success had brought them to Washington. Flora was in her element, entertaining for the bachelor president, her style celebrated by John Philip Sousa's march 'La Reine de la Mer' played by the Marine Band in her honour. Then the president had surprised everyone by marrying the young Frances 'Frankie' Folsom (rather than her mother as the gossips surmised), when he was fifty and she was twenty-two; Flora and 'Frankie' became the best of friends. Privately the Whitneys still mourned Olive, and most privately, disregarding her doctor's advice, Flora decided that only another baby would do, and so Dorothy arrived, their gift from God.

Pauline and Payne Whitney, Dorothy's sister
and brother

Eventually Baby Dot settled into her quiet nursery routine. President Cleveland lost the election in 1888 to Benjamin Harrison and the following year, when Dorothy was just two, the Whitney family returned to New York, this time to the huge mansion on Fifth Avenue at West 57th Street, immediately south of Central Park, which Colonel Payne had bought for them. Dorothy's nursery was high up above the sidewalk with grown-up life carrying on in the stately rooms beneath her; she had few memories of this time, one of playing bear-chases with her brother Payne, who would have been fifteen when she was four. Pauline and Harry, at seventeen and nineteen respectively, were all too engrossed in their busy lives to have much time for their baby sister.[7] Her parents were often absent, her father was working hard, and Flora, fresh from her Washington success, was determined to meet the challenge of New York's demanding and censorious Gilded Age society. It was said that she was 'addicted to activity', to parties, concerts, the opera and even to the White Star Line, which took her on shopping trips to Paris.[8] This was not the outdoor life that, in her heart, Flora would have preferred, and with too many banquets and no real exercise her weight became a problem. Worst of all, Dorothy managed to overhear, with her little girl's sharp ears, talk that she was the cause of Flora's problems: her mother should never have had such a late baby, and her heart was seriously weakened. Dorothy's last memory of her mother came from soon after her sixth birthday in 1893, when she was led into her mother's room where Flora was lying on a couch, and she was told to say 'goodbye'. She was taken from the house, even from New York, for the critical time, and some weeks later, as she recalled, she was told that her mother had died.[9]

Her efforts to remember her mother always ended in tears, and other memories of her childhood assumed a nightmare quality. She clung to her Irish nurse, 'Ma Bonne', but could not give her real name, only that they so often walked down Fifth Avenue to St Patrick's Cathedral where she was left alone in the echoing void while 'Ma Bonne disappeared into that fearsome brown box'. Even more troubling were the annual Ash Wednesdays, when she was taken to the altar to have her forehead smeared with ashes, she knew not why. She had no memories of her father, perhaps because he disappeared for months on end, taking Harry, Pauline and Payne to the West Indies, then to England and the Continent to salve their more grown-up grief. Dorothy's saviour was her first friend, Gladys Vanderbilt, who was a few months older but also inhabited her nursery eyrie in the even more monstrous and grand mansion across the street. They rigged up, presumably with help, a kind of private telephone with a light rope slung across the chasm, which made them feel close, two fluffy chicks on Manhattan cliffs. They went to dancing classes together, and Dorothy always remembered the hot chocolate they drank afterwards, 'the favourite drink of my youth'.

Pauline Whitney came home from Europe engaged to an Englishman, Almeric Paget.[10] They were married on 12th November 1895 at St Thomas's Episcopal Church on Fifth Avenue, a few days after Gladys's cousin Consuelo Vanderbilt had married the Duke of Marlborough. Fifth Avenue existed in a rose-petal storm. Dorothy emerged from her schoolroom at the age of eight years and ten months making her debut as a flower girl in a dress trimmed in sable, with a floppy velvet beret à la Rembrandt. Her father's treasure hunting in Europe had included buying a painting by the Dutch master, the ultimate in Fifth Avenue status symbols. The following year Harry Whitney married Gertrude Vanderbilt in August in Newport – 'our Social Capital' – on Rhode Island. Gertrude was Gladys's big sister, and something of a goddess to the younger girls – she was very tall, willow slim, with a pile of dark curls and green eyes. Harry's and Gertrude's was a boy and girl next door romance: she had looked after Harry's dog while he was at Law School and they had fallen in love. The wedding was a fairytale. The Vanderbilts' new and breathtakingly grand mansion, The Breakers, gleamed like a wedding cake, trimmed with vine-covered pergolas casting filigree shades, overflowing with pink and white flowers and cascades of cooling ferns. Dorothy and Gladys wore white silk with floaty gauze, which they flew as wings in the sea breezes.

There was another wedding in the following month, September 1896, which Dorothy knew little about, when her father left in his yacht for Bar Harbor in Maine, where he married the widow of a British army officer, Edith Randolph, in the little St Sauveur's Church. Later in New York he explained that Dorothy had to choose whether to live with him and Edith, or with Uncle Oliver and her brother Payne. The family had divided over this second marriage. Colonel Payne's grief over his sister Flora's death persuaded him that Whitney was betraying her memory, and Pauline and Payne, listening to the rumours that

Edith had been their father's mistress before Flora died, felt the same. Dorothy chose to stay with her father, and she loved to recall how joyously her life was transformed. Her tall and beautiful stepmother Edith won her over with love and laughter, she was surprised into the delight of being gathered into Edith's arms and given goodnight kisses. Her days were full of fun and activities, and Edith's children, Adelaide and Arthur – Addie and Bertie to Dorothy – became her boon companions. They played musical houses, Whitney giving Harry and Gertrude the big West 57th Street house, which was so full of Flora's tastes and belongings, and commissioning his architect-friend Stanford White to decorate and furnish 871 Fifth Avenue at 68th Street for Edith. For Dorothy, no longer banished to her schoolroom, the world beyond Fifth Avenue opened as a kaleidoscope of adventures as they summered at Bar Harbor where she learned to sail, explored the Berkshires from her father's house at Lenox, travelled by private railcar to his farms and racing stables at Aiken in South Carolina, and most beloved of all by Dorothy, lived out lazy days at Old Westbury on Long Island. Edith loved horses and riding, they all rode with the Meadow Brook Hunt Club, and Dorothy hit her first golf ball – though her golf was always a somewhat comical amusement – at the old course there.

Her happiness was all too brief. Just after her tenth birthday they were hunting at Aiken, and Dorothy, riding behind her stepmother, saw Edith fall, knocked from her saddle by an overhanging branch. Edith lay seemingly lifeless, not dead, but despite the efforts of many doctors she was paralysed. Dorothy's father searched and hoped for a miracle cure but in vain. Edith remained loving and cheerful with them all for just over two years, but she died in May 1899. Dorothy wrote, 'My poor father, he loved her so much and she brought the gaiety of life to him, and to me, and I see her always now with a light around her.'

Once again her father found his consolation in Europe, especially in England for the racing. Dorothy could no longer enjoy riding, and it was only to comfort him that she attempted a brief interest, noting that he had invested in 'some important bloodstock'.

He leased a horse called Volodyvoski, a relative of the legendary Eclipse and King Edward VII's Persimmon in the hope that he had spotted a potential Derby winner.[11]

At home again he became very sociable, giving parties and musical dinners; they called him 'Mr Fifth Avenue', and as a handsome widower he was a favourite with Mrs Astor and the Four Hundred, the most fashionable set of the day. His box at the opera could be safely graced by every visiting grande dame, of whom the grandest and his favourite was Alice Keppel.[12] His most spectacular ball was for his stepdaughter Addie's coming-out, for five hundred guests, with relays of musicians so that the dancing never stopped until buffets of French delicacies appeared as if by magic, the magic of Sherry's, his favourite restaurant. Even though it was December the house was filled with 'American Beauty' roses and lily of the valley, and at the witching-hour a flower-decked, chauffeur-driven automobile, headlights blazing, rolled onto the dance floor carrying the favours.[13] Addie, who had grown as tall and lovely as her mother, was the star of the evening; Dorothy had grown tall but felt herself far from lovely with a mop of unruly hair and rather heavy features – like the schoolroom girls in novels, she had to watch from the stairs.

Weeks later she was on bridesmaid's duty again, dressed in light grey satin crepe with Alice Hay, for the wedding of her brother Payne and Helen Hay. Helen and Alice were the daughters of President Theodore Roosevelt's Secretary of State John Hay, and their mother Clara Stone had been Flora's friend. Colonel Payne lavished presents and a Fifth Avenue house on Payne and Helen, but as the colonel and Dorothy's father were still not on speaking terms but had to share a table at the wedding breakfast with the Roosevelts and the Hays, a stiff-lipped truce reigned. Dorothy's affection for her brother Payne never diminished, despite his rift with their father.

With Harry and Payne married, and Pauline and Almeric Paget moving to England, Dorothy now had more of her father to herself; Cordelia-like as his youngest daughter, she wanted his blessing. Together they explored places and ideas that meant so much to Flora, who had believed with all her passionate soul in the beauty of America and the special good fortune of being American, which is why she had honoured the annual return to the wild or the sea for both recreation and thanksgiving.[14] She had known full well that the pleasant lakeside Cleveland of her childhood was being transformed into an industrial realm, largely by her relatives and their business colleagues. As her husband had become increasingly involved in railroad franchises the progress versus paradise debate had sparked disputes around their own dinner table. Flora's favoured Catskills harboured Washington Irving's 'Legend of Sleepy Hollow', and Hawthorne's image of the locomotive shattering the peace of the legend, the advent of the machine in the garden, was a warning to the would-be despoilers.[15] As a disciple of Agassiz and Harvard President Charles William Eliot's cohort of Harvard natural scientists, Flora had been an outspoken pioneer, and perhaps it wasn't a coincidence that she was in Washington when the government removed exploitative leases and gave protection to some 81 million acres of America, freeing Indian lands and water resources.

Rich men were now obliged to play their part and Will Whitney was not to be left out. He bought thousands of acres and dozens of lakes in the Adirondacks leaving reserves for animals and birds. At Washington in Massachusetts, between the towns of Lee, Lenox and Becket, he bought a mountain, October Mountain, which sheltered buffalo, moose and their kind. At Aiken in South Carolina he created thousand-acre farms, and racing stables to bring employment to a depressed land.[16] These were the places he shared with Dorothy; she loved their springtime visits to the white wooden house, Joye Cottage at Aiken, where she could play hostess to the townspeople who sang her father's praises for putting them on the map. They explored October Mountain and enjoyed summer camps at Raquette Lake in the Adirondacks, with fishing, canoeing and campfire suppers. Just in time, and as Flora would surely have wished, Dorothy learned the summering habit from her father. It supported her forever afterwards; for her it was more than a return to the American garden, it was her return into her parents' embraces, just as they had hugged her as their gift from God.

Yet, once again, hers was all too short a happiness. Just after her seventeenth birthday on 23rd January 1904, her father was taken ill in his box at the Metropolitan Opera, during his favourite *Parsifal*. Appendicitis was diagnosed and characteristically he refused a fuss. It was well known that the 'Napoleon of the railroads', E.H. Harriman, had been similarly struck down on his train in the middle of Wyoming, but he had withstood his doctors until he arrived back in New York and was successfully operated on by Dr William T. Bull. Whitney held out until that same Dr Bull arrived with his team to operate, but it was too late and blood poisoning and peritonitis caused his death. Dorothy, who was present during the days of drama, could not believe that her beloved father, 'so full of spirit and so dynamic', was lifeless. He was sixty-three. On a miserably cold February day his long funeral cortège with black-plumed horses and wagons piled with flowers made its way down Fifth Avenue to Grace Church, silent crowds standing by; in the church a wreath of lilies lay on his empty pew, 'For Father'. Afterwards the family all boarded the train at Grand Central Station, taking them to Woodlawn Cemetery in the Bronx, where he was laid close to Flora and Olive.

It was reported that Dorothy collapsed at the graveside for she was inevitably reminded of her tears for Flora. This was an even greater blow, magnified by her adolescent emotions; she had loved the freedom of her father's house, his houses, he had tutored her growing up as well as being her closest companion for more than three vital years. She was so proud of him; in her imagination she had lived with a merchant prince amidst his treasures, walking beneath blue-panelled ceilings rosetted in gold, dining in the company of old Italian paintings crowding the walls ('a unique decoration for a New York interior'), and practising her skills at conversation before carved mantels of antique Fiesole stone. Jan Paderewski's piano playing and Fritz Kreisler's violin as well as dance music and laughter had echoed from these now silent rooms. The very act of leaving her father's house – for leave she must as Harry had inherited so many houses he had no need for this one – becalmed 871 Fifth Avenue in her mind as her father's gilded carapace, the evidence of his love and need for beauty.[17]

TWO: 'DOROTHY ALWAYS TAKES THE HARD CHAIR'

From beyond the grave Dorothy's father comforted her, his will expressing his confidence in 'her striking American individuality and penchant for doing her own thinking in her own way'. Flora's child was to be given her independence with a legacy of about $7 million in 1904 values, and her own home at Old Westbury.[18] As she was only seventeen Harry Whitney was appointed her guardian and allowed $50,000 a year for her upkeep; in addition, a salary of $10,000 a year was to be paid to Miss Beatrice Bend as her companion, chosen with the approval of Harry, Pauline and Payne.[19] When they were in the city Dorothy and Beatrice were to live with Harry and Gertrude, which meant her return to the house of her childhood at Central Park South, which had been Flora's house and had – the cause of great excitement – a new electric lift.

Most people were kind, and Beatrice Bend was a promising companion, but for Dorothy it was still rather a shock to be pitched into an adult world of competing egos and gargantuan expectations. There were inevitably newsmen and photographers camped at the door of Harry and Gertrude's house, for they were gossip-worthy, and as a pretty orphan-heiress she was also the delight of the columnists of *Town Topics*. After too brief an interval she had to weather the less-than-admiring commentaries on her father's life and fortune-making: how he had played the 'Kingmaker' in Grover Cleveland's rise to the presidency, how he had refused to return for Cleveland's second term, giving Flora's death as his reason but in reality preferring the 'sportive indulgences' of Wall Street and the racing at Sheepshead Bay in Brooklyn. Dorothy had to hear jibes that her money was tainted as unscrupulous gains in the manner of the Vanderbilts, Carnegie, Rockefeller and J.P. Morgan.[20] From the start she decided to 'stick to her guns'; she tackled the shark-infested waters with her candid blue gaze, her smile lighting her face and dimpling her chin, holding out her hand and saying, 'I am Dorothy Whitney.'[21]

She had always been a great reader and kept a record: Mrs Molesworth was an early stalwart; at ten she dismissed *Little Lord Fauntleroy* as 'quite stupid'; at eleven she moved on to Louisa M. Alcott; and at twelve she had found her brothers' copies of Henty, Conan Doyle, Stevenson and Dickens. The remainder of her education had been frankly scrappy (Flora would surely have arranged it otherwise), a series of governesses and false starts. She had attended Mr Roser's Academy, where she found a lifelong friend in May Tuckerman, was adamant that she never saw the famous Mr Roser, but remembered a Miss Tomes teaching her in a private class with seven others 'nothing except Greek mythology and Roman history'. When that class broke up she had been 'whisked away' to Miss Clara Spence's on West 48th Street – the schoolbooks she saved show grammar, rhetoric, literature and drama as her subjects, with 'composition' essays on John Paul Jones, life in Aiken and the Society for the Prevention of Cruelty to Children. Her extra topic was a course of architectural history and her critical curiosity was to lead her into hours of pleasure simply looking at buildings in Beaux-Arts New York and old Europe.[22]

On 10th August 1904, six months after her father's death, she set out on her first Atlantic crossing for her first taste of Europe. For the time being, her independence was quelled and she would do what was expected of her; a party that could have stepped out of a Henry James novel boarded the SS *Baltic*, the ladies in big hats with parasols, the men in blazers and white flannels – Harry and Gertrude Whitney, Dorothy and her friend May Tuckerman, Miss Bend and her mother Marraine, and assorted men friends of Harry's to be trusted escorts and tennis partners.[23] From the outset it had been clear that Beatrice Bend was an 'older sister' and equal; Beatrice was ten years older, tall and rather stately of bearing, not a lady to be trifled with, which was the idea. In the few months they had been together they had become inseparable, Beatrice adoring her charge, Dorothy pliant and affectionate.

Dorothy's debutante studio portrait, c.1905

They landed in England to be reunited with Pauline and Almeric Paget, Dorothy's little niece, Olive, and Addie and Bertie Randolph who now lived with their English relatives. In Paris they found Gertrude's mother with Gladys Vanderbilt on her debut tour; the shrieks of laughter and girlish giggles can almost be heard as Harry piled May, Dorothy and Gladys into his new Mercedes for a drive south – Dorothy noted 'Automobiling great fun!' – and a tour of the Loire valley. May, Dorothy and the Bends intended a long stay; after the sights of Paris and Versailles they went to Amsterdam to see the Rembrandts, then, as it grew chillier, they moved south to Nice, then Rome. They were in Rome for Christmas and Beatrice produced bulging stockings for May and Dorothy. On her eighteenth birthday, 23rd January 1905, Dorothy told her diary that she was 'feeling terribly old'. From her life that had passed almost without record she had graduated to her Line-A-Day diary, that cipher of society existence that allowed space for morning, afternoon and evening engagements, but little more, just as there was little time to draw breath between the parties. She is revealed as a traveller rather than a tourist, making her own choices from the architectural guides, with abrupt comments, 'very fine' or 'a splendid view'. She liked to wander around churches and through street markets watching the everyday patterns of ordinary lives; she seemed immediately at home in European cities and she was undoubtedly popular among the urchin gatekeepers and flower sellers to whom she was unfailingly generous.

May Tuckerman, who always brought a lot of fun into Dorothy's life, left them in Rome and the 'rump' of three went to Sicily, returning northwards in easy stages as the weather improved and arriving in London in the spring of 1905. The Pagets had a house in Berkeley Square and a country place in Suffolk; though Dorothy was not 'out' her sister Pauline – who had many of their mother Flora's organisational abilities – could not resist showing her off, being perfectly convinced that she had grown into such a lovely heiress that she would be well married before she was twenty.

In September Dorothy and the Bends returned to Paris to meet Harry and Gertrude who had arrived for their annual visit. There was an important ritual to be accomplished, Gertrude introducing Dorothy as a client at the House of Worth where she would buy dresses for her debut on her nineteenth birthday and which demanded a 'royal' accreditation – or a Vanderbilt would do. The legendary Monsieur Worth had dressed Flora, but now his son, Jean-Philippe, ruled the Maison in the Rue de la Paix, his effusive welcome hinting that she was expected to maintain the family tradition and order lavishly. Dorothy was more concerned to keep the mannequins and seamstresses in work and she endured her fittings by engaging them in conversation (and improving her French) whenever possible. They returned home on the SS *Kaiser Wilhelm II*. Her Line-A-Day, usually filled as if her life depended upon it, stayed in her case on board, and she was content with a good book and a quiet passage. It was Quarantine at Ellis Island, the prelude to docking in New York, that appalled her, the spectacle of 'the huddled masses' disturbing her dreams for nights on end.

Settled back home with her brother and sister-in-law, Dorothy could not escape their influence. Harry Whitney, in his mid-thirties, was clever, handsome and charming; his tutors had said he had the makings of a brilliant lawyer but he preferred his sporting life. With the lion's share of his father's millions, his houses and their precious contents, his acreages and racing stables, Harry was more inclined to keep an eye on his investments and enjoy his seasonal round of tennis and sailing, racing and hunting, and playing polo, which he did to international standard. Asked once why did he not spend more of his fortune, he is supposed to have quipped, 'I'm saving it for Dorothy for when she has given all hers away.'

Harry and Gertrude (Vanderbilt) Whitney

As Harry's wife and 'senior sister', Gertrude was head of the family. She was thirty, mother of Flora, Sonny and Barbara, and outwardly she personified the regal poise expected of a Vanderbilt heiress married to the Whitney heir; inside her was an artist longing to kick over the conventions. What could she do that was useful? She tried writing – plays, romantic fiction, her self-analytical journals – but her real talent was drawing, and she had dreamed of herself modelling clay figures, and so had begun her sculpture, largely self-taught. Harry had little sympathy for his wife as an artist, feeling her proper role was in patronage, so Gertrude struggled to do everything. She imagined a school, a gallery, perhaps a museum, with commissions for herself and patronage for American artists. She listed those who would help her: Harry obviously number one when she could win him over, and Dorothy at number four, 'young now but that is the time to influence her so that financially she would be interested'.[24]

Dorothy, aware of these tensions, was always grateful for Gertrude's love and 'good companionship'; she saw her struggles clearly, how her money was a double-edged sword bringing hurtful prejudices and jealousies, as well as her expensive sculptural materials and her Tuscan-style studio designed by the architect William Adams Delano and built in their garden at Old Westbury. The incompatibility of being a creative artist and living with the obligations of wealth was starkly drawn. Dorothy knew that she had no choice, or rather that her father had made her choice for her – there was to be no posing in garret or studio for her, she loved and read poetry but wrote none, she attempted no novel nor drawing, nor painting, nor any needlework; she enjoyed classical and choral music but she did not play any instrument nor did she sing. She often joked wryly about her complete lack of 'drawing room accomplishments' – was she to live in a cultural desert? No, but she had other aims in view.

The year 1906 was her debut year: her Line-A-Day became frantic, and she stepped out in the supreme confidence of being Miss Dorothy Whitney. Politics and powerful men interested her and she made the first of several New Year visits to Washington, this time as the guest of

President Roosevelt's Assistant Secretary of State, the ultra-handsome Robert Bacon – the Bacons were her Long Island neighbours and had their eyes on her as a daughter-in-law, though she feigned innocence of this. She was actually busy charming Bacon's chief, the formidable Elihu Root, whose mother was a Whitney as it turned out, and with whom she became a great favourite.[25]

Back in New York her aunt Lilley Barney gave a formal dinner on the eve of her nineteenth birthday; a week later Harry and Gertrude staged her coming-out ball, their house filled with the traditional 'American Beauty' roses and Dorothy, her hair piled high, leading off the cotillion in her Worth gown, partnered by a most dashing beau. 'Princess' Alice Roosevelt and her fiancé Nicholas Longworth were among her guests, and on the following 17th February in spring-like sunshine Dorothy went to their wedding in the White House. It was like playing in the Giant's Castle, their high spirits took wings in those fabled rooms and she long remembered how – in all their finery, hats flying – everyone ran helter-skelter across the East Lawn to wave the honeymooners on their way.

Being 'out' entitled her to membership of the Colony Club on Madison Avenue, founded by Gertrude, Payne's wife Helen Hay Whitney and Mrs J. Borden Harriman, known to everyone as Daisy.[26] Her New York days slipped easily into the pattern of the sisterhood, her Book Class or a gallery lecture in the morning, lunch at Delmonico's, fresh air in the afternoon, tea at the Colony then home to dress for the opera in Gertrude's box, or the theatre and dinner and dancing. She was often at Sherry's on Fifth Avenue three evenings a week, which had been her father's favourite haunt and was the fashionable party venue for her set.

As a pretty girl with a fortune must be in want of a husband, the question of beaux was uppermost, deftly managed by Gertrude from her own list of admirers. Dorothy's early escorts included two architects, who found her knowledge of their profession intriguing: Lloyd Warren, whose firm was by appointment to the Vanderbilts, and Grosvenor Atterbury, a coming star. Atterbury was eighteen years older than

Dorothy and, more critically, shorter; she had reached five feet ten inches in her heels and a hat. His missionary zeal in the unfashionable realms of low-cost housing and hospital building touched her social conscience, and he was not the last to mistake her friendly enthusiasm for his work as an interest in him. More light-heartedly there were Harry's friends in the Long Island tennis set, the Bacons' son Bob, in his last year at Harvard and destined for banking and the Treasury, and for a while the god-like Devereux Milburn, captain of Harry's all-conquering 'Big Four' polo team. Courtland Barnes was briefly a beau until he married her cousin Kate Barney and as a couple they became her close friends. Much the same could be said of the lawyer Joseph Howland Auchincloss, who married Priscilla Stanton, another of Dorothy's set.

The 1906 trip to Europe began in April as Dorothy was to be bridesmaid at Addie Randolph's marriage to Lionel Lambart in London. They sailed on the *Oceanie*, Dorothy, Beatrice and Mrs Bend, now the intrepid four with the addition of Dorothy's red-haired maid Louisa Weinstein, who was to be with her for the next twenty years. After the wedding in early May they made a quick diversion to Spain,

Dorothy's legacy from her father, Elmhurst at Old Westbury

26

to the Alhambra at Granada, and were back in time for Royal Ascot. There, Dorothy purred, 'Mrs Keppel introduced me to the King,' who kindly remembered her father and his racing successes. Additional beaux included sister Pauline's protégé, a Scots Guards officer, Lord Falconer, heir to the Earl of Kintore of Inverurie in Aberdeenshire, Delancey Jay, a Harvard law graduate on secondment to the Foreign Office, and Sumner Gerard, one of the chivalric company of Roosevelt's Rough Riders from the Cuba campaign of 1898.[27] Dorothy was lightly pursued to Berlin, Munich and St Moritz before she returned to Paris – 'I love Paris,' she told her Line-A-Day; to all her suitors she smiled sweetly and said 'No'. The highlight on their trip home on the SS *Kaiserin Auguste Victoria* was her tour of the new Marconi radio room.

It became her habit after an Atlantic crossing to take refuge in her own home at Old Westbury on Long Island. At about the time of her birth her father had bought an estate of inland acres in the Wheatley Hills at North Hempstead in Nassau County as an escape from the city. He left Dorothy the Shingle-style cottage built for Harry and Gertrude, while they moved to his larger house five minutes' walk away; hers was called Elmhurst – the postal address was Roslyn, and it was easily reached on the Long Island Rail Road, Glen Cove branch line, or by motor by wide sandy lanes alongside open fields and woods. This was old farming country, settled for two hundred years, studded with huge barns and water mills. Roslyn was a neat town with boardwalks, a General Store displaying shelves of Campbell's red-labelled soups and a busy blacksmith named Napoleon Forget. The steamboat service along the East River brought trippers to Glen Cove in search of 'Long Island Duck Dinners', and celebrity escapees tucked themselves into clapboard cottages and discreet hotels, but nothing was spoiled, and it had the salty air of a happy haven.[28]

At Old Westbury Dorothy was safe, surrounded by people who had known her all her life. Harry and Gertrude were close, but not too close, and Payne and Helen were at Manhasset not far away. As for her style of living – certainly not rocking chairs, animal skins and elephant tusks as at Theodore Roosevelt's Sagamore Hill at Oyster

Bay, nor did the oppressive grandeur of tapestries, gilded woods and priceless ginger jars filled with ferns ever make it out of Manhattan. She gathered favourite pieces from family rooms, eighteenth-century pieces in the English Georgian manner, Chippendale upholstered chairs with reeded legs, knee-hole desks and dressing tables, block-fronted chests by Duncan Phyfe and other craftsmen of old New York, with pretty floral papers and chintzes: these were the backdrop to her life. A bowl of garden flowers reflected in a polished mahogany tabletop symbolised Elmhurst.[29]

Loyalty to her family and friends was Dorothy's guiding star but she was impatient to have another occupation than that of bridesmaid, and yet she was nowhere near ready to be a bride. The year 1906 brought her another sisterly friendship, important because it broke the pattern of her social whirling before it became a habit. Soon after her coming-out she had been invited to dinner at E.H. Harriman's house where she discovered his daughter Mary, who also thought for herself. Mary Harriman was six years older, the eldest child in an affectionate family, 'a dark, pleasant girl with an infectious laugh' who had been well educated, studying biology and sociology at Barnard College. Her father had a fearsome reputation: Alice Roosevelt was once a guest on his private train when he announced he was trying for the speed record home from the Midwest. Alarmed, the president had wired, 'Please take care of the safety of my daughter on your train,' to which Harriman snapped back, 'You run the country – I'll run the railroad.'[30]

Alice was in no danger for Harriman was noted for his care of his own 'perfect family' who accompanied him on tours to Alaska and Japan, and especially proud of Mary, who had been to California with him dealing with Union Pacific labour problems.[31]

Mary Harriman introduced Dorothy to her Junior League, an association of friends who volunteered to work with the emigrants in the settlements of the Lower East Side.[32] She was eased in, as other Leaguers were, with fundraising sales of work and 'entertainments' but the autumn of 1906 found her on committees discussing women's health and children's welfare, and projects for housing nurses and teachers, which the League funded. Dorothy knew she had a great deal to learn, so she enrolled for courses explaining employment laws and workplace regulations, and at the same time she discovered her natural efficiency: she was a stickler for time-keeping and her confidence in speaking meant that she blossomed as the most naturally talented Madame Chairman. Her friend Ruth Morgan, a civil rights activist whom she met at Grace Church and the Colony Club, described her: 'Dorothy always takes the hard chair and the drumstick – with which she conducts the meeting.'[33] She faced up to the harsh lessons of charity work; she visited a school on the Lower East Side with $500 the League had raised for food, but came away in despair, realising how quickly it would be used up and the children would be hungry again. Playing 'lady bountiful' was of little use and social work of a more serious kind was needed. She confessed, 'I am filled with that terribly absorbing desire to work, and help, and carry through something which may be useful – I can't help realizing every night how much more I might have done.'[34]

Mary Harriman also told her of the two greatest pioneers in America, Lillian Wald and Jane Addams. Dorothy went to see Miss Wald at her Henry Street Nurses' Settlement in the Lower (lowest) East Side and found her very encouraging. They liked each other immediately and became the best of friends. The Settlement housed twenty-two public health nurses who went out into the streets to minister to the emigrants' physical and mental ills of the most horrific kinds – or simply to help with the difficulties of adjusting to life in America.[35] Cooking and sewing classes and advice on housing and employment were available and Miss Wald was working towards a holiday scheme and a music settlement. Dorothy – only too aware that she was useless at nursing, cooking or needlework – was able to work regular sessions in the Advice Centre, a further spur to her learning about children's welfare, employment laws and women's trade unions. 'Was there anything else she could do?' Yes, Miss Wald had long wanted an Emergency Fund they could dip into for things not covered by other allowances, 'small things but worthwhile'. She wrote of a boy of sixteen with incipient consumption, earning $4 a week in a fish store, and his parents could not let him go to a sanatorium. When she managed to get him away he had no clothes to wear, and so the Fund kitted him out. He had been at the sanatorium for six weeks, improving all the while – 'This stay in the mountains will probably save his life,' Lillian concluded. The Fund also paid for summer picnics and Christmas presents; it was regularly accounted to Dorothy, though hardly exceeded $100 at any time.[36]

By the time of her twentieth birthday in January 1907 she had already learned something that so many people never learn, that in order to really help others you have to give of yourself rather more than you first imagined. Harry Whitney heard all his friends' jokes about his 'pink sister' and perhaps scowled, he could do nothing; the society columns still dubbed her New York's 'Number One Marriageable Heiress'. Dorothy had her own conscience about loyalties and she divided her life as best she could. She was bridesmaid to her school friend May Tuckerman who married the banker Herman Kinnicutt, and to her cousin Kate Barney who married Courtland Barnes. In the June of 1907, with the Bends and Louisa, she sailed for Europe on the SS *Adriatic* with Russia in view and *Anna Karenina* in her book bag. She was attracted by the chance of seeing the seventy-nine-year-old Count Tolstoy on his estate south of Moscow where he was known to care for and educate his peasants, and the political mood was sunny that summer with liberal voices in the Duma and an Anglo-Russian entente in the making. Her visit had the blessing of the State Department, from Secretary Bacon, whose son Bob was to meet them in Moscow.

But first, there was Paris, which did nothing to quieten her doubts about her divided life. Her Book Class had just discussed Henry James's *The Ambassadors* and the Master had bewitched her mind's eye. Walking in the Tuileries, treading the 'long dim nave' of Notre Dame, the little pink shades that lit up the faces at restaurant tables, all the impressions of the Paris she loved were suddenly not quite what they seemed. Bits of her own life were scattered through the book:

'We're all looking at each other,' says Miss Barrace, 'and
in the light of Paris one sees what things resemble. That's
what the light of Paris seems always to show. It's the fault
of the light of Paris – dear old light!'
'Dear old Paris!' little Bilham echoed.
'Everything, every one shows,' Miss Barrace went on.
'But for what they really are?' Strether asked.[37]

In Lambert Strether's momentary escape from the burdensome
inevitabilities of his American money, Dorothy glimpsed her mother's
need for Paris. Was she herself as seemingly innocent as Jeanne de
Vionnet, the girl who resembled her 'in a white dress and a softly
plumed white hat' – were they both pawns in a game they didn't
understand? Was her dear Beatrice Bend, now entering her thirties,
as doomed to modest servitude as Miss Gostrey unless she 'landed' a
dry-as-dust lawyer? How many of the beautiful women she met had
dark secrets and cruel husbands like Madame de Vionnet? And young
lovers? For she supposed that Chad Newsome, with his fortune and
niceness, appeared exactly like so many of her own suitors – if Chad
could simulate 'like the click of a spring' that he was in love with one
person when it was really another, how could she ever be sure?

If *The Ambassadors* echoed her own predicament, then by the time
their train had rattled for endless miles across Europe to St Petersburg
– hot and dusty and 'so beautiful it made me shiver' – she had stepped
into Anna Karenina's world. In the care of the American consul they
were surrounded by uniformed attachés and clicking heels, their
wives and daughters dressed as in some grand opera, Tolstoy's Dolly,
Kitty, Betsy and Anna come to life, and gossiping about the Tsarina
Alexandra being in the power of the wicked Rasputin. It was all so
hurried and so unreal; she was trapped in a schedule that did not allow
a visit to Tolstoy's Vasnaya Polyana (or she would surely have written a
whole notebook about that) but for the first time she heard the names
of Dostoevsky, Stravinsky, Diaghilev, Rimsky-Korsakov, Stanislavsky,
the Moscow Arts Theatre and Anton Chekhov, names that would

echo throughout her life. Their train left Moscow bound for Warsaw and Vienna but by the time they reached the Polish border Dorothy was overcome by 'a great Russian tristesse'. No doubt they were all exhausted, relieved to be Americans and not bound to that beautiful land of endless suffering, which made her feel so small and infinitely helpless, that they were leaving behind.

Vienna was enchanting, with a performance of *The Merry Widow* as a colourful coda to her seminars on marriage. Out of it all she had come to a conclusion, 'that a woman on her own, unless she was a fighter and extraordinarily clever could do so little', and she felt she was neither. 'Marriage, my marriage, was the only way.' In Venice on Grand Hotel notepaper, she moved on from her decision:

> When the right person comes along, I wonder if one has doubts, even then? Many of us are swept away into an irresistible current of love – while to the rest of us love comes walking slowly, and yet with sure steps he overtakes us and folds his arms about our shrinking forms – or is that my longing for a protective love? Of course the man one marries cannot be all one dreams of – I can't help longing for certain things – he must be strong, and he must be tender – he must be honest and generous, and also kind and thoughtful – and oh – if he will only love me tenderly, take care of me, put his arms about me, and let... [her sentence is unfinished].[38]

She could not marry a man without ambition because she felt 'a great longing' to be a true helpmeet. She could not admire a man without ambition: she admired Grosvenor Atterbury's architectural mission but doubted he needed her as he said, for she was butter-fingered at drawing and could not assist him.[39] Then Bob Bacon had been in Moscow, calling her 'dearest Dorothy', and 'he has almost all I need and a political future which I find exciting'. But then 'horrid feelings' overcame her with the admission that a political wife had little to do with politics but was chiefly a party giver.[40] Can a woman really be of help to the man she marries? She concludes it unlikely – would her chance of happiness be greater with a man of no career who would need her in their daily life? Would she be happy as Lady Falconer as her sister Pauline wished, wife to a Scots laird keeping up with the shooting parties?

Then she dropped her bombshell. 'I have seen only one man that comes near to what I long for – only one man that I would really like to marry – at least I think I would; altogether he fills up most of the holes and niches and I know he is much too good for me.'[41] She had seen him first at Alice Roosevelt's wedding, and met him properly at dinner at the Harrimans. His name was Willard Straight and he was working for the State Department. He was posted as consul to Mukden in Manchuria, and he was also reporting on railways for 'Papa' Harriman, who was clearly very fond of him. Nothing was said but she had gathered that Mary was very much in love with him. There was nothing to be done.

She kept this admission a secret, even from Beatrice. Back in Paris they met the Bacon family again and she realised that Robert, who had long been as affectionate as a second father to her, was more handsome and attractive than his son. Shades of *The Ambassadors* with herself as Chad, the Bacons as the Vionnets! At home in October she discovered what she had missed, that Mary Harriman and Willard Straight had become secretly engaged, that Mary had gathered her courage and told her father, who was furious, and she had threatened to run away to be with Willard. At home and alone in the August she had been wrong-footed by a *New York Times* reporter who splashed the whole story and 'Papa' Harriman was even angrier; he liked Willard, and loved his daughter, but they were too alike, 'lacking in balance and stability'. Mary had been swept off her feet by a man she hardly knew – 'there had never been an engagement', he growled at the pressmen, 'and would never be a marriage'.[42]

Dorothy's life grew sombre. In late November her uncle Charles Barney shot himself after the declared bankruptcy of his Knickerbocker

Trust, and she tried to comfort her aunt and Kate. Working in Henry Street was easier. Then her oldest friend Gladys Vanderbilt announced her engagement to the Austro-Hungarian Count Laszlo Szechenyi, and she was bridesmaid at their wedding in St Patrick's Cathedral, where she had hardly been since the days of Ma Bonne and the Ash Wednesday ashes. Gladys was going to live in Budapest and they vowed to meet in London or Paris whenever they could, but Dorothy was fearful for Gladys, haunted by her Russian experiences and the rumours about Gladys's cousin Consuelo's unhappiness as Duchess of Marlborough.

Discovering that Jane Addams was to be in New York she managed to spend 'a wonderful morning' with her, hearing how her inspiration as a pioneer social worker had come from a visit to Toynbee Hall in London's East End, meeting Canon Samuel Barnett, Octavia Hill and Beatrice Webb.[43] 'Canon Barnett,' said Miss Addams, 'had rejected a comfortable parish to work in the truly Dickensian slums of the Docklands [Dorothy winced with shame at her ignorance of that part of London] and it was his expressed belief that top-down charity did more harm than good, it demoralised both the giver and receiver, and improving living conditions had to be a shared experience.' She had based her Hull-House in Chicago on these precepts, and they now helped two thousand people every week.[44] Dorothy found Hull-House to be a friendly and busy place, full of good humour and fellowship and she was amazed at the range of facilities which went beyond personal needs to education for all ages, to music, drama, crafts, including a book bindery, and an employment bureau. Miss Addams insisted that Settlement work was not charity, she kept emphasising that there was a crucial distinction between 'doing good to or for other people and doing good with them'. She was determined that 'Hull-House was a collaborative, experimental bridging of class cultures, it was not philanthropy, which – however it was packaged – was likely to be morally disastrous'.[45]

The formidable Miss Addams was hardly encouraging; she may well have thought Dorothy too expensively dressed and too pretty to be serious, or simply too young at just twenty-one. However, Hull-House had a special compensation for Dorothy, for there she first heard the name of John Dewey. He had been professor of Philosophy at the University of Chicago for eight years, and with his wife Alice had run the Laboratory School in league with Hull-House. Dewey believed in education for democracy, that children's talents were to be fostered to make them social beings, finding self-realisation in becoming part of a community. The Laboratory School had just closed when Dorothy was in Chicago, but its ethos lingered. Dewey had moved to New York to become a professor at Columbia, and she was determined to find him and his book, *The School and Society*, for this was worthwhile work that she felt was within her grasp.[46]

In 1908 she took her last trip to marriage-market Europe and it was supposedly full of 'gaiety and fun'. Her sister Pauline (Polly) was in poor health and they needed time together, with Polly's daughters Olive and her name-child Dorothy, aged three. Polly had arranged for them to stay in Scotland with Lady Kintore in Aberdeenshire; there was the son Lord Falconer whom she thought handsome and kind, but she was perfectly able to see that his estate needed her money, and so she said 'No'. Sheldon Whitehouse, four years her senior, ex-Eton and Yale, and secretary to Ambassador Whitelaw Reid, was her escort to Henley Regatta and a ball at Buckingham Palace; he was such good company that she was sad to reject him.[47] In London she and Beatrice contrived to elude Polly's watchfulness and slip out to buy the *Votes for Women* newspaper sold by the Suffragettes, and they managed to see something of the colourful banners and thousands of beautifully dressed women on their demonstration marches to Hyde Park.[48] At home the franchise was creeping slowly from the Midwest (Wyoming had given women the vote in 1869) but progress had stalled in Idaho; Dorothy would revive the cause at the National Junior League level. Grosvenor Atterbury met her in Paris, they walked in the Tuileries, and again she refused him.[49] At least she was now certain she was doing the right thing, but she blushed at the thought of the trail of wreckage she left behind.

In the New Year of 1909 she was in Washington, as the guest of the Meyers – George von Lengerke Meyer was ambassador to Russia and one of the president's oldest friends – for the dinners and balls that marked the end of the presidential term. She found herself sitting next to Willard Straight at a dinner, and later danced with him at the White House. She was there again for President Taft's inauguration in March and the parade in the Mall moved her to tears of pride for her beloved country. Payne and Helen Whitney included her in their party to visit Havana and meet President Gómez. Her feet hardly touched the ground for she was then immediately bound for London for the Albert Hall rally of the Women's Social and Political Union. She had made good her word from the year before and urged the National Junior Leagues to take up the cause, with the result that she was elected their representative. With such an impressive mandate she was naturally seated on the platform, where a press photographer caught her looking pensive as the lively audience cheered speaker after speaker who recounted her maltreatment in prison or at the hands of the police. Dorothy, whose innate pacifism prompted her grave doubts about militancy, the smashing of windows and 'rushing' of the House of Commons, felt increasingly uncomfortable; she was puzzled that such a seemingly intelligent audience could be roused by Christabel Pankhurst's fearsome power into a baying mob, screaming for 'justice' and 'liberty' and so betraying their intelligence. Dorothy thought of 'justice' for her New York seamstresses burned alive in locked factories, and of the chill of 'liberty' for those refugees in her Settlement houses, and somehow protest in Kensington had a hollow ring. Bitterly disillusioned she crept away, only to be rescued by Sylvia Pankhurst, known to differ from her militant sister, and shown around Sylvia's East London Federation of Suffragettes for helping working women.[50]

At the end of her return Atlantic crossing she retreated thankfully to Old Westbury. The May weather was lovely, her neighbours were sociable and she soon encountered Willard Straight, who was between postings and staying with her Long Island neighbours, Harry P. Davison of J.P. Morgan's Bank, Willard's sponsors. On morning rides,

Willard Straight

which Dorothy enjoyed for the first time since her stepmother Edith's accident, and at tennis teas they dovetailed: Willard was tall, taller than she was, slim and carelessly elegant in his dress. His birthday was a week after hers, on 31st January, he was seven years older and also an orphan. His father Henry Straight had taught natural sciences and was a disciple of Louis Agassiz, as her mother Flora had been. Professor Straight had died when Willard was five, and his mother Emma had taken him and his sister Hazel to Tokyo, where she was teaching, until she too became ill. She had brought them home to guardians in Oswego on Lake Ontario, where Willard and Hazel had grown up. He had inherited his mother's talent for drawing and so he had gone to Cornell University to study architecture. He enjoyed Cornell but concluded that progress in architecture was too slow for him, and his flair for languages, and a quickly accomplished course in Mandarin, fitted him for the Imperial Maritime Customs Service, which represented the Great Powers in Peking under Sir Robert Hart, whose secretary he had become. The American Minister in Seoul, Edwin V. Morgan (another of Dorothy's Long Island neighbours), had taken

Willard to Cuba as his assistant, where he had made the arrangements for Alice Roosevelt and Nicholas Longworth's honeymoon stay. Alice's father had made Willard consul-general in Mukden.

Willard had an attractive voice and loved to tell of his adventures. Dorothy listened spellbound as he told her about the Russo-Japanese War and his journey by train, riverboat and on horseback north through the Amur Region to the Sea of Okhosk. He had found a place of ruins, with a wonderful garden that he believed was Coleridge's Xanadu, or Shangtu.[51] E.H. 'Papa' Harriman had found him his new job as American Representative for the quartet of Western bankers making loan agreements with the Chinese government. As Imperial China crumbled the aim was to encourage the Chinese people into the modern world. Dorothy gasped, 'What great and worthwhile work!' When, at the end of June, Willard called to say goodbye as he was off to Peking, she laughed, 'Another wonderful adventure?'

'Well, you must come,' he replied.

THREE: 'DESTINY AND INTRICATE AFFAIRS'

Dorothy did not stop to question why she would cross America and the Pacific Ocean to meet a man she really did not know very well; she leapt into action. She wrote to Senator Root, who replied saying that he had such fond memories of her father and her family since she was a baby that she 'fell heir to his affection'. He sent introductions to the American Representatives she would meet on her journey along with the State Department's carte blanche:

> Miss Whitney is not a mere sightseer but a close student
> of human events able to appreciate most thoroughly any
> insight you may give her into the destiny and intricate
> affairs of China.[52]

'Papa' Harriman's Union Pacific office arranged their travel, and the intrepid four, Dorothy, Beatrice, Mrs Bend and Louisa, set out in mid-July. It was a royal progress in the Whitney family's private railcar, *Wanderer*, which was attached to the Chicago express, then presumably shunted around to meet their travel plans. They stayed at Denver to visit the Grand Canyon, then travelled north to Seattle, the Northern Cascades and Glacier Peak, where they explored and rested, eventually reaching San Francisco. Dorothy did not explain their rambling course (did the train schedules force *Wanderer* to be true to its name?), but she did note how strange it felt to be so far from her usual haunts when she heard of Harry's triumphs in England with his 'Big Four' polo team, and that Louis Bleriot had flown across the English Channel on 25th July.

At San Francisco they boarded SS *Korea* bound for Yokohama and Tokyo. Dorothy's great-uncle, Commodore Matthew Perry, in his frigate *Susquehanna* had sailed into these very waters some fifty-five years earlier, his 'gunboat diplomacy' persuading the Japanese to sign the Treaty of Kanagawa, thereby opening trade with America and the West after two centuries of isolation. Dorothy does not mention this, nor does she say much about Japan. The people she met in diplomatic circles had westernised manners overlaying the infinitesimal courtesies of the Orient, and she may have found them dull. A few years earlier Mary Fraser, the wife of the British Minister, had been bewitched by the beauty she found, she thought Tokyo one of the fairest cities she had ever seen, its streets and houses 'seemed to have grown up by accident – and are of no importance as compared with the flowers'. Dorothy was there in the chrysanthemum season and the huge golden blooms were everywhere with their sombre scent, perhaps a poor second to the springtime azaleas and plum and cherry blossoms? (Japanese cherry trees and azaleas were later to be her garden favourites but she was never to share the American popular taste for 'Mums'.) Undoubtedly, simply travelling occupied them, settling in and out of hotels, encountering the strangeness of the food and everything else: Dorothy's maid Louisa Weinstein quickly adapted to the cities of the East because she found cheerful and willing hands to help with her three ladies' wardrobes, keeping them happily dressed.

From Tokyo they went south to Mount Fuji; Mary Fraser felt that the merest glimpse of the perfect cone-shaped Fuji-San was enough to lift her spirits, and surely Dorothy would have appreciated her sentiments: 'That one cannot think of Fuji as a thing, a mere object in the landscape – she becomes something personal, dominating, a factor in life. No day seems quite sad or aimless in which one has had a glimpse of her.'[53] These travellers apparently passed by and onwards to Nagoya, where Dorothy complained that the hotel was 'horribly dirty', then to Kobe and Kyoto – where surely the sublime temple gardens detained her, or was she simply getting impatient for Peking? It was not until 22nd October that they sailed from Shimonoseki, crossing the Korea Strait to Busan on the southern tip of the peninsula, and then taking the train to the French colonial capital of Seoul. Willard had expected them much earlier, for his welcome to Dorothy was dated in early September, saying that China awaited her, 'red carpets and brass bands straining at the leash – we place the keys of the American compound in your hands, they are of brass and very heavy'.[54] She did not dare tell her fellow travellers of Willard's impatience, or her own. Seoul was within his diplomatic reach and he smoothed their path north to Mukden (now Shenyang) where there was a fire at their hotel – 'a very fortunate escape', reported Dorothy, a bad memory soon banished by seeing the Great Wall by moonlight.

On 1st November they arrived in Peking, at 8.20 in the morning. Willard was there to meet them and walked them to their lodging, returning to accompany them to the Legation for lunch with the president of the Board of Chinese Foreign Affairs. '*Such* a nice day,' recorded Dorothy; 'Miss Whitney v charming,' noted Willard.[55]

Willard shared his house with Henry Prather Fletcher, a career diplomat of thirty-six and former Rough Rider from Roosevelt's Cuban campaign. Fletcher, or Prather as Dorothy called him, was a tough and touchy bachelor and a bit of a cynic, and as opposite temperaments he and Willard suited each other. Willard called him 'Elder Brother' from the reverential title *Ta-a-ko*, 'Great Elder Brother', given to the Qing dynasty heir apparent P'u-chun. Between them they decided that their guests must have their house and servants, and they would sleep in the Legation.

The next day they explored the Legation Quarter and walked through the five courts of the 'wonderfully picturesque' Lama Temple. Their first dinner was with Legation friends and Prince P'u Lun –

P'u Lun Beitzu, one of the claimants to the throne the previous year when Hsuan-T'ung (Proclamation of Fundamental Principles), born P'u-Yi (whose story is told in the film *The Last Emperor*), had been enthroned.[56] A dust storm kept them indoors the following day, and on their fourth morning Willard sent greetings in French, asking what they would like to do. 'Such gorgeous days,' wrote Dorothy, 'Mr S took us this morning to the Drum Tower, where we climbed for the beautiful view. Then we went outside on the walls of the Yellow Temple. Exquisite.' With some Legation ladies they called on Princess P'u Lun, while Willard was playing polo; on the Sunday morning he arranged a picnic, the ponies and the lunch ready at noon. The next day, Monday 7th November, was 'One of the Golden Days!!' They drove out to the Summer Palace '& after going through that glorious place took "rikishas" to the Imperial Jade Spring where we had a picnic lunch – purple hills on one side, distant Peking on the other. Long talk tonight with Mr Straight – so long and interesting.' The 7th November remained a special anniversary for Willard: he wrote, 'Summer Palace and Yu Chuan San – quiet dinner and long talk by lantern light – the best day for many moons.' The Summer Palace was a favourite residence of the Empress Cixi who had it restored when she returned in 1902 after the Boxer Rising. She had died the previous year, but the 'civility of bribes' would have gained entry for Willard to this enchanted world – to the Garden of Harmonious Interest with the porcelain pagoda, the ornate boat houses fringing innumerable waters, the Fish-knowing Bridge and roofed walkways, the ancient twisted trees and Fragrant Hills.[57]

Dorothy managed to ride alone with Willard, 'the best ride I have ever had'. His version was, 'Record breaker. Beautiful day, lunch at Wan Show Sze – rode along the Jade Canal afterwards, quiet dinner *en famille*, with a juggler afterwards. A little music.' Music meant that he played his guitar in the firelight, and sang 'his own melodies to Kipling's songs of the East – songs of the far flung battle lines of Empire'.[58]

They went by train to the Great Wall, and on their next-to-last day by train to the Ming Tombs. Mrs Little's description of four years earlier held good – the approach through millet fields and persimmon orchards with all the ornamental trees felled, then 'clumps of foliage become visible in the distance, enclosing the golden roofed buildings clustering around the different tombs, some at three, some at four miles distance, but all alike beautifully enshrined in the bosom of the hills, at the upper end of the long wide valley'.[59] For Dorothy, isolated as she was from all reality in a landscape pitched between great antiquity and imminent destruction, the wreckage wrought by the 'Harmonious Fists', the Boxers, all too evident in the smashed statues and broken trees, was travelling in a fantasy land, wonderful to her yearning nature. The visit to the Ming Tombs was her never-to-be-forgotten day; they dined alone, Willard reading to her from his travel journals. He kept her up too late and apologised the next morning; 'Cannot though – honestly – say that I am penitent,' he told his diary.

On their last day they inspected the house Willard had chosen for his permanent quarters: 'The Princesse went through the house with me, and suggested here and there. It was hard not to ask her to stay on and live there.' After a 'wonderful' ride into the sunset they had a quiet dinner with 'a little choking at the throat, I think'. Next morning he saw them off at the station.

Leaving Hankow, Dorothy wrote:

> Oh Wise Man of the East – you have made us very lonely and very homesick for the purple hills and for your own companionship. I don't think I realized what a sad break our departure was going to be until I stood on the wall with you yesterday morning and said goodbye to the great city and the distant hills – and hardest of all to you. And then when we stood on the station platform and the whistle suddenly blew and we all said goodbye, I had a lump in my throat that was very hard to smile away, for the veil was being drawn then over two of the happiest weeks I have ever known.

Walking beside the river at Hankow she and Beatrice had talked of Willard and Prather, 'but we can't even tell each other how much we think of you both'. On deck in the starlight Dorothy lit an incense wand for Willard, breathed a prayer for him and for herself, 'that I might be more like you'. She felt that if she tried to thank him for all his generosity and consideration, 'words would only belittle the gratitude I feel, and I know you understand how much it all meant. I can only thank you for being the sort of man you are... and have faith always that there can never be in the future such a thing as lack of understanding between us. Goodbye – and may you find true happiness in the future, for you deserve the best there is... Goodbye.'[60]

Willard had written, 'Princesse – I thank you for coming here – and for all the sunshine you have brought us with your bonny laugh – Peking will be very different now – dearer because you have been here – and more lonely because you have gone – please be careful, you are very precious, WS.' Her letter from Hankow made him 'proud and happy', but he ended, 'It is not Goodbye – is it Princesse?'

Dorothy, sailing from Shanghai on 26th November, addressed her 'Dear Guardian of Borderland'.[61] His letters and telegrams had made her feel close but now they were turning southwards and sailing farther and farther away: 'I think the incense will have to burn twice as long these months when a vast distance separates us.' She had been reading Emerson, 'which reminded me at once of you – it is easy in the world to live after the world's opinions; it is easy in solitude to live after our own – but the great man is he who in the midst of the crowd keeps with perfect sweetness the independence of solitude'.

'A perfect trip from Shanghai to Hong Kong' was enjoyable for finding three Ivy League college boys on board, 'so we all had meals together, played bridge and did tricks in the gymnasium and laughed at our fellow passengers'. At a last night dance on board she was amazed at herself 'waltzing on the decks with strangers'. Dorothy and Mrs Bend explored the curio shops in the backstreets of Canton and climbed a five-storey pagoda; Dorothy's nightmares were peopled with Buddhas, figures dressed in mandarin coats and curious carvings of jade.

They took the ferry across the Pearl River to Macao – 'light and sunny and flowery Macao' – where they eyed the gambling casinos with interest but thought the Dutch merchants in their 'pyjamas' very unattractive. Back in Hong Kong it was dinner at Mr Murray Stewart's of Jardine Matheson, whose table talk put up Dorothy's rating of the place by fifty per cent. She scoured the market stalls for books, especially copies of J.O.P. Bland's *Houseboat Days in China* with Willard's illustrations, for him and for her friends. On 10th December a postcard from Saigon headed Willard's way: 'We think the Frenchmen here in their pure white clothes are just lovely!!' to which Beatrice added, 'We almost disappeared for months to Cambodia and Siam but think we will be safely on our way tonight to Singapore.' It became clear that Beatrice and Prather Fletcher were tip-toeing into a relationship.

On Raffles Hotel notepaper, with which she was well stocked, Dorothy wrote her longest letters to Willard. On 27th December (still 1909):

> The great excitement of Christmas morning was the opening of your large envelope containing our three real gifts of the day, and I don't believe that any gifts were ever more appreciated. Marraine and Beatrice were tremendously touched by theirs, and as for mine – the poem and the picture made Borderland seem very real and wonderful – the purpling hills, the misty plain – remain as they were that last afternoon for you have painted the picture for me.

With the New Year, 1910, Dorothy was coming out of her oriental dream, thinking about her old life at home, and preparing those she loved for her new: to her cousin Kate Barnes she wrote:

> Peking was so wonderful – the best part of it all was the real friendship we made with Messrs Straight and Fletcher and they are two of the strongest men I have

ever known – every evening we used to turn out the light and sit by the fire, Mr Straight brought out his guitar and sang to us. He is really a very remarkable person with a great deal of force and a really wonderful power of sympathy. He is a famous man all over China – we used to hear words of praise of him on every side... it is really extraordinary the power which he and Mr Fletcher wield in China, they are serving their country in a way that makes one proud.[62]

In Peking Willard made light of his New Year gloom:

'Strange Action of Heretofore Docile Guitar' – in local musical circles comment has been caused by the strange obstinacy of Mr W. D. Straight's guitar. Its frets are of no avail. Nothing will bring the strings into harmony – a sensible old thing, having served you, will serve no other... Today I rode alone – over the Northern plain, where we went that day to the Yellow Temple – I silliquized [sic] and told the scenery that it couldn't plume itself any longer, that India had won your heart, and that [China] now lay thumbed and a little ragged, like a month-old magazine – still on the table, eclipsed by the Special Indian Number.

The intrepid four had indeed reached India, Dorothy reading Kipling's *Kim* on the way. She celebrated her twenty-third birthday in Benares en route to Delhi, where Elihu Root's diplomatic reach ensured that they were entertained by the Viceroy, the 4th Earl of Minto, who had known Dorothy's father while in his previous posting as Governor-General of Canada. Willard need have had no fear; India did not win her heart. She telegraphed him on his thirty-first birthday, and he thought her message 'the best of the day'. Then there was the long trip from Bombay across the Indian Ocean and through the Suez Canal to Cairo, where they were in mid-March. Dorothy found thirty letters waiting for her, some from Willard, but also disturbing news of her sister Polly's poor health. To her delight the Theodore Roosevelts were in Cairo, Kermit and his father on their return from shooting in Africa meeting Ethel and her mother who had been holidaying in the Mediterranean. As a family the Roosevelts liked Willard and were happy to have news of him and Dorothy's adventures. For Dorothy it was relaxing: 'Ethel and I played around together every day'; Ethel Roosevelt, aged nineteen and rather shy, conceived an almost worshipping affection for Dorothy and theirs became a treasured friendship on both sides. As for T.R., Dorothy thought him 'simply splendid, and I was overcome by his sitting down and talking to foolish, ignorant me… he sure is a great man – and I am all for him!' The girls accompanied him to the Moslem University where everything was very solemn and dignified, 'although T.R. gave Ethel and me the wink once or twice'. To Willard, she finished in triumph, 'Of course he is going to be President again – don't you think so? Then you will be Secretary of State – and USA will immediately annexe China!! Banzai!!'[63]

She 'had a grand welcome from Sister & the kids' at St Raphael south of Cannes where Polly was recuperating, and after a week playing bridge – Polly's favourite pastime – Dorothy headed back to Florence and the Bends. Displaying every symptom of 'in loveness' she wandered alone, in and out of churches, around the Piazza del Duomo, climbing the 414 steps of Giotto's Campanile for the views. 'Oh, I love Florence,' she told her diary. Then in quick despair, 'The weather is overcast & tomorrow Halley's comet is going to finish off the earth,' her earth that was now so much more familiar and full of treasures. To Willard she questioned, 'And so are you really coming – are you?' He had given her his deadline, 28th April, for completion of the loan negotiations when he would leave Peking for London. He was going to leave in any case to avoid 'loss of face', but the Agreement was not yet signed. In Florence Dorothy bought an expensive present for Beatrice Bend, a string of pearls, as a thank you for their great journey; or was Beatrice anxious to get home and being persuaded to stay? For Dorothy was frankly kicking her heels.

Willard left on the Trans-Siberian express: 'I am crossing half the world to see you, Princesse. I want to see you more than I want anything else – I know I am right and hence have no smiting conscience – one learns somehow as one grows older that even one's elders and betters have to be told what to do.' This last meant that he was going to deal severely with the laggard bankers, even the great Mr J.P. Morgan, as he believed his first-hand knowledge of the Chinese circumstances was the soundest. In Berlin he found the Roosevelts, T.R. being feted by the Kaiser, and he joined their special train, arriving in London in mid-May. At the Morgan Grenfell office in the City he found that Mr J.P. himself and Mr Davison were not expected from America for three days. Three free days! He leapt on a train for Milan and Dorothy.

> Willard arrived at 6 this morning – there were no pretenses then. After one brief word of greeting he told me why he had come. Standing against the door of our little sitting-room with his hat still in his hand he poured out the yearnings of his heart. I, who had been living for six months in anticipation of this day, suddenly found myself weak and uncertain. Confronted with the reality I drew back in hesitation and doubt.

That she did not fall into his arms was a shock. Beatrice and Marraine were unfailing chaperones, having breakfast with them and joining them on a drive to Stresa. This was Dorothy's favourite place of all, and they took the boat onto Lake Maggiore to Isola Bella, where she and Willard sat in the garden, alone but not out of view. Travelling took two of his precious days so he had to leave on the Simplon express at 6.15 p.m., after just twelve hours. From her hotel Dorothy wrote:

> It's just five hours, Willard, since you went away, and I have been standing on the balcony and thinking of you as you cross the mountains tonight – as you left the clouds began to gather, and a mist crept over the lake, so that

when the sunset time arrived we had no sunset, and now
instead of a starry sky and moonlight on the waves, there
is only an impenetrable darkness above… so in leaving
you took light and colour away with you.

She was glad for their day together in Italy, 'the land that has always
meant so much to each of us in our dreams'.

This was 22nd May; she had been travelling, buffeted by the winds
of the world, for ten months, lost to her family and her beloved home.
In her heart she knew that Harry and Gertrude and many of her
friends would disapprove of Willard, as perhaps her sister Polly had
already done. She continued to Willard:

And I wondered if you know how much I appreciate the
high ideal of truth you showed me yesterday – when you
told me all those things about yourself – after you had
told me I knew that our relationship was on a higher
plane and that you had given me your truth as a part of
your love.

While they were in Milan, and out of Dorothy's hearing, Beatrice
had challenged Willard on the nature of his relationships with Mary
Harriman and Katherine Elkins – Mary was marrying the artist
Charles Cary Rumsey but there was still gossip about Miss Elkins,
an heiress he had supposedly abandoned for a richer heiress – and
these were the things about himself that he had confessed, winning
Dorothy's assurance. In Paris he brightened with the 'Great Hope'
that she would tell him she loved him, and he rediscovered his sense
of humour:

You have asked me to wait. Do you know how hard it
is. Do you know that I can't wait long – and that any
moment I am apt to let the spirit of the Moyen age sweep
me away – to ride for you and swing you into the saddle

before me. I shall be quite terrible then – on a very big
horse – and all in tin clothes. Are you not afraid?

She was afraid, afraid of his vibrant sexuality as well as the rumours
of his fortune-hunting. She wanted him to have the success of the
Chinese loan agreements, for which the Paris and London papers
were already feting him in anticipation. In Paris he talked for hours
without a conclusion and he was ordered to New York. Dorothy had
reached Paris and they had a short time together before he sailed on
the *Lusitania* – cablegrams and flowers, posies of lily of the valley and
a daily single red rose descended on Dorothy. He dashed mercurially
from Wall Street to Washington, to Oswego to see his sister and aunt
Laura, then back to New York catching the *Lusitania* like a riverboat
on her return trip. He realised, 'I am not *in love* but *I love* and there's
all that difference – it is very wonderful and very terrible – it makes
me ache.'

In Paris Dorothy and the Bends were being sociable with
Ambassador Robert Bacon, and the coterie of Edith Wharton
and Henry Adams.[64] Their host in Peking, Prather Fletcher, now
appointed Minister to Chile, stopped over to renew his courting of
Beatrice. Willard, fresh off the *Lusitania*, spent three days with them,
before leaving for St Petersburg to tussle with the Russian bankers.
Dorothy gave him a gold locket with her portrait; she hung it around
his neck, and he thanked her, writing, 'Without you paradise would be
a wilderness – the Great God that rules us – and shapes our lives – has
meant this to be. The hand of Providence has led us together – and
together we must be.'

Dorothy reached London, finding it in sober and uncertain mood
at the ending of the Edwardian era with the death of the king in
May; she was too late for the black and white Ascot in mourning, and
everyone she knew had gone to the country. Sister Polly, who loved to
rent a different house each summer, was installed at The Deepdene,
near Dorking in the Surrey hills, a fantastic Italianate palace in its
own garden valley.[65] Making her preference clear, Polly had invited

Lord Falconer to the house party, but Willard also arrived, commuting from gruelling days in the Morgan Grenfell office, and prickly with frustration. Dorothy, tossed on emotional seas and exhausted from travelling, took to her bed, though she was not excused from sitting for her portrait. Willard was reduced to plying Louisa with notes, 'Buongiorno princessa mia – before going to pose will you tell Louisa to knock on my door – and see me for a moment in the hall – today you must be kind princessa mia.' Trysts in the dark panelled corridors, knocking on heavy doors, dodging the hawk-eyed servants, no wonder Willard felt driven to medieval tactics, and he certainly felt that everyone was against him. Polly had summoned Harry, who was in England for his polo anyway, for a family conference, but it is unlikely that he faced Willard. Harry admired him for his work but had heard on good authority that he had declared himself to be deeply in love with Katherine Elkins.

Dorothy, finding The Deepdene claustrophobic, headed back to Paris, closely followed by Willard. His attentions were becoming tumultuous, but then he knew he was being sent back to America and then directly to Peking. One of his many bouquets of roses came with this note:

> You may shake you may scatter
> Your Boy if you will
> But the scent of his roses
> Will cling round you still!

He had found his old Cornell professor, Henry Morse Stephens, in London and persuaded him to write his testimonial. 'Without parents or means he has made himself what he is,' the professor wrote.

> Without any backing but his own brave heart he set out
> to play the game and he has played it like a man [with
> no one to guide him or play influence for him] – he has
> kept himself clean and wholesome and brave, when many

51

a young man would have gone down; he has steered clear of cynicism and credulity, he has made his way in the world by sheer merit, held his head high and asked no man anything.

The letter is dated 8th July 1910 and Dorothy kept it.[66]
    They had six days together at Divonne on Lake Geneva at the invitation of Mrs Wharton, who had just relinquished her romance with Morton Fullerton. Walter Berry was there too; Judge Berry had been at Dorothy's christening, and he had just returned from working on a tribunal in Cairo in his role as an international lawyer, experience of special interest to Willard, and Dorothy. Willard left for New York on 30th July.
    Poor Dorothy, her feet were itching and cold at the same time; marriage to Willard 'would be such a complete break with the past, such a plunge into new surroundings and new circumstances, such a separation from people I loved'. However much she wanted to go home she felt she must not weaken. Willard wrote from New York to Beatrice urging her to persuade Dorothy to come home, and Dorothy lost her usual equanimity:

> You foolish child to have written the way you did to Beatrice. Of course she doesn't understand what right you have to expect us to change all our plans and go home earlier to see you and I'm afraid she thinks it somewhat fresh of you to ask it. If you and I were engaged, or even if I knew I cared, it would be entirely different. Your nerves must be on edge, poor Boy.

It was unsaid and unwritten that Dorothy's closest companion Beatrice Bend was completely opposed to her romance with Willard, and this also unnerved her; there must have been many a long silence as they avoided the subject while staying in France and England through August and September. They all arrived in New York on the *Lusitania* on 13th October; Willard met them, and he was invited to Old Westbury. He had little time for he was due in Washington prior to his return to Peking, via London, and he was working desperately hard. The American bankers had increased the loan for the Chinchou–Tsitshan–Aigun railroad to $300 million, but he had to get the British, French and Russians over the final hurdles, in the face of opposition from those in Washington who preferred to make loan agreements with the Japanese. Something has to be said for his persistence under pressure, especially to those who thought him too volatile. While Dorothy cheered him on and sympathised with his exhaustion, Willard must have felt it would all have been so much easier had 'Papa' Harriman not died – he so wanted to achieve Harriman's last dream of influencing the Chinese 'so that we can show them how to do it right & and thus get a real lasting American influence'.[67]

After just twelve days on the same continent as Dorothy, Willard sailed for London and headed east. From Moscow he wrote:

> Here tonight I am starting out across Siberia, and you
> are four thousand miles away – even though you say the
> Miracle has not yet been granted – there is that bond
> between us – the bond that makes me wake with thoughts
> of you – that gives you my last waking thought, and
> weaves you through my dreams.

In New York Dorothy did not appear concerned that the gossip columnists seemed affronted that their 'Number One Marriageable Heiress' should have abandoned 'both common sense and tradition in becoming involved with an outsider whose status as an heiress chaser seemed generally accepted'.[68] She stayed close to her friends in her Book Class, at Henry Street and Grace Church; she was often with the Roosevelts at Sagamore Hill where Ethel was sympathetic and T.R.'s sister, Corinne Roosevelt Robinson, became her affectionate champion.[69]

Harry Whitney had announced that he intended to buy back their father's palatial 871 Fifth Avenue, which he felt they had mistakenly sold to James 'Silent' Smith, who had died. Mr Smith must have been the veritable one careful owner, for it was all settled in a month (for something like $2 million) and Gertrude and Harry were able to move in immediately, on Dorothy's twenty-fourth birthday, 23rd January 1911. She was pleased that her father's treasures were safe, but she and Beatrice were actually occupied in moving into their own apartment in the Lorraine Building at Fifth Avenue and East 45th Street. Dorothy's tactics became startling. Putting on her prettiest hat she called at the Morgan Library to beard the great man in his lair. 'JPM was lovely to me,' she reported to Willard, 'he laughed and said he wished I would go there every single week – dear Mr J.P. he's such a sweetie underneath the sternness.'[70] Wearing a slightly less becoming hat she presented a large donation ($25,000) to the Red Cross, in the person of none other than her Long Island neighbour Harry Pomeroy Davison, who was the Red Cross Representative *and* the Morgan partner most closely associated with the Chinese loans.[71] She talked with Theodore Roosevelt whenever the chance arose because she felt he was Willard's greatest ally. She also told him about the Henry Street Settlement; he visited the new Music Settlement, and thanked her: 'They mentioned incidentally what you had done, and your interest in that new working-girls' home or hotel or boarding house, or whatever it is – I wish you would take Ethel and me to it.'[72]

Was it possible that she had made up her mind? That Roosevelt's high opinion of Willard, that with the Chinese loans to his credit, he would become a prime political asset with a great, perhaps the greatest, future role? Had she pierced the rosy glow of *in loveness* to see Willard as the husband who would enfold her in his arms, and also the partner who needed her, or at least her fortune, for their great work together?

Her friend Ethel Roosevelt met a storm of publicity when she felt unable to accept Dr Richard Derby's proposal of marriage – and Dorothy liked him so much that she urged him to keep trying. 'He really is a wonder,' she wrote to Willard, 'and Ethel simply must marry him – I'm afraid Ethel is terrified by the great wonder of marriage just the way I am – I believe in it so much Willard, that I don't dare believe in it too much – that's all. But I do get panics now and then.' She and Ethel talked into the small hours, and Ethel told Richard Derby that she would not marry him unless Dorothy married Willard! Derby immediately threatened to go to Peking and fetch Willard home. Fortunately Miss Elkins spoke out, exonerating Willard from any dishonourable conduct: there had been no promises and none broken. Dorothy cheered him on:

> I know how dreadfully hard and lonely it must be for you –
> but I have great faith that you will pull the loan through –
> and then, oh Willard – won't that be wonderful! Wouldn't
> it be the greatest triumph ever, if you won! Don't be too
> positive – especially with men – for it antagonizes them
> and really, humility is always one of the characteristics of
> a big person... Oh Willard, don't be in a hurry to leave
> the Group for the [State] Department. I'm sure it is far
> wiser to continue for a while in this way with Mr Davison
> and Mr J.P.

Then, suddenly everything came together, and on 15th April the $300 million loan was agreed and ensured. Willard cabled and then wrote:

> O Dorothy child – before this letter reaches you I should
> be started on my way... the loan was signed today without
> any further quibbling... and 'Dollar Diplomacy' is justified
> at last. Oh child – if only you had been here to celebrate,
> but you were – for it was your Victory, and the courage
> you gave, and my hope for you, Dorothy mine – alone
> carried me through – and I've you to thank for it all.

She went to church singing glad hymns of praise. But there was also the second, smaller Hukuang railroad loan, and she felt he should stay until that too was completed. He wrote, 'My – but you are such a greediness oh Dorothy mine! So you want the Hukuang too, do you? As a matter of fact we seem to be in a very fair way to get it – inside a week.'

It took until 20th May and Willard finally left Peking. He was a physical wreck, full of aches and pains and influenza, and he felt 'a little more twisting on the strings would have snapped 'em, I know'. Dorothy was pleased and proud, but 'when I think of you being here with me again I just gasp for joy – and the next moment I just shiver inside and feel just as terrified of you as I used to, last year'.

Willard's success made headlines as he travelled westwards, so that by the time he reached New York, on 21st June, he was feted, and many of his critics, most importantly Harry Whitney, were mellowed. Dorothy cautioned, 'Please be humble with everyone, they all know what you've done, and I know best of all.' At Old Westbury he proposed again, and she accepted, but it was to be a secret. She wanted a quiet wedding, not a circus. Her passage, with the Bends and Louisa, was booked on the *Olympic* at the end of the week, and so Willard sailed with them. Harry announced their engagement to surprise 'heard on all sides – the match is one of the most amazing in many years. Straight is a poor man – and Miss Whitney is the last heiress of her set remaining unwed – [she] has had untold chances to marry. For five years she has been the most sought-after and most talked-of girl in New York.'[73]

Ethel Roosevelt was among the first to know; she wrote to Willard welcoming their friendship, and to 'Best Beloved Dorothy – how very happy I am for you both… some-day Dick and I will join you'. She sent on a letter which perhaps typified the feelings of those who hardly knew Dorothy: 'I hear Dorothy Whitney is engaged to Strait [sic] – he has got to do some flying to get to her… in my estimation there is nobody as fine, splendid, big and humanly Olympic as she in the whole wide world.' From Henry Street, Lillian Wald wrote of her genuine pleasure 'to know that you were as happy in your own right as well as through the happiness of others', and that hers would be a marriage of true minds as well as of hearts.[74]

They had landed from the *Olympic* and gone their separate ways, Willard to London, and Dorothy and company to Paris to buy her trousseau. Then they were installed at the huge Caux Palace Hotel in Montreux and letters and cablegrams flew backwards and forwards with wedding arrangements. At the end of August, Dorothy told Lillian Wald, 'Willard and I expect to be married very quietly in Geneva next week – and soon afterwards go out to China, but we are planning to be home by the beginning of January.' She told Lillian to expect $50,000 sometime in the winter, 'but please, say nothing, will you?'[75]

Their wedding day was 7th September, Willard's special number. Everyone was to foregather at the Grand Hotel National which sprawled palatially along the Geneva lakeside, though Willard's bachelor quarters were at the Tennis Parc. Dorothy was nervous, she had been reading through the marriage service, 'and oh Best Beloved, it is so beautiful that I felt a dreadful lump in my throat at the thought of what it all meant'. Willard feared she would be tired from staying up too late and talking to Beatrice, who – even at this last moment and having come this far – was still opposed to the marriage of her dearest Dorothy. On their wedding morning he wrote, 'Oh, my Best Beloved – I miss you. I love you everything. I'm looking forward to 3.45!'

That was the time they would get away. Before that seemed rather an ordeal, and the bride, who had been suffering from tension headaches, looked weighed down by her veil of antique lace. Willard looked hardly more cheerful. A civil ceremony was followed by a service at the Episcopal church. Harry gave the bride away, and afterwards the wedding breakfast was served on the terrace of Polly and Almeric's suite. Olive and Dorothy Paget were Dorothy's bridesmaids, and Willard was supported by William Phillips from the American Embassy in London, as both Prather Fletcher and Harry Davison were too far away. In the wedding photograph Marraine and Beatrice Bend are apparently in tears. The bride and groom were driven to Lausanne to catch the Simplon express for Stresa, to spend their first night beside Maggiore, in view of Isola Bella on her lake of dreams.

FOUR: PORCELAIN AND
POLISHED MARBLE[76]

Two weeks in Venice 'meeting experiences side by side', as Dorothy put it, transformed the fearful bride into an ecstatic wife. Afterwards Willard had to dash briefly to Berlin necessitating his revealing note to 'My Wonder of the World', full of staccato intimacies and ending, 'it seems impossible to write – my heart is too full of your dear heart – it is all aching, aching within me – you give so much – your love is so rich'. Dorothy, left at Versailles, felt alone 'without the presence of the one person who means more than all the rest of the world together'. In fact the Bends were with her, though for the last time, and she cabled to Willard with the message that Beatrice was 'all right'.[77]

In early October they set out on the Trans-Siberian Railway for the three-week journey to Peking. Dorothy was overjoyed to find her house ready, the furnishings she had helped to choose, the big living room 'full of lovely Chinese things' and the remembered Chusan palm in the front garden. They each had a suite of bedroom, bathroom and sitting room, and the maid Louisa had a suite of her own. They settled down to recreate their idyll of almost exactly two years before, riding out and exploring their favourite places, returning to quiet evenings by the fireside which ended with a serenade from Willard and his (restored to

Dorothy and Willard on their honeymoon

health) guitar. But they were on borrowed time, and Willard noted his extended honeymoon experience as 'a bit thick with excitement'. They were issued with service revolvers to keep by them, and warned to take extra care and secure their valuable belongings. Dorothy reported, 'We have just hoisted our American flag – it waves a hands-off warning to any intruders. It is the first time in my life I have lived under our flag, regarding it solely as a protection. It is quite a thrilling sensation.'

The trouble came from the south. An accidental explosion in a revolutionary headquarters in Wuchang sparked a panic in a group of army officers who, fearing their collusion would be exposed, ordered rebellious uprisings which spread to fifteen provinces. A bomb exploded outside Willard's house in early January and they were advised to leave for a while, which they did, travelling to Manila. Willard was anxious to secure the future of his loan agreements with the advisers to the westernised republican leader Sun Zhongshan and he appears to have been successful. After six weeks they returned to find that the Last Emperor had abdicated and that General Yuan Shikai was president of the new republic.[78] Things appeared to be as before. The Fabians Sidney and Beatrice Webb arrived with a letter of introduction to Willard, and were warmly entertained – he 'about five feet high with a shaggy beard', and she 'with a sweet face but great intellectual superiority', reported Dorothy. A few evenings later they were dressing for dinner when a fire-fight and looting erupted, and they had to take refuge in the Legation, Willard returning through the dangerous streets to rescue Louisa. Next morning their house was surrounded, 'smoking ruins on all sides', and three days later the Marines arrived, marching into the American compound. Dorothy was thrilled and impressed. Government reprisals followed and she was soon revolted at 'a horrible day of executions & dead bodies are to be seen lying around in all the streets'.

In New York they were headline news: 'Peking set on fire and looted', 'Mr and Mrs Straight in Peril', and 'Great danger from flying bullets and fire brands'. Harry Whitney cabled his concerns, but an even greater power, J.P. Morgan, personally ordered their recall.[79] Dorothy and Willard seemed the only people who took it all in their stride, giving farewell parties, Willard playing polo, then together they 'took a last wonderful walk on the wall'. The Webbs were able to leave on the last crowded train because the conductor was a keen Fabian Socialist. Dorothy and Willard, the Marines at their backs, were given a rousing send-off. It was 26th March 1912, and Dorothy, 'feeling so sick', knew that she was pregnant.

Trunks full of their 'lovely Chinese things' were shipped home to Old Westbury, the souvenirs of their happy hunting through the bazaars of old Peking: porcelain vases glazed in peacock blue and powder blue, and with apple-green or ox-blood crackle glazes were packed with antique flower pots, jardinières and more vases coloured in soft green celadon and pink and green splashed peachbloom.

They had found endearing figures of Buddhas, immortals, warriors and ladies in various guises, and animals – horses harnessed and free, a trotting horse, a laughing camel and miniature carvings of jade and ivory. Chinese landscapes painted on silken scrolls, some of the Ming dynasty, were Dorothy's favourites, and a collection of Tibetan bronzes, incense burners, teapots, tobacco pots and altar decorations came from Willard's travels to the north. With these treasures around them the happiness they had found in China could not fade.[80]

April found Dorothy in Paris having dress fittings for her expanding waistline. They reached London with the news on 15th April of the 'terrible Titanic disaster'. They were to stay for three months in a rented house at Amersham-on-the-Hill in the Chilterns, which was close enough to the station for Willard to commute to Morgan Grenfell's office. Dorothy spent a quiet time, guarded by two West Highland White terriers that came with their house. She went to Nancy Astor's Cliveden for tea – Waldorf Astor was a friend of Harry Whitney – and found a friend for herself. Nancy was thirty-three to Dorothy's twenty-five, she had been married to Waldorf for five years, and had recently given birth to their third child, David. Despite Nancy's being a Southerner, a Virginian, and wearing a Conservative label (she said, 'If I thought it would work I would be a Socialist'), they had common causes in women's and workers' welfare. The Astors' lives intrigued both Willard and Dorothy, for being radicals and American they found themselves outsiders in English society. Waldorf Astor had just bought the Sunday newspaper the *Observer*, which was to forward the broad liberal agenda of his friends of the Cliveden 'Round Table'.[81]

From America Beatrice Bend had been agitating for Dorothy to come home and 'be properly looked after'. They sailed on the *Mauretania* on 10th August, arriving in a sweltering New York, from where Beatrice whisked Dorothy away to the Catskills. Beatrice was still uncertain about Prather Fletcher's proposal, Dorothy did not wish to force the issue, and found it impossible to say that she and Willard did not need her in their married life. Beatrice, in her mid-thirties, proud and strong-willed, devoted to Dorothy, seemed more than ever a subsidiary character of Henry James – a Maria Gostrey from *The Ambassadors* doomed to be an arranger of tours, a meeter and greeter, or companion to some upper-crust widow. If she lost her salary from Dorothy's trustees what would she live on? Dorothy could only insist that Beatrice come to Old Westbury to help her with the baby's birth.

Their baby boy, named Whitney Willard Straight, was born on 6th November 1912, the day after Theodore Roosevelt's renewed presidential bid was defeated by Woodrow Wilson. Dorothy, a nursing mother, had her long confinement in the quiet warmth of Old Westbury, with an outing on Christmas Day when Willard took her, on an improvised sleigh, to Kate and Courtland Barnes at Manhasset, a 'most exquisite day'.

She intended to move gradually back into her public life; in early 1913 she gave $1,000 in response to her sister-in-law Gertrude's request that she support the New York Armory Show of Modern Art.[82] Then, in early March Willard was summoned to Washington with Harry Davison to see Secretary of State William Jennings Bryan, who 'hedged diplomatically' in their presence, but later recommended to President Wilson that the Chinese loans be cancelled. The new administration soon announced that it did not approve of the conditions of the American Group loans, and the 'implications of responsibility' that seemed too much like interference into the politics of 'that great Oriental State just now awakening'. The administration by Morgan Grenfell in London (and partner-agents in Hamburg, Paris, St Petersburg and Yokohama) was, said the communiqué, 'obnoxious to the principles upon which the Government of our people rests'.[83]

That was final. It was such a blow to Willard, a personal insult seeing how hard he had worked, throwing back into his face all he had argued and travelled for, those endless miles and endless hours. Morgan's Bank was willing to keep a place for him for his knowledge of the Far East, but his lack of banking experience meant that his position would no longer carry the status he was used to; even Dorothy's charms would no longer work, for her 'sweetie' Mr Morgan died at the end of March. They attended his funeral.

In early April 1913 Dorothy noted in her diary, 'Ethel's wedding to Dick [Derby] took place this morning at Oyster Bay at 12. So simple – wonderful all through. Nice, happy reception afterwards, home by 3.30.' She and Willard settled to architectural pursuits, all done in his name as Dorothy was so sensitive to her 'poor' father's feelings when Flora held the purse strings. Their new town house at 1130 Fifth Avenue at East 94th Street was commissioned from William Adams Delano and Chester Aldrich, the coming men, who also enlarged the Old Westbury house and built Willard's new stable block. This was thought 'a stimulating lesson in sociology' and a revelation of modernity, that a building of such high quality should be devoted to servants, horses and motor cars. 'Bill' Delano, who had built Gertrude Whitney's sculpture studio, also introduced them to the landscape architect Beatrix Farrand, who was Edith Wharton's niece and a great favourite with the Roosevelts.[84] Beatrix shared their deep conviction that it was vital to live in harmony with their natural surroundings, and she added that making a garden was the most vivid expression of this harmony. They planned Old Westbury's Chinese garden together.

An aerial view of Old Westbury, 1914, with the Chinese garden at the bottom

Marriage had infused both Dorothy and Willard with the elixir of love; they were changed beings, joyful in each other and in their baby son. They took parenthood very seriously, and Dorothy read the handbooks aloud to Willard as he painted his watercolours. And yet, as they approached their second wedding anniversary, it must have seemed that the frisson of destiny was subdued. Woodrow Wilson's extinguishing the Chinese loan 'with the hose of presidential rhetoric' was a humiliating blow to Willard – from his lone assumption of the White Man's Burden (as Kipling had written of the United States and the Philippines) striving for the greatness of America, he was reduced to a Wall Street commuter. He had plenty of ideas for foreign business but as Harry Davison tactfully pointed out Willard had not earned by experience in banking any right to such initiatives, his 'pay grade' did not allow him to influence bank policy. It was Dorothy who had to keep her head: 'Almost every evening he would come home from the office with the same words on his lips, "I had a new idea today",' she wrote. 'In spite of myself I was forced to become the critic, for though many of the plans were sound in conception, the means of execution were often not at hand – [and] I often had to break the blow of his disappointments.' Willard's estimated annual salary was $20,000, which would not go far in New York, even in 1913; Dorothy's $7 million wisely invested might yield $250,000 annually – but then she was perfectly likely to give away $50,000 at a time to her favourite causes.[85]

Moreover Willard hated routine banking. Their hopes were pinned on Theodore Roosevelt who was leaving for Brazil. Dorothy sent him God-speed flowers, and he responded from the *Vandyck*, 'As soon as I come back I shall want to see you both. I shall have much to tell you.' Dorothy found his Bull Moose Progressive agenda, or New Nationalism, exciting with his endorsement of women's suffrage, schemes for health and welfare insurances, for reform of the labour laws and a 'clear and definite programme by which the people would be the masters of the trusts', instead of vice-versa.[86] She firmly believed that he would stand for the presidency in 1916, he would be triumphant and there would be a big job for Willard.

Willard, Dorothy and baby Whitney, *c*.1913

Meanwhile, they worked things through by reading and talking together – they talked of the Astors' *Observer* and of the news that the Webbs were launching their radical *New Statesman* with a capital of £5,000 (£1,000 from George Bernard Shaw), with a captive Fabian and Labour Party readership and Shaw's promised contributions. At T.R.'s suggestion they were reading Herbert Croly's *The Promise of American Life* published in 1909. Croly was in his forties, humanist and a journalist by upbringing and an academic by inclination, and by a circuitous route he had arrived at the editor's desk of *Architectural Record* where Willard found him.[87] At first he was wary of the Whitney reputation and the imagined splendours of Old Westbury, but soon realised that Dorothy was unconventionally serious, and he confessed that it was his dream to edit a paper to perpetuate and extend his thesis of *The Promise* – that America must 'become more of a nation' and assume 'a more definite and more responsible place' in the world. To do this, the education of her people of an 'awareness of the world in general' was essential. Dorothy's first opinion of Croly's rather squashed visage was as 'having the look of a disappointed frog', but they warmed to each other. Legend has it that she said,

> 'Why don't you get out a weekly yourself, Herbert?'
> H.C. 'But where would I find the money?'
> 'I will find it,' said Dorothy quietly.
> H.C. 'It would take a lot of money, it might take five years to make the paper self-supporting.'
> 'Yes, I understand. It may take longer, much longer. But let's go ahead.'[88]

On Sunday 16th November 1913 she noted in her diary that it was the 'Great Republican Conference' at their house. Willard chaired the gathering of Herbert and Louise Croly, Judge and Mrs Learned Hand, Phil Littell – a Harvard classmate of Croly's who would edit the book page – and Felix Frankfurter from Vienna, then a law lecturer at Harvard. Croly's prize recruit was the journalist Walter Lippmann at a salary of $60 a week, and he also found two young economists, George Soule and Alvin Johnson. The byword for editorial policy was 'looseness' – Croly said, 'We'll throw a few firecrackers under the skirts of the old women on the bench and in other high places.'[89]

The paper was to be called *The New Republic* and its mission was 'the enlightenment and enrichment of the nation', its politics were liberal and progressive, in the hope it would be the flagship for Roosevelt's campaign in 1916. Willard and Dorothy were joint proprietors and the first issue was scheduled for a year's time, the fall of 1914. The paper's home was at 421 West 21st Street downtown, bought from the Crolys and refurbished into a comfortable clubby atmosphere with an editorial round table and a well-equipped kitchen for serving good lunches.[90] Croly wrote to Judge Learned Hand, 'The vision I have... will, I fear, set angel Dorothy back some hundreds of thousands of dollars, but she will get a little education for her money, and so will I, and so, I hope will you and the others.' Walter Lippmann suspected that she was 'laundering' her father's tainted fortune in liberal causes.

Not long after *The New Republic* conference Dorothy realised she was pregnant again. This time, as her baby grew during the early months of 1914, there was the blessed harmony of making their Chinese garden. Mrs Farrand's design was for a walled garden at some distance from the house, the entrance guarded by two Chinese stone dogs – the surrounding wall pink-washed and topped with heavy pantiles. Beds of spring flowers were to be followed by larkspur, poppies, columbines, peonies and meadowsweet for summer. Beyond the flowers were matching tip-tilted roofed pavilions wreathed in soft blue *Wisteria chinensis*, with rounded 'moon' doorways and carved and painted bargeboards hung with musical bells. Beyond them was the swimming pool with twin changing pavilions. The flower garden was ready for planting when Beatrice Whitney Straight – 'such a cunning little girl weighing 7–9 pounds' – arrived on 2nd August. Two days later, though it must have seemed a world away, Europe went to war.

They summered in September in the Catskills, and returned to find their friends all concerned about the war, even though President Wilson insisted that it was none of America's business if others 'had lost their reason'. Roosevelt in his lair at Sagamore Hill was the magnet for those able to see that America would be drawn in and must arm herself for the fight. The first issue of *The New Republic* appeared as planned on 7th November 1914 with Croly's editorial warning that the conflict may have consequences 'as profound and far-reaching as our self-made Civil War'. Dorothy had paid for her own subscription, $4 a year; she was one of 875 opening subscriptions and this first issue sold a few thousand copies.[91]

Three weeks later, at very short notice from Harry Davison at Morgan's, Willard was ordered to London; motherhood or no, Dorothy could not let him go alone, and leaving their babies, almost certainly with Beatrice Bend in charge, they left on the *Adriatic* – it was winter, memories of the *Titanic* were fresh, and rumours were rife. Dorothy noted the news of attacks on shipping in her diary, but avoiding the danger area of the English Channel they arrived safely if shakily in Liverpool on 3rd December. In London she went directly to Claridge's, took a deep breath, and 'spent all afternoon at the Red Cross office packing kit bags for British soldiers'.

London at war had a nightmare quality for her. She found her stepsister Addie Lambart with her husband and her brother Bertie Randolph in uniform, she found her sister Polly frailer than ever but working for the war effort, and heard that her dear Gladys Szechenyi was rescuing refugee children with the Red Cross in Switzerland. Gertrude was also in London as she and Harry were sending a fully equipped field hospital to France, and it was her sacred mission to break through the red tape on both sides of the Channel so that the hospital was established in a boys' school at Juilly, near Compiègne. For some inexplicable reason, perhaps to convince herself that it wasn't just a nightmare, Dorothy went with Ethel and Richard Derby to Scarborough and the Hartlepools to see the damage from the bombardment by German destroyers, when more than one hundred people were killed.[92]

Back in London the zeal for the fight screaming from the headlines pained her, and then she detected the dreaded word 'profiteering'; Willard explained that he had said to Harry Davison, 'If I were running [Morgan's Bank] and wanted to help the Allies I would suggest that... they co-operate on a joint financial policy just as they were doing in a military and naval way.' Apparently Davison said nothing but went straight to 10 Downing Street where the suggestion was promptly adopted.[93] Willard grumbled that he didn't get any credit; Dorothy suspected that Morgan's role as purchasing agent for supplies from America was going to look like profiteering. *The New Republic* of 5th December had published a letter warning America of exploitation 'to promote its own business and trade', fairly swiftly followed by the Wilson administration's infamous note to the effect that the British blockade of German ports was harming America's trade. It was a bitter taste of the hatefulness of war. Dorothy left on the *Lusitania* with Gertrude and Ethel and Dick Derby, leaving Willard behind.

The crossing was bad. 'Captain Dow says the ship is "under water" part of the time,' noted Gertrude. In New York Dorothy shopped hastily for presents and spent a quiet Christmas with her children, Ethel Derby, whose husband was working, and Daisy Harriman who was recently widowed.

The first weeks of 1915 are silent, an indication of troubled times, or simply that the winter weather had prevented her from shopping for a new diary? Her silence extended to Willard who cabled, 'Please cable me Dorothy about yourself and the kids,' and adding 'whether she regarded him as too costly a plaything?' He returned at the end of January but was gone again after a month. They had talked things out and love's banner flew in the face of the world once more. Willard sent a letter to Whitney Straight Esquire, aged two and a half, 'We went through all the heart yearnings of those who part before action... she didn't sleep much [and] showed it in the morning but there was no word, no tear, only smiles and cheerfulness. If you ever amount to anything it will be because of your mother.'[94]

The German Embassy's warning to passengers travelling 'at their own risk' was on everyone's mind. The Cunarder *Lusitania* was flying the Stars and Stripes when Willard looked over her rail and watched Dorothy as she 'walked cheerily down the dock as the big ship slipped along out into the stream'. He continued to Whitney, 'This I shall never forget... this and the time we went through in Peking before you were born. These are the things that knit you close, for all the fluff is stripped away and you realize how much you care.'

From on board he wrote even more introspectively to Dorothy, 'But are we going on like this? Are we going to continue as privates in Wall Street – when we might be captains of our own ship?' He watched the turquoise water 'glistening, foaming under the bows and swirling alongside – purpling under the shadows of the clouds that tumbled overhead'. He was reading *The New Republic* about America's role, echoing their beliefs of 'a certain mission in the world' and the need for showing how things had been done so differently from Imperial Britain, and how 'from the old days we may gather inspiration to face the modern task'. In London he was sociable, dining with John Maynard Keynes, who contributed to *The New Republic*, and also meeting Colonel Edward House, President Wilson's envoy whose job was 'to knock heads together' and bring peace; the colonel hinted at a job for Willard in the peace negotiations and asked him to deliver a message to the French Foreign Minister. In Paris, after his visit to Morgan Harjes, Willard came to his decision to leave the bank. He was at home with Dorothy in April.[95]

On 7th May the Germans sank the *Lusitania* as she neared the end of her eastward crossing off southern Ireland. The *New York Times* of the following day howled in thick black headlines:

> *Lusitania* **sunk by a submarine, probably 1,260 dead; twice torpedoed – sinks in 15 minutes; Captain Turner saved, Frohman and Vanderbilt missing; Washington believes that a grave crisis is at hand.**

It was Gertrude's and Gladys's brother Alfred who was missing, and drowned. 'I feel,' wrote Gertrude, 'that if the loss of the *Lusitania* brought this country to a realization of its responsibilities and roused our apathetic citizens to action, it would be some consolation.' She was laid low by grief, exhaustion and an operation for appendicitis. Dorothy, haunted by her father's fate, was consoling and kind. Willard committed himself to a civilian training camp at Plattsburg with Dick Derby and two young Roosevelts, Theodore junior and Quentin. After a brief brush with international law he was appointed a vice-president of the American International Corporation, a bankers' consortium promoting overseas trade, and he was back on the dining and speaking circuit.

For the world in general, 1916 was hardly an inviting prospect, but Dorothy challenged it with her new diary, a large, sleek volume bound in black leather with a silver edging and purple plush lining. She entered the phone number of Miss Anna Bogue, who became her secretary and the stalwart of her life. Willard arranged a surprise party for her birthday on 23rd January, her twenty-ninth, and she realised that she was pregnant, the baby due in late August. Willard went to Europe in mid-March and was gone for ten weeks, writing long essays home for little Whitney to read some day. He learned that Bertie Randolph was killed, and he found the Pagets in Eastbourne, where the guns in France could be heard thundering all the time, and Polly was devoting her last energies to caring for wounded soldiers. Like Nancy Astor she had discovered Christian Science.

Willard had a warm welcome home, and they gave summer parties in their Chinese garden. A cottage at Southampton suited their holiday, which began with a party for Beatrice's second birthday on 2nd August, instituting a happy tradition. Dorothy did very little; she had to refuse their invitation to her niece Flora's coming-out at Newport, but then she never really liked Newport. She waited impatiently doodling in her diary until Michael Whitney Straight was born on 1st September. He had 'fair hair & blue eyes & a real nose' and was most like his father. Whitney was four on 6th November, and the following day President Wilson was elected to serve his second term. Dorothy was reading H.G. Wells' latest novel, *Mr Britling Sees It Through*, in which Mr Direck from Massachusetts visits his ancestral village Matching's Easy in Essex in wartime. Then on 23rd November she noted, 'News came this morning of Pauline's death in England.' Polly was forty-two.[96]

Events had meant that Dorothy and Willard were perhaps less attentive to *The New Republic* than they had hoped, though they read it assiduously; a Vassar graduate Charlotte Rudyard was appointed as an editorial assistant, and Dorothy had suggested that Walter Lippmann should interview Jane Addams at Hull-House in Chicago for her opinion on the election. Sadly the paper had veered away from Roosevelt, and Lippmann's star-column 'Washington Notes' was ushering its stance towards President Wilson, both inching towards American intervention into the war on the moral high ground of procuring the peace. By the start of 1917 the paper found itself with friends in high places; Herbert Croly and Lippmann 'were known' to make weekly visits to Colonel House's New York apartment and they

Soldiers three – Willard, baby Michael and Dorothy with
Beatrice and Whitney in uniform. A hasty snap, 1917.

were deemed to be in his confidence. The circulation doubled, rising
to twenty thousand copies a week.[97]

Dorothy and Willard went to Washington to stay with Daisy
Harriman – the vivacious and politically astute Daisy was a democratic
insider whom Dorothy saw as her ally in the cause of getting Willard
into the State Department. There was a vacancy, he applied, and
they went house-hunting in Virginia, but events moved too fast,
and prompted by the start of revolution in Russia and German attacks
on American merchant shipping the president told Congress that
'right is more precious than peace' and America would enter the war
for democracy's sake.[98] This happened on 6th April. When Daisy
approached Colonel House he said she was 'too late', the vacant post
would not have suited Willard, but 'I have a very high regard for him
and at the first opportunity I shall suggest his name for service'. Later
he added that 'he was most anxious for the sake of the administration
that Willard be drawn in' rather than joining the army 'as he threatens
to do'.[99]

FOUR: PORCELAIN AND POLISHED MARBLE

It might seem that Dorothy had another ploy because her friend, the young reformist Mayor of New York John Purroy Mitchel, appointed Willard as chairman of his Committee on National Defense; Dorothy was on the Women's Committee. However, Willard took his army exams, and in late May he was commissioned as a major in the reserve corps. Dorothy threw herself into the war effort, juggling her resources, fundraising for the Red Cross, and turning their home at 1130 Fifth Avenue into a hostel for war workers. On 25th July Beatrice Bend and Prather Fletcher were married in Dorothy's sitting room at Old Westbury and given a warm send-off on their journey to Mexico City where he was appointed ambassador. August and part of September were spent at Southampton with the children, this time making jams and preserves and digging vegetables.

Returned to the fray, she was immersed in City Food Conferences, Consumers' League and child welfare committees and *The New Republic*. Willard was sent to training camp at Fort Sill in Oklahoma, where she was present at his passing-out parade in late October; she was the toast of the officers' mess, who gave her the film-star treatment. It was Herbert Croly who delivered a message from Colonel House saying that there would be an assignment in London or Paris for Willard, at the peace conference which would come soon now that America was involved. This would be a coup for *The New Republic*. In reality Willard was made organiser of the War Risk Insurance Bureau as serving men were now offered low-cost policies; with a company of sixty men, and his valet George Bennett who had enlisted as his batman, he left on 11th December. He and Dorothy had a few quiet days as a family, in part fitting Whitney and little Beatrice out in soldier suits, and having their photograph taken. Dorothy knew that his ship had to keep radio silence but even so she burst into tears when Louisa wished her a 'Happy Christmas'; the next day Willard cabled to say they had arrived in Liverpool – she felt 'as if the world had suddenly burst into song'. Typically Willard's men were noted as the smartest and most cheerful, he had not wasted the voyage and, equally typically, when he saw Nancy Astor in London he bought her a soda fountain to

73

comfort the American boys at her Cliveden hospital, and left the order and wherewithal at Fortnum & Mason's to keep it stocked.

Dorothy was immersed in endless committees and her vigorous support for Mayor Mitchel's re-election, which failed. She was observed as she presided over a war work meeting at City Hall:

> Mrs Straight called the meeting to order, and in an easy manner explained the object of the gathering – the hope to establish a clearing house for the different charities. Every syllable was heard even by those standing near the door. She is far too slender now, and very tired and pale, but she has gained much in manner and self-possession.[100]

Her New Year's Eve was at Harry and Gertrude's with:

> many young aviators from Mineola and hydro-fliers from I don't know where – and of course dozens of officers from Upton. When midnight struck and we all formed a big circle and sang Auld Lang Syne, one tried not to think of what the New Year would bring forth to the majority of the people in the room! I think it best to have no imagination these days.

The war closed around her. Gertrude and Flora left for Texas to be near Sonny Whitney training at Fort Worth; Flora was secretly engaged to Quentin Roosevelt who was on flying duties in France, one of four Roosevelt brothers in uniform. New York suffered in a bitterly cold winter with fuel shortages, and schools, shops and offices closed. The pipes were all frozen at 1130 Fifth Avenue so Dorothy stayed at Old Westbury; she discovered a stock of twenty tons of coal and sent out enough for dozens of families. She told Willard that she was 'amused' that her rich neighbours were stock-piling – 'I wonder why there are not more Socialists in the world!'

FOUR: PORCELAIN AND POLISHED MARBLE

In Paris, Willard, pleased with a high rate of take-up on the soldiers' insurance, was playing (and paying) as host for a wedding breakfast at the Ritz for Daisy Harriman's daughter, and Cole Porter played the piano for them. The party was followed by an air raid into the morning of Willard's thirty-eighth birthday, 31st January. Some of Dorothy's friends felt, but did not say, that he should not have left her alone for a young man's war. He confessed that he had paid Daisy's bills and Dorothy agreed that Daisy was 'a luxury'. Daisy sent her a lovely sepia postcard of the tables laid on the Ritz terrace: 'I will tell you all news of Willard, he looks so well and has been such an angel to me.'

On George Washington's Birthday in late February she took Whitney and Beatrice to watch the huge tickertape parade for the 77th Division from Camp Upton marching to their embarkation. They were 'her boys' – for weeks she had been taking (sensible) Junior Leaguers dressed in neat blue overalls to the bleak camp, the huge wooden sheds hastily erected on the Long Island sands at Yaphank. They had served teas and handed out books, finding that the soldiers were eager simply to talk to a woman and 'not a single man was fresh'. She was convinced of the importance of some 'home comforts' to the thousands of young men, culled from the cities and backwoods all over America and destined for they knew not where. One of them was Irving Berlin, who composed 'Oh, How I Hate to Get Up in the Morning' for an Upton concert party. Dorothy was appointed chairman of Camp Work Committees for the whole country, 'An enormous job but I can't help doing it – we women have to play a part worthy of you,' she told Willard.

Having completed his insurance selling to everyone's satisfaction Willard was now at the American Expeditionary Force Staff College at Langres in the Haute-Marne, billeted with Major Grayson Murphy, who also had a wife and family on Long Island and shared Willard's taste for Chaucer and Kipling. As part of the course they were taken up the line to Toul, west of Nancy, to the brigade commanded by Douglas MacArthur. Willard thought MacArthur, who was about his age, 'a corker – the best in the business', but confessed to his diary that

75

the experience terrified him, especially the gas, and he was scared to death.[101] To Dorothy he wrote, 'I took off my glasses and we splashed along – shells sang overhead, and next four German planes – & it seemed as if everything had broken loose – the sky was speckled with bursting shells.' She replied, 'I love you for saying you were scared all the time – my love must help protect you.' His letters become full of his conviction that he is ready for action, that he could handle a regiment, or a brigade or even a division: 'I'd rather have you mourn me and have [Whitney] say that I died fighting over here than to come back and feel that I had shirked.' It was not to be, it was Major Murphy who was posted to MacArthur's 42nd Division, and Willard was sent to the 3rd Army Staff at Remiremont, to the east in the Vosges. On liaison duties he found himself travelling across country to Reims, in a position to watch the Marines of the 2nd Division in action defending Belleau Wood, a defence they converted into attacks on the German positions and then to an advance. The courage and determination of the young Marines – in the presence of the demoralised French – impressed him deeply; these were the Americans he desperately wanted to lead, and lead them safely home.[102]

At home Dorothy was still playing her part, now canvassing 82nd and 83rd Streets on foot for the Liberty Loan schemes. She was deeply shocked at the news of the death of John Purroy Mitchel on 6th July. He had joined the Air Service and was in training at Lake Charles in Louisiana, and mysteriously fell out of an aircraft. He was the same age as Willard. Dorothy sent all her summer flowers from Old Westbury to be strewn on the cortège on its journey from Washington Square to St Patrick's Cathedral. Worse was to come; Quentin Roosevelt was killed flying in France at the end of July. The family were devastated and Dorothy's adored T.R. was never to get over his loss. She comforted her niece Flora, who, in her twenty-first year, was so pathetically young for such a blow – she found herself having long talks with both Flora and Olive Mitchel. Later in August at Southampton she would gaze out into the Atlantic and imagine herself with Willard. She sent him a small gold-covered notebook as she had read the story of a gold cigarette case stopping a bullet. His letters concerned her: in ever smaller writing, which becomes almost impossible to read, he theorises at length about command techniques – she pleads, 'Please Best Beloved it wouldn't be right – I wish you would heed the words of your friends and remain in the work for which you have been specifically trained and not fly off into line service – really Willard, it isn't sense is it?' In return he chides her for overworking and worries about her radicalism, being 'a little restive and uncertain about some of these forward looking people – so many of them aren't honest'. He tells her not to give away everything, 'remember you have a husband in the army to support' as well as costly magazines.[103] He finishes, 'I'm becoming a filthy conservative,' he is afraid, 'don't go too far my Dorothy.'

He went so far as to write to the State Department, to his best man William Phillips, now Assistant Secretary, about 'scourging pot-bellied Major Generals, incompetent brigadiers and rotten colonels' – that such men could keep their positions 'it makes me sick at heart'. To Dorothy he went further, saying that nobody liked him on the staff or appreciated anything that he had done, or realised that he had that rare quality that brought out the best in fighting men. He confessed to using his letters to express his troubles (he may never have sent the letter to Phillips) but he was clearly under great strain. His batman George Bennett persuaded him to see a doctor, who ordered him off to the hospital base at Trouville on the Normandy coast for rest and sea air. Unfortunately – did Dorothy admit it? – he was no longer the athletic polo player of Cecil Davis's portrait, he was approaching middle-age, he had put on weight and was losing his hair, and that pathetic image of him taking off his spectacles as he 'sloshed' along in the mud (could he even keep up with the younger men?) must have pained her. He had a wound on his leg that refused to heal, a persistent cough and insomnia.

He returned from Trouville refreshed, and was assigned to personnel work at First Army headquarters; 'I'll make the best of a bad job,' he told Dorothy, 'but I need your wise head and your comforting voice.'

For their seventh wedding anniversary on 7th September 1918, George Bennett arranged a dinner and they drank to her health. Worryingly Willard's reading was *A Connecticut Yankee in King Arthur's Court*, that disturbing fantasy by Mark Twain, which he had not read since childhood.[104] Every piece of news took his fancy – could he go as an envoy to the Russians? Mention of reviving the Chinese loan made him think of going back to Peking – and withal he is so endearingly candid, he knows he has not the right background, that he has not been to West Point, just as he had no banking training, and he understands that because he is married to Dorothy he has access to people that otherwise would not notice him, particularly Colonel House. He is being shunted around the Western Front, never in danger. Dorothy, writing when she is exhausted and sometimes through the night, draws phrases from her memory: 'I'm so proud of you – you are such a really big person that I feel I can never truly deserve you – your spirit is the most magnificent thing I have ever known, and I thank God that men are made such as you.'

She had been leading her friends in a marathon harvest of vegetables and fruits, picking, bottling and jam-making for the Settlement houses. She was following the Allied advance on her map, and went into the city to hear the president on his conditions for peace, his famous Fourteen Points, and his hopes for the League of Nations.[105] Then a more insidious enemy, the Spanish influenza, invaded America and she struggled to keep her YMCA work parties together, which meant harrowing journeys, one to Philadelphia where the streets were 'just a long funeral procession'. 'You can't imagine how terrible it is – it is just a hideous plague,' she told Willard.

He was happier, transferred to Marshal Foch's headquarters at Senlis, north of Paris, at the end of October. In early November, with the Germans in retreat, he met a jubilant Colonel House who assured him of an assignment at the peace negotiations. On 10th November with the news that the Kaiser had fled and Germany had capitulated, he drank champagne with his brother officers and wrote to Dorothy:

When the Armistice is signed I'll close this letter – this
is the last line written during war time – you have been
so wonderful – all these hard months you have grown so
tremendously – and been such an inspiration to all about
you, my Dorothy – you are the Wonder of the World –
I am grateful that you have given me your love – My
Sweetheart – I pray that I may be worthy, always.

There was a postscript: '5.40 a.m. Nov 11th – hostilities will cease at 11
a.m., it is Peace, Best Beloved, think what it means.'

Later he dined with friends, Martin and Eleanor Egan, and wrote
from the Hôtel Crillon that Paris was alive with dancing and singing
in the streets. It was also rapidly filling with people he knew, Harry
Davison, Walter Lippmann, Daisy Harriman, Dorothy's friend Ruth
Morgan who was with the Red Cross, Grayson Murphy and Bill
Delano (bearing gifts from Dorothy). He cabled 'Peace Greetings'
and 'going strong – our day someday soon', and he was already busy
at the Peace Commission, 'a whale of a job!' On the Sunday after the
Armistice he went on a motor tour with Colonel House and Gordon
Auchincloss, House's assistant and son-in-law, to the battlefields around
Château-Thierry and Reims. The next day both the colonel and Willard
were ill; the colonel soon improved, Willard did not. In his room at the
Hôtel Crillon he was attended by army doctors and nurses, and Daisy
Harriman, who had always been so fond of him, appointed herself his
guardian. On 25th November he was no better and severe influenza had
been diagnosed. Daisy cabled Herbert Croly to tell Dorothy, who was in
her office at the YMCA. In Paris Willard, hazily aware it was Thanksgiving, asked Daisy to take some money from his dressing table and buy
a turkey – 'I love people to be happy.' In New York Dorothy was trying to
keep in touch with Washington, for news via the State Department and
because she intended to sail on the *George Washington* that was taking
the president and Mrs Wilson to France on 3rd December. On 28th
November she cabled Daisy, who was at his bedside, saying 'Please hold
his wrists for me – it helps him. I am there with him every moment.'

But, as Daisy later wrote – it was 30th November – 'Walter Lippmann came in and at 11.30 that night we realised he was going fast.' They sent for the Reverend Billings who had married Daisy's daughter, and he 'made three beautiful prayers and two minutes after he stopped Willard quietly stopped breathing. Just as he went I kissed him and said "that's from Dorothy" – there was no struggle, no suffering so far as human sense could see, only a great weariness from the long fight.'

Once again it was Herbert Croly who carried the news to Dorothy. She sent a cable with her thanks to all who had cared for him: 'No words can express my gratitude to you. I should like to have Willard buried in France somewhere with the American soldiers he loved and admired so much. Will this be possible? Please do not worry about me. I know that he is safe and that is all that matters.'

FIVE: 'DWS, THE ARGOSY OF GRACE'

Their marriage had lasted for seven years, Willard's magical number. A flurry of crossings-out surrounds 1st December in her 1918 diary, and then it is silent. Words of sympathy and love fell on her as snowflakes from everywhere, from her brother Payne, from her godmother Frances Cleveland Preston, from Beatrice and Prather, from her closest friends, sometimes with a touching formality as from her Book Class – 'we want to try and tell you of our sympathy', the signatures headed by Harriet Aldrich and tailed by Gertrude, who, with Harry, had certainly been with her. Beatrice Fletcher wrote again quickly, saying she would come and look after the children if she needed to leave. But Dorothy stayed, reading Daisy Harriman's careful accounts of Willard's ending: 'There never was any look of pain or suffering, but at the last moment a decided look of relief – like a tired child dropping asleep – passed over his face – dear, darling Dorothy, how I ached to hold him here for you.'

Daisy, though exhausted from her vigil, felt she must write everything that Dorothy might need to know. Pneumonia and septicaemia were the causes of his death.[106] Colonel House, who told Dorothy that Willard's death 'has troubled me too deeply', asked a personal favour of the Secretary of War that Willard's body might be taken home, but then Dorothy's wish was made known. He was laid to rest in the American military cemetery at Suresnes, on the opposite bank of the Seine from the Bois de Boulogne, on 3rd December. There were many mourners and more than three dozen wreaths and bunches of flowers, red roses from General Pershing, white roses from the staff at *The New Republic*, roses and violets from J.P. Morgan and Company. Bishop Brent's committal address spoke of Willard's 'living a long life in a few years' and that 'by added purpose and activity [we will] endeavour to make up what has been lost to us by his going'. Daisy made sure Dorothy knew who was present, and that the cards and ribbons, including the tricolour ribbon from Marshal Foch's tribute, came home to her.[107] The last flowers mentioned were a bunch of carnations from George Bennett, and his letters perhaps caused her most pain: 'Oh! Madam, how could God take him?' Bennett had been badly injured in a motor accident some weeks earlier and he felt certain that the Major would never have become so ill had he been there to look after him. Daisy went to see Bennett in hospital and wrote that she had never seen such distress. Bennett's long testaments to Dorothy spoke of the Major's endless kindnesses to his fellows – 'I think it's too cruel that one of God's best men should be called away like this' – of how he should have stayed longer at Trouville, 'but just like the Major he would never rest up'. He knew that Willard didn't care for his work and was always trying for his battalion, 'but for all that he was cheerful', and making plans for when the war was over to take Dorothy to Langres and other places he had seen; 'everywhere he went everybody adored him especially the French people'.[108]

The very efficient Miss Bogue, for whom Dorothy was truly grateful, would leave the letters in piles on her desk for her to read when the children were in bed. They came from afar in time and space. 'I first knew Willard as a handsome four-year-old,' wrote a stranger to her. 'Pardon an old soldier intruding,' wrote Lieutenant Healy who had served under Willard – 'always my idol'; they came from the high command of the American Expeditionary Force even now advancing into Germany, from friends from Peking days, from Chester Aldrich with the American Red Cross, from the Reverend Slattery at Grace Church, where a memorial service for the war dead included a prayer for Willard, from Lillian Wald and friends at Henry Street, and from Dorothy's favourite, the Music Settlement. Letters from people who searched for their words, who didn't know how to write but managed anyway; a simple tribute: 'with love, your friend T.R.', sympathies from 'Papa' Harriman's widow, from Mrs Edward House, from Beatrix Farrand, from all the Junior Leaguers working at Camp Upton, 'even the maids'. There were formal *In Memoriam* addresses from the staff at *Asia* and *The New Republic*, high-flown eulogies from those she knew well, led by Herbert Croly and including Walter Lippmann, who had been at Willard's bedside and was now home.

The letters and cables continued in their hundreds, 'My dear Dorothy' falling from page upon page, tumblings of shock, distress and sympathy and outpourings of love.[109] One in particular could not help being noticed: it was from May Kinnicutt, her school friend with whom she had had that first carefree jaunt to Paris and Rome (was it only fifteen years ago?) – perhaps May spoke for them all, her generous rounded handwriting filling each page with few words:

> Carina, I always want to tell you when I'm with you how much I love you & how wonderful I think you've been but I'm such a poor one at expressing myself & I never can trust my voice without crying – all I can say is that I never knew what real goodness was before & to have been with you at all has been the greatest privilege I could have ever asked for. I resent so terribly that Willard should have been taken from such a wife & children – I would rather have had this thing happen to anyone but you, because you didn't need it. But I suppose the way you have taken it all will be a lesson to all who know you & will be an inspiration for always.[110]

Theodore Roosevelt died on 6th January 1919. 'The old lion is dead,' Archie cabled to his brothers Kermit and Theodore in France. Dorothy went to the little church at Oyster Bay and sat with Ethel and Flora for his simple funeral service, and they stood together for his burial in the Young's Memorial Cemetery nearby. The president's sister, Corinne Roosevelt Robinson, a loving champion of Dorothy ever since her engagement to Willard, had written to her, 'You have the power of giving & therefore you will always carry other people's burdens.' To Flora, who had been enfolded into the Roosevelt household and making herself useful as T.R.'s secretary, Dorothy wrote, 'You have been wonderful – I feel that you and Quentin are more truly one in spirit than you have ever been before.' Louisa Weinstein had told George Bennett, 'You know how very quiet Mrs Straight is, she is now more so than ever – [she is] so sad and still keeps up her appearances as if she is interested in everything [and] in the meantime her poor heart flows over with grief.'[111]

She had no rest. Herbert Croly and Louis Froelick at *Asia* magazine were full of questions for articles about Willard's life and work. Willard had written fully of his experiences at every stage of his life, there were notebooks and journals, diaries and letters, hundreds of paintings and drawings as well as his extraordinarily vivid photographic record of life in the Far East. They decided that Herbert Croly should write a biography but Dorothy took upon herself the task of reading and sorting all this material. In the quiet of her evenings this brought him close, though sometimes she found herself in tears. She worked until mid-July then took the children to summer camp on Raquette Lake in the Adirondacks, to Camp Deerlands where she had been with her father. They did lazy, far-away things, fishing, stalking beaver, lying out on the porch; 'too heavenly', she wrote. They caught trout and cooked them on the campfire, tossing scraps to the fox cubs that came out to watch; Beatrice's birthday on 2nd August was celebrated with a boating party, then their idyll was interrupted by a cable from General Pershing suggesting Dorothy should go to France. Her arrangements were hastily made, and gathering up Flora along the way – they would cheer each other along – they sailed on 14th August.

The Versailles Peace Treaty had been signed in June but there were still many Americans in Paris. Daisy Harriman met them, taking them first to the Christian Science church as a preparation for what they were to see – the Suresnes cemetery was all heaps of bare earth and rows of unfinished graves, the rawness of its purpose all too painfully evident. Later, at dinner at the Hôtel Crillon, where Willard had died, it was hardly surprising that Dorothy was sick and collapsed into a faint. The blessing of having Flora with her was that they comforted themselves with some shopping. At lunch at the Ritz with General Pershing and the expatriate sculptor Herbert Haseltine (a friend of Gertrude's), the purpose of the invitation was made clear: they rather hoped that Mrs Straight would pay for the fencing, gates and memorial pavilion for Suresnes, and that Jo Davidson's tribute figure 'Doughboy' would be placed there.

Dorothy and Daisy were taken to the Louvre by Bernard Berenson to polish their 'taste'. Was there a suggestion that the young widow needed an occupation for her mind, as well as her fortune? She found herself surrounded by the many converts to Christian Science, dining with Philip Kerr, Nancy Astor's great friend who shared Nancy's enthusiasm for the teachings of Mary Baker Eddy, and Arthur Balfour, the British Foreign Secretary and a discreet sympathiser with his sister Eleanor Sidgwick's Society for Psychical Research. There was much talk about *Raymond*, the best-selling account of the physicist Oliver Lodge and his wife's conviction of their meetings with their son, who was killed in 1915, through the medium Mrs Leonard, who 'spoke in the voice of a young Indian girl called Feda'. The desolated parents needed to believe, but only when they visited his grave at Ypres and saw 'the great company' all dead and laid in the earth, could they accept the truth.[112]

Flora and Dorothy were driven to Château-Thierry and north to Chamery where Flora found Quentin Roosevelt's grave. Dorothy realised she was in a countryside familiar to Willard, 'the towns all destroyed but [the] country green and smiling'. She spent a 'most wonderful and happy day' going alone on the train to Langres, where she found his house and the staff college, and spent time in the cathedral, as Willard had done. On her last day she went to Suresnes in the late afternoon on her own, and sat by Willard's grave, and found 'such a peaceful experience of Reality there'.

After crossing to England to meet her widower brother-in-law Almeric Paget, she and Flora sailed home on the *Mauretania*. The shipboard company was good, the adventurer Moreton Frewen, Sir Arthur Whitten Brown – the half of Alcock and Brown who had flown the Atlantic in record time – and Viscount Grey of Falloden, the new British ambassador to Washington.[113] It was 'too lovely coming up harbor', she wrote.

The Dorothy that returned from visiting Willard's grave was ready to pick up his fallen banner. She had his love for always, she would be his 'Wonder of the World', as if time had simply stopped when he wrote that, the night before the Armistice. From the deck of the *Mauretania* she had gazed out to sea, as she was always to do, 'with an intensity that burned something out'; she admitted 'although my own pain now seems only the smallest part of the world's suffering, still it is always there – and always part of my bond with the rest of humanity'. At home she had her luxuriant hair cut to a sleek shingled bob, her skirts were shortened to calf-length, her waistbands dropped and she entered the 1920s as a modern woman, slim and sleek and invariably dressed in black, her heeled court shoes clipping along the Fifth Avenue sidewalks with serious tread. She bought a motor with a self-starter, a Buick, so that she could drive herself and the children. In April, Flora Whitney married Roderick Tower, a friend of Quentin Roosevelt's. They managed a crowd-pleasing procession of limousines along Park Avenue, one carrying Dorothy with Beatrice and Whitney. Whitney stood tall, a determined 'little man' despite his white satin trousers, frilled shirt and posy of flowers. Beatrice and little Gladys Szechenyi were the smallest flower girls. It was a family reunion, especially for Dorothy and her childhood friend, Countess Szechenyi; it was almost like all those other weddings in the world before the war. Almost, but not quite.

To her friends she was the 'Samaritan of all', in a child's mishap or a kitchen crisis:

> She sails, the Ship of our Delight, To every little port,
> Nor rests by day, nor sleeps by night, nor gives herself
> a thought.
> Her cargo is the gift of Light, the Mariners' report.[114]

Did she sail on, to everyone's delight, because she felt that in giving of herself and all she owned she could melt into the arms of the world, her only consolation now? To a private notebook she confessed that she felt God had deserted her. She plunged into ever harsher philosophies, reading Bertrand Russell, who bolstered her pacifism with his warning of what he called 'cosmic impiety', meaning man's intoxication with his apparent power over nature, it 'is the greatest danger of our time'.[115] The advent of theatrical realism made a timely bulwark for her grief. She saw Eugene O'Neill's *Beyond the Horizon*, his first Broadway success in which 'gloom spreads over the stage like a sea mist', and even his father's verdict was, 'What are you trying to do send them home to commit suicide?'[116] Dorothy was instinctively interested in O'Neill and she had most probably met him in 1916 when on a visit to Gertrude's studio in Macdougal Alley downtown she had strayed into the impromptu theatre where the Provincetown Players were presenting his *Bound East for Cardiff* to a casual audience gathered on wooden benches. The fervent playwright was there attending to his own sets, and she already knew the Players' activist John Reed through his work for trade unions; but for the presence of Reed's lover Mabel Dodge, who bank-rolled the Players, Dorothy's role as impresario might have started there and then. In the fall of 1917 with Willard away in Oklahoma, she had coyly noted several 'Players' entries in her diary which suggested she had volunteered to help – were these the 'forward looking people' Willard had warned her about? Now she became an O'Neill devotee, as partly a return of her youthful passion for the theatre, which had lain dormant with Willard occupying her mind, and partly because of Willard's loss. O'Neill never let her down, he was writing for her and for others like her at sea in their own emotions when, as he said, 'From his own life he excavated the pain and overwhelming loneliness of living in the first century of which it could be truthfully said that God is dead.'[117]

John Dewey was another lodestar. Her discovery of his educational philosophy and Laboratory School in Chicago long before her marriage had to some extent lain behind the educational aims of *The New Republic*. She had followed his career at Columbia and heard his lectures on psychology. Her turn of mind being naturally pragmatic (she even ventured into William James's *Pragmatism*), it was Dewey, sixty-ish, professorial and well married, who was her natural master, launching her on her own questing and metaphysical journey that was to be essential to the rest of her life. As she struggled to regain her equilibrium, she learned to ameliorate her private needs by her recognition of the public good. She became a director of Dewey's New School of Social Research, and also of the Columbia Teachers' College, which trained teachers in his methods of child development, to foster communication skills, their curiosity, creativity and self-expression. She enrolled her own three children with their widely differing personalities into the offshoot Lincoln School.

In her last letter to Willard (which he could not have read) she had exploded in fury at the misrepresentation of the war's casualty figures, grossly underestimated in the American press.[118] Two years on from the Armistice people were shocked at the slaughter of their innocent 'doughboys' on the Western Front, in that horrific trench warfare that seemed utter madness, and they shied away from President Wilson and his League of Nations. America would look after her own, and Warren Hastings came into office in March 1921 with the promise of a return to 'normalcy', the small town values of the rural heartland. Dorothy, as elected president of the National Association of Junior Leagues, was an observer, with John Dewey and Ruth Morgan, at the armaments' limitation conference in Washington at the end of the year.

She found the French 'impossible', the Japanese 'more conciliatory than expected' but the power of the United States 'the thing that frightens me – power that has come through accident'. She found herself sitting with H.G. Wells who pronounced himself 'sick of world affairs'; she sensed his physicality and 'need to indulge himself' and perhaps he slipped down her chart of favourite novelists. She marched behind the Honour Guard for the burial of the Unknown Soldier at Arlington, and thought it 'rather fine' to hear the vast crowd repeating the Lord's Prayer with the president.

Her friendship with John Dewey led her into the greatest liberal cause of the day, championed by *The New Republic*, the campaign to rescue Nicola Sacco and Bartolomeo Vanzetti from a miscarriage of justice. The two Italian immigrants were accused of attempted robbery and murder on weak – and some said contrived – evidence, and sentenced to death. Their poor English meant that they did not understand the judicial process, and their disillusion with the way they felt America had broken her promises to new arrivals had led them to be activists, labelled as anarchists. Vanzetti, who was well read and something of a mystical philosopher, asked why the judge seemed to hate him so, 'But now I think I know – I must have looked like a strange animal to him, being a plain worker, an alien and a radical to boot,' he had concluded. They were both in their early thirties and friends in adversity; Vanzetti, a pastry cook, had lost several jobs because head chefs were paid for every new employee so consequently dismissed existing ones – and he had taken to outdoor labouring. Nicola Sacco worked in a factory and had a wife and two children, he had never been out of work and had saved up enough for their return passage home to Italy. Their appeals against their sentences galvanised an influential defence committee, led by Dewey, supported by Bertrand Russell, Albert Einstein, Wells and Anatole France, who fought for years against fallible judges and a right-wing popular opinion who thought 'the bastards' deserved to die. Dorothy was not involved in the judicial process but she gave generously, as she always did, towards the defence costs.[119]

She had also given $1,000 to Rose Schneiderman's campaign as the New York Labour Party's candidate for the Senate in 1920. Rose was defeated by the Prohibitionist and the Socialist candidates, but she had established herself as a brilliant orator, passionate in the cause of the Women's Trade Union League (WTUL), now a well-organised scourge of sweatshop conditions.[120] Dorothy gave a tea party at 1130 Fifth Avenue to raise funds to buy 247 Lexington Avenue as WTUL headquarters, and on this occasion Rose met Eleanor and Franklin Roosevelt who became her great allies. Eleanor had worked side by side with Dorothy at the Camp Upton welfare centre in the war, but of late she had been the stalwart of her family since her husband had contracted polio; this tea party was one of his first outings on crutches as he struggled to return to active life, and probably Dorothy's first meeting with him.

The New Republic was her anchorage – in the dark days to cheer Willard she had written, 'The paper is really extraordinary – I believe it is going to do more for the education of the country than any other one force that I know of –[it] is the best thing you and I ever put over.' It was (almost) their fourth child. Herbert Croly and Willard had their differences, but Croly was devastated by his loss; Dorothy became the lone proprietor, arranging Christmas presents for the staff and dinners for the editors, she read almost everything that was published and she was often present at the weekly editorial post-mortems. Her influence was subtle – 'all the most important things were indirectly felt' was her rule. She did not interfere editorially, but then she did not need to if she was there – a smile, a lift of her eyebrow, or gentle drawing aside of the offender and a suggestion of lunch, that was her way. She did increase the paper's coverage of women's concerns because it increased the readership, the franchise for women over thirty having been won in 1920.

In late December 1922 Croly redefined *The New Republic Idea* for the post-war world, in an editorial printed under the paper's masthead of a galleon in full sail, and Walt Whitman's words:

> O To Sail to Sea in a Ship! Passage to more than India,
> Passage to you, to Mastership of You, Ye Strangling
> Problems.[121]

Dorothy's copy, bearing her and Willard's bookplate, was referred to so often that it is torn and falling apart, and has been carefully mended with sticky tape.[122] Croly began:

> The group of men who founded the New Republic in
> 1914 [the woman wishing invisibility or taken as read?]
> had a definite conception... we called it a journal of
> opinion. Its object was less to inform or entertain its
> readers than to start little insurrections in the realm of
> their convictions.

The Great War had thwarted their intentions, it was no longer a prodding of America's apathy and contentment that was needed, but 'a full-scale campaign to save the structure of western civilization'. The 'good ship America' was drifting into dangerous waters, he could have said iceberg-ridden, and in a prescient passage he located the sources of the 'bergs':

> ... from a science which multiplies machinery much
> more than it illuminates human nature, from an industry
> which saves so much human labor and wastes so much
> human life, from a technology which – while prodigiously
> productive – is still too sterile to cultivate craftsmanship
> and creative work, from a nationalism which is opposed
> to imperialism but which insists itself on being pettily
> imperialistic, from a liberty which... remains consciously
> negative and unedifying.

Like Eugene O'Neill he finds religious faith redundant, 'for the first time in history the human spirit is the captain and the only possible captain of the ship on which the human race has embarked'. Croly's faith is in American federalism, 'the first great political symptom of an emerging humanistic culture'. His friends attested to him being too honest and self-knowing to truly believe that a weekly paper's contribution to 'so vast and pretentious an idea' could only be woefully inadequate. Perhaps 'something to keep *faith* alive in those members of the community who believe in the power of the truth to set men free' would be enough? Dorothy was wholly in support of Croly's first 'practical watchword', the reform of working conditions and labour relations by means of 'full and fair' discussions, which would 'break up the unmanageable class conflict into minor specific manageable conflicts'.[123]

She now summered with the children on Cape Cod, in the tiny fishing village of Woods Hole on the southern tip of the Cape. It had the great asset that the scientists from the Oceanographic Institute had set up a children's summer school, much enjoyed by Whitney who would be ten in November, Beatrice eight on 2nd August and Michael, whose sixth birthday on 1st September now signalled the end of their holiday.[124] As company for Whitney, 'a warlike child' with abounding energy, she had found a Harvard student John Rothschild, organiser of the inter-collegiate liberal league and of the student disarmament campaign, to spend the summer with them. She confessed to losing her heart to him, 'there being nothing so enchanting as a youth of that age'.

The attractive young widow with the campaigning heart had become something of a magnet for idealistic young people who flocked to purposeful gatherings at 1130 Fifth Avenue. Benjamin Seebohm Rowntree, whose reports on the living conditions of the poor in his native York in England had shocked social workers and governments alike, was one visitor who became her friend.[125] Albert Mansbridge, founder of the Workers' Educational Association (WEA), took home her funding for Toynbee Hall and also her friendship.[126] The Reverend Phillip 'Tubby' Clayton, the army chaplain who had set up Talbot House at Poperinge near Ypres as an 'oasis of sanity' for soldiers, was also her visitor.

Talbot House, shortened by the soldiers to Toc H, its symbol a lamp, was just as necessary now for thousands of ex-soldiers struggling to find peacetime work. The Toc H aims – friendship, service to one's fellows, fair-mindedness and Christian witness – had steered the Reverend Clayton to Dorothy, and he did not leave empty handed.[127] Her wavering religious faith did not deprive her of the so-called Christian virtues. But she seems to have been more comfortable with another of her young visitors, Kenneth Lindsay. Lindsay, invalided home after the 3rd Battle of Ypres and now at Worcester College, Oxford, was 'good-looking, clever, amusing and as much interested in workers' education as she was' – he was leading an Oxford Union debating team on an American tour. He found No. 1130 'the centre of discussion on educational and international matters', with often several meetings going on at once, and with an enlightened atmosphere that was to influence him all his life. He was invited to Old Westbury, probably with his debating colleagues because of Dorothy's perennial need for tennis partners and young male company for Whitney and Michael. Lindsay might have been fazed by her artlessness, however: 'I spent many hours in his room reading and talking to him,' she wrote. 'He is a bit of a genius, that lad – and his future is gleaming with possibilities... I love him dearly.' Lindsay, whom family tradition maintains was in love with her, perhaps recognised her widow's cry, but also that Willard was ever present, with his belongings in her house and in her life.[128]

Croly's biography was growing, using much of Willard's own writing on his experiences (it eventually made 596 pages) and publication was planned by Macmillan for 1924. Dorothy had already arranged for an exhibition of his watercolours and drawings, which had opened at the Arden Gallery at 599 Fifth Avenue in the spring of 1921. Two and a half thousand cards were sent out for the preview, which brought another deluge of thanks and appreciations, while the watercolours travelled on to other galleries. Less publicity, at least for Dorothy, attended the unveiling of James Earle Fraser's statue of Alexander Hamilton on the south façade of the Treasury Building in

Washington. Hamilton, the 'Founding Father' who had championed Eli Whitney's industrial inventions but died from duelling injuries in 1804, was also her mother Flora's ancestor. She paid for the statue in Willard's memory but only a few people knew of this.

If she was trying to fill her every unforgiving minute then she was not finished yet. Her most daunting task was in fulfilling Willard's wish to make his university, Cornell, 'a more human place'. Where to start? In his letter dated 23rd January 1919, her thirty-second birthday, Willard's former tutor and drawing master, Olaf M. Brauner, was simply sorrowful. 'For what Willard Straight was to me, I thank you,' he wrote, and so, later that year when she had needed to find out about Cornell, she turned to Professor Brauner. They met quietly in the city, and he responded with ideas for Willard's memorial – an architectural travelling fellowship, a chair in international law, or history, or art, or maybe an art gallery or a college of fine arts? She wanted a scholarship for Willard's old school, Oswego High, to send a pupil to Cornell, and approaching Cornell's President Schurman about this, she added that she 'had it in her mind' to carry out her late husband's wishes. Despite her discretion the Cornell community was soon speculating as to what Mrs Straight might do, and humming with assured gossip as to her wealth. In October 1920 she spent a day on the Ithaca campus with a cohort of professors, ending in an agreement that Willard's memorial should be a new student union building, and that his friend and hers, Bill Delano, should be her architect. She quickly learned that she had to tread as on eggshells through the Cornell politics for in early 1921 she had been warned of a 'sex war' – the talk had been blithely of male undergraduates when a quarter of the students were women, as Ezra Cornell had intended 'an institution where any person can find instruction in any study'. She of all people had hardly overlooked this, but the faculty of Home Economics headed by Martha Van Renssaeler and Flora Rose had to be reassured. Bill Delano sent her his first design for a beautiful stone building of restrained gothic, with a big gable end for a hall and memorial window, and separate rooms for various student activities.

Outsiders, particularly the parsimonious professors at Cornell, did

not understand her attitude to the cost of the union building, that
– as with Henry Street, Sacco and Vanzetti's defence and *The New
Republic* – her word, once given, meant that she would find what was
genuinely necessary. They were so accustomed to jostling for funding
that they continued to quibble and question over the siting and details
of the design, and her architect had to put up a stout defence. Matters
were made easier with the appointment of Livingston Farrand as
Cornell's new president, the brother of Professor Max Farrand and
therefore Beatrix's brother-in-law. Dorothy saw 'something rather fine
and idealistic in his make-up'. She saw Beatrix fairly regularly as she
continued to oversee the maintenance of Old Westbury's Chinese
garden, and as she was now the doyenne of campus designers (working
at Princeton, Yale and Chicago) the massed Farrands' expertise on
academic life was at Dorothy's disposal. They suggested that Hart
House at Toronto and the union building at Ann Arbor in Michigan
were the best models for Cornell. Dorothy visited them both and
polished her expertise. Delano and Aldrich's design had grown in
gothic majesty, providing for a lounge, writing room, women's lounge,
co-op, library and theatre, with upper rooms for music, games and
committees. Dorothy was adamant about the theatre, and she sent a
typed list of additional requests – that the union should be managed
by the students, there were to be no heavy-handed controls, and a
standing committee of trustees were to take a light stance, and in all 'a
maximum of decency, order and cleanliness should be the ideal'.

In June 1922 her gift to Cornell was formally announced, and her
architect promised to keep her informed of any changes to the design.
In the following October Professor Lincoln Burr wrote, hoping that
the evident progress would bring her and the children to Ithaca – the
professors had become paternal and sent love 'to the kiddies'. Finally
she was sent the formal resolution dated 7th March 1923, 'That Mrs
Dorothy Straight is hereby granted permission to erect upon the site
designated, and in accordance with the Delano & Aldrich plans, a
building which will be presented when completed to Cornell University
for social and recreation purposes and maintained as a Union.'[129]

In June a cable arrived from Louise Croly in Venice to say that Herbert was ill. Dorothy had crossed the Atlantic only once since the war; now she sailed on the *Homeric* on 16th June, arrived in Paris eight days later and made a dash via the Simplon express to reach them. She found Herbert improving, but that the crisis was over the proofs of Willard's biography, which he could not finish correcting, so she shouldered the task, put them in her bag and headed for home. She went to Suresnes; Daisy had told her that the cemetery was being reorganised and the bodies all reburied in steel coffins, 'and dear Willard's body will be placed where it won't ever have to be moved again'. The work was finished and the cemetery had been rededicated on Memorial Day at the end of May, so that the posies laid by French schoolchildren were still on the graves.[130] Once again she seemed to find the reality comforting; she wrote of her acceptance, of 'having given up the man I love at least there is no further struggle'. She tripped gaily into London in early July, meeting Almeric Paget and his new wife Edith Starr, whose wedding she had attended in New York. She lunched with John Maynard Keynes, dined with Kenneth Lindsay and Albert Mansbridge, and treated herself to Shaw's *Fanny's First Play*. After seeing her beloved stepsister Addie Lambart in Dorset she sailed on the *Elizabethan* on 17th July.

The rest of the summer at Woods Hole became stressful. She was trying to be the 'Samaritan of all' but it became more and more difficult. Louise and Herbert Croly arrived directly from Venice, Herbert being nervous and touchy about his long manuscript and Dorothy still absorbed in proof correcting. As August progressed she felt sicker and sicker, she noted that her heart was racing all the time, she was short of breath and had constant indigestion – hardly right for a slim and active woman in her mid-thirties. She made such a good job of disguising her distress, as usual, that no one apparently noticed. She grew hysterical with exhaustion, she said she felt 'poisoned'. She hung on for Michael's birthday on 1st September and her wedding anniversary on the 7th, which she realised four days later, 'I rejoiced and was glad in it.' In New York in mid-October she finally collapsed. Her doctors ordered complete bed rest for an unspecified period with no contact at all with the outside world. She was moved to Old Westbury, where Mrs James, Louisa Weinstein and George Bennett – with Miss Bogue managing everything – constituted a guard no one would pass.

As the year darkened and winter closed in so her life was reduced to her own room where only the crackle of logs on the fire or the lift of the curtain in a breath of fresh air broke the quiet. Her committees and causes, 1130 Fifth Avenue, Henry Street, *The New Republic*, her Book Class, the Colony Club, Grace Church and her friends all had to do without her. Miss Bogue fielded all requests and messages, she kept the households running, but almost everyone was kept away. Dorothy's breakdown laid her low through Christmas and into the spring of 1924. It is impossible to know what nightmares roamed the drug-induced haziness of her mind, but when she was recalled to life, she was changed. Her closest friends visited, and it seems that Ruth Morgan, who became her spiritual confidante, restored her religious optimism. It is also to be hoped that someone she loved released her into a cathartic outburst of anger at Willard for dying. His death seemed so implausible, so unnecessary. If he and Colonel House had caught the Spanish flu at the same time, why did the hypochondriac desk-bound Texan more than twenty years older than Willard survive, and Willard succumb?[131] The influenza killed younger men in their thousands but in battlefield conditions – Willard was in the luxurious Hôtel Crillon with the best army doctors and nurses.[132] Or, terrible to contemplate, had he given up 'like a tired child', as Daisy Harriman had written? Had Theodore Roosevelt's failure to return as president in 1916 ended his political hopes, followed by his humiliation at President Wilson's cancellation of the Chinese loans, leaving him only the role of war hero to merit Dorothy's love, and even that was denied him? He had so often joked about being her expensive luxury, or was it always a joke? He had written so pointedly to the young Whitney, 'If you ever amount to anything it will be because of your Mother.' Had poor Willard died of shame?

He is dead and gone, lady,
He is dead and gone;
At his head a grass-green turf,
At his heels a stone.[133]

She had done her very best for him, to the point of endangering her own life. On 15th June 1924 there was 'an affecting little ceremony' at Cornell when the cornerstone of Willard Straight Hall was laid. A copper casket was buried beneath it containing a copy of Herbert Croly's *Willard Straight*, just published, the letters of offer and acceptance for the building, views of the campus, newspaper cuttings, a copy of the 1901 class book, Willard's registration card, a photo of him, and his sketch of his admired Professor Morse Stephens.[134] Those present included several of Willard's former friends and colleagues and Dorothy was represented by her secretary, Miss Anna Bogue.

SIX: 'ALL THINGS CHANGE'[135]

In the last week of July 1924 Dorothy was released by her doctors to go to Woods Hole for her holiday with her children. Those who knew her respected her frailty, all except for one, an Englishman named Leonard Elmhirst, who had journeyed from India and overland from San Francisco to see her – how could she refuse? She managed a wan note: 'I'm glad you've come.'[136]

Up until now Dorothy had lived her life on her own terms, that famed independence of mind that her father knew so well, and those she wanted to share her companionship had been her chosen ones. It was not so with Leonard Elmhirst. Leonard, hearing of her name and her riches from the campus gossip at Cornell, had confidently, brazenly, stormed the feminine bastion of the Colony Club and persisted until they were face to face – 'There was Mrs Straight, tall and slim, all in black except for a little sable fur around her neck and a very fetching hat,' he later recalled. Leonard's English male and matron-dominated upbringing had in no way equipped him for such an embodiment of the former colonial race: 'She was not only charming to look at, but there was a graciousness and style about her bearing [and] when I mentioned the business shortcomings of professors, her face lit up and the laugh she gave will not easily be forgotten.'[137]

He was a twenty-seven-year-old postgraduate studying agriculture at Cornell, and he hoped she would support the university's

Cosmopolitan Club for foreign students, in danger of closing for lack of funds. With a disarming chivalry he had escorted her from the station to the Cornell campus on her first nerve-wracking visit to Ithaca in October 1920, lightening her dealings with the professors with his insights into student opinions. She had promised to make the 'Cosmo' her concern for she realised 'there was an absence of any real intellectual curiosity on the part of the average American student', which was a 'discouraging aspect' of college life. In her own way she cheered him on: 'I am glad that you are at Cornell and that you are making yourself a force for liberal thinking. Keep your courage high for it all counts tremendously.' That was enough for Leonard to keep writing to her, confessional letters full of crimes against his childhood with the whiff of the boys' changing room, full of earthy Yorkshire tales, which Dorothy had not really the time nor the inclination to read.[138]

She felt sorry that he was lonely at Cornell, and guilty that she could not keep up with his flow of letters, and so she invited him to Old Westbury in June 1921 where he proved good at adventure games with Whitney. He had met the Indian poet and mystic Rabindranath Tagore, who had asked him to manage his community farm and school in Bengal, but Leonard insisted he had no means of getting there. The polished – if rather theatrical – Guards officer-type with a wide smile and bristling moustache who appeared at the Colony Club had been replaced by an impoverished-looking student reduced to one battered suit and his last dollar. Leonard brought out the Samaritan in Dorothy, and she cheerfully turned out her purse for his train fare; 'I do need your guidance in regard to the Union,' she smilingly said, as an excuse for suggesting ways of making him money. He could write 'Letters from India' for *Asia* magazine (she would clear this with the editor Louis Froelick) and being so enamoured with her own new Corona portable typewriter she ordered one for Leonard as a 'serious necessity'. 'Why don't you sell the Corona typewriter when it finally arrives then I can send you another – and we can go on doing that indefinitely! Brilliant idea!' Finally she 'realised': 'When Tagore was here I saw him two or three times but through inadvertence on my part, I let him get away without really doing anything for him – and it has worried me ever since.' Should she give Leonard, say, $5,000 or $10,000 a year for five years for the benefit of India?[139]

Leonard accepted the challenge of India and he was to leave in the August, so Dorothy invited him to Woods Hole, partly because Whitney asked if he could come, and partly because she knew he had nowhere else to go. Leonard, brought up in chilly Yorkshire, revelled in the unbelievable Cape paradise of sun, sands and sea, sailing, picnics, crab suppers, exploring Kennebunkport, all the glories of New England summering. Dorothy was the queen of the glories, to whom he addressed his slavish affections: 'Your every look makes me feel like a veritable worm of a man and want to grovel at your feet,' adding that he had 'adopted' her as his 'mother and sister and everything else'. After he had left, she supposed for five years in India, she replied philosophically:

> Love and understanding are the great gifts we humans can
> bring to each other and we all need them so dreadfully,
> in spite of our fine self-sufficiencies. For some reason or
> other the harmony of spirit between man and woman
> seems greater than any other and so I am going to count
> on you always and be grateful to you always for all that
> you have added to my life.[140]

She wrote in her usual hurry, and her sermon-like phrasing seems caught – as she was apt to do – from the marriage service for her brother-in-law Almeric Paget and his new wife Edith Starr Miller, which she had dashed into Manhattan to attend. She meant a farewell. Most people, friends or radicals, knew her signals – 'always be grateful' signifying the end of a spell of meetings or companionship. It was her only armour against the myriad of people who could make her life impossible. But less than six months later, in January 1922, Leonard surprised her with an agonising proposal of marriage sent from India:

'The cry of a floundering kind of helpless, homeless, comfortless pilgrim – my soul calls across the chasm – would she meet him in Bombay?' No, she would not, marriage 'was out of the question'. Leonard had the grace to confess that in his heart he 'knew nothing of marriage – and I know still less about the real nature of woman'.[141]

He continued to write, and she managed perhaps one letter to his six or seven. Isolated in the backwoods of Bengal, Leonard's fantasy of Dorothy possessed his mind; this lovely American woman with a fortune, to win her would astound his family, all his high-achieving brothers, and justify his position as now the eldest son and heir.[142] He grew stronger in his determination, while she grew weaker, sinking under strains and exhaustion. The nadir was that summer of 1923 when, after her flight to Venice, they were all at Woods Hole. The children, Whitney now ten and a half, Beatrice, nine, and Michael, seven, were his secret weapons; he introduced Whitney to boyhood skills with a pen-knife and fishing rod and spent hours watching birds with Michael. They called him 'Jerry' and sometimes Dorothy joined in, coyly thanking him, 'what a gift you have for reaching children'.

Her inner child had always made her good at children's games but of late her energies had sunk so low. She was well and truly trapped between Willard's importunate ghost and Leonard's vigorous presence; she was still living through every word of Willard's life in the proofs of his biography. Leonard was wiry but strong, the thick downstrokes of his writing told her that, his presence was very physical; if Willard's character had been porcelain then Leonard's was of sawn English oak, with a thin veneer of spirituality assumed from his time spent in the company of the mystical genius Tagore. Everyone with them assumed he was the holiday tutor, and in a friendly gesture Herbert Croly suggested he might like to read the proofs of his *Willard Straight*. Herbert was deeply upset; he told Dorothy he feared 'Leonard had not liked the book at all'. It was not the book's fault it had aroused, perhaps confirmed, Leonard's jealousy of Willard's sainthood, and Dorothy had to apply balm to Herbert's hurt feelings. To Leonard she wrote of having 'hurled myself back into the life of the world' at the end of her holiday, signing herself 'Yours and Willard's Dorothy'.[143] No one seemed to notice that she was on the verge of her complete breakdown.

So, there they were, back at Woods Hole again, at the beginning of August a year later in 1924. Leonard had continued writing from India, oblivious of her illness, and Miss Bogue had filed his letters under 'Financial' as he had lectured Dorothy on her money, that her resources would be better spent on a single project than on her many causes. Now they had much to talk about, or Leonard had; he proposed again, and her reply emerged as 'an understanding' that 'we are to try and be content to be married in spirit and in absence'. Did that mean on opposite sides of the world? Their second decision was more sensible: their aim, their great project, would be a school 'such as has not happened yet', drawing on Indian, American and Chinese ideas of education, involving a few men of ideals and spirit (no politics and no 'isms') and nurturing children for service and fellowship – 'a Jerusalem' to set their faces towards. Leonard intended Jerusalem to be in India, but he had identified Dorothy's deep interest which survived from her discovery of Dewey's Laboratory School in Chicago in 1908 (and conveniently pre-dated Willard). He left Woods Hole for the city, writing from Dorothy's 1130 Fifth Avenue, 'This is to say good-bye and never good-bye for we are bound for eternity,' and Dorothy replied, her bruised brain unearthing impressions from Peking:

> I'm glad I have lived in heaven, Jerry! The afternoon at
> our rock was that – the yellow tufted hills, the sea and
> the birds and the broken stone wall. And through it all
> a sense of understanding as deep as life itself. Never was
> there such a communication of soul between two people.

Leonard warmed to his mastery of the situation: 'I don't want to see you drift back into the old life and be caught in the old net – the world can't afford to lose you again and you know it.' Touching her Achilles heel, for she felt so strongly that Whitney needed a man's guidance, he added, 'Life has been too easy for him, he's too ready to sacrifice truth for his own immediate ends – life has come to mean possession and having, not enough of earning and creating.'[144]

In part her rescuer came out of the ether, for in the late August she read E.M. Forster's newly published *A Passage to India*, which she found 'extraordinary' and 'oppressive' except for his 'flashes of insight'. The India he portrayed, she feared, was of 'muddle, muddle, muddle' and it would be impossible to get anything done; 'suspicion in the oriental is a sort of malignant tumour' was her verdict.[145] She would not go to India. Leonard, now in England, seeing people who knew nothing of Dorothy but heard the magic words 'American' and 'heiress' and told him that he was a 'lucky dog' and what was he waiting for, wrote on 18th September with his third proposal:

> Will you join me in Europe in April and transfer your
> dreams from the night – to the day, to reality, to marriage,
> and permit me to give a hand in bringing them to fruition?
> We've played with our dreams long enough.

She read this fifty times; her answers are enumerated:

1. Dr Connor says that her thyroid condition has weakened her system and she is not sure she can have any more children.
2. She has to consult Whitney, Beatrice and Michael, but not yet.
3. 'There is my age, in ten years I'll be an old lady.' (She would be forty-seven.) She finishes, 'But how wonderful your letters are – that I can keep my nationality and my name if I want to, angel, angel, that's what you are.'[146]

Leonard was impatient from four years of 'aching and wanting' and being unable to convince her that she was 'his only one right person'. She cabled him, 'Not Now Please Wait Till I Recover Fully.' She promised to keep April in mind. Leonard was now on the high seas to Bombay and, accepting that India was not for her, suggested that their school might be in England. Dorothy was overwhelmed: 'You know I adore England and always have since I stayed with my sister – and Dorset? Shall we really live there?'[147] The children's doctor had advised telling them everything, to keep their confidence – Michael, aged eight, said it would be 'dandy' if she married Jerry. Herbert and Louise Croly thought he had 'in a rare degree that purity of heart and that luminous moving simplicity of mind' that any man she married 'ought to have'. They thought that Leonard would simply marry her in New York and everything would remain the same, and that he was more suited to the quietly spiritual Dorothy that had emerged from her illness than any of her American friends and former suitors.

She spent a quiet autumn; Leonard was now acting as companion and secretary to Tagore who had been invited to visit Peru. They arrived in Buenos Aires in early November where Tagore was taken ill and they were both given refuge by his disciple and muse Victoria Ocampo in her luxurious villa.[148] Dorothy was intending to meet Leonard in April but for now he seemed very far away, and she had time to recover her spirits.

Whitney was enrolled at Groton School in Massachusetts, her brothers' old school, and this decided her that Beatrice and Michael too would be educated in America. She saw Shaw's *Saint Joan*, which made her think about patriotism – she, who had always been such a devout American patriot – could she ever relinquish her beloved country? Was there nowhere for their school in all America? Her 1925 diary, of gold-embossed mauve leather, marked the return of her *joie de vivre*. She would take Whitney and Beatrice to California for an adventure and a holiday, and so on the morning of 10th January they all trooped into the Natural History Museum with John Rothschild and Ruth Morgan to look at birds, as a treat for Michael who was being left behind.[149] Later Dorothy, Whitney and Beatrice boarded the sleeper train for the long haul, two nights and nearly two days, to Green River in south-west Wyoming, where they changed to the Western Pacific for Salt Lake City, some sightseeing and a recital in the Mormon Tabernacle before another train to San Francisco. There they stayed for over a week, spending a day in Berkeley with friends, seeing the La Honda redwoods, Palo Alto and Stanford; Dorothy celebrated her birthday in the Yosemite National Park. They acquired a driver and 'in a nice Cadillac' made their way south through the olive groves of Sausalito to San Raphael, then along the Santa Clara Valley to Monterey. They spent 'two gorgeous days' at Pebble Beach before continuing southwards along the Salinas Valley (the coastal highway was not yet built) to El Mirasol and Santa Barbara, and viewed the Ojai valley in the rain. Pasadena and Hollywood were their planned treats for Beatrice, where they visited Douglas Fairbanks's Studio and watched the filming of *Don Quixote* – from then on the stage-struck girl had few doubts about her future career. The next day they went to Rockwell Field and the Naval Air Station especially for the speed-struck Whitney.

In the meantime Leonard and Tagore had left Buenos Aires, and Leonard had reached England. He presented himself at the Hanover Square office of estate agents Knight, Frank & Rutley to be greeted with a polite wall of scepticism on announcing that he was looking for a large agricultural estate in south-west England. They smiled indulgently when he mentioned marriage to a rich American. He persevered (he dined out on this story for ages afterwards) and found himself with a long list of estates in Dorset, Somerset and Devon – country houses were falling like ninepins, it was a desperate decade – which he narrowed down to seven in Devon.[150] So much for Dorothy's dream of Dorset. He bought a small car and took one lesson in driving it, and, with his brave young sister Irene Rachel Elmhirst[151] as passenger, set off for Exeter, and westwards on the Plymouth road. He rejected Marley as it was then called, elegant eighteenth-century Syon Abbey, which can be seen now sitting in its wide green vale when turning south off the A38 at Rattery.

A little further south he found, with difficulty, Dartington Hall nestling in the valley of the brown and bubbling River Dart. Nosing their way up an overgrown track and peering through the ruined gatehouse, it was 'like love at first sight'. He was once again upon his knees. He wrote to Dorothy, 'I wanted to kneel and worship the beauty of it all – unlimited farm buildings with roofs and windows and doors like a fairy land, and such farmer folk, and the garden and trees you must see for yourself, the orchards, the river and the boathouse.'[152] He looked no further, his mind was made up while she was gazing down canyons in Colorado.

Dorothy, Whitney and Beatrice had come by 'California Limited' to the Grand Canyon, then south to Phoenix. They stayed at Chandler with army friends of Willard's for a sociable four days, before being taken north to Holbrook on the Colorado River, and more army friends, to see the Painted Desert, the Petrified Forest and more spectacular canyons. Dorothy's journey was followed by letters from the Crolys, motherly Louise's pleasure that she would 'once more enter upon and take up the activities that a young woman naturally has', softening Herbert's pessimism. His longer letters were filled with warnings, that she would find it difficult to adjust to living in two countries, that she would legally be a British citizen by marriage, and 'the major part of your wealth will be demanded by the British government for the support of the British Empire', and that Leonard's 'roving experimentalism' made it more important than ever to have a settled home for herself and the children. Without this, he prophesied, 'Your life may develop into a series of excursions tied together by a purpose which will have but little relationship to any national affiliation or background.'[153]

Dorothy's verdict on California was, 'I'm so glad we came – it has been infinitely worthwhile – much of it I don't care for at all – but Yosemite, Pebble Beach and the Ojai valley – these remain a picture of deep and stirring beauty.'[154] Taking Whitney and Beatrice to meet their father's army colleagues bequeathed memories of Willard to his children. From somewhere in Colorado they caught a train which delivered them home to New York on 20th March. That same afternoon Dorothy went to the dock to meet Leonard, having found a long letter of assurances from him, ending, 'Please don't be afraid.' She 'waited from five until seven' as the *Berengaria* was late. She had been wise to absent herself while the news travelled round. Anna Bogue's icy business letters to 'Mr Elmhirst' were negated by a warm hand-written expression of, 'My feelings of joy in the happiness that has come to you and Mrs Straight – my loyalty and feeling for her is unfailing and I hope that now we can work together.' From Marraine Bend in Rome with Beatrice and Prather Fletcher, for whom Dorothy was the 'most unselfish, devoted and loving daughter', Leonard received a frosty reply saying, 'Dorothy has never mentioned the subject to me.' After hearing from Dorothy she changed to calling him 'Dear Leonard' and ending, 'Please let me know – when you will become my son-in-law.'[155]

There were a thousand things to do. Leonard took the boys to Aviation Field and went riding with Beatrice. Then he went into the city and Ruth Morgan stayed with Dorothy for some time in quiet, prayerful talk. Then Dorothy went into Manhattan for shopping and a visit with Leonard to her doctor who, in the way of medical men, probably told her to enjoy herself. This she seemed eager to do, she was ready for a new sexual relationship, a photograph shows her posing coquettishly, and it is most likely that the complete withdrawal of her sedatives had fired her libido into an eager and erotic desire to be ravished, no matter how inexpertly. They bought a Havelock Ellis handbook on sexology and read it together.

Leonard's brother Victor, who had followed him to Cornell, was to be his best man. Victor told Leonard that 'he must have Dorothy for a sister because he feels he grows sizes bigger' every time they met! Harry and Gertrude Whitney were less easy. Gertrude was famous after the triumph of her Buffalo Bill Monument in Cody, Wyoming, and embroiled in the difficulties of casting her memorial figure standing on the wings of an American eagle for Saint-Nazaire in Brittany. Harry was in pain from a bad fall from his polo pony, which aggravated other ills, and their three children – Sonny with legal problems, Barbara recovering from the difficult birth of her daughter and Flora's five-year marriage ending in divorce – made it 'all a horrible spring'.

Harry's ills, wrote Gertrude's biographer, 'probably neutralized' his pleasure in Dorothy's new marriage, though 'it is unlikely that, under any circumstances, Harry would have taken his new brother-in-law to his bosom'. Gertrude's old friend Charles Draper described Leonard to her as 'quite a nice crank'.[156] It was Payne Whitney who came up trumps and offered them his yacht for their honeymoon. And so, after a lot of walking and talking, and a dash to Manhasset for a licence, Leonard and Dorothy were married by Bishop Wilbur at ten o'clock on the morning of 3rd April 1925 under the pine trees on Old Westbury's lawn. There was a small lunch party before they walked across to visit the ailing Harry, then they caught the 3.50 p.m. train for Miami, via Washington. Leonard had cabled his solicitor brother Pom Elmhirst in York, 'Happily married complete purchase Dartington immediately.'[157]

As pampered passengers on Payne's yacht they drifted around the Florida Keys, reading and birdwatching. On the way home Dorothy showed Leonard around Aiken and some of the sights of Washington. In New York she had three days of gynaecological attentions, pronounced herself 'as fit as a flea', did more shopping and had 'last talks' with everyone. Their truly last supper was with the children before they boarded the *Majestic* late in the evening. She slipped her moorings at six the next morning, 23rd May, bound for Southampton, the original of that name, in England.

The newly-weds landed on 29th May to be met by Leonard's sister Irene Rachel, and another brother, Richard, who took them to Exeter and the Royal Clarence Hotel. The following day they drove to Totnes and then to Dartington where they spent the morning – 'too heavenly' was Dorothy's verdict. As Leonard had written, 'a fairy land' or at least otherworldly, for what they were looking at was an ivy-covered ruin with roofless Great Hall and agricultural squalor predominant in all the surroundings. After lunch at the Seymour Hotel in Totnes they returned for a second inspection; 'interior difficult' noted Dorothy, presumably referring to the abandoned rabbit warren that might one day be her home. There was nowhere for them to live in the foreseeable future. Her old life crumbling behind her, her prospect only ruins. The next morning they went to 'a lovely service' in Exeter Cathedral, and afterwards she broke down and 'wept idiotically'.

After a day on Dartmoor in lovely weather and her third Devon teashop cream tea in three days, they headed for London and the Haymarket Hotel. They went to Knight, Frank & Rutley and to Hamptons as the Dartington purchase was not going well. They had offered £25,000 against an asking price of £30,000 for the 820-acre estate, and the seller, Arthur Champernowne, tenth owner of that name since the mid-sixteenth century, was not willing to proceed.[158] They discussed matters over dinner at the RAF Club with yet another Elmhirst brother, Tommy. Next day they watched the Trooping the Colour and dined at the Berkeley, and the following day they set out to buy a new motor and also called at the architect Henry Tanner's West End office, seeing the Carl Rosa production of *Madame Butterfly* in the evening. Freed from trains they drove back to Devon on the Friday, having a picnic in a field and looking at churches at Wyle and Mere. The following day, 6th June, was Leonard's thirty-second birthday, spent in more exploration at Dartington.

Dorothy and Leonard Elmhirst at Dartington, 1925

In the middle of June they motored to York and lunch with the Seebohm Rowntrees, then back southwards via Bawtry to the Elmhirst home, a 600-acre holding of that name near Worsborough, south of Barnsley. To Leonard's parents the Reverend William and Mrs Mary Elmhirst Dorothy smiled, held out her hand and said, 'I'm Dorothy,' and her victory was apparently complete. On the way home they stopped at Stratford-upon-Avon to visit Shakespeare's grave in Holy Trinity Church – de rigueur for an American, especially one with a place in her heart for the sonnets and plays, or was there something more? They drove south over the Avon to the still-feudal hamlet of Clifford Chambers, its one gravelled street bordered by wide lawns and leading to the gates of a lovely Queen Anne manor house grouped with a medieval church and stunning E-shaped timbered rectory, reputedly the haunt of the poet Michael Drayton and his drinking friend 'Mr Shaxpere'. Had Dorothy's appearance at Hamptons or Knight Frank & Rutley improved their client status beyond ruins to plum estates? Who sent them there if not? The manor was owned by Mrs Douty, the former Kathleen Wills of the Bristol tobacco family, but she was recently widowed with a young son, and had perhaps given 'the right buyer' a thought. They drove on to Broadway to tea with the actress legend of the New York stage, Mary Anderson de Navarro, who presided over a literary, gardening and cricketing society with a strong American flavour which embraced Major Lawrence Johnston and his garden at Hidcote Manor.[159]

Their gypsy life continued into July, the chance of Clifford Manor faded as Mrs Douty decided to marry Colonel Rees-Mogg, and Leonard was determined to have Dartington. Manorial rights and the valuation of the timber had complicated matters, Arthur Champernowne was digging in his heels, and on the 23rd he wrote, 'I can see no certainty of any agreement,' nor could he hold himself under any obligation. With the advice of Charles Elmhirst, Leonard's solicitor uncle in York, and brother Pom, a younger solicitor, they increased their offer to £30,000.

This might be the moment to introduce Susie Hammond's considered reflections on her friend's second marriage as 'self-denying, filled with generosity and consideration for others, serious [and] creative'.[160] This was never going to be a marriage as before; that Dorothy could not be given again as she no longer existed. Now, she had reached outside herself, she appreciated and admired Leonard's 'luminous simplicity of mind' and purity of heart, and she gave him her loyalty to their great project, her loyalty that would be unshakeable. She would find the money, he would make it work, that was their agreement. She paid for the Dartington estate and everything they did for the first four years, though thanks to her, or Harry Whitney's, clever lawyers and accountants, comparatively little of her wealth fell into the hands of the British government as Herbert Croly had feared. She remained an American citizen for more than twenty years, though she did call herself 'Mrs Dorothy Elmhirst'. She was also generous to herself, and to Leonard, in that they would continue to live in the style to which she was accustomed. Herbert Croly was right about the difficulties of living in two countries and here her 'consideration' verged on the courageous; as she gazed out into the Atlantic from the deck of the *Majestic* carrying her to England she made a silent pact with the great ocean that she was destined to cross, not for pleasure or at will but for love and duty, at beck and call, for the rest of her life. The great liners became part of her life, her transatlantic crossings became her 'decompression chambers', with always her own cabin and often a sitting room, where she could read and think and calm her fears. Poetry became her great solace, from this time she was hardly ever without a poetic hero to whom she could turn; at the moment it was John Masefield and the haunting cadences of 'The Passing Strange':

> For all things change [...]
> They change, and we, who pass like foam,
> Like dust blown through the streets of Rome,
> Change ever, too; we have no home.[161]

The serious nature of her sacrifice, that her part of their bargain was to let Leonard have his own way, would have denied her Clifford

Manor in its enchanting countryside, with a group of ready-made friends, all basking in the theatrical glow of Shakespearean Stratford, even had it become available. Her dream for her school beckoned her onwards. On their way to Yorkshire they had called at Oundle School in Northamptonshire on the strength of H.G. Wells's admiration of the headmaster Frederick William Sanderson and his progressive methods.[162] She found Sanderson's influence rapidly weakened after his recent death, which disappointed her, deterring her from following any English pattern and deciding her to rely upon her American experience.

In the middle of August 1925 their despair over Dartington turned to relief as the purchase was agreed. Work started on the restoration of their house, three Elizabethan storeys with attics at the west end of the Great Hall. Dorothy knew she was pregnant. They lived in a rented house called Elmsleigh in Totnes, somewhere to leave their belongings as in October they went separate ways, Leonard to Denmark to learn about modern dairying, and Dorothy to New York.

Willard Straight Hall at Cornell, December 1925. Photograph by Leonard Elmhirst.

113

President Farrand of Cornell had written of the exciting and inspiring opening days of Willard Straight Hall, now soaring elegantly from the Libe Slope on the Ithaca campus, and urged her, 'Do come and see for yourself what a beautiful thing you have done.' Almost five thousand people had roamed its gothic halls, full of admiration, and Willard Straight, 'WS' and soon simply 'the Straight', had been happily accepted into the life of Cornell.[163] On 14th December 1925 Dorothy gave a modest address at the opening, thanking everyone who had made the building possible, including Willard's old friends George Lincoln Burr and Charles H. Hull, and most especially her architect, William Adams Delano. Leonard had joined her in time for the opening, and they spent Christmas at Old Westbury with Whitney, Beatrice and Michael. She told the children about her new baby, and encouraged Michael to feel it moving inside her, which made for a difficult parting. Her added disappointment was that Louisa Weinstein, who had been around the world with her and lived in Peking, wanted to remain in America, as she really did not like the isolation of the Devon countryside.

Dorothy was not long back in Totnes before leaving for London to be near her consultant, the royal surgeon-gynaecologist Mr William Gilliatt. She needed to rest a great deal of the time but managed some outings with Kenneth Lindsay, and gentle forays to her favourite Floris and other Jermyn Street bazaars, and to Heal's in the Tottenham Court Road, the Arts and Crafts emporium and the first shop in London to sell Bauhaus modernist designs. Leonard, working hard in Devon, arrived in London in time for the birth of their baby daughter on 28th March 1926. She was named Ruth Whitney Elmhirst – Ruth in honour of Ruth Morgan.

SEVEN: A SCHOOL 'SUCH AS HAS NOT HAPPENED YET'

Dorothy, Leonard and baby Ruth were settled into their temporary home, the Old Parsonage near Dartington church, by the beginning of the summer. Ruth was in the care of her nurse, Miss Edith 'Jeff' Jefferies, and Whitney, Beatrice and Michael soon arrived for their holidays. A photograph of Dorothy was taken (probably) by Leonard as she sat in the garden typing the first Dartington school *Outline*. This pioneering document, strongly aligned with Dewey's theories on education, can be briefly summarised as follows:

1. Education is conceived as life (and not merely a preparation for life) and thus the centre of gravity shifts to 'the immediate instincts and activities of the child' rather than to textbooks and traditions.
2. 'Learning by doing – handicrafts will be regarded as of vital importance both for co-ordination of hands and brain' and also for bringing access to 'the world of form, colour and line in the handling of stone, wood, clay and textiles'; Dewey was particularly keen on geography, 'the unity of all the sciences' and so 'doing'

also meant the exploration of immediate surroundings, identifying resources, inventing and using tools.[164]

3. Adults were to be friends, not authority figures; at Dartington adults were 'seniors' and the children were 'juniors' and everyone used Christian names (though Dorothy's butler Thomas and chauffeur Rushton were excepted).

4. The school was to be organised as a miniature society, as Dewey saw a microcosm of 'the developing, democratic, larger society'. At Dartington this meant a self-governing commonwealth, with the students as decision-makers and with discipline enforced 'by the students' own court and judge'.

Leonard had persuaded a friend from Cambridge, the introverted piano-playing Wyatt Rawson, to teach, with assistants, one being Victor Elmhirst, and the other Miss Marjorie Wise who came over from Columbia Teachers' College. On 24th September 1926 Dorothy noted the arrival of the first children, brought from Totnes station and introduced to Whitney, Beatrice and Michael over tea and games.[165] The three Straights had not wanted to return to America at the end of their holidays and so it was decided they would attend Dartington's school. It was rather like 'home schooling' to begin with, an extension of home life in the Old Parsonage, and Dorothy was completely involved, cheerfully describing their evenings to Susie in America:

> Every Monday night we sew together, the children learn to darn socks and do their own mending – on Tuesdays we have Dancing Class for the older students, workers on the estate and the maids of our household. We feel very proud of ourselves for achieving the Charleston, and even Whitney [now fourteen] is no longer scornful of our efforts. Then on Wednesday evenings Mr Heuser [of the poultry department] is dissecting chickens and giving

the most wonderful lessons in physiology, anatomy and biology – the children are thrilled and really learning a lot of elementary science. On Thursday evenings Boxing comes along – I wish you could see Michael and the younger ones with great boxing gloves on, trying to look fierce – Friday and Saturday are free evenings, and then on Sunday we all sit on the floor around the fire in the Music Room and either read aloud or have discussions.[166]

With school life in full swing in the November her diary has a note of a trip to London to see Mr Gilliatt, who confirms that she is pregnant. They spend Christmas at Dartington and then go to Lenzerheide in the Swiss Alps for ten days, returning in time for Dorothy to see Mr Gilliatt again before they are back home for the school opening on 14th January. Their house in the corner of the Courtyard is ready for them to move in, some twenty-one months since Dorothy had first gazed upon it in ruins, and now they and the school activities are at the heart of things. The Great Hall is still roofless, being subjected to a patient process of restoration, with trees on the estate being felled for the roof timbers.[167] The distinguished seventy-year-old Henry Avray Tipping[168] took his first look at the garden, and the potter Bernard Leach came over from St Ives with his assistant Jane Fox-Strangways, 'the foremost lady potter in England', Dorothy tells Susie:

[who] is going to live and work here. We are fixing up a shed for her where she will have her wheel and all her materials for pottery and designing, and both Beatrice and Michael are planning to study pottery from the ground up. It is really a beautiful craft I think, and a person like Miss Fox-Strangways puts real originality into it. Her pottery is like no other I have ever seen, and to hear her talk about form and its meaning gives one a new insight into the value of Art.[169]

Then, on 6th March she was overcome with 'dreaded pains' and the next morning her baby girl 'slipped away' gently. She held the tiny foetal form, 'quite red and soft but complete and unblemished' in a little soap dish. Next day Leonard came in to see her before lunch and found her weeping; she wrote that he 'showed me my own weakness and, incidentally, his strength'. He said, 'Don't let yourself want things so intensely.' They read the words of St John together, Christ's answer to Nicodemus:

> The wind bloweth where it listeth, and thou hearest the sound thereof, but canst not tell whence it cometh, and whither it goeth: so is every one that is born of the Spirit.[170]

Leonard apparently urged her, 'Be yourself, don't always strive for results, for action. Learn to become yourself.'[171] Unsurprisingly tears spattered the beginning of her letter to Susie written a few days later while she was still in bed: 'I miss you dreadfully, and so often long for your companionship.' She confesses that losing her baby was her own fault as she had been moving heavy furniture around in their new house, which hardly lessened her misery. On the other hand, Ruth, coming up to her first birthday, 'was adorable, and just reaching, I should say, one of the really dangerous stages, when she scales heights and drops off, tries to fall out of the window, and puts everything in her mouth'. Ruth's nursery was on the top floor of the tall house.

Of their general progress she became philosophical:

> Things are going very well here, though at times we have a fearful sense of the inadequacy of it all. The possibilities of education are so vast, and the glimpses that one gets at times of what it might be make one conscious of all one's shortcomings. But I suppose the great thing really is to make a start, and provided one can keep one's eyes open and respond to the demands of the moment, the future will take care of itself.

She finished more cheerfully:

> We are at present on the trail of two musicians for the staff, both of them composers and from all accounts intensely alive to the need to bring music home in simple ways to the lives of everyone. We hope to have a school orchestra as well as a big chorus before long and even now in our amateur efforts at chorus singing we are finding enormous satisfaction.[172]

The Easter holidays were spent in New York. Dorothy had reluctantly decided to part with 1130 Fifth Avenue – which had been built for her and Willard's political ambitions – as she had an offer from a lawyer who could afford to keep it intact.[173] Their new base was an apartment at 1172 Park Avenue, with a housekeeper to look after friends who stayed in her absences. It was a dull and hard-working trip, there are signs that she was feeling not at all well, perhaps not fully recovered from her miscarriage, and she had now passed her fortieth birthday.

At home in mid-May her diary shows nothing but visits to her doctor and dentist and her school duties. In late June she had the shocking news of the death of her brother Payne, who had collapsed after a game of tennis at his home at Manhasset. He was only fifty-one. Her homesickness for New York, losing 1130 and grieving for Payne made her sensitive to her loneliness in Devon, where she had not exactly had a warm welcome. Leonard had brought his 'Socialist' wife to the most deeply Conservative of counties, to Dartington, which had been owned by the same family for four centuries, and was now being subjected to lavish and speedy expenditure of American money. They did not deal in 'public relations' and were too busy to explain what they were doing, the schoolchildren could be seen 'running wild' in their great adventure playground rather than walking in crocodiles, and so there were inevitably lurid rumours. Leonard, in his tweeds, merged in with his farming fellows well enough, but Dorothy, expensively dressed and usually in her big American car, was seen as an alien being metaphorically clothed in dollar bills.[174]

The truth was Dorothy had become uncharacteristically shy, and not a little fearful. She realised that this was not the England of her pre-war visits to her sister Polly, and she had not understood how the formalities of Polly's house parties and high society junkets at Ascot and Henley had protected her with a kind of armour plating, which she had now lost. Leonard's urging her to 'be yourself' and that she should not 'want things so intensely', apart from being tactless to the point of cruelty to a mother who had just lost her baby, depressed her; had he no idea how much of her 'self' she had sacrificed? She had written that 'we came together to England' and it was 'no longer her personal story'. She had merged her 'self' into the duopoly – the indivisible Leonard-and-Dorothy – which united their decisions about Dartington. To outsiders this seemed a fortress mentality, and Dorothy's clothes, which she continued to buy in New York, and her car, were her defences of her frail remnant self.

The more tangible evidence of the 'fortress Dartington' was the amount of building of cottages and school departments that was going on – Dorothy may have joked about 'our village' after she and their Clerk of Works Albert Fincham had chosen the sites for some new cottages – but this amount of development could only have been carried out in a private world even in those days of an embryonic planning system.[175] Dartington's country neighbours were innately suspicious of new buildings, and the wider mood was strongly in favour of conserving England's 'green and pleasant land' from too much concrete; the Council for the Preservation of Rural England, founded in 1926, had strong support in Devon. The net gain was in local employment. A school-style photograph taken on a fine day in 1927 shows no fewer than eighty-eight Dartingtonians, including two infants, one being Ruth sitting on 'Jeff's' lap. An absurdly young-looking Dorothy and Leonard are surrounded by rows of forestry, farming and building men, male and female teachers and household staff. In the front row sit eight school seniors and seven juniors.

Dorothy struggled to the end of the summer term and to a first community effort, the Dartington Cottage Garden Show – which put her and Leonard to shame as hardly anything had been done to the Hall's overgrown garden. Mr Avray Tipping could not understand why they had not leapt into action on his recommendations, and Leonard had explained:

> It is quite impossible to do everything at once; and as you know, with a gang of 200 men on construction work of one kind or another, with a school into the bargain, it has not been easy to find the time and leisure which are essential if one is to take the right kind of interest in garden reconstruction... I have insisted from the start that the bread and butter end of this experiment must come first, and that we are not an ordinary country house for entertainment.[176]

Tipping was not used to coming second after 'bread and butter', and after he had renovated the tiltyard terraces and planted good yew hedging he closed his 'professional connection'. Dorothy resolved to write to Beatrix Farrand.

Their summer holiday was in Spain, with Whitney, Beatrice and Michael but not little Ruth. For a while Dorothy's energies were renewed, but when school started she soon tired, simply with the amount she had to do. On hearing that Nancy Astor was speaking in Totnes she invited her to Dartington, but Nancy's schedule was too tight. The rebuff hurt more than it should, for she needed allies. Early in 1928 she made a mercy dash to New York, accomplished in three weeks so spending little more than a week there, because Beatrice Fletcher had written to say that her mother Marraine was ill. Marraine Bend, not a lady to reveal her age, must have been over eighty; she had been Dorothy's adoptive mother for more than twenty years, and now they were together for the last time. What remained of her visit was spent with her Committee on Commitments, for far from devoting her resources to one big project – she gave Leonard all he needed for Dartington – she still maintained her charitable giving of $100,000 a year.

The year's causes illustrate her thinking – Carrie Chapman Catt's Women Against War, the Museum of Natural History's project on American Indians at Pueblo Village in New Mexico, Barnard College's summer school for women workers in industry, the League of Women Voters, the progressive Bennington College in Vermont, and her Willard Straight fellowship at the New School for Social Research. Miss Bogue listed ninety appeals for the current six months, page after page headed 'My dear Mrs Elmhirst', recalling meetings or friends in common, or simply forwarding their worthy cause. They reflect Dorothy's unfailing loyalty to the places and people she knew – Chinese Famine Relief, German Student Exchange (John Rothschild's introduction of the new Youth Movement into American universities), the Bulgarian Folklore School in New York, the Edward MacDowell Colony for artists and musicians at Peterborough, New Hampshire, the Arnold Arboretum at Brookline, Massachusetts, the Long Island Biological Association, George Washington's Sulgrave Manor in England, the Actors' Fund, the Red Cross, kindergartens, bible societies, cancer research, the Willard Straight Agricultural School in the Philippines, Pioneer Youth of America, mass education for the Chinese, co-operative banks and the New York Society for the Suppression of Vice. Her Committee – Herbert Croly, Edouard Lindeman and Ruth Morgan – usually met in Dorothy's absence; their decisions were collated by Miss Bogue and Dorothy authorised the grants for each session.[177]

Back at Dartington, 1928 only merited a Collins Diamond Diary, a modest object which recorded her doctor's appointments and activities with the children, her own and the school's. In June they escaped to Aviemore, Nairn and the Gairloch for some golf and fishing. On 29th June Dorothy saw Mr Gilliatt in London who confirmed her pregnancy. This time she would be careful. Anna Bogue and Ruth Morgan visited Dartington in July, and in August she and Leonard sailed from Newcastle for Bergen, for a month in Scandinavia which included some time at an Oslo conference on internationalism. In September she was clearly feeling better and shopping at Heal's for her new retreat. To her great joy they had managed to buy an Alpine (or

Adirondacks) style chalet overlooking Whitsand Bay at Portwrinkle on the Cornish side of the Tamar. The Chalet, with a pretty wooden balcony and upper storey of fir logs, was built in 1908 for Lady Beatrice Carew Pole; it was secluded and quiet and allowed her to sit in peace and gaze out onto the ever-changing sea.[178]

Once again, with her baby growing inside her, other desires weave themselves into reality. 'From the earliest days at Dartington,' she wrote, 'we have tried to infuse our life with the elements of theatre... one day we resolved to invite a touring company to give a performance here.' Friends had mentioned Maurice Browne playing in *The Unknown Warrior*, and Dorothy found the text immediately and read it, finding it 'the most profoundly moving of all the war plays'. She was so deeply affected that she 'could not rest until it had been given here'.[179] Browne was in his forties, disillusioned with soldiering in the South African War, a poet, bookseller and actor/producer in America, reduced to nine happy months in a shack on Telegraph Hill in San Francisco until his mother sent him his fare home. Fate had brought him *The Unknown Warrior* role, and fate conspired – as his mother lived in Devon – to arrange his meeting with the Elmhirsts. It was rather a replay of the birth of *The New Republic*, with Dorothy perceiving another's passion reaching out to her own, and her quiet response. There was her love of the theatre, and her adventure with the Provincetown Players who were part of the Little Theatre movement, and so, she discovered, was Maurice Browne; with the American actress Ellen Van Volkenburg he had started the Chicago Little Theatre, putting on Rupert Brooke's play *Lithuania*. 'Little Theatre' was the guardian of the 'eternal verities', of beauty and 'its articulation in art' and the players' service was 'not lightly to be given, nor to a light cause, nor for profit'.[180] Miss Van Volkenburg, a Pre-Raphaelite beauty and experienced as a director, was keen to work at Dartington, but the flamboyant Browne, in teddy bear fur coat and gold earrings, might be less easily settled.

About ten days after their first talk in November, Browne reported that he had seen a Sunday night run-through of a 'wonderful' play called *Journey's End* by R.C. Sherriff, with an actor called Laurence

Olivier playing the lead role of Captain Stanhope. Robert Cecil Sherriff was an insurance salesman who wrote plays to raise funds for his Kingston-upon-Thames rowing club. *Journey's End* was based on his own experiences in a dug-out at Saint-Quentin on the Western Front, and he felt it was his best yet. Browne said it was 'difficult', meaning it was too serious a portrayal of the hopelessness of war and that no commercial West End theatre would touch it – would the Elmhirsts put it on? Dorothy knew immediately that they would, but Leonard cautiously asked for some costs – being a theatrical impresario had not been included in their great project, as far as he knew! Browne came up with the Savoy Theatre and addressed Leonard and Dorothy as 'My dears', in the way Rupert Brooke had written to him and Nellie; 'everything settled, *Journey's End* to open around 21st January' – the start of a six months' lease at £400 per week all included.

Journey's End did open at the Savoy Theatre on 21st January 1929, making theatrical history. Browne was the producer, it was directed by James Whale, and Stanhope was played by Colin Clive, as Olivier was committed elsewhere. The critics found the first night 'flawless' and wrote rapturous reviews. Almost everyone connected with the play was working in memory of someone maimed or killed in the war; the audiences sensed this and as so many felt the same the play's success grew by word of mouth until it was confirmed a 'smash hit'.[181]

At Dartington Dorothy had retired into her pregnancy and a family Christmas. Then it snowed, and snowed, and they became snowbound. It was not until a Sunday in mid-February that they managed to get to London with Jane Fox-Strangways, who was off to Egypt, and Marjorie Wise, who stayed with Dorothy while Leonard returned home. Dorothy and Marjorie saw *Journey's End* on Monday the 25th, with no fuss, as no one knew that Dorothy was their fairy godmother. On the Tuesday afternoon she felt 'signals of disturbance' and went into the nursing home; she noted a 'friendly visit' from Mr Gilliatt at 5.30 p.m., his return at 8.30 p.m. when she was sedated and the birth of her baby son at 8.50 p.m. He weighed 6 lbs. 4 oz., had dark hair, a wide brow and tiny pointed chin and she called him Bill. The next day she wrote, 'Can't sleep from sheer happiness – what blessedness to have a boy.' Leonard, she noted, was 'quietly happy'.[182]

'Bill' was baptised William Knight Elmhirst at Easter in the Old St Germain's church as they were all staying at The Chalet. His godparents were Beatrice Straight, now fourteen and a half, Leonard's brother Richard, Louise Croly and Maurice Browne, the last two being 'over the sea'. Dorothy noted Easter Sunday as 'a day of peace and joy with the grandparents' – William's middle name was for his grandmother Mary Knight Elmhirst, which Dorothy added 'suggests romance and poetry and adventure and high surprise'.[183]

At the end of the summer term, and less than six months after William's birth, Dorothy and Leonard set out for India, taking Michael, now nearly thirteen, with them. Michael remembered the trip as the first time he had been alone with his mother and stepfather, and for the discomforts they encountered. From the ship at Bombay they travelled by train to Tagore's estate near Bolpur in West Bengal. Naturally Leonard wanted to show Dorothy the Institute for Rural Reconstruction, Shriniketan at Surul, which he had established on her scholarship in the early 1920s, and then they were Tagore's honoured guests at the ashram at Santiniketan, a beautiful place with its marble-floored prayer hall. Tagore was approaching seventy, with the appearance of a white-haired prophet of great spiritual beauty, his presence was hypnotic. His worldly honours were laid aside and he preached the virtues of education and enlightenment to his community and the wider listening world.[184] Dorothy and Leonard were both busy and absorbed, leaving Michael to the mercies of boys of his own age who were not spiritually inclined. Michael's abiding memory was that there was only one water closet, which he was allowed to use only after Tagore had completed his toilet. He recalled his parents as uncaring. 'At times my stepfather was remote and my mother naïve.'[185] It seems more likely that Dorothy was half-stupefied in waves of post-natal depression brought on by the alien surroundings and diet and lack of bathrooms. At Nice on the return journey they found a letter from Victor Elmhirst waiting for them; he had been left in charge at Dartington and things were not going too well.

There were bad reports about the school. It had always seemed puzzling that Dorothy, usually so open-minded and thorough in her researches, had disregarded the experience of other English progressive schools – notably Bedales in Hampshire and A.S. Neill's Summerhill – and gone her own way with Dartington. She must have been conscious of this, and perhaps fearing her independence of mind might appear as hubris, they had asked the school's doctor for a report on the children. He had noticed symptoms of fatigue, which he thought due to lack of any rules about rest periods or bedtimes; he thought periods of quiet reading would be more beneficial than Dorothy's lively Question Club sessions and sing-songs. Even more hurtful was a report from visitors from her revered Teachers' College at Columbia University which indicated that Dewey's principles had not been successfully translated into the school's life, and it was vital that they appointed a professional and experienced headmaster. This paragon would have to be found, so in the meantime Victor Elmhirst and John Wales were acting heads.[186]

In the September of 1929 the school reopened with twenty-five pupils between the ages of eight and eighteen. Michael Young recalled how his introduction had been the sight of a 'big boy', Whitney Straight, on his back under a Model T Ford: 'He gave me a ride in it, reversing at speed up perilously steep fields as though that was what the Ford was made for.'[187] (Michael Straight, more reliable on cars, said it was a Riley 9, with which Whitney became an enthusiastic competitor at hill-climbs.) Cars and motorbikes were allowed for the seniors and Whitney was a good advertisement, steady and responsible and settled into his English life, too absorbed in his passions for speed and jazz to be worried about his unconventional home. He had earned some local fame by turning up at Haldon airfield, a newly opened flying school, proffering a £1 note and asking for as much flying as that would buy. Haldon's owner, William Parkhouse, put Whitney to work driving a tractor with a roller crushing flints on the runway, and taught him to fly so that he had earned his first pilot's licence just after his seventeenth birthday, and soon bought a De Havilland Gypsy Moth.[188]

Serendipity had stepped into the search for a headmaster. The companionable Marjorie Wise had returned to America, to Philadelphia where her sister Ena was married to the head of Oak Lane Country Day School, a twenty-nine-year-old Briton called William Burnlee Curry. Curry was presumably willing, and Leonard and Dorothy liked the sound of him, and planned to see him in America. For the time being they were embroiled in the plans for Dartington's consolidation, the second stage of development, as their project had outgrown their sole charge, Leonard's single-handed management and Dorothy's sole financing in four short years. Now, in 1929, Dartington Hall Limited was set up as a private company with a share capital of £65,000, with Leonard as chairman of the Board of Directors and Dr W.K. 'Bill' Slater as managing director. The company was to manage and promote the commercial departments, the farms and orchards, the textile mill and Staverton Builders' contracts, each under a departmental manager. Later the Dartington Hall Trust was formed as a charity vested with the estate and its maintenance, including the Hall, and with responsibilities for education and research. Dorothy was a trustee, and their meetings assume regular places in her diary and frame her activities.[189]

They discovered that Mr Curry, as Dorothy steadfastly called him, while he became 'Bill' to others, had degrees from London and Cambridge, had taught at Bedales and gone to his headship at Oak Lane, a progressive day school run on John Dewey's theories. Dorothy warmed to him when she knew that Oak Lane had a special relationship with Leopold Stokowski and the Philadelphia Symphony Orchestra, and also with a young modern architect, William Lescaze, thus giving the pupils two most desirable extra perspectives. She found both Currys, William and Ena, to be 'extraordinarily fine' human beings. The financial organisation of the Trust allowed Curry's appointment as 'Director of Education to the Social and Educational Experiment at Dartington Hall', at a salary of £1,000 a year.[190]

Headmaster Curry demanded a new house and insisted on bringing his own architects, the Howe & Lescaze Partnership from Philadelphia. They built his very expensive and glamorous 'celestial house with wings' as Dorothy called it, referring to the blue exterior finish on some walls which 'on a fine day match the sky itself'. She thought it 'clean, stark and beautiful' and wondered 'whether in a few years we shall regard every other type of architecture stuffy, suffocating and artificial'.[191] The interior was spacious, with chairs designed by Mies van der Rohe, a fitted kitchen complete with Aga cooker, guest and staff rooms and sleeping terraces. Two garages housed the motors that the headmaster owned at various times, vintage Rolls-Royces, a Bentley and the huge Hispano-Suiza that was to be used in Carol Reed's film *The Third Man*. Curry delighted in 'the special clarity' of his house, and told *Country Life*, 'Serenity, clarity and a kind of open-ness are its distinguishing features, and I am disposed to believe that they have important psychological effects upon the occupants. Of this, however, it is too early to speak confidently.'[192]

Before too long Headmaster Curry was seen to be a resounding success, the numbers of pupils soared into the hundreds and Dartington Hall School fulfilled the trustees' hopes. The style, charisma and particularly the laughter – 'he talked so well, laughed so much, sometimes deep, sometimes high, at his own jokes even more loud and long than at other people's' – of the headmaster marked him out as the star in the Dartington firmament.[193] Inevitably he had usurped Dorothy's role, and the clause in his contract that demanded complete freedom from interference 'in all matters of educational administration' seemed aimed directly at her. Ena Curry became one of Dorothy's closest friends, one of a small literary discussion group that took the place of her beloved Book Class in her English life. Her relationship with the headmaster was always visibly correct, appointments were made through their respective secretaries for their frequent morning meetings, and for his invitations to business lunches or dinner with important guests. It has to be admitted, though no one may have uttered the words, that Dorothy's dream school had been wrenched from her grasp.

EIGHT: 'THE YEAST IN THE LEAVEN', THE ARTS COME TO DEVON[194]

Once more, consolation came out of the blue, this time from the old grey stones of Dartington. The builders working on the porch of the Great Hall had uncovered a carved ceiling boss of a white hart couched on a huge red-petalled rose, the rose of Lancaster. The hart was chained with a golden coronet around its neck. Leonard's researches into Dartington's history revealed that it had been the home of John Holand, or Holland, a nephew of John of Gaunt, Duke of Lancaster, into whose mouth Shakespeare had put his 'scept'red isle' speech in *King Richard II*. Coincidentally there were newspaper reports of the 'Wilton Diptych' being acquired for the National Gallery – this was King Richard's travelling altarpiece, and there on the gilded panels were angels wearing the same white hart badge.[195]

There was more to come. On behalf of Whitney, who was now curious about his forebears, Dorothy had sent to New York for the solid volumes of Whitney pedigree which her father had commissioned. Melville's *Ancestry of John Whitney* had identified the Lord Marshal, who orders the joust between Harry Bolingbroke and the Duke of Norfolk in Act 1, Scene 3, to be in reality Robert de Whitney, who died in battle in 1402. This Robert de Whitney was the real King Richard's Knight Marshal but he was also Sheriff of Hereford where the Whitney lands lay, and so naming him in the play would have exposed his partiality for Bolingbroke, Duke of Hereford and his liege lord. In all probability they were not the first Whitneys to come to Dartington, which was a comfort, and this discovery warmed Dorothy's passion for Shakespeare and his plays into life. She had found, where the hill rose on the far side of the tilting ground, her favourite outlook to where 'the land in the distance seems to take the form of soft green waves, silently rolling in', Gaunt's 'precious stone set in the silver sea'.

Maurice Browne, one of William's godfathers, was absent from the christening because he was in America persuading Paul Robeson to play Othello in London. Robeson had been successful in O'Neill's *The Emperor Jones* in Greenwich Village, enough recommendation for Dorothy. She had been to one of his Albert Hall concerts of spirituals, her favourite was 'Steal Away', and Michael Young remembered that Robeson sang spirituals in the evenings at Dartington when they were rehearsing *Othello*. Peggy Ashcroft was Desdemona; Dorothy noted her 'most beautiful voice' and that 'physically she and Paul Robeson made an astonishing picture'. With *Journey's End* transferred to the Prince of Wales Theatre, *Othello* opened at the Savoy on 19th May 1930, pioneering Shakespeare in the commercial West End. The reviewers applauded a brave production.[196] Audiences were good at first but then faded away and the play came off in June. *Journey's End* also came off in June after six hundred performances – 'Messrs. Sherriff and Browne have good cause to congratulate themselves upon the last eighteen months,' purred the *Evening Standard* on 9th June. Browne boasted he had made a fortune; he celebrated rather too well and blotted his copybook by 'outing' his backers, 'the couple who do good by stealth' whose identities everyone longed to know.[197]

In America that May, Herbert Croly died a disillusioned man who had been 'drifting slowly off into the ether of mysticism' in the footsteps of the elusive Alfred Orage. Croly's hopes of the post-war revival of *The New Republic* had foundered in falling circulation figures and new rivals; as Edmund Wilson recently arrived from *Vanity Fair* pointed out, 'The editors, who started out as gay young free thinkers, have become respectable to the point of stodginess... they are also very much at odds with each other.' Wilson never minced words and had already told a friend, 'When you become a regular editor at the *NR*, you draw a large salary and never go near the office, but stay home and write books.'[198] Had Croly's work on *Willard Straight* created this impression? Croly never came to terms with Dorothy's leaving, and her continued financial support of the paper was not enough; his letters to her have the sadness of a lost soul. 'I would give anything to have the right and opportunity to do something for your protection,' he had written, with a little consolation 'that you are fully capable of protecting yourself. For you are not only brave and generous but you are wise and strong... and incorruptibly independent.'[199]

For Dorothy an even worse blow came in late October when Harry Whitney died, aged fifty-eight. Her glorious elder brother had given her joy and comfort and her education into the ways of the world. There was poignancy in his passing: she remembered how people remarked on his wasted abilities, how Willard's friend Grayson Murphy had written from France saying that Harry should be with the Red Cross – 'He could have done great things in developing the entente between our country and our Allies – I should hate for anyone as fine as Harry to be out of it all.'[200] Now, at his end it turned out that Americans loved him for being a great sportsman; his polo, his sailing, his racing successes and the manner of his success had been good for the nation and they were lauded in long obituaries of praise. His expectedly quiet family funeral was overcome with more than a thousand mourners, from stable lads to senators, who crowded into St Bartholomew's church. Harry was buried at Woodlawn in the Whitney plot. Gertrude came home and shut herself into his room for days on end; Dorothy, who remained in England, cabled:

> My heart is with you all it has been a great experience
> to have such a generous warm hearted and loyal brother
> my love to you dear Gertrude you have been a good
> companion bless you for it.

At Dartington the profits from *Journey's End* funded the drama under the lively influence of Nellie Van. Beatrice Straight, seventeen in August 1931 – 'charming and obsessed with theatre and dancing, movies and lipstick', in her brother Michael's opinion – had never wavered in her acting ambitions. She served her apprenticeship with Nellie, and together they put on an open-air production of Milton's *Comus* (as Rupert Brooke had done at Cambridge) and *Woman of the Vaux*, a play about Mary 'Perdita' Robinson, the Georgian actress and playwright and favourite of the Prince of Wales. Nellie and Beatrice travelled to Seattle together, to the Cornish School of Arts for additional training for Beatrice and to recruit artists for Dartington. Dorothy had mourned her school for a moment, and then found her new vision: prompted by images of the past, the 'white hart' and Shakespeare, King Richard's knights, be-wigged Jacobeans and graceful Georgians, she saw that once again Dartington's Courtyard could be, not the filthy farmyard they had found, but the backdrop to colourful and creative lives, the working lives of the painters, potters, actors, dancers and musicians who would teach and perform there.

The puppeteer Richard Odlin and dancer Louise Soelberg were the first arrivals from Seattle. Richard Odlin and Nellie Van set about converting the sixteenth-century barn at the entrance to the Hall's Courtyard into a theatre. Louise Soelberg taught dance and was soon married to Richard Elmhirst. The painter Mark Tobey arrived, trailing his considerable reputation as an abstract artist of mercurial personality.[201] Tobey was forty-one, skilled in Chinese calligraphy and a convert to Baha'ism; Dorothy was fascinated and enjoyed his company. 'Today we have been to three galleries with Mark,' she reported home to Leonard from London, 'he has discovered for himself and for us a young English painter who is "the real thing". His name is Ben Nicholson – in a moment of weakness I bought two.'[202]

She had caught the phrase 'the real thing' from gallery talk, it was the grail for Ben Nicholson and Christopher 'Kit' Wood in their landscape painting. One of the Nicholson paintings was *Cumberland Landscape (Hare Hill)* painted in 1928 from Bankshead, where he lived with his wife Winifred and their son Jake; Wood was staying with them and had painted a similar view, and when he thanked them he wrote, 'I am absolutely on the verge of the real thing after what I saw and learnt at Bankshead.' That summer they had all gone to Cornwall, to Feock and St Ives, where Nicholson and Wood had found Alfred Wallis, who painted his primitives on card and odd pieces of wood with 'the restraint of colour and the sense of movement of a master'.[203] Dorothy soon acquired Winifred Nicholson's *Fishing Boat, Feock* and *The Island, St Ives*, but she really treasured Winifred Nicholson's flowers – Winifred had found 'flowers the perfect subject to combine her interest in colour with the aspiration to give a spiritual dimension to her art'. Dorothy went on buying Winifred's flowers – including *A Nursery Posy, Flowers from Malmaison* and *Allwoodii Pinks in a Glass Vase* until she owned seven or eight. Dorothy's other Ben Nicholson was his 'cubistic' *Charbon*, one of his finest paintings.

In August 1930 Kit Wood had died in tragic circumstances aged only twenty-nine. Ben Nicholson wrote to Jim Ede, 'We did try to help him – tried and tried & Winifred especially gave him one of the most beautiful affections I have ever seen.'[204] Gallery owners and Wood's friends were anxious to establish his reputation by selling his paintings, and Dorothy was invited to a preview in the November, which she visited with Jane Fox-Strangways, and then made a return visit with Leonard, when they bought *Pony and Trap, Ploare, Brittany* for £450. This was about three times as much as she usually paid, there was apparently some confusion over the price, and they were given two Frances Hodgkins watercolours 'which they had admired'.[205] *Pony and Trap, Ploare* was always to hang in her music room, and Dorothy bought more of Kit Wood's works, his *Crocuses in a Flower Pot, Dancing Sailors*, a watercolour of Chelsea showing the bridge and Lots Road Power Station, a charcoal and chalk drawing of Monte Carlo and *Fish in a Basket*, which she had in her bedroom.

In far-away Seattle the personable Miss Cornish, 'Miss Aunt Nellie' to her pupils, was so fascinated by stories of Dartington that she came over to see for herself, and noted that on her first morning:

… we were invited into the dining room for breakfast. A battery of huge platters under silver covers were aligned on the massive sideboard. With Richard Odlin as my guide, I discovered under these lids delectable kippers, lamb chops, and American ham and eggs. A butler who looked and played the part served us very formally and very politely.

This butler, over six feet tall, was Walter Thomas, who made many such impressions; he was supported by two footmen, a cook and kitchen maids and four housemaids. Thomas had been trained in the household of the Marquess of Bute, and Dorothy paid him £120 a year. His soon-to-be-wife Emily, a clever needlewoman who had come from Ludgrove preparatory school, had arrived at Dartington for the first time in the bleak darkness of a winter's night, and Thomas had taken her under his wing. In addition to these indoor staff there were also two chauffeurs for the several motors and four gardeners growing fruit and vegetables for the table.

After her breakfast Miss Aunt Nellie's time (she noted 'the whiff of English comedy about it all') was spent 'visiting the activities, including the newly-equipped dance school where Louise Soelberg taught her classes. There I became acquainted with her fourteen-month-old daughter Eloise, with whom I could play only when her very strict nanny graciously permitted it.'[206] The strict nanny was Miss Jefferies, as the marriage of Louise and Richard Elmhirst had been short-lived, and Eloise had been gathered into Dorothy's nursery with Ruth and William. They were soon joined by Dorcas Edwards, whose mother Bridget taught at the school, and all four were brought up together. In Dorothy's mind her nursery was now full, some of her joy at William's birth stemming from her relief that she had given Leonard a son, and since then she had sought advice and was attending a birth control clinic.[207] Michael Straight felt that his mother and stepfather found other people's children easier to relate to than their own – for a strange child in distress Dorothy had a tendency to light upon one of her own children's favourite toys; Leonard insisted on being called 'Leonard' or 'Jerry' but never Papa, Daddy or Father. He was detached from them, while Dorothy sometimes discounted them – Michael recalled, 'One of the disadvantages of the Hall as a home was that Whitney, Beatrice and he never knew who might be in their bed.'[208]

Mark Tobey was the most exciting teacher of drawing to children and adults, or anyone who wished to attend his class, for that was the Dartington way. 'Mark did not teach by any ordinary standards, yet he taught everything, even by silence,' observed Bernard Leach. 'One fine day some of the class were missing, some were bent over their drawing boards, but their teacher was also missing – Mark entered quietly, stood in the open doorway, paused and said, "I too have been out for a stroll watching some of you move freely in the sun on the tennis-courts. Is there a piano? Play – now leave your boards – dance – let go! – That's better – dance you emotionally tied up English! Now stand up and dance with your chalk on your drawing boards."'[209]

Beatrice, Whitney and Michael standing, and William and Ruth sitting. A rare photograph of all five together.

Tobey's magnetism brought the thrill of creativity, a 'buzz' to life around the Courtyard. Bernard Leach had returned to teach in the pottery because Jane Fox-Strangways was unwell, eventually leaving his son David in charge. Dorothy's largesse afforded a holiday trip to the Far East for Leach and Tobey, which allowed Leach to renew his friendship with Shoji Hamada and the Japanese craft potters who were his greatest inspirations. Richard Odlin travelled with them for a time and they collected fabulous Balinese puppets and oriental textiles for a growing collection at Dartington. It was Dorothy's continued support of Bernard Leach which enabled him to write *A Potter's Book*, which was to acquire biblical status for modern craft potters when it was published in 1940.

The arts thus gathered their own momentum. Dorothy's way was to welcome newcomers as long as she found them inspirational teachers and they fitted temperamentally into the community's 'campus-style' life. Quietly, however, she was running a rather different agenda with friends who came to stay as her house guests. One was Noel Brailsford, a left-leaning war correspondent whose interest in arms limitation and the causes of war had led him to her discussion groups at 1130 Fifth Avenue, and now – after another spell of travelling – he had found her at Dartington. He had given a winter series of lectures on 'The World Today' and she paid for his visit to the New School of Social Research in New York, and possibly also for his trip to India which resulted in his book *Rebel India* – controversial at the time for its anti-imperialist stance but now a classic. He became an affectionate sender of postcards from wherever he was in the world, and Dorothy was generous in her invitations to stay when he was in England. He brought the wood-engraver Clare Leighton in April 1931, having joyfully announced to Dorothy that they were married – he perhaps thought decorum was necessary even if it could not be as he was trapped in an unhappy marriage.[210] Dorothy gained a friend in Clare Leighton and she owned at least two of her illustrations for *Wuthering Heights*, and also *Breaking Camp*.[211]

The liberated air of Dartington was attractive for lovers. The philosopher Gerald Heard, 'pacifist intellectual' friend of the Huxleys and Bertrand Russell, was a most frequent visitor during the 1930s, 'grateful', he said, 'for what Dartington was doing for us two'. His significant other at that time was a young pianist named Christopher Wood, who found Dartington 'the one civilized place in England'.[212] Heard had been at Cambridge with Leonard, but it was his little book of 1924, *Narcissus: an Anatomy of Clothes*, that first attracted Dorothy. She was intrigued by his artful opening, 'The Life Force is like a juggler; it is always contriving that we shall watch the hand with which the truth is not being done – and when we look back we realise that we were studying the symptoms and not the causes.' Her copy is well thumbed; it is something of a guide to the undertones of life through the signals conveyed by costume, an actor's stock in trade. Gerald became something between her sage and her confessor; she started a 'Gerald' notebook and wrote down his maxims, 'Psychology is the science of the soul', 'self-examination and repentance are the first stages towards holiness', these the clues to her yearnings.[213] He persuaded her to find time for a daily meditation, and that her pursuit of self-knowledge would calm her fears about her past life and her present. Appointments with Gerald, friendly 'psychiatric' sessions, became regular reasons for her trips to London.

Heard also made a wider contribution to Dartington with his support of Leonard's philosophy that the countryside must not be a museum, nor a 'peasant's reserve', and its future economy needed careful planning – the framework of his article 'The Dartington Experiment' published in *The Architectural Review* in April 1934. Heard stepped perceptively from the rural economy to the quality of life in the countryside and the 'real tragedy' of its depletion:

> The inventor, the artist, the men of ideas, originality and design, must not be let run off to the town studios, and there immure themselves in hermetically sealed groups and sets... the creative type must not be let evaporate,

leaving the soil caked and hard – he must be retained as
yeast in the leaven.[214]

Dorothy was grateful for this airing in the *Review*, their debut into
the world of ideas via the liberally progressive minds of the paper's
readers. She harboured a quiet hurt at the lack of encouragement from
people she admired, particularly Nancy Astor. Following a chance
meeting in London she had written 'My dear Nancy', almost begging
her to come down and see 'more of what we are trying to do – you
are not very clear I know'. Once more Nancy was too busy. Sensing
this, Gerald Heard went on something of a crusade on Dartington's
behalf, telling his friends that 'the structure of a complete philosophy
of life' might be found in this Devon valley. He brought Wystan
Auden, then a teacher at Larchfield Academy in Helensburgh.

Harold and Vita Nicolson were staying in the district 'and want
to know if they may come over?' Harold was anxious to bring
Oswald Mosley 'to let him see that planning is already taking place
in England'. Dorothy and Vita Sackville-West liked each other and
– considering it was a long way from Dartington to Sissinghurst –
their meetings had a rarity value and their lightweight friendship
lasted for twenty years. Dorothy, who had already heard from
Maynard and Lydia Keynes, Duncan Grant and Roger Fry and
had enough imagination to suspect that Mrs Woolf might be in
the offing, did not wish Dartington to become a Bloomsbury out-
station like Garsington. They may live in country house style with
silver salvers and breakfast-laden sideboards in their house, just as so
many depictions in *Country Life* magazine, but this was for Leonard's
expectation, let alone the self-respect of her butler Thomas and the
staff. Now she had discovered *The Architectural Review* – 'the guide-
book, totem and art object' of the age – and the design revolution
of the decade, and her tastes would change.[215] Had her instinctive
appreciation of the paintings of Ben Nicholson and Kit Wood led her
into the fresh air of modernism – surely more fitting for her youth-
oriented Arts Department at Dartington?

Jane Fox-Strangways had been her partner in crime. Jane had taught in her pottery for two years before her mental and physical health gave way, and in her frailty Jane became Dorothy's companion, at least one afternoon a week set aside for 'reading with Jane'. Jane's artistry was turned to flower arranging in the manner of Gertrude Jekyll's naturalism, at which she was brilliant, and to writing poetry.[216] About once a fortnight they went to London on the train, and as Jane knew many of the young painters from her time in St Ives, she gave Dorothy her opinions as they went round the galleries together. Dorothy's purchases extended to other members of the avant-garde Seven and Five Society, works by Ivon Hitchens, Henry Moore, David Jones and Barbara Hepworth. Prompted by the *Review* they went to the 1933 exhibition of contemporary design at Dorland Hall in Regent Street, where Dorothy discovered the work of the Russian émigré architect Serge Chermayeff. His clean-cut and 'fitted' interiors, furnished with geometric-patterned rugs by Marion Dorn, the newly dubbed 'architect of floors', had an immediate appeal. Dorothy felt that here was (at long last) the design complement to her own radicalism, her recognition of modern art as 'a stimulation to living' as Henry Moore had written in *Circle*.[217] If one had to stiffen one's sinews to participate in the *Brave New World* (Gerald's friend Aldous Huxley's novel was published in 1932) then it was as well to have *le style sympathique*.

Dorothy had leased a flat at 42 Upper Brook Street in Mayfair (the area known as Little America, as her compatriots' clubs and societies gathered around the embassy in Grosvenor Square) which she commissioned Chermayeff to remodel. Behind the conventional sash windows, now masked with long gauze drapes, the flat became open-plan, with oak flooring and walnut veneer on the walls. The living-dining area, doubling as a meeting room, had sleek fitted sideboards and compartmented units on spindle legs for easy cleaning of the floor; the furniture was lightweight and there were wall mirrors reflecting uplighter lamps. The living room was warmed with two luxurious multi-pile rugs in a Greek key design of muted browns by Marion Dorn, and one of her more strongly geometrical rugs in darker browns was in the dining area. One photograph was published, amassing much praise for Dorn and Chermayeff, though the client was never named.[218]

Dorothy's quiet voice easily became lost amidst the Dartington building spree of the 1930s and the expansion of corporate governance that it generated. She had hoped that Bill Delano and Chester Aldrich would build for the school, but their Aller Park for the juniors was expensive and unsatisfactory. Leonard turned to the stylish Oswald P. Milne who had built Coleton Fishacre for their neighbour Rupert D'Oyley Carte, so Milne built the main school Foxhole, the new textile mill on the Dart, the Dance School and several 'well-mannered residences' for senior staff, all by late 1932, when he was dismissed. The success of the headmaster's house by William Lescaze was in his favour (and he had little work in Depression-hit Philadelphia) and so – working with his resident assistant Robert Hening – Lescaze designed the three school boarding houses, 'extremely impressive and indefinably American', cheap and quickly built. Departmental administration had far outgrown the Hall's Courtyard and so Lescaze and Hening also built the utilitarian Dartington Central Offices at Shinners Bridge and more houses for staff along Warren Lane.[219]

Fate, in the guise of Dorothy's perception, stepped into the brief vacuum between Milne and Lescaze, and almost launched Dartington's fame into the stratosphere. Ben Nicholson, now parted from Winifred and living in Hampstead with his new love Barbara Hepworth, wrote to say that he and Barbara would like to visit Dartington, bringing new friends, the German architect Walter Gropius and his wife Ise. This was in 1933, on Gropius's private, unpublicised first visit to England; he was fifty, with lean and intellectual looks, but a poor grasp of English. Except for the coterie of modern architects and artists who had travelled in Europe, and *Review* readers, few people knew of his work, only that he was the former director of the Dessau Bauhaus, now increasingly marginalised by the Nazi regime. Gropius found Dartington 'a sort of English Bauhaus', he was dazzled by the lavish budget for education and he and Dorothy understood enough of each other to realise their mutual interest in social housing and theatre

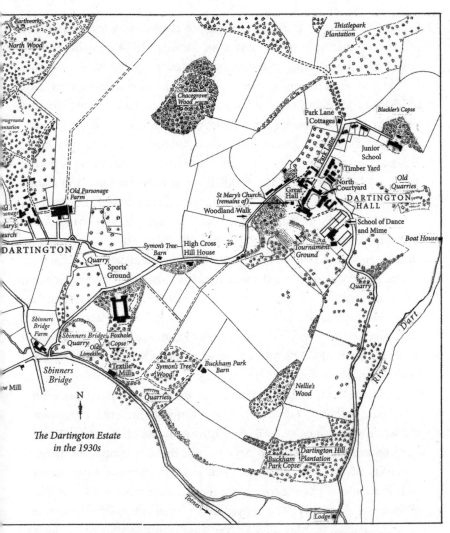

The Dartington Estate in the 1930s, showing the Great Hall with Dorothy and Leonard's home at the north-west end overlooking the old church tower, the buildings around the Courtyard and the Barn theatre at the north-east corner. New buildings include the dance school, the junior school and the staff cottages. The drive leads westward, passing the Headmaster's High Cross Hill; it divides northwards to the church on the Buckfastleigh road and south-west to Shinners Bridge, the offices, textile mill and on to Totnes.

design. He found it difficult to make up his mind to leave Germany and it was only after another year, in October 1934, that he and Ise arrived as refugees with little money and few possessions.

They were taken in by the architectural community led by Jack and Molly Pritchard, given a flat in the modern Lawn Road block in Hampstead, and Maxwell Fry took Gropius into partnership.[220] In the December he visited Dartington, where Dorothy was now convinced of his genius and hoped he would be appointed as architect for future housing schemes. Some cross-fertilisation had occurred as Gropius had met Henry Morris, the pioneer of village colleges in Cambridgeshire, for whom he was to build Impington Village College.[221] Morris was probably the one man in Britain who was on Dorothy's wavelength; he drew inspiration from the New York Settlements, and his colleges were to give an involvement in the arts to those 'who learn by practice and action' and had 'lost out' in conventional education.[222] Dorothy did go to see Morris, at least once, and what she and Gropius learned fuelled her desire for a 'college' of domestic design and furniture making, which would be 'a sort of English Bauhaus'. Leonard, who could not be such a free spirit as his wife, with the expectant Lescaze and Hening waiting for their next commission, could only see Gropius as an occasional consultant, and for goodwill asked him to specify for a manager's house and workers' cottages at the New Piggery on the estate at Yelland. As every farmer will understand his new pig unit was clearly the light of Leonard's life at that moment, but to Walter Gropius – Gropius who built the famous Fagus factory, who was director of the Grand Duke of Saxony's Academy, who designed a Ukrainian State Theatre, the Moscow Palace of Soviets and the Reichsbank in Berlin – had his pride. He dashed off a brief technical note with some measurements and added his opinion that William Lescaze was 'a second-class modernist' (which of course he was), and that was the end for the time being.

Dorothy fared better with her Dance School. She had seen Martha Graham dance in New York but found that free or German dance, dance-mime, were little known in England. One of Graham's pupils,

Margaret Barr, had come to Dartington and she and Louise Soelberg had trained a small group, but dancers did not seem to grow in Devon fields and Dorothy wanted a larger company now that she had Milne's Dance School. Coincidentally Whitney Straight's arrival at Trinity College in Cambridge had prompted the bursar of neighbouring King's, John Maynard Keynes, to remember his meetings with Whitney's father, then to write to his mother in early 1932. To Dorothy he recalled 'our common friend Croly', that they both supported 'an organ of the Left' and were interested in dance.[223] Keynes was also 'getting into farming' at Tilton, his Sussex home, and he would appreciate an opportunity to look around at Dartington. He did so, and he and Leonard were happy in farming talk. It was a friendly overture, and Keynes being so much more at the centre of things, Dorothy invited him and his wife, the ballerina Lydia Lopokova, to the opening of the Dance School in April 1932.[224] They could not make the day but came soon afterwards, and suggested a joint performance with their Camargo Ballet, which Lydia ran with Frederick Ashton, and could Dorothy help with their overspend? Dorothy pleaded poverty but sent £20 for goodwill. It became a delightful friendship, both Leonard and Dorothy enjoying the company of the miniature vivacious Lydia, who had been Diaghilev's principal ballerina, but wore her fame so lightly. Of course her lanky, looming husband was even more famous, and also 'charming and kind' to Michael Straight when he arrived in Cambridge in 1934. 'He is a very nice boy,' he told Dorothy.

The Keynes' neighbours in Gordon Square were the dancer Beryl de Zoete and sinologist Arthur Waley, another pair of lovers who became regulars at Dartington.[225] They were all in the audience for the Kurt Jooss Company's galvanising presentation, *The Green Table*, which foretold how the iniquities of the Versailles Peace Treaty would surely lead to another war. Kurt Jooss danced the role of 'Death'. Dorothy found it disturbing on behalf of Willard's ghost, hearing again Walter Lippmann's words from their last conversations, 'that what we had meant, and what alone could justify it all, was not the meaning and justification of those who will decide'.[226] She recognised Jooss as the supreme director of his immaculate company. She approached him backstage, nervously, apparently 'pushed' by Beryl de Zoete, and asked him to come to Dartington, but Jooss was as hesitant about leaving Germany as Gropius had been. Also the press reception for *The Green Table* was lukewarm – London was not ready for dance on the O'Neill spectrum of harrowing – though Lydia declared it 'a masterpiece' and Maynard told Dorothy not to be discouraged. Surely enough and soon, a matter of months, at his home at Essen Jooss was instructed to dismiss the Jewish members of his company, which he refused to do – and they were able to escape just in time as they had friends and sponsors at Dartington and knew where they would find a welcome. The company, '20 dancers, a manager, a stage manager, 2 pianists along with 23 students and 3 teachers', duly arrived; a large house, Redworth, on the road to Totnes was bought for them, and Kurt Jooss, his wife Aino Siimola and their daughter Anna soon moved into their own house in Warren Lane, effectively becoming Dartingtonians.[227]

Dartington Hall in the 1930s: the south front, the Elmhirsts' house at the west end of the Hall, is prominent. Also the stony remnants of the south court, Dorothy's sunny border and the Apostle Yews; and the Tournament terraces have been neatened for the occasion of the photograph.

For light relief Dorothy now had her garden. Beatrix Farrand had paid her first visit in the early spring of 1933 concentrating upon the Courtyard and the garden on the south side of the Great Hall. She had gone to Wisley and Kew to refresh her memory on English plants, and to Oxford and Cambridge to look at courtyards before spending ten days at work. Dorothy watched from her window as 'she worked incessantly – scrutinizing every corner and angle, setting up her stakes, taking meticulous notes, planning, planning every hour of the day and night'. It was a sheer pleasure to have an old friend there, to whom nothing needed explaining. Beatrix was now well into her sixties, a tall, elegant woman, muffled against the February weather, with stout boots, and when it rained a mackintosh cape, so that her dramatic figure stalking the tiltyard was christened 'Queen Elizabeth'. Her plan for the Courtyard – a farmyard space of awkward levels – envisaged a serene oval, paved with setts and cobbles around an oval lawn; she ordered *Magnolia grandiflora*, wisteria, roses and honeysuckles for the grey walls and camellias and azaleas for the garden walks. Later Dorothy recalled, 'In a short fortnight she had shown us the way to proceed.'[228]

In America it was Harry Whitney's legacy that Dorothy should have the use of Camp Deerlands in the Adirondacks, where she had stayed with their father, and where she now took her family for their annual summering. That August, 1933, after Camp Deerlands, she and Leonard had gone to Washington to see Beatrix Farrand's most famous garden at Dumbarton Oaks, but it was all rather a rush and the Oaks' owner Mildred Bliss was still away. Beatrix was pleased with their verdict:

> No mother ever purred more audibly with praise than I do over commendation of the joint work which Mildred and I have done… she had imagined the box ellipse when she was a child, so that its actual existence only wanted a spade and level to make it come true.

Dartington's Courtyard, being longer than it is wide, gave itself to the oval lawn, but it does seem that Beatrix had the Oaks ellipse in her mind, especially when she concluded:

> If you like Dumbarton Oaks let us all three, Leonard and you and I, work to make Dartington its English fellow.[229]

Beatrix came to Dartington again in February 1934; she forwarded her vision for the three magical paths, the Spring, Camellia and Rhododendron Walks that were layered along the hillside above the tiltyard. While in London Max Farrand sounded out his distinguished colleagues for their opinions on their educational experiment, finding great interest and enthusiasm among younger men, but the older ones – so typical of the English Establishment – were 'sitting back and doing nothing'. On leaving, Max wrote to Leonard from the Athenaeum in early March, 'It is a big thing you're attempting and thoroughly worth doing,' and he added that he had 'nothing but admiration' for the standards they were setting. He also added that he was happy to see Dorothy 'looking at least ten years younger' than when he had last seen her, when she was actually nearly ten years older.

NINE: 1935, SITTING FOR MR BEATON
IN HER SCHIAPARELLI HAT

It may seem strange that a museum director from California, albeit a
distinguished Ivy League historian, should have to take news of the
educational and farming experiments in the West Country to the
opinion makers of Pall Mall. Also strange that in encouraging Leonard
and Dorothy in their 'big thing' Professor Farrand omitted to say that
few people he spoke to had ever heard of the place. True, if he had
asked in the Crush Bar at Covent Garden some would have known
of an outpost of the dance, and in public school common rooms some
would have cursed another so-called progressive establishment; some
architects and the journalists at *The Architectural Review* would know
of the building spree, and at the Society for the Protection of Ancient
Buildings there would be praise for William Weir's restoration of
the Great Hall; but in general, in the mid-1930s, Dartington was a
secret place. In a way Leonard Elmhirst had intended this; in choosing
a fortified manor house set in fields that wore the River Dart as a
chastity belt, in a tree-girt valley in that remote country beyond Exeter,
served by one road and one railway line, he wanted to work away from
prying eyes and the criticisms of his peers. South Devon was almost
as far as he could get away from his family in Yorkshire, as well as
distant from the Home Counties stamping grounds where Dorothy

had enjoyed herself in her previous life. Was Dartington her refuge – did her increasing shyness dictate her preference for the nunnery that de Tocqueville had identified as the American woman's lot in marriage? Or was it her prison? Her weakness for big hats had been subdued of late but her mother-of-the-bridegroom hat from Elsa Schiaparelli floats through 1935 as her banner of her independence, still flying.

Dorothy was forty-eight on 23rd January 1935. She had been married to Leonard and in England for almost ten years. Herbert Croly's prophecy had come true, her life was divided between two countries with dwindling perspectives on both sides of the Atlantic. New York was still fun, she shopped at Saks and Abercrombie and Fitch, bought piles of books and American magazines, and their Park Avenue apartment had been decorated, with lily-flowered chintz for her bedroom and rose hips and leaves in Leonard's. She was still close to her sister-in-law Gertrude whom she loved, but the deaths of her brothers Harry and Payne had shaken her identity as a Whitney, and she felt isolated. On their 1934 holiday in the Adirondacks she had wandered away from the picnic party to find a knoll where she could sit and contemplate the beauty of the land she had relinquished. She recorded in her notebook her need to 'keep a tryst' with her spinster aunt Etta Whitney, who had recently died at a great age, 'but it was more than a tryst, it was an act of renewal with my father – with my forebears'. Summering at Camp Deerlands on Raquette Lake in the Adirondacks, which she so wanted her new family to enjoy, was now the immovable event of her year.

In England her constant companion is her slim navy leather, week-at-a-glance diary from Frank Smythson of Bond Street, which it has become her habit to use, and will be for the rest of her life. Inside, in green ink, she always writes her addresses – 42 Upper Brook Street (Mayfair 6782) and Dartington Hall, Totnes (telephone 193). Her diary encapsulates her English life, she is slim and often dressed in navy blue, she exists between the poles of Dartington and Mayfair, only rarely leaving her allotted path, and the diary is a model of confinement, its pale blue pages crammed with the pencilled minutiae of her days.[230]

Her New Year of 1935 began at the Chalet at Portwrinkle with walks along the sands, 'soppy golf' and a party for Ruth, William, Dorcas, Eloise and their neighbours' children. She was rather pre-occupied with Whitney and Michael who were piloting themselves home from South Africa, where Whitney had won the East London Grand Prix. He had previously raced his Maserati at Brooklands and Monaco, but never gone this far before; she plotted their stops, 'boys at Khartoum' on Sunday 6th, then Cairo two days later, Benghazi on the 9th – the day the school opened and they all returned to Dartington – then the boys reached Tunis on the 10th. Dorothy left for London on the Saturday afternoon, had dinner with Gerald Heard, and was at Heston aerodrome on the Sunday for the heroes' return. She gave them a celebration dinner. Michael Young, who had been part of her family for his teenage years, called 'Youngster' to distinguish him, and was now at the London School of Economics, was with them. Michael Straight, about to begin his second term at Cambridge, needed more of her time so they went to the Tate Gallery then a film and on the Tuesday evening they saw Gielgud's long-running *Hamlet* before she caught the midnight train to Devon.

At Dartington her daily round of interviews, meetings, lunches, teas and evening events is relentlessly crowded, but gradually, as the days go by, there is a sense of something growing out of apparent confusion. Kurt Jooss comes for a morning business meeting, the business of dance and also of making Redworth, the house at Totnes, a comfortable home for his company. Dorothy spends a great deal of her time there. A few evenings later Kurt and Aino Jooss are at dinner, a social occasion, with a 'Mr Martin' – formality indicating a first meeting, which is very soon, in early February, warmed into 'Chris and Cicely Martin'. Christopher Martin, whose only fault was that he was the nephew of the disapproving Reverend J.S. Martin of St Mary's church at the end of the drive, had been appointed arts administrator by the Dartington trustees. His first task had been to produce a report identifying the ways to unite the rather opportunistic gathering of painters, potters, dancers, actors and musicians into Dorothy's dreamed-of Arts Department. He had given her a choice: was the Department's ethos to be professional 'having amateur work with the Estate as an offshoot... or, primarily amateur and dilettante with professionalism only as a chance consideration?' Without hesitation Dorothy opted for the former.[231]

Walter Gropius, always Gropius in her diary, Herr Gropius across the dinner table, stays overnight in early February as she is trying to woo him back. She loves his vision and talk of unifying the arts as he had done at the Bauhaus, and she realises that he is a born teacher and organiser who is, unusually, a good listener. His enthusiasm for low-cost housing and system design reminds her of her architect-beau Grosvenor Atterbury, and also of her ancestor Eli Whitney, the patron saint of systems design.[232] She asks Gropius to redesign the interior of the Barn Theatre, to ensure his return. 'Mr and Mrs Collins' were also at that dinner, this her first meeting with the surrealist painter Cecil Collins, and his artist wife Elisabeth Ramsden, whom Mark Tobey had suggested as teachers of drawing in his stead.[233] Whitney comes for the weekend bringing his fiancée Lady Daphne Finch-Hatton for a first meeting with her prospective mother-in-law; Dorothy had arranged for the maestro Arturo Rubinstein to give a recital, playing on the gleaming black concert grand piano which had been bought for the Dance School.[234] As February is the month for nursery ills she spends some days with Ruth and William, and she is equally attentive to Dorcas and Eloise. All their birthdays are religiously celebrated, William's sixth with a film shown by George Bennett. February closes with the trustees foregathering for their quarterly sessions, three days of intense talks, with inspections all under Leonard's chairmanship about the workings of the Dartington departments. Dorothy doodles her way through milk yields and poultry economics, but now at least the Arts Department is included, and in Chris Martin's capable hands. Between them they persuade the trustees to appoint Walter Gropius as consultant and controller of design.

As the last meeting closes Dorothy and Ena Curry catch the train for London for a meeting of their philosophical group with Gerald

Heard. Unsurprisingly he steers them to the metaphysical, and they are studying Francis Thompson's *The Hound of Heaven*, the writings of Kahlil Gibran especially *The Prophet* and *The Rock*, the recently performed pageant-play for which T.S. Eliot wrote the choruses.[235] Dorothy manages tea with Whitney, perhaps to tell him how happy she is with his fiancée and their plans to marry in the summer, and they see a film together before she catches the midnight train home. It is Michael who concerns her, and she goes to Cambridge to see him, perhaps staving off his problems until they have time together after his term ends on 15th March.

Unfortunately for Michael, Dorothy's March is frantic. All her usual meetings and she is out and about more than usual to Paignton, Plymouth and Exeter, stung by the criticisms that the denizens of Dartington were more familiar with the streets of New York than of Devon towns. She finds a local hairdresser and a dentist, though still keeps her appointment with Mr Gilliatt in London, after a visit to the birth control clinic.

Michael emerges from his second term at Trinity College, they manage some theatre dates in London and he makes a brief visit to Dartington. With much attendant publicity he and Whitney are moving into a house belonging to P.G. Wodehouse, who has moved to Le Touquet, in Norfolk Street at the Marble Arch end of Park Lane, where they have a pet monkey.[236] The gossip columns make much of the monkey. Whitney, whom she meets often for tea or dinner in London as she is trying to persuade him to give up motor racing, is well able to cope with the celebrity lifestyle, but Michael is vulnerable. He seems younger than even his eighteen and a half years, and so like Willard, tall, fair with his candid oval face and *faux* insouciance; a young man who never knew his father, always in Whitney's shadow, and now the older half-brother quite understandably jealous of his mother's new children, let alone her new husband.

March closes with a rush of 'meetings all day', a housing committee, a performance of Chekhov's *The Seagull*, another visit from Gropius, Ruth's ninth birthday, and Whitney brings the racing driver Richard

'Dick' Seaman to dine. It transpires that Whitney wants to set up his company, the Straight Corporation, with Seaman as a director, and Fred Gwatkin of their London lawyers McKenna's as their legal adviser. He intends to acquire operational rights on a dozen or so of the new municipal airports and run first-class travel and flying training courses. Will Dorothy arrange for the money? She shelves that one for the moment as a string of people need her attention – Christopher Martin, Jane Fox-Strangways and Kurt and Aino Jooss – and on Tuesday 2nd April her oldest friend Gladys Szechenyi arrives in London and they meet for the first time in years. The next day, after having her hair fashionably waved, she meets Daphne's parents, the Earl and Countess of Winchilsea and Nottingham to be correct, and after a session with Gerald she meets Leonard at Southampton and their much-labelled trunks are delivered on board the *Majestic* and they sail for six days of peace.

Beatrice Straight, who will be twenty-one in the summer, had chosen to resume her life in America, and she waits on the dockside in New York. She has already telephoned excitedly (to Dartington's newly installed telephone) to say that she has found just the teacher for Dorothy's drama school. The following afternoon they are on the train to Philadelphia to see a performance by Michael 'Tchekov', Dorothy's spelling, and his company of Gogol's *The Government Inspector*. It is in Russian, but Dorothy is bewitched, and apparently without a second's thought she invited the company to Dartington, and was accepted. At Old Westbury she sees friends and Beatrix Farrand, then goes into the Sloan Hospital for two nights, for she still prefers New York hospitals. They spend Easter with Louise Croly at the St Simon's Island resort off the coast of Georgia, returning to the city for her doctor's check and lunch with Gertrude. Four days at the Park Avenue apartment are filled with serious business catching up with Miss Bogue and the Committee on Commitments, seeing her trusted American lawyer Milton Rose, and the men who guard her money, on Whitney's behalf. Lunch with Louis Froelick at *Asia* is pleasant for the magazine causes her few problems, and the stable-mate *Antiques* even makes a profit.

Lunch with Bruce Bliven, now editor at *The New Republic*, is less easy; Bliven is quiet, 'mousy', and admits he was 'frightened' when asked to take over from Herbert Croly, but now feels proud that 'almost all the ideas of the New Deal had been thrashed out in our pages'.[237] Dorothy's light touch is evident; they published W.H. Auden's cynical *Song* for 'a world that has had its day', Noel Brailsford wrote a piece from London on Armistice Day (1934) and Newton Arvin on Robert Herrick is a homage to one of her favourite poets. It becomes clear that in the midst of all the activities at Dartington she must read far into the night to keep up with *The New Republic*. President Roosevelt, just over two years into his rescue of 'the stricken nation', is 'such stuff as dreams are made on' to Dorothy for 'his grim and stern determination to oppose the evil and selfish forces' – the right-wing extremists that she so feared. His New Deal powers to provide employment, work schemes for conservation and social insurance, improved industrial relations, plus relief for home owners in 'negative equity' and 'agricultural adjustment' on farm prices and production, all these testified to an America that she had imagined. Did it cross her mind that if FDR had come into office earlier, for his struggle with polio had cost him eight years, she would never have left? Her enthusiasm for the president and all his works was not wasted on Editor Bliven, who went to Colorado to assess the effects of the Boulder Dam, part of the nation-transforming Tennessee Valley Authority scheme, on which he wrote a feisty article. He could also report that the New Deal 'gloss' had increased *The New Republic*'s weekly circulation to forty thousand, but twice that number was needed to break even.

After dinner with May and Herman Kinnicutt they left on the *Aquitania* on 27th April. Whitney and Daphne meet them at Southampton, eager to discuss business and wedding plans. It is King George and Queen Mary's Jubilee, London is en fête and expectant, Dartington is quiet and fine enough for lunch outdoors, and then its own Jubilee Fête on the Bank Holiday Monday. For Dorothy meetings come tumbling in, with Architect Lescaze and Christopher Martin – where are they going to put Chekhov and Company? – with

Headmaster Curry and Kurt Jooss, and then thankfully tea and quiet reading with Ena. Evenings at home are now blessed with music broadcasts on the BBC's Third Programme – this time Bach's *B Minor Mass* from the Queen's Hall in Langham Place. Rabindranath Tagore comes for a brief visit, which allows Leonard to show how the fruits of his experience in Bengal are ripening at Dartington. Hot on his heels another demi-god, Walter Gropius, arrives. This time Dorothy has invited him and Ise, with a cheque, as she has heard they are in difficulties. Her hope that Dartington would manufacture modern furniture on Bauhaus lines has come to little, partly because Gropius has been involved with a big scheme for Isokon's flats in Manchester, but this has failed for lack of finance. Bridget Edwards, the mother of Dorcas, comes to dinner, and after seeing Ruth's school play, the hairdresser in Paignton, Gropius yet again, Dorothy and Leonard are off to the Glyndebourne opera in Sussex for the opening season performance of *The Marriage of Figaro*.[238]

From Glyndebourne it was but a charmed journey to another stage-set, the renowned and beautiful Leeds Castle near Maidstone in Kent, set in a moat so large that it appeared as a lake. The castle was the home of Dorothy's niece and sometime bridesmaid Olive, her sister Polly's elder daughter, fairly recently married for the third time and now Lady Baillie. There were striking similarities, and differences: Olive was twelve years younger than Dorothy, she was thirty-six, tall and elegant, reserved and quiet, with her steady blue gaze and Whitney strength of will – 'the assumption that she would get her own way'. Unlike Dorothy she smoked cigarettes and wore glamorous gauzy dresses; they both hated publicity and valued their friends. Lady Baillie's castle was her passion. She had bought it in 1925, it had cost her six times the price of the Dartington Hall estate, and each year she spent as much on restoration and decoration as Dorothy dispensed through her American charities. Lady Baillie had two daughters from her first marriage, Susan and Pauline Winn, and she and Sir Adrian had an infant son, Gawaine. Sir Adrian was planning to enter politics as a Conservative. Leonard cannot have found their visit congenial, and it was perhaps forced upon Dorothy by her sense of duty to Whitney, who understandably wanted to gather up some relatives to come to his wedding. Whitney had found the Baillies for himself, for his name appears in the castle's visitors' book alongside his friends the Duke and Duchess of Kent, Anthony Eden, David Niven, Joan Kennedy and Errol Flynn.[239]

At Dartington June opens with the usually crowded days and familiar faces, but wedding fever is in the air. Dorothy flits to London for 'a fitting' and then, on Friday 14th, she takes wing for the first time on the Croydon Airways late morning flight to Paris, which allows her to reach her appointment at Worth at five o'clock. On her return she sees Whitney and Daphne, to be debriefed, and then has an appointment with Gerald, to calm her nerves? The long, even tenor of life in Devon resumes, the roll-call of all the usual names, to which Irene and Gilbert Champernowne are now added. Irene is a Jungian psychotherapist and they are both skilled in healing through art therapies; they bring a deeper meaning to the practice of the arts in the serene surroundings of Dartington. Dorothy's conscious understanding of living with music, painting, dance and drama as the texture of her days is heightened. She is both the spirit and the substance of the place, a presence more often seen in the audience or passing in her motor car by the majority of musicians, dancers and other students as her shyness prevents encounters. But she has all their interests at heart, she has to keep everyone's desires and problems in her mind, and be prepared for the next big event or trip across the Atlantic. Her diary is essential to her juggling act.

Maurice Browne comes for four days in mid-June to discuss the arrival of the Chekhov company, and his own future. Suddenly Dorothy realises that Beatrix Farrand, whose time is so precious, is already halfway across the Atlantic; she meets her at Plymouth on Tuesday 25th and Beatrix gets down to work immediately, watched with half an eye by Dorothy while she is having lunch or tea on her sunny terrace, the Loggia they call it, with an array of visitors. On a weekend in London she manages a Worth fitting, a session with

Gerald, lunch with Gladys and Lady Winchilsea, who are soon to be mothers-in-law, and she arrives home in time to entertain a party from Bedales who have been invited by Mr Curry. She has noted on 24th June, 'Michael's friends to dinner' – Leonard's sister Irene Rachel, whom Dorothy likes very much, is their house guest, so it is family for dinner plus the fiery Cambridge radicals John Cornford and Hugh Gordon.[240] Michael, who has to keep his head for long enough to be Whitney's best man, is excited about going to Russia in August with a group including Cornford, Gordon, the brothers Anthony and Wilfrid Blunt, and Michael Young.

Weddings come apace; first in July there is Irene Rachel's engagement party in Yorkshire, she is to marry George Barker who is huntsman of the Badsworth in the famous hunt country near Pontefract.[241] On 11th July Dorothy attends the St Paul's, Knightsbridge wedding of Gladys Szechenyi's daughter, also Gladys, to Daphne Finch-Hatton's brother Christopher. The next day Beatrice arrives from New York to be one of Daphne's attendants, and Dorothy has an appointment with her wedding hat at Schiaparelli's. A folk dance festival, the quarterly trustees' meetings (how does she sit still for long enough?) and a party at Redworth with the Jooss dancers fill the weekend before she catches the noon train on Monday for a final Worth fitting, and dinner at Whitney and Michael's house. On Tuesday there is a rehearsal at St Margaret's, Westminster – where seventeenth-century Whitneys were baptised and married – and later Leonard arrives with Miss Jefferies and Ruth and William, who are bridal attendants. Dorothy has a hair appointment early on Wednesday morning, 17th July, so that she appears freshly Marcel-waved – her Schiaparelli hat in hand – when she meets Cecil Beaton.

He is already a celebrity photographer, thirty-ish, elegant and excruciatingly thin. He darts around the room in Park Lane being brilliant, flipping tulle drapes and adjusting the light, before he rather casually clicks his camera. His portrait of the afternoon's bride, Daphne, as a porcelain beauty swathed in tulle, had appeared in *Vogue* in June, but Mrs Elmhirst's portraits, he had been told, were strictly private and not for publication. Dorothy withdraws behind her powder-blue gaze, she is out of practice at sitting for her portraits, and she suspects that Mr Beaton's camera will detect her edginess at the thought of her crowded afternoon to come. At least he is quick.

The mother of the bridegroom, serene Dorothy by Cecil Beaton

The afternoon's wedding is a starry affair and *The Times* carries fifteen column inches of report, more than half that the tightly printed roll-call of guests. Dorothy's relatives include her stepsister Addie Lambart, Almeric Paget now Lord Queenborough, and the Baillies, her friend Gladys Szechenyi and her two younger daughters and Pamela McKenna, with Christopher and Cecily Martin, who is a McKenna, from Dartington.[242] Whitney's friends include Ian Fleming, a mediocre stockbroker and man about town at this time, and his business partner Richard Seaman. To the majority of the guests Whitney's mysterious mother, of whom there was much gossip but whom none of them knew, was an object of gush and awe, almost an exhibit. She sailed through, Leonard standing stalwartly at her elbow looking a little like a figure from *Menswear Magazine*.

Dorothy and Leonard escape to the opera, and on the way home they visit Bedales at Steep in Hampshire, enthused by their recent visitors. There is a happy, active end-of-term disarray about the place, which is set in beautiful countryside. They do not envy the large brick main building in Tudor style, but Ernest Gimson's heavily timbered library cannot but impress – fine memorial libraries are becoming fashionable, but there will not be one at Dartington because book learning is less revered than activity and experience. After the end-of-term festivities they – plus Beatrice and Ruth and William – are off on the *Aquitania*, arriving in New York on 30th July. They go straight to Raquette Lake and Camp Deerlands in time for Beatrice's birthday on 2nd August with 'a wonderful supper' by the lake. The newly-weds Whitney and Daphne arrive for a short stay before going to take the more glamorous airs of Saratoga Springs, the racing resort that Whitney's grandfather had helped to create. The remainder of August is given over to tennis, swimming, canoeing, sailing and shopping; the most onerous duty was listening to a First Aid talk, and the most momentous was William 'catching a big fish'.

Dorothy, windblown, coming out of St. Margaret's with Lord Winchilsea;
Leonard walking behind with the (invisible) Lady Winchilsea

They return to the fray in New York on 2nd September, the absent
Michael's birthday the previous day still signifying the end of the
holiday. A week later they sail on the *Manhattan* and Dorothy's diary
has several days marked 'in bed', code for shutting herself in her own
cabin to be alone with her thoughts. Whitney's wedding, and the alien
crowd of English society to whom she has nothing to say, overlaid with
her summering dose of nostalgia in the midst of the mountains and
lakes of upstate New York, alongside the realisation that her home at
Old Westbury had little place in her life now, all this had emphasised
her rootlessness. Ever since Willard's death and the war her Atlantic
crossings had given her this space for her own thoughts, but these
Manhattan notebook entries dated 13th September reveal her to be 'at
sea' in many senses:

> The practice of religion, then, must be the conscious
> effort to find perfection, as we approximate it. One means
> of doing this might be found, I believe, in the attempt
> to clarify for ourselves the moments, the incidents, the
> individual qualities in people, which have penetrated,
> further than the rest, into the ideal world. Perhaps one
> form of meditation might be the concentration on
> someone we know, someone we love, to find the essential
> quality of that person which makes him divine and so
> greatly deserving to be loved.

These notes can be seen as holiday-work for her therapist, Gerald
Heard or Irene Champernowne, but they end in such a pitiable
longing for an anchorage. Is there such a person of 'essential quality'
as to 'make him divine'? Her elusive artistic genius is not Kurt Jooss,
who is too severe and too safely married, nor Walter Gropius, who
is too wavering in his attachment to Dartington, and to England.
Her notes begin to replay her analytical thinking from twenty-
eight years ago, when in that hotel in Venice she had put down her
reasons for choosing her husband, except that now it is something

of herself, her own innate creativity so long suppressed, that she is searching for:

> And, as with people so with beauty – to recall, and by recalling to dwell with it. And so, I believe, I must gather up for myself as I go the values, the experiences which belong to my real world and which will enable me, perhaps, in moments of fleeting insight to apprehend God... I can no longer call to Him out of the void, nor can I any longer pray... I must begin with something more immediate – with human beings, their lives, their thoughts, their creations – then conceivably I can recognize the divine there instead of continuously passing it by.[243]

She goes no further, and if she did have a notion of a creative beauty that was within her grasp, it was all swept away the moment the *Manhattan* spilled her onto the Southampton dockside, where Michael, just back from Russia, met them. The 'Socialism in action' that the Intourist guides had set before the loose-knit group of young travellers, the busy modern factories, collective farms and workers' housing, had made them feel that Tolstoy's society was in the making, even if only halfway through the first Five Year Plan. The contrasts between the Tsarist court that Dorothy had found intact in 1908 and Michael's impressions kept them talking for the short time they had together. Term started for Dartington's activities on 21st September, but Dorothy and Leonard soon headed north for Manchester for the Jooss Ballet's first night, then on to Leonard's parents for a short stay, which featured a trip down a coal mine at Barnsley. Their stay in Cambridge included seeing the new film *Sanders of the River*, starring Paul Robeson and Leslie Banks, a homage to goodness in people and deeds, in darkest Africa. While going about her motherly task of making Michael's rooms comfortable Dorothy noted in her diary that she met more of his friends, Maurice Dobb and Brian Simon. Dobb was the 'fair-haired, pink-cheeked' dandified doyen of the Cambridge left, a member of the Communist Party of Great Britain since it was founded in 1920, a delightful, charming, cultured man, enjoying the new-found enthusiasm for his cause. Brian Simon, like John Cornford and Hugh Gordon, was of the younger contingent of clever and passionate activists, extraordinarily gifted young men drawn to the opinions of distinguished members of the university, like Dobb, and J.D. Bernal, the crystallographer and X-ray pioneer of the Cavendish Laboratory. Bernal's expressed 'intellectual's' opinion was that the USSR was the only nation 'moving on' and providing 'the antithesis to the whole catalogue of cultural reaction represented by Fascism'.[244] Dorothy hoped Michael would remain level-headed and keep to Socialism, but she feared that he felt isolated, and homeless (rather as she did) and susceptible to hero-worship and the Communist ideal of comradeship, the force which drove his brilliant and fearless friend John Cornford.[245]

On Friday 11th October at 11 a.m. she noted that Michael Chekhov was to be given a tour of the estate.[246] He is 'Mr Chekhov', he seems older and less handsome than his photographs, but there is an elasticity in his step and he glides along in his loose-fitting suit, and when he is talking and something sparks his interest he becomes a magician. The moment is good, the trees are sheened in gold, especially the beech trees, and the tiltyard 'theatre', the legacy of Richard Odlin, has been freshly mown. The beauty of the place is irresistible and Chekhov is delighted that he will come to teach there. Dorothy is walking on clouds.

But Walter Gropius was still putting the finishing touches to his transformation of Barn Theatre when, late in 1935, he was 'poached' as Isokon's Controller of Design for their new furniture making enterprise. Dorothy may have allowed herself a scowl, but it would have had to be in private, for both Jack Pritchard of Isokon and Gropius's partner Maxwell Fry were involved in the policy discussion group soon known as Political and Economic Planning being nursed into life under Leonard's and Dartington's wings. When, a few months later, Pritchard appealed for help in paying for Cambridgeshire's Impington Village

College, construction costs having doubled the estimated £20,000 as Gropius had not used standard components, it was Dorothy who answered the appeal. She paid some, if not all, of the architects' fees of over £1,000.[247]

December begins with a weekend trip to Yorkshire for Irene Rachel's and George Barker's wedding. Christmas shopping in London and seeing Whitney and Daphne are mixed with the usual parties and carols at Dartington, ending with 'our party' for Christmas Day at home, but without Whitney and Daphne. On 28th December, true to pattern, they all pack up and go off to Portwrinkle to the Chalet, for long walks and games on the beach. Dorothy's holiday reading is Dr Ian Dishart Suttie's *Origins of Love and Hate* just published and probably given to her by Gerald Heard, who had been to Cambridge to see Michael at her request. Dr Suttie dealt with the breakdown or loss of a closeness between mother and child, and the child's subsequent craving for companionship and to love and be loved from another source, not – as Freud insisted – necessarily sexual. Dorothy was blaming herself for Michael's yearnings for the comradeship of Communism at Cambridge, and it was also no accident that they had seen *Hamlet* together, the starting point for a discussion on a mother who married a second husband.[248] The year ended with 'a terrific storm', and after it had passed she and Leonard played golf, only this time it was not so 'soppy' and she managed three holes.

King George V died at Sandringham on 20th January 1936, and the next day the new King flew himself from Norfolk to London for his Accession, which seemed a good omen to his modern subjects. A few days later Whitney Straight applied for British citizenship, the notice appearing in *The Times* on 4th February, and prompting a family conference.[249] Whitney had made his choice and put his faith in Britain and his British company, and therefore it was Michael, as yet only twenty, who remained an American citizen and who would fall heir to the American family trusts and properties. Dorothy still had her American passport, though she had applied for British citizenship in April 1935. As this was one more estrangement between brothers who had depended upon each other Dorothy continued to be watchful of Michael, and it seemed her new policy was to keep him as close as she could, whenever possible. She was in Cambridge in early March when he was elected to the Apostles, after his nomination by David Champernowne. On 26th March she and Leonard sailed on the *Berengaria* for an unusually sociable crossing, for her, cocktails with the Captain and Buster Keaton films. It was a hard-working trip spent at Old Westbury where a great deal of her past was exorcised. She had left in such a hurry in 1925 (was it really eleven years ago?) that there were piles of boxes and trunks to be sorted through, to see what Whitney, Beatrice – now settled in America – and Michael might like to keep. Willard's carefully packed mementoes from China, porcelains and bronzes by the dozen, and boxes of her father's Georgian silver and dinner services, things she could not quite bring herself to part with were all destined for a holding station, the caverns of Manhattan Storage. Anna Bogue was kept busy with mammoth lists and labelling marathons. Leonard went to Ottawa, leaving Dorothy to see her old friends, and go to Washington for tea at the White House with Eleanor Roosevelt.

Back at Dartington in May, on the 6th, Michael Chekhov comes to dinner and confirms that he will open his teaching studio in the autumn.[250] Dorothy is overwhelmed, but keeps her bubble of excitement to herself, nor does she write anything down, yet. She has been delving into his theatrical past, as well as her own, and can hardly allow herself to suspect, let alone believe, that a creative force that verges on the 'divine' is coming to Dartington. It is her most blessed (and least troublesome) child Beatrice who has guided her into this, Beatrice, now twenty-two and confidently pursuing her acting training in New York, who 'found' Chekhov and realised that his experimental methods would suit her mother's dreams. Chekhov's Moscow Arts Theatre background matched Stanislavsky's, and as with Lee Strasberg's Group projects in New York the actors were trained in feelings rather than techniques, in nourishing their 'emotional memory' and 'finding themselves in the character that the author had written'.

Beatrice elaborated in excited telephone calls as she learned more, that the Group was 'based on two propositions: that art should reflect life, and that through art it is possible to make life better. Theatre had to provide for society what society had failed to provide for itself'.[251] These actors had a role in the community, and as teachers. It seemed to Dorothy that in her latent, almost secret, love of the theatre she had found the extension of John Dewey's hopes for education – to a larger justification for life itself beyond the schoolroom.

Just in case her flight of fancy took her over she was brought to earth, and by Chekhov himself. She had been out in her garden placing new shrubs with her head gardener David Calthorpe, gardening came into the conversation and Chekhov gave it his blessing, saying that he liked to teach outdoors whenever the weather was suitable, urging his students to be at one with nature, to 'feel what it is like to be a tree' and to experience the tenderness of flowers. The very next day she noted in her diary, 'Digging in garden,' thus announcing the birth of Dorothy the gardener, rather than merely the garden owner who instructs her gardener. She will no longer pass by the beauty around her, at least people keep telling her that she lives in a beautiful place, and now she begins to recognise this. For the first time, unbelievably, she and Leonard take a weekend motor tour around Somerset and west Wiltshire, to the cathedral at Wells, to Bath and Bradford-upon-Avon, and they discover places that had been there all the time, unnoticed. Returning home, Dartington now appears in context, and she realises what Beatrix Farrand, the most contextual of designers, has been working towards with her insistence on traditional materials and native plants. Through the entrance arch their beautiful Courtyard oval is a reality, its focus on the Porch entrance to the, now restored, Great Hall, rather than on the discreet door to their house in the far right corner. The Courtyard lawn is surrounded by cobblestones, and through these the twin wheel-tracks of smooth stone run as necklets, allowing in the motors of their visitors and themselves.

At the last minute before the holidays her new mindfulness deposits a playwright at her door, and her diary notes the name of

Sean O'Casey. He and his wife Eileen are coming to live in Totnes and want their children to attend the school. O'Casey's three wonderful plays, including *The Plough and the Stars*, 'a dissenting patriot's history of the birth of the Irish Free State', surely set him in the footsteps of the Russian masters?[252] He had escaped from the tumult of Dublin theatricals to his preferred peace in Devon – could he be persuaded to write for Dartington's new drama company?

There is no summering in the Adirondacks this year.[253] The whole family, including Michael, climb aboard the sleeper for Fort William and two weeks of happy holiday, walking in the hills towards Loch Eilt, sailing in the Sound of Arisaig, dancing at a Highland wedding, shopping in Morar, picking blackberries and driving to Glenfinnan, all in rain and shine. After an interlude for the Jooss dance festival at Dartington the others went their own ways and Dorothy took Ruth and William, seemingly even without Miss Jefferies, to the Norfolk Broads, taking a boat from Wroxham, armed with flashlights, extra dishcloths, candlesticks and wellingtons. As in the Highlands she revelled in the earthiness – or wateriness – of it all, the morning mist on Hickling Broad, the joy of a hot bath, even of fetching milk in a can at Ranworth, of finding 'a most interesting church' and the 'lovely breeze' as they returned to their mooring. As Dorcas and Eloise had gone to spend a holiday with their respective families, this was a rare if not unique experience for Ruth and William to have their mother to themselves, and for Dorothy to take notice of her youngest children. Where was Leonard? He was committed to his fellow agricultural economists, fast becoming his habit as he gave some of his energies to his own particular interests. Though, as Dorothy had written, they had come together to England, and her life was no longer her personal story, their togetherness had really come down to a public display, and each had drifted into leading almost separate lives, often only in the same room in the evening after dinner when they listened to the BBC news bulletin or a radio concert. Dorothy's return to high society 'junkets' on Whitney's behalf had left Leonard rather bemused at his own role of dog-like devotion to 'a person with a strong sense of world-unity and mission' and yet 'driven and confused by [her] imaginative tensions'.[254] Now there was Mischa Chekhov. Leonard was not about to be embraced into the golden glow of her new-found appreciations, at least not yet.

TEN: MISCHA AND *THE POSSESSED*

Since the holiday in Scotland Michael had been at home and working at campaigning on behalf of the Independent Labour Party in Totnes, an occupation arranged for him by Leonard and Headmaster Curry at Dorothy's request. In early October she went to Cambridge to see him settled into what would be his fourth year and she was pleased to find he had friends outside college, with an Anglo-American academic family, the Cromptons, with three daughters. Michael was smitten with Belinda, the youngest.

Dartington's Chekhov Studio opened on 2nd October 1936, and Dorothy was soon absorbed in explaining to the trustees and the world in general what this was all about. As she had once before, just ten years earlier, typed out the prospectus for the school, now she did so for the Studio, beginning with Chekov's experience:

> As a young man of twenty he entered the Moscow Arts Theatre under the direction of Stanislavsky. It is here that he learned to prepare the parts that later made him famous in Russia, and from Stanislavsky he learned also the value and importance of a method. Chekhov's name became synonymous with the great roles he created [including Khlestakov in *The Government Inspector*, Malvolio in *Twelfth Night* and Hamlet].[255]

She noted that as director of the Second Moscow Arts Theatre Chekhov ran 'an organization of nearly two hundred people' for four years from 1923. 'His aim was to deepen and ennoble the work of the Theatre,' and he found the plays of Shakespeare most rewarding, enlarging the repertory to include *King Lear* and *The Taming of the Shrew*, alongside the Russian classics. 'Leaving Russia in 1928 he determined to study at closer range the European theatre – he worked in Germany with Max Reinhardt, and then in Paris and in Riga.'

Dorothy only wrote of her own feelings at the opening of the Studio in 1936 in her 1959 memoir. In 1936 she clearly felt that she had to justify the introduction of this avant-garde Actors Studio and present it as part of their steady progress. She started with her own love of the theatre as a means of 'refreshment and renewal', she recalled Maurice Browne and *Journey's End*, Richard Odlin and their attempts at open-air performances including Milton's *Comus*, Nellie Van and her productions of Ibsen, especially *A Doll's House*, and their newly refurbished Barn Theatre, and continued:

> For me [this] all leads up to the day when Mr Chekhov came to Dartington – one day [afternoon of Monday 12ᵗʰ October] I went over as a visitor to his class. Several people were sitting with me on the little balcony and I watched an exercise. Mr Chekhov was showing the different qualities of emotion in the way we approach someone. He walked across to Esme Hubbard in one tempo, and then in another, taking her hand and saying 'how are you?' It was a simple exercise, but what he gave to it was such a revelation to me that I knew I had met the man who was for me, the Master.[256]

Michael Chekhov in the garden at Dartington, *c*.1936

After that first visit it was Beatrice, on the phone, who urged her mother to join the group 'for an hour a day'. Dorothy continued, 'I did this with certain misgivings, but soon it was 2, 3, 4, 5, 6 hours a day and even more. I hardly dared ask myself where I was going. I only knew that the work opened up new vistas of life for me.' Her diary is the evidence as the sessions grow, first her morning sessions then the afternoons, and 'Mischa's' classes replace her usually multifarious activities. Soothing friends such as Arthur Waley with his 'mask-like face', who talked of the Chinese poets, and his devoted companion the dancer Beryl de Zoete were welcomed as regular guests.[257] Also Jim Ede, a curator at the Tate Gallery, who had been once before and thought Dartington 'an oasis of light, of activity + of friendship' and was overjoyed that Dorothy's taste matched his own, for the works of Kit Wood, David Jones and the sculptor Henri Gaudier-Brzeska, as well as Henry Moore and Ben Nicholson. Ede suggested that

Dartington should have a gallery, partly because Dorothy's collection was growing too large for the house, but for some reason this did not happen, possibly because this was Ede's last visit for twenty years as he was on the point of leaving to live and work abroad.

It was less easy to cope with 'several talks' with Headmaster Curry, who had left his wife Ena at High Cross House while he moved into the school to live with his new love who was a school housemother. His reasoning was that he wanted the children 'to see what a really happy marriage was all about'. Dorothy noted that she must call a meeting of housemothers. There was no question of losing Curry, he was too valuable a headmaster, but the liberal excesses of his regime – at least in the opinion of the Dartington Sales Department's staff – contributed to the racy reputation that undermined their marketing efforts, reduced to ridicule by stories of the school's pupils bathing naked in the Dart then leaping about as the Totnes trains went past.

Dorothy's 'Master' and his rarely seen wife were installed in an elfin-style thatched cottage at Yarner. Everyone was fascinated by his Russian mystique and the rule was that no one was to disturb him. In class he was wholly serious, but outside he was enchantingly child-like, enthusing over their tea-and-biscuit breaks and substantial lunches. Classes were held from 10.30 a.m. to 12.30 p.m., then lunch and a rest afterwards, before resuming at 3.30 p.m. until 5.30 p.m., and sometimes later. A peep through the door of the large studio revealed the Master in his loose-fitting suit conducting his class of sylph-like figures, both male and female, clothed from neck to ankle in a supple navy blue fabric, wearing slippers of the softest suede, and moving elegantly to the music played by Patrick Harvey on the piano. On the end wall of the studio huge letters exhorted 'GET THE RIGHT FEELINGS THROUGH THE RIGHT MEANS'. The exercises were for suppleness and consciousness of one's body, then the class would move into the exploration of their emotions through responses to mythical or Shakespearean characters and situations. This was necessarily an analytical process which brought tears and laughter to the surface, the end result being that the actor arrived on stage not only physically attuned, as Stanislavsky taught, but emotionally involved, and so able to project the feelings of their character to the audience.[258]

Dorothy's life narrowed to the essentials. She had for some time been noting events which marked the worsening situation in Europe, and she listened carefully to Edward VIII's Abdication Speech on 10th December. She would have found it hard to sympathise with one who put love before duty, and could not help wondering if the public's disdain for Mrs Simpson would rub off on other American women, especially in Devon. Into this esoteric existence a letter from Noel Brailsford – 'I want to tell you that I am joining the International Brigade in Spain' – came later in the month. 'I know your pacifist principles,' he continued, 'at one time of my life I came near to holding them as strongly as you do, but can one in this muddled world be sure of any theoretical guide to conduct?' He made his case fervently, that indolent Britain must wake up, that 'the Brigade, if we back it wholeheartedly, can save our souls as well as the soil of Spain', and that 'if the Republic goes down, the whole Spanish Left will be massacred'.[259]

He asked her for money for his recruits. She was in a terrible quandary, she loved the Spain she knew, and made herself reply immediately, on 21st December:

> I hardly know what to say to you... I can hardly bear the thought of your going to Spain. My heart is torn between the desire to restrain you and the urge to encourage nobility and greatness when one sees it in action of this kind. What can I do? I think I must ask you to take a gift as a kind of personal testimonial to yourself and to ask you to spend it in any way that you think best. I can't quite bring myself to contribute to a fighting brigade direct, but if you make the contribution for me perhaps that is a way to salve my conscience. It sounds terribly dishonest, doesn't it? But you will understand how torn and confused and miserable I feel about it all. The purity and integrity of your motive is about the finest thing I see. Bless you.[260]

Others among Brailsford's friends dissuaded him from fighting – he was rather old at sixty-three – and he was able to take his recruits and supplies to Spain, and return unharmed. No amount of pleading would have detained Michael's friend John Cornford, a determined hero who left behind his former girlfriend Ray Peters and their infant son, as well as his poetic muse Margot Heinemann, and who was killed in the fighting on the Cordoba front on 28th December, the day after his twenty-first birthday. Cambridge, the city of the Darwins, was deeply saddened at the death of Charles Darwin's promising great-grandson, and his poor parents, Professor F.M. Cornford and the poet Frances Cornford, who were close friends of Rupert Brooke and had named their son Rupert John, suffered an echoing tragedy. It was Michael who kept his head and managed the duties of a friend, sorting out Cornford's papers and belongings, and – with Dorothy's assistance – he found a refuge for Ray Peters and her son James with his friends, the Ramsdens, who worked for the Labour Party in Totnes.[261]

For Michael, Cornford's death brought on the crisis that had been hovering about his college life. Cornford, with his fierce Byronic looks and vehement Marxist outbursts, had been Michael's shield, their friendship carrying him into a well-connected company who would otherwise not have had much time for the tall, fair and frankly lightweight American, with his sports car and the epithet 'millionaire' dropped every time he entered the room.[262] With Cornford holding the stage Michael could be, as he admitted, a bystander in political arguments, which suited him. Poignant images of Willard arise like spectres, Willard who had no banking training, who had not been to West Point, and who found that the gremlins of Morgan's Bank and the American Expeditionary Force defeated him – and Cambridge and Trinity College in the 1930s were no less demanding. Michael was ill-equipped, he had been educated with dancers and actors at Dartington, followed by a year's cramming at the London School of Economics, rather than with his peers at Eton or Rugby; he felt exposed and isolated, that nobody liked him (shades of Willard's desperation) and most of all that his 'final examinations loomed like monsters' on his horizons, and he dreaded failure. These seem common enough as final year fears, except that Michael went further and told his mother that he felt like the student Razumov, in Joseph Conrad's 1911 novel *Under Western Eyes*, swept out of his depth in the current of history. The unworldly Razumov moves from St Petersburg to Geneva, finding himself a pawn in a revolutionary underworld in which he is forced to become 'a secret agent' against his will.

Michael's sense of the dramatic had concocted the 'secret agent' idea (perhaps he had been reading too much John Buchan in Scotland or even Erskine Childers?) and the situation, at least in January 1937, was really rather different. True, he had been approached by Anthony Blunt, at the prompting of Guy Burgess, to 'work for anti-Fascism' but this was seen as putting one's ideals into action, and supporting all those who went off to Spain. Burgess was especially admired 'as one who in the most real sense had sacrificed his personal life for what he believed in'.[263] If he was valued as an American, Michael protested, he had left that country when he was ten, and from what little he knew it seemed fanciful that in its increasing isolationism America was interested in events in old Spain. He also believed that Blunt told him not to worry about his finals for his degree did not matter, whereas Michael knew very well that in his mother's eyes it was of the greatest importance.

Dorothy's diary notes that Blunt, with Michael Eden and Guy Burgess, visited Dartington in the Easter holidays, though it is not clear if she invited them, or if it was their own idea. Anthony Blunt was rather desperately searching for a job and knowing Dorothy's interest in art perhaps hoped that she might do as Victor Rothschild's mother had done for Guy Burgess, and pay him a retainer as an adviser.[264] Or perhaps they just wanted to see if Michael's tales of the important people his mother knew were true? Guy Burgess was remembered as amiably playing cricket on the lawn, though less appreciated when, after too much to drink, he ogled the Jooss male dancers. Dorothy and Blunt walked in the garden talking about paintings; did he tell her of his opinion of her young favourites of the Seven and Five Society, that he

Louise Croly and Dorothy at sea, Naushon 1937

had called them 'a bedful of dreamers' – or did he steer her towards his rather grudging opinion of Picasso as making 'almost the only form of serious art that could be produced in the given circumstances'? Did he happily take her commission for buying her Picasso?[265] She asked Blunt to keep an eye on Michael for his last term, and they agreed to keep in touch as she put his Cambridge and London phone numbers into her diary.

At the end of the holiday when Michael said he could not go back, Dorothy reached her own crisis point: did he not realise that she had given up her country, and lost Whitney to Britain, and that now she looked to him to succeed where Willard had failed? Did he not realise that talking to so-called Marxists was child's play and mattered little, when his Cambridge Honours would fit him for carrying on her work with her liberal connections in America, and directing her newly founded William Collins Whitney Foundation?[266] She actually lashed out at Michael, using Harry's failure: 'My brother Harry was a brilliant student at Yale... But he ran away. He ran away from every hard challenge: he couldn't face the possibility that he might fail. He squandered his great gifts, and that is something you cannot do!'

It was Michael's turn to be shocked at his mother's rarely seen passion, and he returned to Cambridge to work hard. Undoubtedly Dorothy wrote to Maurice Dobb – who held up the example of Kim Philby as a brilliant student to Michael – and to Maynard Keynes.

William, Leonard and Ruth Elmshirst, Naushon 1937

If it was a battle for Michael's ideological soul then it was Round One to his mother; Michael duly gained his First Class Honours and left, announcing that he would be working in America. Dorothy had already written to Eleanor Roosevelt on his behalf.[267]

They all left for America, and that August of 1937 Leonard and Dorothy (though perhaps not Michael) with Ruth, William, Miss Jefferies and Louise Croly were guests on the Forbes family's Naushon island, off Cape Cod. It was a particularly idyllic summering, captured by Leonard with his new camera, his snapshots carefully arranged into a small album. He labelled this unique album *Naushon 1937* – did he fear it was to be the last of such summerings, the last of those magical happenings of which the first two had changed his life?

Dorothy was contemplating her second year of Mischa's classes. She thought that Leonard was jealous and fended him off by thanking him for his patience 'during this strange new experience of concentrating all my energies on one thing, one idea'. She added, 'I see, with a kind of overwhelming gratitude, that perhaps only you would have been capable of supporting and helping me in this way – asking nothing in return, and only eager to see new vistas of life opening for me.' Michael Young suggests that her fondness for Mischa, whom she loved, had flowed over to Leonard, that she had conjoined them.[268]

Chekhov had decided upon Dostoevsky's *The Possessed* in its 1916 translation by Constance Garnett for his first production, which, in

175

Dorothy's words, 'In the winter of 1940 his students will take out to the cities and towns of the old country and to distant regions of the new [world].' If things went according to plan, at the age of fifty-two, Dorothy would open on a Broadway stage in the substantial role of Varvara Stavrogin, a woman of 'possessions' of many kinds who shares a deep, platonic love with Stepan Verkhovensky, played by Chekhov. From her growing experience she continues to explain the training:

> A method is unfolded, so precise that no vagueness is possible; so profound that only by continuous and gruelling effort can the student become aware and sensitive in his body and aflame in his imagination. Never is praise or blame given, but instead doors are opened, one by one, through which the creative power of the student may emerge. Watching [Chekhov] teaching one becomes aware of a new art of communication. Every word that he utters is spoken with his whole person; every movement he makes is rhythmical; no part of his being is inactive. In fact, through him activity seems to achieve a new dimension of intensity.[269]

Not everyone was convinced, Sean O'Casey for one. He felt that the theatre 'must find itself again in literature', and his wife Eileen wrote that 'while appreciating that Michael Chekhov was a clever man, he could not endure a set-up in which the actors wore long blue robes and went round capering and bowing to each other'. She felt that Dorothy 'was ignoring something splendidly worthwhile upon her own doorstep'.[270]

Or perhaps it was that O'Casey did not need rescuing? Rescuing émigrés was a dubious activity at this time with public fears that they would turn into collaborators when the invasion came. Dorothy was undeterred and to the Jooss dancers and Chekhov company she now added, in the first week of February 1938, the choreographer and 'dance artist' Rudolph Laban. Laban was almost sixty, his career had culminated in the spectacular dance presentations by schoolchildren and amateurs in the Eckert Open Air theatre that launched the cultural activities surrounding the Berlin Olympics (he had steadfastly refused to choreograph the Opening Ceremony in the Olympic Stadium). Alerted by Kurt Jooss, Dorothy had sponsored his escape; she was not too absorbed to appreciate this additional soulful genius, but the dancer Lisa Ullman took him under her wing, looked after him 'and probably saved his life'.[271]

Dorothy was too absorbed in her classes, though, to go to America and support Michael in his interview with the First Lady, but Leonard was going on agricultural economics business and rather nobly offered himself for the White House. He was horribly embarrassed, he had cold feet, and felt 'just a four flusher, putting one over, barging in on the White House [as] just an exercise for my sudden self-conceit'.[272] Michael was given an unpaid position writing reports, and Dorothy wrote her thanks to Eleanor Roosevelt on 23rd February 1938.[273] She did not hear, and neither did Eleanor Roosevelt, of Michael's cloak-and-dagger last meeting with Anthony Blunt in a pub on the Great West Road, when Blunt had torn a small drawing in half, giving half to Michael saying that the other half would be produced by his contact in Washington. Michael said that he 'lost' his half.[274]

For the early weeks of 1938 Dorothy was rehearsing the Dostoevsky; 'Mischa kept telling me to be more commanding'; later, 'my voice was like a weak mouse'. But on 30th March she was on her own on the Cunard liner *Queen Mary* enduring an uncomfortable crossing, immediately met by Michael and Belinda 'Bin' Crompton, and soon seeing her own daughter 'Biddy' and also Beatrix Farrand. Unusually she kept her place card for dinner on Easter Sunday, 6th April, at the White House, with Michael. A fellow guest was the Secretary for Agriculture, Henry Wallace, who had been to Dartington for one of Leonard's conferences on agricultural economics, had written for *The New Republic* and was now the rising hope of the Democrats. This was presumably Michael's first meeting with Wallace, who became one of his heroes, and who was shortly to be appointed as Roosevelt's running mate for the 1940 election. Dorothy, and the absent Leonard, won presidential approval for their work at Dartington, and Dorothy's friendship with the First Lady was cemented in her willingness to support Mrs Roosevelt's good causes. It seems unlikely that harsher subjects were discussed – America's isolation or Chamberlain's appeasement and that the president's newly appointed ambassador in London, Joseph P. Kennedy, had reported that the British view 'was that it was certainly not worth going to war over such matters as the *Anschluss*, the Sudetenland, or the persecution of the Jews'.[275] Dorothy had added the *Anschluss*, the 'union' declared by Hitler's troops marching into Austria, as one of her 'fearful' notes in her diary. Coming home on the German liner *Bremen*, holder of the Blue Riband and interesting for her catapult-launched aeroplane which speeded mail delivery, she wrote that the Atlantic was like a millpond.

She is soon at rehearsals: 13th June, 'found difficulty with "Now I know you love me" – Mischa asked me to say it to him, quite simply and directly, and then it seemed to come more easily'. Gerald Heard had left for America and was settling in California so his letters now come to replace their conversations, but they overflow, like his talk, with classical allusions and biblical allegories and end in conveying little, except his real affection for her. There is a slim chance that he will lure her back to another God than Mischa Chekhov in time to come. Whitney and Daphne bring their daughter Camilla, Dorothy's first grandchild; also Vita Sackville-West comes to lunch with her sister-in-law Gwen St Aubyn, and they walk around the garden. Otherwise it is classes, rehearsals and unavoidable duties until term ends, and Dorothy finds herself crossing the Atlantic for the second time this year, on the *Britannic* with Ruth, William, Dorcas and Eloise, but no Leonard, for summering at Woods Hole. Still on the *Britannic* Eloise goes down with mumps and as Dorothy stays with her in the ship's hospital (which Eloise never forgets) when they reach their cottage she has it too, then so do William and Dorcas. The children are up and down but Dorothy is unwell for the rest of August, spending time writing in green ink in her green diamond patterned notebook:

'Mischa says "find the creative idea in everything". This morning I think I discovered the creative idea of a sailboat – working with natural force, accepting, using and welcoming the wind, and at the same time preventing chaos by the use of [wo]man's intelligence and conscious control.' And again:

> Coming up from the beach a moment ago I became aware of two general types of plants – those with flat tops outspread, and those with pointed steeple forms – for one we have, as it were, the democratic idea, the whole flower reflects and receives the sun equally in all its parts – the other has lifted itself to a peak with a kind of aristocratic distinction!

They are all well enough to move to Old Westbury for Michael's twenty-second birthday. He is still happy in the State Department, still rapturous over Belinda Crompton, and ready for marriage and more responsibility, and so he becomes president of the William Collins Whitney Foundation. Dorothy attends a *New Republic* conference in New York where she is plunged into politics. The paper had been basking in the successes of the New Deal and domesticity, 'isolationism' by more ordinary names, but now Bruce Bliven was smarting from a long-running argument with Walter Lippmann over the need to confront German aggression, Lippmann telling him, 'I see no way of putting any stop to [Fascist] aggrandizement except by convincing them that at some point they will meet overwhelmingly superior force.' Dorothy would have winced, though she had heard something of the sort from Vita Sackville-West, whose husband Harold Nicolson was in touch with Lippmann, who told him how 'we [Americans] watch with a kind of dread what looks to us like the failure of Great Britain to arouse herself to the danger she is in'. Bliven denied that he was under pressure to shift his paper's stance to warnings of Hitler's evil intentions, but this he did so as to wake up some opinions at least. Dorothy must have swallowed hard as she realised that her pacifism was no longer enough.[276]

She went on to Washington to help with Michael's house-hunting, then sailed for home on the SS *Paris*, 'a delightful ship'. Now she watched the headlines, and by the time she reached Plymouth Prime Minister Chamberlain was on shuttle diplomacy to Berchtesgaden and Bad Godesberg, bargaining over Czechoslovakia. She went immediately to the Chalet where Mischa was, as she wanted to tell him that America was relaxing the strict immigration laws against Jews from Europe, but there would be quotas, and they would have to plan carefully. Anti-refugee feeling was rising in New York and she feared it would soon increase in England. She listened to Chamberlain's broadcast, read the reports of the fiery debate in Parliament, and waited for the news from Munich, 'Hitler promised peace if all he took was the Sudetenland'.

Dorothy had never expected that the Atlantic would loom so large. She realised that Beatrix Farrand would not come to Dartington again, the death of her aunt Edith Wharton in France in August 1937 had severed Beatrix's links with Europe. 'The very last of my family,' she mourned, as she wrote to Dorothy of her 'added glow of affection' for them and for Dartington. She had given them so much, and besides the lovely Courtyard, the spring walks through flowering shrubs and Dorothy's Sunny Border, she had left design and planting ideas for so many more garden schemes.[277] She had been to Hillier's Nursery in Hampshire and personally chosen the cedars now growing on the lawn, soon to become the grandest images of Dartington. She had bequeathed to Dorothy the role of guiding spirit to their garden, which proved an unexpected kind of satisfaction that was to give her strength to endure the bitter years to come.

She was not deluded by the public hysteria over Chamberlain's return from Munich, and even before the November terrors of *Kristallnacht* Dorothy had decided what to do, as she explained:

Then when the Crisis came and the supply of students fell away and the Trustees decided there would be a better chance for Mr Chekhov in America, I realised then that

I could never entirely dissociate myself from the group and that if Beatrice and Mr Chekhov needed me in the immediate future I should stand ready to serve them, provided no other interests were sacrificed.

The class that had worked so hard gave a farewell performance in the Barn Theatre in December, which included a scene from Ibsen's *Peer Gynt* in which Dorothy played the peasant widow Aase. Michael Young remembered how everyone was agog to see this – how 'she was intensely concentrated on her part and full of feeling which was, however, more fully directed inwards than outwards. The wonder, to the audience, was that the shy Dorothy they knew (or rather did not know because she was so shy) could get up there with a white wig, a radiant face, a hank of wool – and perform at all'.[278]

Beatrice Straight had found a large house in Ridgefield, Connecticut, where Chekhov planned to resume his classes in January 1939. He insisted that he needed Dorothy for her part in *The Possessed* which he wanted to stage the following autumn. Dorothy's justification was: 'Leonard has not only acquiesced, but urged me to go. There is one other reason for going – if I can be of any use to Mr Oppenheim's students in the future, as a teacher of Miss Crowther's method, my own knowledge and personal experience will be greatly enlarged by another six months with Mr Chekhov.'[279]

Leonard had set sail for India in mid-December so that Dorothy had Christmas at home with Whitney, Daphne and Camilla, and then went to the Chalet. From there on 3rd January she wrote a long letter to Anna Bogue, thanking her for her carefully chosen Christmas gifts for all the family, indulging in her appreciation of the moment, and her own present:

The writing case is, altogether, a work of genius. It is by my side at this very moment, and I carry it up and downstairs, and in and out of the house – in fact it is rather like Mary's lamb! It is so complete that it carries all my essentials for work, and what is more, it is so convenient and handy to use that I can't resist having it beside me at all hours of the day. I have placed the little memorandum cards where they belong, and my fountain pen and stamps are fitted in too – and it is all become both a toy and a tool for my constant use and enjoyment.

After the presents, the people: George Bennett is in good spirits and has plenty to keep him busy, but he is worrying about Willard's drawings and sketches which have been returned from various galleries – will Miss Bogue have them put into portfolios and added to Willard's things at Old Westbury? Finally, 'I can sit back now and tell you how much I've enjoyed your many letters and reports – and the long summaries of our many "personal dependents". You are the real benefactor and guardian of many, many people, dear Miss Bogue, and your advice and help is given with the right discrimination.'[280]

On 14th March 1939 she noted 'Czechoslovakia ceases to exist' and the following day Hitler entered Prague. On 30th March she sailed on the 'delightful' SS *Paris* again, in her cabin of grey rosewood, and was met by Michael and Beatrice on her arrival on 6th April. She is keen on helping a campaign to show British films to garner support in America and attends a White House reception for this before going to Ridgefield. Their William Collins Whitney Foundation has granted the Chekhov Studio $4,000 and things seem to be going well. On 21st April rehearsals resume and detain her until the end of June, with just a break for another trip to Washington on 6th June for a family gathering at the Natural History Museum where the Whitney Memorial Wing, endowed in Harry's name, has an added collection of birds. Surprisingly Gertrude has acquired these from the very Victor Rothschild who was so much a part of Anthony Blunt's circle at Cambridge, who is now Lord Rothschild and has inherited his grandmother's Tring Park with all its natural history collections.[281] Back at Ridgefield *The Possessed* rehearsals have gone through the fishing scene, the drawing-room scene, the nightmare scene – 'My epic!' – and on 10th July reach the 'Painful Parting', scene or reality? She leaves anyway the next day, her passage booked on the Holland America Line's *Statendam* .

Mischa Chekhov has given her a copy of Rudolf Steiner's *Knowledge of the Higher Worlds*, and her reading results in a lesson for herself, dated 13th July, in her *Statendam* notebook:

> Let go: sit lightly – live fully in the moment neither in the past (with regret) nor in the future (with fear) but fill the present with intense awareness – then past and future fuse with the present, and the concentration of intense awareness brings all together into the Eternal moment – into Timelessness.[282]

Arriving on 20th July in Plymouth the evidence of 'mobilisation' takes her by surprise, the First Aid centres, the sandbags and air raid shelters, the taped-up windows and posters shouting about the blackout. After a week at home she has gathered up the four children and Miss Jefferies and they are all back on the *Queen Mary* and landed back in New York on 7th August. They will have their holiday on Raquette Lake as planned, Leonard joins them in mid-August, and they tell Ruth, William, Dorcas and Eloise that they are to stay in America, mostly at Old Westbury and go to schools in New York, living with Miss Jefferies with Michael and Beatrice at hand. Dorothy's diary counts the days, Hitler's demands, the French Prime Minister Daladier's promise to Poland, then Hitler's march into Poland on Michael's twenty-third birthday, 1st September, the British ultimatum on the Sunday, which expires, so that 'England Declares War'.

Michael and Belinda Crompton are safely and joyfully married at Nantucket, and Gertrude Whitney is at the wedding and suggests that Sonny Whitney's new Pan American Dixie Clipper seaplane service might be their safest way home. Dorothy and Leonard take to the air, landing at Gander in Newfoundland before the long sea crossing to Foynes in the Shannon estuary, where they arrive on 18th September.

William, Dorcas Edwards and Eloise Elmhirst at the Dartington
summer house just before they left for America

With lunch at Adair – this is still travelling in leisurely style – they catch a train at Limerick for Dublin, the ferry and home.

At Dartington in that autumn of the 'phoney war' she had to do some explaining. When she had spoken after the Munich Crisis of being 'ready to serve' Mr Chekhov some had thought she was saying farewell. When she left at the end of March and had not returned after her usual month-long trip, others thought they had seen the last of her. Apart from her fleeting visit to pick up Nanny Jefferies and the children in late July, she had been missing for almost six months. When Leonard left in the holiday month of August they speculated that he had gone to bring her home, 'like Orpheus bringing his Eurydice back'. Two brief additional entries in her *Statendam* notebook are clues to her struggle within herself: on 13th August before Leonard arrived she noted, 'One unhappy day at Ridgefield due to egotistical sense of separateness.' Could she just not quite give herself to her part? A fortnight earlier she, Beatrice and Michael had spent an evening with Gertrude, who had made a note of their 'lovely voices' all speaking of their artistic interests. In this family bonding, or re-bonding, of like minds did Dorothy shed her 'Russian-ness'? Her notebook also confesses that she had 'learned the beginnings of conquering fears – the fear of acting, the fear of flying, the fear of people' and she had learned how to say 'No'.[283]

She had come home that September to a Dartington where the peacetime brilliance still glowed, where the Courtyard resembled an Elizabethan playhouse or Renaissance piazza teeming with beautiful people of many nationalities. The grey stones of the buildings were the backdrop for the colourful dress, and undress, of the dancers, singers and actors, upwards of one hundred souls chattering and laughing. According to Michael Young, 'Leonard swore that there were more beautiful women per square yard at Dartington than anywhere else in the world.'[284] Occasionally, after Thomas had served dinner, Leonard would look across to Dorothy and ask, 'Shall we go down?', to which she might reply, 'Mmm... mmn... n... yes, in a minute.' The party in the Courtyard felt that half an hour with 'the duke and duchess' was a restraint, and they were glad when it was over. How little they knew. Although Leonard took it all in good part, the 'duchess' was most relieved as she climbed her stairs, for she had been shaking in her shoes.

And what of their marriage? What if Dorothy had not come back? Would Dartington have crumbled and been sold and forgotten? Would Leonard have returned to India and become one of Tagore's heirs?[285] He had worked hard for his part of their bargain, he had become a familiar figure in the South Hams and further afield, elected as a Devon County Councillor where he enjoyed peppering their conservative conversations with his enlightened viewpoints. He had become used to his cars, his Savile Row suits and shoes from Mr Lobb and he dressed his part fastidiously – people called him 'dapper'. He knew that he would take nothing away from Dartington, other than his own earnings, but – and was it really only fifteen years ago – he had been astute enough to pin his future not only on Dorothy's money, but on her unshakeable loyalty that would not fail once her promise was given. If any one moment marked the change in their relationship it was when they climbed aboard that

Dixie Clipper seaplane, she was not completely sure she had conquered her fear of flying, and she would have needed to lean on his arm. She now refers to herself as 'Mrs Leonard Elmhirst' rather than 'Mrs Dorothy Elmhirst' as before, a small point but significant.

In New York Michael Chekhov's production of *The Possessed*, with Beatrice Straight as the beauty Lizaveta Nikolaevna, and Nellie Van in the role of Varvara Stavrogin, opened on Broadway in the October. For Beatrice it was the real beginning of her stage career and her road to Hollywood, even though the play did not have a successful run.

In England the mood darkened – the Jooss ballet performers left for New York although Kurt Jooss remained to look after his students. Lisa Ullman spirited the frail Rudolf Laban away into the Welsh countryside. Internment as aliens threatened many – Hein Heckroth, Hans Oppenheim and the sculptor Willi Soukop among them, seeming a cruel betrayal by the country that had given them refuge – and Chris Martin and Dorothy spent long hours writing letters and pleading with the authorities in the interests of these people they knew so well. For many of them there were miserable conditions to be endured in the camps at Paignton and farther away, until the regulations were thankfully relaxed.

This was merely Dorothy's opening campaign as she prepared for whatever the war would ask of her; make no mistake, the war had saved Dartington because she knew, as she had told Willard twenty-one years before, 'We women have to play our part.' She listened to the King's Christmas Broadcast, and she was so deeply moved – along with many others – that she copied his words into her Commonplace Book:

> And I said to the man who stood at the Gate of the Year:
> 'Give me a light that I may tread safely into the unknown.'
> And he replied:
> 'Go out into the darkness and put your hand into the Hand of God
> That shall be to you better than light, and safer than a known way.'[286]

ELEVEN: THE CHILDREN OF LIGHT

Three names spring from the front of her 1940 diary, the people uppermost in her thoughts: first Whitney, then Jane Fox-Strangways and Christopher Martin. Whitney always came first and, with Beatrice and Michael now settled into their American lives, he was nearest. Whitney had a string of addresses and phone numbers as he was in the RAF Volunteer Reserve and forever on the move, for the moment based at Biggin Hill in Kent and flying with the 601 (County of London) Squadron of well-heeled and already-qualified pilots. His business interests in airfields at Ipswich and Clacton, in Devon and at Weston-super-Mare (operating a shuttle flight to Cardiff for 9s. 6d. return) had all been subsumed into the war effort.[287] She met him as often as possible in London, taking him and Daphne for dinner at Boulestin's or Prunier's, or for tea and buns at J. Lyons and then a film at which they could laugh together. In the April Whitney disappeared on a secret mission to Norway to locate a landing field for the RAF, and was invalided home after a German attack. He was awarded the Military Cross and appointed an aide to Prince George, the Duke of Kent.

Jane Fox-Strangways was three years older than Dorothy and they had been friends for more than a dozen years since Jane had come to Dartington as a vibrant and talented potter. Dorothy admired Jane's artistry, which had not faded, though her health had given way and she was no longer able to work. In theory Jane shared a house in Totnes with her younger sister Elinor, but in practice she spent more and more time at Dartington as Dorothy's 'artistic pensioner' spending her time drawing and writing poetry as she felt able.

If Jane was her light cross to bear then the Martins, Christopher and Cicely, were most nearly her kind of people at Dartington and she held them in great affection, perhaps guiltily and in gratitude for their keeping the Arts Department going in her absences. Now she had frequent meetings with Chris Martin to discuss how they would start afresh with a new arts programme. Dartington had always gathered artistes, teachers and students into its fold, now it was to be 'outreach', a new word for the initiative into public patronage, via the county education authority's committee for Music and Drama, and the government's CEMA – the Council for the Encouragement of Music and the Arts – of which John Maynard Keynes was the first chairman. Dorothy had drawn back from Keynes's overtures for her money and her presence on his committee, feeling that her place was to support Chris Martin in his pioneering of the role of 'Arts Administrator' in their quiet corner of Devon.

On the domestic home front she was determined to economise, which in general meant freeing Dartingtonians on her staff for war work or service, and in the particular her decision to close her house kitchen consigning the silver-service breakfasts to history. Everyone was to eat in the White Hart dining room together. A stray sheet gives the workings of her budget for February 1940 – the largest sum still for household wages, £67, the next largest £25 for meals in the White Hart, and with fuel and other small bills the total was £156. 19s. 0d.[288] Also on her desk, and not unconnected, was a volume of Alfred Tennyson's later works, open at his long mystical poem *The Ancient Sage*, from which she copied some lines:

For more than once when I
Sat all alone, revolving in myself
The word that is the symbol of myself,
The mortal limit of the Self was loosed,
And passed into the Nameless, as a cloud Melts into
heaven.[289]

She needed her dialogue with the *Sage*, for to resign herself into walking into the crowded White Hart each day for her lunch, conscious of the whisperings about her dress or shoes or something she said, was no mean feat for her, far harder than the economising. She accomplished it with grace so that both residents and visitors expressed surprise that she queued for her lunch and chatted to her neighbours. The artist John Piper was one guest who was definitely not amused at having to queue for his lunch, but no exceptions were made, not even for Cabinet ministers nor, as the war went on, American colonels.

Nor indeed for the captains of industry and commerce who were Leonard's colleagues in Political and Economic Planning (PEP), the research group given birth at Dartington nine years before, in April 1931, and now preparing to tackle the unpopular causes of war aims, peace terms and post-war reconstruction.[290] Leonard had taken over the chairmanship of PEP from Israel Sieff of Marks & Spencer Limited, and they worked closely together, planning a trip to America in the spring. In his *Memoirs* it is Sieff, later 1st Baron Sieff of Brimpton, who dubbed Dorothy and Leonard 'the Children of Light' for their war work and their patronage of PEP; he admired Leonard, identifying him as 'one of the makers of the way of life, a leader because he really loves the led', and counting him among his three finest friends outside of his family, the other two being Max Nicholson and Aneurin Bevan.[291] PEP was an overwhelmingly male organisation of businessmen, professionals and academics, which we would now call a 'think tank'. The conservationist Max Nicholson, its ideological father, took several pages to explain 'what kind of body it was', and for present purposes it might be called *a club of extraordinarily clever men who applied their experience to planned solutions for the problems in national life, within the framework of a free-enterprise society.*[292] Conventionally Dorothy was regarded as their 'constant support'; she and Leonard gave them money, and she presided at lunches and teas in London, and weekend gatherings at Dartington for their deliberations, though it is unlikely that if asked most of the clever men, even Israel Sieff, would have acknowledged her as anything more than a figurehead, with money.

However, one of those who happily queued for his lunch knew rather differently, for the first General Secretary of PEP and long-serving council member was Kenneth Lindsay, who as a young war veteran had sat at her feet at 1130 Fifth Avenue discussion groups in the early 1920s and fallen more than a little in love with her. The young man she had called 'a bit of a genius' acknowledged her social work as part of his inspiration to be a founder of PEP, and a glance at the subjects of their early publications – on conditions of employment, consumer affairs and co-operatives, social services, 'the economics of having children' and Roosevelt's New Deal – suggest that he still had her inspiration in mind.[293] Now, in 1940, Lindsay was Independent National Labour MP for a Kilmarnock constituency, which could hardly be farther from Dartington, he held various political appointments and had not married. They must have met frequently during PEP's existence, and on the late April weekend when PEP gathered at Dartington Lindsay stayed on for an extra day, according to Dorothy's diary.

Soon after that meeting Leonard and Israel Sieff left on their trip to America. Dorothy's May diary takes on liquorice allsort tones of pointillist pleasures mixed with black perils: tea at J. Lyons in Coventry Street with Jane, then the new film of the Broadway success *Ladies in Retirement*, a domestic thriller starring Ida Lupino and Louis Hayward; a performance of *King Lear* [7th–9th May the government crisis, Hitler crushes Holland and Belgium, Winston Churchill becomes Prime Minister]; at Dartington on the 11th she has a visit from Max Nicholson and Tom Hopkinson of *Picture Post* and on Sunday 12th her garden is open to visitors. Bandaging instruction classes are held [21st May Germans reach the coast, the evacuation from Dunkirk was under way, 23rd Germans take Boulogne]; Basil Liddell Hart, their Devon neighbour and friend, prophesies 'the Germans would land at Start Point, wheel right and take Exeter', which would mean marching through Totnes. Liddell Hart is an invigorating guest, he is a brilliant military historian and his strategic expertise gives him what seems like foresight, but he also has the ear of Fleet Street's finest as he is a columnist for the *Daily Mail*.[294]

[Italy declares war on 10th June]; at Dartington evacuee workers arrive, the children from Blackfriars and Southwark are already here, being occupied with ballet classes and walks beside the Dart, some are delighted, others run riot; [14th June, Paris falls, Dorothy if given to such phrases might say her heart is breaking for Paris and all it has meant to her, though in another life]. The sociologist Barbara Wootton comes to stay overnight, she is a Conscientious Objector and perhaps hopes to find agricultural work in the sympathetic air of Dartington; Noel Brailsford calls as he is researching a piece about Devon in wartime. [18th June, the first big raid on the East Coast]; Dorothy sees the film of Daphne du Maurier's *Rebecca*; Arthur Waley and Beryl de Zoete come to stay, Beryl says that the Vic-Wells Ballet need to escape from London to work on Frederick Ashton's new ballet, can they come to Dartington? On 2nd July and in gloomy mood Dorothy writes to Michael of our 'veneer of easy-going democracy' that has blinded us to the 'rottenness of the system which tolerates poverty and unemployment and exploitation':

> Soon, of course, the invasion will have begun... we shall
> presumably be cut off from you, from one another, from
> the world – but I can't believe we will be easily conquered.
> As I look at these antique terraces and trees and buildings
> I know, if they are spared, they will bring new life to birth,
> as they have done for the last five hundred years, and it
> matters little whether we are here or not.[295]

Later in July after false alarms, delays and silences Leonard arrives safely from America, full of plans for a return trip. Dorothy is busy with Dartington trustees' meetings, and a visit from Professor and Mrs Cornford who wish their grandson James to become a pupil at the school in the autumn; she warms to Frances Cornford and her poetry and hopes they can become friends. The absent Biddy's birthday on 2nd August, so often a day for celebration, is marked with a First Aid Demonstration. After an influx of Fabians and Local Defence Volunteers, she and Leonard snatch a day out, driving north to the lovely Exe valley route beside the sparkling river to Bampton, taking the by-road across the Brendon Hills then turning east to Bridgewater and on to Glastonbury. The comforts of this English landscape, and of Leonard's presence, are seeping into her heart. The next morning, Wednesday 21st August, Leonard is off to London, resuming his weekday work on war transport, hoping for weekends at Dartington; [22nd August, 'bombing', 24th the first raid on London].

Dorothy is shown around the textile mill at Shinners Bridge by Hiram Winterbotham, who is very tall with thick tortoiseshell-framed spectacles. He is making beautiful and colourful furnishing weaves and she realises that the mill is a Dartington enterprise she has hardly noticed; Hiram proves an interesting companion and their friendship flourishes. With Leonard she steals another day to look at the beautiful stones of Dodington, Dyrham, Bath and Ashton, just in case they don't survive. The Pilgrim Players arrive, very late, to present *Murder in the Cathedral* and *Tobias and the Angel* and eventually all turns out well, largely thanks to Chris Martin's young assistant Peter Cox, who keeps a cool head. The following week in London she has Tuesday lunch with Lady Colefax, attends the National Gallery concert and lunches with Arthur and Beryl on Wednesday, and on Friday when leaving she discovers the Crowther's treasure house, or yard, of garden ornaments in North End Road, Fulham, where the beautiful *Flora* awaits.[296] At Dartington she takes stock: 'We now have 150 soldiers quartered in the Dance School and the Chekhov Studio, and our own Junior School buildings are filled with evacuees.' Merely housing and feeding were not enough, at least for Dartington, and she could foresee 'a new kind of community life opening up, based on singing and dancing, painting, acting and all the activities we love so much'.

September opens with a lecture on manure. Either she has no news of Whitney or she would not write it down, but he is flying his Hurricane in what would soon be known as the Battle of Britain. For the first weekend they go to her parents-in-law, the Elmhirsts at Barnsley, and she steels herself to go out with the shooting party just because Leonard does and it is expected. The little ironies of the spatter of the guns followed by 'All Creatures of Our God and King' on Sunday morning are fading, when quite late on the fine evening, 8th September, they board their train for King's Cross:

> Half an hour before we were due the lights suddenly went out... and we slowed to a crawl – Air raid? Slowly the train crept along until finally one hour late we drew up in the station. Still no lights. The porters had small torches and with the help of these we collected our baggage and walked to the entrance. What a scene as we stepped out into the night. The sky a great sheet of crimson to the east – and a stillness like death in the streets – not a sound – no taxis – no buses – no human beings. Deserted city yet glowing with sinister crimson light – planes overhead buzzing like angry mosquitoes, thuds and crashes.

They took themselves to an air raid shelter where Dorothy concentrated hard on learning a Shakespeare sonnet by heart, 'it seemed the best thing to do'.[297]

The raid continued all night and eventually they reached Upper Brook Street. Next morning the PEP executive, including Israel Sieff, Max Nicholson and Kenneth Lindsay, arrived for their meeting, and afterwards Dorothy took 'a quiet walk with Kenneth'. The next day she has lunch with Whitney and the Duke of Kent, and the following day with the Sieffs. Back at Dartington she 'slept all day', then gardened; [16th–22nd September is 'the worst week for shipping losses'.] The end

193

of the month is lightened by Arthur and Beryl bringing Frederick Ashton and the Australian dancer Robert Helpmann for a long weekend. While they talk about the practicalities of the Vic-Wells Ballet coming to Dartington she is absorbed with her rockery; a letter has come from Mischa Chekhov who has heard from Beatrice about her gardening. 'If I dare say something,' he writes, 'it would be the following. I think all your experience with flowers is the bridge which links you with us, and your acting... and with your flowers you are undoubtedly rehearsing your future parts.'[298]

Her quiet New Year at her adored Chalet with *The Ancient Sage* is her last, as it has now been requisitioned, surrounded with barbed wire as a lookout station. She has to go over and check that all their belongings have been removed. Will she ever see it again? On 4th November President Roosevelt is returned for a second term and he and Eleanor remain in the White House, at least there is some stability. William and Mary Elmhirst celebrate their Golden Wedding, which Dorothy has to accomplish on her own – they are Papa and Mamma now – as Leonard has gone travelling again, in secret.

Home is a matter of meetings, the Dartington trustees have worries over the school as Headmaster Curry is preoccupied and frequently absent on his 'war work', which is promoting world government as the only way of saving the situation. Dorothy tells Leonard in a letter that there is nothing to be done about Curry, or rather that she is too exhausted to do anything, and she takes to her bed in mid-December – there is no one left for her Christmas anyway. [29th December is fire over London, the City and the East End reduced to smoking ruins.] Snow in Devon.

For the New Year of 1941 she has no Chalet and little hope. Even the ballet dancers have succumbed to the mood for they give a farewell performance of Ashton's *Dante Sonata*, his interpretation of the struggle between 'the children of darkness and children of light', before they leave to be transformed into the Sadler's Wells Ballet and enduring fame.[299] 'My drama class' means that Dorothy is teaching now, which is something. She has cut from a newspaper a map of Europe to put in the front of her diary; it shows most of France, and Belgium, Holland, Poland, Czechoslovakia and Norway in enemy occupation. Another cutting is a report of Beatrice playing Viola in *Twelfth Night*, triumphantly in New York. On a Sunday in early February Chris Martin is taken ill, and as Cecily is away, Dorothy and Peter Cox go with him in the ambulance to Exeter; it will be April before he comes home.

[20th/21st March, Plymouth is bombed.] The King and Queen had been visiting, having tea with the Astors at their house in Elliott Terrace, and when they left for the station the siren sounded. No one paid any attention but that evening the city centre was almost obliterated. On Wednesday 26th Dorothy goes to see Nancy Astor; 'Plymouth is a tragic sight,' she tells Leonard. 'In answer to my offer of hospitality Nancy decided to send us 20 Nursery School children, and they have been housed here in the Courtyard gym and the Barn studio above.' On 1st April she goes to Buckingham Palace to see Whitney receive his Military Cross – she notes, 'He is full of airman's talk of dogfights and near misses, all wonderful and terrible.' He is now sometimes with the Duke at Northolt, sometimes at Manston in Kent and sometimes at Stapleford Tawney in Essex; she can only try to pray.

The bombing does not stop, it goes on and on; the *Blitzkreig* was to continue to the year's end. On 7th May, 'Nancy my dear, my thoughts are with you every day and all day,' as the Astors struggle to help their beleaguered city. Dorothy feels 'it is a comfort – perhaps the greatest comfort in the world – to feel that one can still be of some use to people'. She is reduced to tears by the text of a talk Noel Brailsford has given on American radio, his theme that 'Life in England is not all struggle and destruction'. Brailsford, it is the key to their continuing friendship, was brought up in South Devon, and remembering the things he did as a child he follows the fate of some of the London children now here – 'groups of boys shouting and laughing were wading in the usually silent Dart'. He allows that many of them had lived through 'days of terror', that they missed their mothers and that they found the countryside 'dreary and uninteresting'. But there was a chance that some of them were about to be transformed – they were growing vegetables and flowers, absorbed in trying to catch a salmon with a lasso, helping the farmers' wives with their dairying and poultry; they were acting, dancing and singing. At least one hundred and fifty children lived at Dartington, another one hundred and fifty were fostered in good homes; they were clean and healthy, their manners were gentler, their horizons widened. 'We have stumbled in our half-conscious English fashion,' concluded Brailsford, 'into a social experiment of great promise.'[300]

The hope of rural futures, or simply holidays, for city children was not to be entirely lost at the war's end, but in 1941 it was the message of hope that counted, the message to America that, in the almost dying words of the British ambassador Lord Lothian, 'If you back us you won't be backing a quitter.'[301] Leonard had returned from a tour speaking to American farmers on his pet subject of agricultural economics and telling them that 'Uncle Sam and John Bull needed each other now'. His tour was made with the blessing of the Department of Agriculture, in the person of Assistant Secretary Milburn L. Wilson, a honeyed relationship that sprang from that White House dinner of Easter Sunday 1938 when Dorothy had asked to meet Henry Wallace and Wilson on Leonard's behalf.[302] Even though America still stood aside from the battlefield, the New Deal successes in soil and water conservation, the reduction of surpluses and support for prices of Roosevelt's first term were all being adjusted to the wartime president's Lend-Lease programme, and his declaration that America would become 'the arsenal of democracy'. A nationwide system of War Boards urged American farmers to meet new targets for producing grains, oil-bearing soya, peanuts and flaxseed and vegetables, the 'food and fiber' in government language needed by America and her allies.[303] The disappearing surpluses and rising prices made the farmers happy but persuading them that it was worthwhile to grow food to put into British mouths was a delicate task; there could be no taint of politics or propaganda. Wilson, who had worked for years on experiments in rural revival in Montana and was steeped in agricultural economics, was Leonard's alter ego in ideologies, and he and his department liked Leonard's transparent honesty and practical approach. His talks had been well received, and they hoped he would make another tour. Only a few people knew of this plan, and of them only Eleanor Roosevelt would have remembered Dorothy as a convincing public speaker for her causes during the Great War.

Dorothy's response to Leonard's suggestion that they make a long public-speaking tour is not recorded, but if they were wise and the request came from the Roosevelts she would not have had a minute's hesitation. She would also have an unexpected chance for a holiday with her children. She had time to prepare her talks on subjects of her very own, on community life at Dartington, more generally on the arts in British life, and on her own experiences of the bombing and the incidental benefits of country life to refugee city children. She would reach out to women in colleges and universities and gatherings of farmers' wives, while Leonard told their husbands of British efforts to feed their beleaguered nation despite shortages of every kind. It was all very secret. Dorothy had a few visitors for the sake of appearances: her new gardening friend Constance Spry, and Stephen and Natasha Spender, Natasha giving an impromptu concert on the Great Hall's piano.[304] Then, at more or less their usual time so as not to cause comment, they were spirited away to Bristol on 20th July, and flown to Lisbon, where they had to wait a week for seats on the Pan American Clipper seaplane which took them on the southerly crossing, via Horta in the Azores, then Bermuda to La Guardia. They landed at 4.30 p.m. on 29th July. Leonard was whisked away to planning meetings, while Dorothy went to stay with Susie Hammond in the city, where she was on 1st August when her diary has a note, 'news of Whitney missing'.

She went out to Long Island, surrendering herself to Old Westbury, 'walking in a dream', and finding the rest of her family. Ruth, William, Dorcas and Eloise were in high spirits because Nanny Jefferies had found them a holiday house on Chappaquiddick, 'such a lovely island off the Massachusetts coast', with its own beach, sailboat and tennis court, and a barn for William's pet goats and the pony which Dorcas and Eloise, both being lightweights, rode together. Biddy came too, and Michael and Belinda and Leonard all arrived; they swam, sailed and baked clams, and after William and

Dorothy had weeded the tennis court, Michael and Dorothy played William and Leonard, 'such a good four', Dorothy reported to Mamma Mary Elmhirst. Dorothy and Ruth went for a long walk and talk, as Ruth, now fifteen, home from her arts studies at Sarah Lawrence College in Westchester County, missed her mother dreadfully. Chappaquiddick was base camp until the end of August with Dorothy returning between trips to Washington, to Cornell for a talk and dinner in Willard Straight Hall, and from several days in collegiate New England.

Dorothy and William at Chappaquiddick during World War II

A little to the north of Maine President Roosevelt and Prime Minister Churchill were having a secret rendezvous at sea agreeing the Atlantic Charter, the war aims and 'hopes for a better future' of the Allies, including Russia. Germany responded by attacking the American ships guarding North Atlantic convoys and making a pact with Japan and Italy to declare war on any nation that attacked any of them. Japan's disunited government and renegade generals meant that, freed from fears of invasion from the north by a non-aggression pact with Russia, the army turned to harassing American interests in the

Pacific. Roosevelt made Willard's hero General Douglas MacArthur commander of all the American forces in East Asia. As Dorothy read these headlines, and of the Atlantic Charter's reliance on President Wilson's (and Walter Lippmann's) Fourteen Points, which she had heard the president utter twenty-three years ago for that other war, she must have bit her lip, uttering her characteristic 'Mmnn... n... n' and renewed her vow to live in the present, thankful that she had something useful to do.

For Michael's birthday on 1st September they were all at Woods Hole, their old haunt, with 'a great sail on high seas'. Dorothy saw Biddy playing Viola in *Twelfth Night*, several performances as if to store up her pleasures. Then came news of Beatrice Fletcher's death on 9th September; she was sixty-four, and Dorothy felt with sadness that her life had not been happy, that her late marriage had been but a quiet reverie after all the excitement that Beatrice had found as her companion for those nine brief, youthful years. She attended the funeral at Arlington, and promised to meet Prather Fletcher for a quiet talk when her schedule allowed. From Washington where, she noted, Leonard gave a talk on the same day as the president's broadcast explaining the Lend-Lease programme was relayed on the Columbia Broadcasting System, they left on the train to Kentucky. A meeting at Louisville on the Ohio River was followed by others at Lexington and Bowling Green, where they were kept talking for six hours. From Cincinnati they continued northwards to Toledo, Detroit and Lansing – the meeting at the students' union at Lansing was 'very worthwhile' – and then on to Chicago, speaking at the Madison and Purdue campuses. At Lafayette, Indiana, they had meetings at breakfast, in the afternoon and evening, and the next day at Urbana, Illinois, found themselves eating a soya bean dinner with six hundred farmers. Secretary Wilson's department had mastered the organisation of their train travel, hotels and destinations well, and even-handedly, for Michigan and Indiana (along with several Midwestern states) had voted Republican in 1940, supporting the local hero, 'a Hoosier farm boy' with 'disheveled charm', Wendell

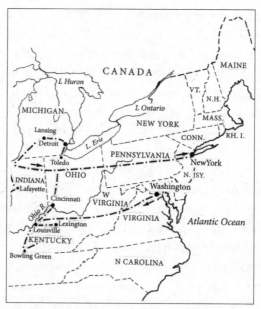

Washington to Indiana, the beginning of their first tour, August to October 1941

L. Wilkie. Wilkie had been only an 'occasional' Republican and he strongly supported the food for the Allies campaign, so it begins to seem that Leonard and Dorothy were carried along on a wave of enthusiasm, and characteristically warm American welcomes. They had been allocated a rest day, Friday 26th September, at Urbana but Dorothy was persuaded to give her talk on their work at Dartington, especially on her Arts Department, using slide illustrations made from Leonard's photographs. She included Noel Brailsford's theme of the evacuee city children whose horizons were broadened by country life, which found a sympathetic echo with these Midwestern farmers and their wives who believed themselves the stewards of God's Own Country.

From Urbana they went south to Decatur, on to St Louis and to Columbia, Missouri, to a meeting at Salina in deepest Kansas. On 1st October they were driven to the Manhattan campus of the University of Kansas where Dorothy spent two hours with the women of the university staff and had 'a marvellous lunch'. Next

St Louis to North Dakota, winter 1941–42

day it was Lincoln, Nebraska, for a student convention at eleven, a faculty lunch and an afternoon meeting of farming women. More meetings with always a barrage of questions about everyday life in England, then on to Ames in Henry Wallace's Iowa, and more meetings before they were shown the fall glories on a tour to Sac City and Sioux City in the hill country of the Missouri River, where Iowa, Nebraska and South Dakota meet. No time for a leisurely stay, even at Sioux Falls, but another meeting before they boarded the midnight train to St Paul. They saw a lot of midnight trains. From St Paul they went to the agricultural school at Morris, Minnesota where there was a huge crowd, then on to their northernmost stops, Fargo on the Red River, where Dorothy spoke at a ladies' lunch, and Valley City, North Dakota, where Leonard broadcast. A flight to Chicago for a meeting of the English-Speaking Union allowed them to continue to New York. At some point along all these ways Dorothy had heard that Whitney had crash-landed and was interned as a prisoner of war.[305]

She had been travelling and socialising rather frantically since the beginning of August, even Chappaquiddick had hardly been a holiday for her, and it was now the middle of October. Leonard had an appointment at the British Embassy in Washington, and together they reported on their tour to the First Lady at Hyde Park-on-Hudson.[306] Then they went separate ways, Leonard to Canada, Dorothy spending a few days in Manhattan seeing friends – Bill Delano, at the Colony Club and Bruce Bliven at *The New Republic*, who assured her that he and George Soule had been so shocked at the news of the Blitz, fearing that Hitler would win the war, that he had changed the paper's line to support of America's entry.[307] She went to Ridgefield and joined some of Mischa Chekhov's classes, saw Prather Fletcher at Old Westbury as she had promised and lunched with Gertrude Whitney. November passed in this way – she needed the reviving influence of those she loved – she saw Biddy's Viola yet again, more than once, and on 7th December she took Biddy and the man she wanted to marry, Louis Dolivet, out to lunch, the first meeting with her future son-in-law.[308] While they were lunching the news came through of the Japanese attack on Pearl Harbor and other Pacific bases: she and Leonard were due to start another tour the following day and her diary has a definite note that they were due at the White House 'at nine' – for a briefing that the story was now changed and America would be at war.

Leonard and Dorothy set out as planned to a Lions' charity lunch at Blacksburg in Virginia, then on through Tennessee Valley Authority country to Knoxville. The TVA was not only building dams and generating power, it was also producing fertilisers and advising farmers on crop management and forestry, and mining metals for aircraft production – it really was Roosevelt's war work-horse. From Knoxville they headed deeper into the South, to Birmingham – 'very sociable' all day meetings, noted Dorothy – to Tuscaloosa, Starkville, Vicksburg, Baton Rouge and finally New Orleans, where their treat was to dine at the legendary Antoine's. Next stop was Houston where the 'good discussion' reflected the enthusiasm of Lyndon Baines Johnson, then champion of small farmers and conservation in

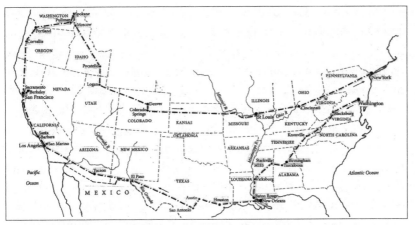

The second tour, winter 1941–42, Dorothy added up that she had made 40 speeches, caught 15 night trains and travelled about 8,000 miles

mid-Texas. After stopping at Austin and San Antonio they took the night train on the long haul to El Paso on the Rio Grande border with Mexico, then westwards through desert land to Tucson in Arizona. This was already a fashionable retirement spot and Dorothy records seeing, of all people, Cecil Davis who had painted Willard's portrait in 1912.[309]

Continuing northwards Leonard spoke at the Los Angeles Veterans' Patriotic Hall, the Agricultural Hall on the Berkeley campus, then at the County Court House in Sacramento, while Dorothy spoke to the Berkeley Women's Faculty Club and revisited some of the sights of San Francisco. On New Year's Day of 1942 they reached Corvallis, home of the University of Oregon, where the next morning Dorothy spoke to a women's group, and they both spoke at a 'big meeting' in the union in the afternoon. They drove on icy roads to Portland and relaxed seeing the new John Ford film of Richard Llewellyn's *How Green Was My Valley*; in below zero temperatures they progressed into Washington state, to Pullman and Spokane then across the state line to Moscow, both speaking in all these places, before making the long journey south through Idaho's spectacular mountains and plains to Pocatello.

They reported to Washington on what they had seen and heard, and by her birthday, her fifty-fifth, on 23rd January 1942 her New York and Old Westbury commuting life resumed, except for one more talk, her 41st, given at Wellesley College. She invited Louis Dolivet to lunch on his own and was immensely taken with his dashing looks and air of mystery, and – needless to say – he had a scheme to put before her, for her investment in his new magazine. She saw Martha Graham dance, she met Clare Leighton, she did blissfully ordinary things with her old friends. In mid-February they were summoned to the White House to dinner, and lunch again the following day, and they saw Gershwin's *Porgy and Bess*. There was one more trip to make, and on 20th February, with Leonard, William, Michael and Belinda, she flew to Des Moines in Iowa, where Biddy's *Twelfth Night* company was performing, for her marriage to Louis Dolivet the following day.

With Leonard she left for New York the next day, the 22nd, Washington's Birthday, but her mind was already on England, and she noted down the names and posts in Churchill's Cabinet reshuffle. At some moment she had the news that Whitney had escaped from his château prison and been spirited to safety and the Royal Navy by the French Resistance. She went to Poughkeepsie for the wedding of Willard's niece Dorothy Sanborn, made a farewell visit to Ridgefield and Mischa Chekhov, gave a last hug to Biddy and Louis who were now in New York, met Jim Ede who was in town on a lecture tour, and then they were gone once again – from La Guardia on Tuesday, 24th March to Bermuda and ocean-hopping. They reached home late on Thursday evening having been away for eight months. Dorothy spent the Friday going around her garden with David Calthorpe.[310]

Spring in her garden welcomed her home and she snatched every moment to go out and look for the awakening treasures, for Beatrix Farrand's legacy of anemones, scillas and primroses planted along the Camellia Walk, for the uncurling spires of Solomon's Seal beneath the trees, and everywhere the advancing cavalcade of blossoms. The green filigrees of the newly hatched beech leaves were her favourite effects: she found these signs of new birth that floated above the bronze carpets of the dead leaves the most comforting of all, especially when she had just returned from London, a strange city now, brimming with uniforms and sandbags, everyone grimly forgiving of the craters in the streets and shortages in the shops. Before they had been home a month the Luftwaffe bombed Exeter in a series of 'Baedeker Raids' from late April into May aimed at the heart of the city. Almost three hundred people were killed, many more were injured, and something like twenty buildings were destroyed or damaged, which meant that much of the historic High Street and the city's 'old world charm has disappeared for ever'.[311] Leonard had already noted how she was 'using her spade and trowel as a means of defeating Hitler', and now Dorothy admitted to herself, 'Despite the war – or perhaps because of the war, I have begun to concentrate on the garden. I find I have a great desire to add to the permanent beauty of Dartington in these days when everything else seems so transitory.'[312]

Dorothy the gardener

But it was not just her garden; in herself Dorothy had moved on, yet again. Her wartime philosophy had been resolved as, 'when one thinks an end has come, then there is a new beginning – there is no end that is not also a beginning'. Months of wayward jaunting across an unfamiliar America, at the apparent whims of a nameless officialdom, had left her feeling profoundly grateful to be home. It appears that in convincing her audiences – forty-one times over – of the virtues and values of life in England she had convinced herself. Despite the dips back into her old New York life, she now felt she belonged at Dartington. Her private philosophies, her vows to live in the present, appreciate everything in her surroundings and identify the spark of the divine in the people around her, all lightened her step. If asked about that spark of the divine she would have named her daughter Beatrice playing Viola; she would have to admit that Mischa Chekhov had been deposed by Franklin Delano Roosevelt whom she believed was the leader of the free world and the apostle of international goodwill. And what about the man nearest to her, what about Leonard? Their American journeys had been graced by warm welcomes and generous hospitality but for all that they were journeying among strangers, across vast distances in the dark and the cold, and they had been alone together for longer periods than at any previous time in their marriage. For Dorothy this had brought Leonard closer than perhaps ever before, and she valued his stability and talent for lightening the direst circumstances. As they resumed their English routines, weekdays in London where Leonard was working and weekends at Dartington, she was both chastened by her former inability to appreciate him and surprised that he had become so precious to her. In her diary she noted the things they did alone together, a walk in Hyde Park, a visit to the theatre, she savoured these moments knowing that he had to leave for the Middle East in the middle of August.

She saw Daphne and her grand-daughter Camilla regularly in London, but nothing of Whitney until he was free to come to Dartington on Friday, 21st August. On the Sunday he accompanied her to church – a new beginning? – followed by lunch with Bridget D'Oyley

Carte at Coleton Fishacre. Whitney was already destined to return to flying duties in North Africa, and it seemed that circumstances saved him, for on the Tuesday his friend Prince George, the Duke of Kent, to whom he had been ADC, was killed along with his colleagues when their plane crashed into a Scottish hillside.

Another new beginning had already been made, for no sooner were her talks from America filed away than she was preparing talks on America to be given in England. The Ministry of Information (MoI) – responsible for 'domestic morale' – had realised that the promised arrival of one million American soldiers into England, and Devon was to be one of the most militarised of counties, could be an unmitigated disaster. 'There is no limit to the harm that is capable of being done if relations between the American soldiers and the local inhabitants go awry,' warned the Ministry directive. It was not just a clash of cultures, as General Eisenhower told the Pentagon, 'for in allowing any friction to develop between ourselves and our Allies we are playing entirely into the hands of our enemies'. He further regarded 'that to bring the US soldier into touch with the British private home would increase the effectiveness of the combined forces as allies'.[313] So Dorothy's second campaign began in the late summer of 1942 and ran through to 1944. She conducted it alone, driving her black 1939 Ford saloon, only taking extra petrol coupons when it was really necessary, until she discovered the Women's Voluntary Service Car Pool in Plymouth for long journeys. Working for the MoI Officer in Plymouth she spoke of 'Our American Allies' and 'Our Friends the Americans' to new recruits, WVS volunteers and Civil Defence Wardens in training, at Topsham, Dawlish, Tiverton, and on 27th September, a Sunday afternoon, to the inmates of Dartmoor Prison. She was understandably nervous about this last date, and assured by her MoI Officer, 'The combination of what you have to say and your personality... will be entirely acceptable.'[314]

Through the autumn and into 1943 her targets were broadened and more demands were made: on 7th November, after lunching with Nancy Astor in her patched-up home, she found herself speaking in

Plymouth Council Chamber with the Lady Mayoress in the chair, and taking part in a Brains Trust. Two days later in her garden she praised the autumn colours, 'God's Day of Days', and two days later still, when she remembered the Armistice, noted 'a perfect day'. The Brains Trust must have gone well for she was co-opted for another the following March, the 'brains' advertised as Lady Astor, Mrs Elmhirst, Harold Nicolson MP, Colonel Clement and Professor Arthur Newell.[315] To close they sang 'Mine Eyes Have Seen the Glory of the Coming of the Lord'.

With the appropriate passes she found her way into a number of 'stone frigates', HMS *Impregnable*, the Signals Training base at Devonport (who requested a return visit), the Artificers Training base at Torpoint, and also Glenholt at Crownhill (a dismal place, a former naturist camp) with a new talk on 'Co-operation with US Personnel'. 'American Viewpoints' was her talk to the Wrens (WRNS) who ran HMS *Foliot*, the 'very comfortable' transit base for landing craft crews. Her name was added to the Voluntary Speakers' Panel which brought requests from schools and youth clubs, the WEA (she remembered her first meetings with Albert Mansbridge and his dream of setting up a country-wide educational organisation and here it was in action), the Women's Institutes, never to be left out, and the Townswomen's Guilds. Whether it was the prospect of the handsome young GIs with their money, silk stockings and chewing gum, but a rash of Americanism broke out, seminars, day schools, whole 'American' weeks. She spoke on 'Women in America', and took days schools in her stride, 'Society and Politics' in the afternoons, 'Education and Culture' in the evenings. She enjoyed speaking on 'The Arts in America'. She took along her large map of North America and whenever possible she showed slides of the photographs that Leonard had taken on their tour, of the Smoky Mountains, the Tennessee River, the Colorado River, neat New Hampshire, tumbling Niagara, cattle grazing in Idaho, wheat on the plains, cantaloupe and strawberries growing in California. She was meeting a wider cross-section of British people than she had ever encountered, standing up and speaking in schools and village halls all over Devon and Cornwall; for Thanksgiving in November 1942 she gave a talk, followed by the traditional turkey dinner, at Totnes Senior School, where Leonard was on the Board of Governors. In the local papers it was constantly noted that Mrs Elmhirst gave 'another of her popular MoI talks' and sometimes she confided to the women of Bickleigh, Broadhempston or East Portlemouth how in America she had found 'a touching sympathy' for the women of Britain. She still noted the war news as the days passed, and could often comment on places she had once visited but were mysteries to most of her listeners. She was not shy of her favourite topics, for instance William Beveridge's proposals for national insurance, and his Five Great Evils – want, disease, ignorance, squalor and idleness.

Two small photographs are stuck into the front of her 1943 diary, of Michael and Belinda's home in Virginia, and of her with their baby son, David Willard, born the previous October. Michael had volunteered and was piloting B17 Flying Fortresses; he was about to publish his first book, titled *Let This Be the Last War*, a plea for negotiation rather than annihilation, and unenthusiastically reviewed.

Was it another landmark that Dorothy awoke on 3rd April and wrote 'Wedding Day' in her diary, when for so long it had been her September wedding that she marked? With Leonard she walked beside the Dart among the wood anemones and the daffodils. On 14th April Tom Eliot came to lunch. On Saturday 15th May Dartington celebrated its First Foundation Day, a festival, part pageant with music and dancing, part speech day, at which she and Leonard presided and which became a fixture in the calendar. John Piper came for four days in mid-June, perhaps at the prompting of Frederick Ashton for whose ballet *The Quest* he had just designed the scenery and costumes, perhaps in search of a commission, and certainly in the company of Stephen and Natasha Spender. Piper's paintings of the Great Hall in his picturesque and 'stormy' style made famous in his studies of Windsor Castle the year before were outshone by his description of his experience, embellished in a letter to Osbert Sitwell:

Dartington was wonderful. The most Godless place I have ever been in; queues for meals and rota washing-up; hundreds of bad musicians with red ties and flannel bags, H.N. Brailsford, several failed artists (though art is not quite the thing) and dozens of girls talking in whispers and either on holiday from unartistic mothers or escaping from doing factory work, or deciding whether they were conscientious objectors.

Piper gossiped with Stephen Spender and enjoyed Natasha's piano playing 'in a great over-restored Hall with good taste white and green glass windows and rush mats from Heals'. He continued:

Dorothy Elmhirst is a much maltreated and very intelligent woman who, unlike her poseur of a husband, retains an attractive American accent, and ought to (and would with encouragement) kick over the traces and throw everybody out on their ears. The whole thing is indeed an interesting survival, very much dated. There ought to be a Batsford book written about it in the 'British Heritage' Series, with coloured photographs of the bronzed inmates and the beautifully hideous rolling red-earthed fields that surround it on all sides, punctured by the concrete walls and flat roofs of the houses all around that were designed by the now-forgotten famous architects of the early thirties.

Some of this comes strangely from one who was fully involved with the delightfully recherché *Shell County Guides* and John Betjeman and Faber, and whose own *Oxfordshire* was published by Batsford. Maybe it was the sight of Dorothy's redundant dining room and being forced to café-style meals that unnerved Piper; according to his biographer Frances Spalding, there was also something Freudian about Piper telling his wife Myfanwy of the love among the bushes, of 'every path in the garden the scene of 100 illicit and very unhappy affairs', when 'an affair, or something akin to an affair' was unsettling his own home.[316]

Two months later, in early September of 1943, the American anthropologist Margaret Mead visited Dartington. Mead was married to the Cambridge anthropologist Gregory Bateson but she was also working for Roosevelt's agency the Office of War Information to explain the military and civilian societies to each other. She was the official ambassador for fraternising whereas presumably Dorothy's role was perceived as merely amateur. Dorothy was fresh from addressing eighty people, mostly women, at the Chartered Insurance Institute in Plymouth on 'Home Life in America', and she had, as usual, done her homework reading Mead's *And Keep Your Powder Dry, an Anthropologist Looks at America*. It is to be hoped that Mead was as well prepared; at least it seems she was visiting Dorothy and not Dartington, in view of her much publicised interest in the sexual politics of primitive societies.[317]

At the end of September Dorothy and Leonard allowed themselves a heavenly five days visiting the cream of Cornish gardens including Carclew, Trebah, Penjerrick, Glendurgan and Tregothnan. They had no petrol but instead went to Falmouth by train, then resorted to ferries, rowboats, bicycles, hitching lifts and finally a taxi. Dorothy returned to 'a heavenly day' in her own garden and a trip to Westonbirt with Hiram Winterbotham, who did have some petrol, coming home to a musical evening in the Great Hall with Benjamin Britten and Peter Pears. They had come to Dartington at the request of Imogen Holst, who had just arrived to cheer the later months of the war with her music. It was a passing of the flame, for as the music soared so the art studio closed with the departure of Cecil and Elisabeth Collins for Chelsea; John Piper had helped to arrange a London exhibition for Collins at the Lefevre Gallery, so was his remark about the 'failed artists' just a tease?

Cecil and Elisabeth Collins had come to Dartington at the start of the war, Cecil as assistant to Hein Heckroth in the Art and Design Studio, taking over while Heckroth was interned, and Elisabeth willingly helping wherever she could, often with the apple and potato harvests. Collins not only painted, he thought and wrote, and his essay, *The Vision of the Fool,* with the accompanying paintings of the Fool in various guises are acknowledged as his most important works. 'The Fool rejects modern society (including the depictions of war),' he wrote, '[and] represents that profound fertile innocence' from which we have fallen – 'The Fool was there at the beginning of life and thus can offer a whiff of paradise to fallen mankind.' Dorothy bought several Fool paintings, the cross-legged, cross-gartered *Happy Hour* Fool with his jousting tent, and the *Procession of Fools.* Conversations on Shakespeare's fools – Jacques' 'I met a fool i' the forest. A motley fool', Lear's Fool and the Clown Feste in *Twelfth Night*, these were an intrinsic part of Collins's inspiration and Dorothy's delight. The Fool allowed her to believe that Dartington's ancient stones and trees would survive to foster new life.[318]

She noted the day of his Lefevre Private View in her diary but for some reason did not make it. Collins wrote of his disappointment on 5th February 1944, 'I had looked forward so much to showing you the exhibition, especialy [sic] you, who have understood, and helped me during these recent years… by giving me sanctuary… how I miss the garden! Especialy[sic] now, living in the vast ruined desert of this city.' On 23rd February the St James's area was bombed and the gallery damaged, but somehow the delicate drawing of *Procession of Fools* and others belonging to Dorothy survived; in March she wrote to Collins, 'I am afraid you have been suffering great anxiety over your pictures, but it is good to know, isn't it, that they have all escaped and that my own four treasures are here at Dartington? I called for them ten days ago… and brought them back by hand.'[319]

In early April she sent flowers for Dartington's church, which had become her habit, and she attended the Easter service. An Easter Sunday lunch party included their friend Philip Hendy from Temple Newsam, Cicely Martin and Chris Martin's young assistant Peter Cox; Chris Martin was not well enough to come and it was his failing health that concerned Dorothy in these weeks. Another lovely spring had come to South Devon, with carpets of white violets, primroses and the early blossoms, but also the United States 4th (IV) Infantry Division, 'the Ivy Boys' with their lumbering transports heading for the beaches of Start Bay to practise assault landings. They were part, and a large part, 'of the largest amphibious operation in history', shrouded in secrecy as General Eisenhower and his British counterparts attempted to dupe the Germans into expecting the invasion much further to the east. Who could have imagined that a vast invasion force could be mustered along the tortuous coastal lanes of Devon and Cornwall? Dartington was immediately ready to help and their Welcome Club saw more and more Americans. Dorothy and Leonard probably knew more than most people of what was happening, especially from Basil Liddell Hart, but Dorothy wrote nothing in her letters or her diary.[320]

On 1st June, a Thursday, her youngest son William Elmhirst, now fifteen, arrived in London and she rushed to meet him at Euston. On his own initiative he had decided to come home, crossing the Atlantic in a convoy to Liverpool. She was so pleased to see him and so thankful for his safe arrival that on the Sunday she spent most of the day washing his clothes.

On 5th June, 'Rome is ours!' D-day, 6th June, was Leonard's fifty-first birthday, and like the rest of England they only learned that the invasion was launched from the streams of aircraft overhead and the sound of the guns. For Dorothy the memories came flooding back: the Ivy Boys were so like the young Doughboys she had joked with as she gave out coffee and books at Camp Upton twenty-seven years ago. It was impossible to know how much to believe of the newspaper reports of the landings and they were constantly in her thoughts, until in mid-July she noted that Commander James Van Allen came to lunch. Then she learned of the 4th Division's landing at Utah Beach and their perilous progress through the marshlands of the Cotentin Peninsula.

On the first Friday in August came a crisis over Chris Martin's health and he was taken into hospital at Exeter. There, after an operation, he died on the Sunday afternoon. Dorothy wrote her tribute for *News of the Day* for 9th August recalling how he had found the 'brilliant individuals' Tobey, Jooss, Nellie Van and Richard Odlin and harnessed their creativity into the Arts Department. In the late 1930s, when 'the Courtyard was the centre of an intense life', she wrote 'the heart that added human meaning to it all' was Chris's, and his vision had carried the name of Dartington Arts into a wider British society.[321]

She plotted the progress of the Ivy Boys noting 'tremendous US advances in Normandy' and that they liberated Rennes; on 23rd August she noted 'Paris freed', and – twenty-six years on from Willard's joyful moment – the people were dancing in the streets once more. With the end in sight her energies faded, she struggled with the approach of autumn, her war had exhausted her. The departing US army are much in evidence, they join in the carol singing and on Christmas Day they provide and serve lunch for everyone in the Great Hall. Perhaps 'Our Friends the Americans' and 'Co-operation with US Personnel' had been worthwhile after all? One way and another she seemed to have graduated, with honours, for being in England and coping with the war, more than coping, making her positive war effort; her flowers for the church in the spring, and now the chrysanthemums and hollies she sent for Christmas marked her diploma status, for it seems she had once committed one of the higher crimes of rural society by taking flowers and putting them in the church unheeding of the Flower Ladies' sacred rota. Now all was forgiven, at least in the earthly realms, and she could attend the Sunday service as an accepted lady from the big house rather than a foreign upstart.

TWELVE: 'THE HASTING DAY'

Fair daffodils, we weep to see
You haste away so soon;
And yet the early-rising sun
Has not attain'd his noon.
Stay, stay,
Until the hasting day
Has run
But to the evensong;
And, having pray'd together, we
Will go with you along.[322]

Dorothy's diary for 1945 is an odd one out, a Smythson 'Wafer' diary, a lesser affair than her usual 'Featherweight', which speaks of austerity, or that some well-meaning person bought the wrong one. She is fifty-eight on 23rd January, which William, now happily at home and at school at Foxhole, and Leonard attempt to celebrate, but she brushes them aside. Her long absences and then her preoccupations with her talks and the evacuees have left the larger Dartington carrying on without her and she seems content to leave it this way. She is still the trustee and only begetter of the Arts Department, and Chris Martin's natural successor, and after some deliberations his actual successor as arts administrator, was Peter Cox. Peter was in his early twenties, handsome with a rather leonine mane of hair; he had come down from reading history at Cambridge to be rejected by the army, the law, and apparently his family. The Martins had given him refuge and he became Chris's amanuensis and then assistant, at £3 a week. Dorothy had come to know him well through Chris's illness, and that final August afternoon when Chris died it was Peter who waited – sitting on the cathedral lawn working at a report – to drive her home. At first she was watchful of his youthfulness and of his ability to cope with capricious artistes, the touring company that arrived late, and the soloist who refused to play on the German-made grand piano, but she soon accepted that he was both determined and resourceful. She was also reassured by his early success at working with Imogen Holst.

'Imo', as those at Dartington called her (though not Dorothy), was Gustav Holst's only child. She was in her late thirties, neat, round-faced, and often dirndl-skirted; she was full of musicality, and totally unselfconsciously would happily break into a jig if someone's voice or a phrase from an oboe inspired her. She believed that everyone could sing, she was a brilliant teacher, and her small groups and classes brought music to wartime Dartington – 'we sightsang unaccompanied every morning – Palestrina, di Lasso, Vittoria, from 9 a.m. to 9.30 – nobody dreamed of calling that compulsory, because it was such a joy'. There were songs in the sunny Courtyard and to the lunch queues and serenades to parting guests; they sang rounds, which Dorothy enjoyed, and Imogen had arranged two rounds by William Boyce as a Christmas gift to her and Leonard. Everyone, the land girls, evacuees, soldiers, convalescent airmen and Dartingtonians, all joined in her musical evenings.[323] Peter Cox called this musical life 'essentially organic, rooted in the Courtyard but growing out beyond its confines'. Together he and Imogen joined these roots to the flower of the musical world, bringing Benjamin Britten, Peter Pears, Clifford and Lucille Curzon, Alfred Deller, Joan Cross and other soloists to inspire and lead the students.[324] Imogen believed that her most callow beginners could advance with Britten's genius in conducting his own *A Ceremony of Carols* or, even more ambitiously, in performing Bach's

St John Passion with distinguished soloists. She still inhabited her father's musical world with many of his connections, and yet 'she felt it to be a great privilege, and a very real responsibility, to be the resident musician of an enlarged private household'. Dorothy cherished her 'court' musicians, and she was even persuaded to play the guitar for the orchestra; Imogen remembered 'we found the happiest look on her face during the week was when she came out of the house swinging her guitar on her way' to play – she was 'awfully good' and 'very musical' but her shyness restricted her. Also, Imogen said she understood well that Dorothy had so many other worries and responsibilities that were far removed from their Devon valley.

The sudden death of President Roosevelt on 12th April 1945 from a cerebral haemorrhage came as a great blow. Dorothy's immediate reaction was to cable sympathies to Eleanor Roosevelt; for herself she analysed her feeling of 'the irreparable loss the world has suffered' for he had been taken in the midst of his work for a durable peace. 'In the struggle to hold together the great family of man,' she wrote, 'there is at present no outstanding leader – no one with the moral force and political wisdom who can speak on behalf of a powerful country, and help to dispel the clouds of fear and distrust that threaten to black out any hope of co-operation.'[325] When VE Day was declared on 8th May, and Imogen and her students sang 'Alleluia and Glory to God' from the Porch tower, Dorothy was thankful but not cheerful. With the release of the atomic bombs on Hiroshima and Nagasaki, noted in her diary in the first week of August, she feared for 'the euphoria of power' in her own country, and felt FDR's loss even more: 'How can we get on without him? How can we hope for peace in the future without the guidance he gave? He was indeed the leader of democracy – all the world over, the focus of the democratic faith, and the source of international goodwill.' Her ending was for Eleanor – his right hand – her 'sustaining him in the hardest of times' – 'the part that you have played all along is perhaps one of the noblest parts a great woman has ever played'.[326]

Dorothy was grasping at every large piece of paper she could find (the war shortage was evident) to write – scrawl in pencil – her emotional eulogy, and its purpose is unclear. Was it for a talk she never gave or was it just something she had to write? Was it the fate of the world or the loss of FDR that moved her so deeply? Once upon a time FDR and Willard were much alike, in stature, appearance and prospects, it was just that one had a future and the other had not. Of Franklin and Eleanor the attraction had always been Franklin, and if Dorothy had been a less just soul she might have questioned why Eleanor, not so rich nor so good-looking, not so intelligent (though perhaps less radical and more pliant) than herself, had been handed the role of 'great woman'.

Was she inwardly cursing her lot? Peter Cox glimpsed this harsher Dorothy one day:

> I was standing with her in the Courtyard and she called Thomas the butler over to give him some message. A minute or two later she saw that Thomas had stopped to talk to someone on the way back. Scarcely raising her voice she called across the Courtyard – *Thomas, I asked you* – the message was received like a bullet, Thomas scuttled back to his pantry.[327]

Walter Thomas's embarrassing moment belied his value, and his status; every difficult guest or importunate visitor could be calmed and charmed by his gracefully serving tea on the Loggia lawn. Emily, the once lost young seamstress, was now his wife, and greatly admired for her home-making skills, especially her flowers – natural arrangements of flowers, leaves and berries according to their season set in beautiful containers, often hand-thrown studio pots – which made such a memorable contribution to the atmosphere of the Hall, house and Courtyard rooms.

When the evacuees, the army and the war workers had all drifted away Dartington sometimes seemed quiet, rather tired and careworn, the whole estate badly in need of a boost to recover from neglect and dilapidations. Dorothy could see this but she could not give the orders and she wrote rather tetchily to Leonard, 'I don't believe many people have a second chance like this,' urging him to finish 'the India job' and come home to 'give the best of your thought and vision to Dartington'.[328] India had remained the subject on which they could never agree. Ever since 1929, she had vowed never to go again, nor did she, but Leonard's visits had only increased with the war and looming Indian partition and independence. His association with Tagore, who had died in 1941 but was more revered and celebrated than ever, had made him acceptable as an agricultural adviser. More than that, Leonard's war had brought him national as well as international distinction as chairman of Political and Economic Planning and for his work on all aspects of post-war reconstruction. Dartington was the platform for all he did but she felt he was taken away too much, her instinct being that Dartington must be seen to shine again, before they could influence the world outside.

Her heart and her head told her that her best work would be to revive the garden. In the darkest days when survival seemed such a fragile notion she had started to write diary descriptions of the most wonderful flowering moments, and these she continued and elaborated into her *Garden Notebooks*:

> July 1945 – the smoke bush is a dream – *Rhus cotinus purpureus* – in full flower, like spun sugar dipped in claret. I love it madly. The group of blue hydrangeas in the Loop is a great success and *Cornus kousa* is my greatest joy of all. *Cornus capitata* is having a sabbatical! [This creamy flowered shrub beside the Sunny Border soon revived.][329]

Constance Spry had suggested that Percy Cane might be the garden designer for Dartington, and with the 'spun sugar dipped in claret' in flower, he made his first visit.[330] Cane could not have been less like the lean and hungry pair of demi-gods Walter Gropius and Michael Chekhov who had both bewitched Dorothy; he was Essex-born, over sixty, a confirmed bachelor, practical and hard-working and uncharismatic. His private practice had been successful for twenty-five years and his gardens were well illustrated in many magazines and several of his own books. He liked to ease his planting out into the semi-wild, with mown paths curving through carefully sited shrubs and trees; a widening of the path into a mown glade was his favourite device.

After an opening skirmish when she feared Cane wanted to change everything, even to deprive her of her treasured *Davidia* which she thought lovelier than any she had seen at Kew or Westonbirt, the dust settled: 'Mr Cane came to help us over the contours... and showed us the advantage of intensifying the great heights and depths. He said you must take full advantage of the dramatic contrasts that have been smothered or lost to view.' In the September, 'We've started with a vengeance making the Glade from Upper Ranges down to the Heath Bank. The tractor pulls the trees with little effort. So far a larch has come down, 2 oaks, 1 fir.'

In October 1945:

> Tremendous clearance is going on by means of the tractor. Great chunks of stuff pulled out of the Woodland and the Dell, and of course the new Glade. We are going to see our great trees (ilex, Spanish chestnuts, Scots pines and Turkey oaks) at last. I hadn't realised how terribly cluttered they had been. These are the days! The perfect autumn days – absolutely still, slight frost in the morning – hot sun at mid-day and a deep blue sky.

In the November she came back after a few days in London to find 'a great change had taken place here – so many leaves have fallen. Only the beeches glow with sun on them – burnt orange. They are so wonderful – the beeches. And now two have been cut down – it's agonizing (though they were rotten and dangerous).'

Clearing the Glade was opening the windows, letting air and light

1 North Courtyard
  (Beatrix Farrand 1933)
2 Spring Walk   } Beatrix Farrand
3 Camellia Walk   1933–6
4 Rhododendron Walk
5 South Lawn
6 Gallery Arcade
  (remains of
  Hall's South Court)
7 Sunny Border
8 Tournament Ground
9 Twelve Apostles
10 Azalea Dell
11 Woodland
12 Pool
13 Heath Bank
14 Steps
15 Glade   } Percy Cane
16 Henry Moore Statue   post 1945
17 Tai Haku Cherries
18 Meadow
19 High Meadow
20 Upper Ranges
21 Valley Field
22 Great Lawn

DARTINGTON
HALL

Plan of Dartington's garden in the 1960s. The Great Hall is at A, the Porch Tower at B, the Elmhirsts' house at C and the White Hart, the wartime dining room, at D. The East Courtyard rooms are at E and the West Courtyard rooms are at F, with the Entrance Arch and adjoining Barn Theatre at G.

flow through – there was now an airy perspective from the Hall to the farthest Upper Ranges, and from the top of the grass sweep of the Glade one could look back, down into the depths of the tiltyard and across to the Sunny Border, which was planted along in front of an old stone wall. This Sunny Border was Dorothy's personal garden, and no one dared touch it without her knowledge. On the opposite side of the path along the border stood the row of Irish yews known as the Twelve Apostles which she thought 'may have been planted to hide an eighteenth-century bear-baiting pit in the tiltyard from the eyes of the children in the house'.[331] At the top of the Heath Bank was her favourite look-out to the rolling green and wooded hills that in some lights seemed like the sea, and here Percy Cane built her a paved circular belvedere, the

221

Whispering Circle. The only way down the steep bank was by Beatrix Farrand's 'little goat track' for the agile, now replaced by Cane's beautiful stone steps, ingeniously nine separate flights of graduated lengths, unadorned, and flanked with bays, magnolias and large heaths. These steps made a tour of the garden possible by connecting the Glade to the lower levels; everything was coming together and ever more often Dorothy noted, 'How I bless Mr Cane!'

Her confidence and happiness in her garden are self-evident, but Imogen Holst's observation about her shyness stunting her musicality identifies the enigma that was growing around her, the shadow that fell over these crucial post-war years. The Dorothy that toured America speaking to hundreds of strangers in vast halls, and then came home to repeat her performances all over south-west England, did not survive the war. She could not face Dartingtonians en masse – at concerts in the Great Hall, on Foundation Days, at church on Sunday mornings she would slip quietly into her seat, and if a speech of welcome or thanks were required then someone else would have to make it, usually Leonard. She was as she had been before the war, as Michael Young had observed, a familiar presence, but one that nobody knew because of her shyness. [332]

The extent of her shyness was infinitely variable, a miasma distilled from inner doubts and outer circumstances, and elusive. Sheer physical exhaustion and the problems of finding a role amidst post-war chaos were the lot of many women, and she was by no means unusual in her affliction. So much was said about women winning their rightful place in society because of their war work, but society quickly resumed its misogynistic bias. The New Year of 1946 confronted Dorothy with two vivid illustrations of this as she set out for London early in January to meet Eleanor Roosevelt and to see the exhibition of paintings by Picasso and Matisse at the Victoria & Albert Museum. Her own Picasso 'jeune fille' with rosebud mouth and cherry cheeks was enchanting (and for all the head was on a table it could still be imagined as attached to the girl's body) but these paintings were perplexing and puzzling with his overtly 'distorted' images of his muses and lovers. It would have seemed less threatening had he painted more men with their orifices rearranged and cubistic limbs. Attitudes would change but at the time they had been frozen by the war, there was controversy, and apparently a riot, as there had been in 1919, and it was unnerving for any woman to be surrounded with such violence inspired by every woman's body.

It might be thought that Dorothy's 'great woman' who had been America's First Lady for a dozen years, Eleanor Roosevelt, was immune from nerves and fears, especially as she was in London as an American delegate to the First Assembly of the United Nations held at Central Hall, Westminster. Mrs Roosevelt, told bluntly by her colleagues 'that we did all we could to keep you off the US delegation', knew well that she had to 'walk on eggs', and that as the only woman representing America to this 'New World Organization' she felt that 'I was not very welcome'. She continued, 'If I failed to be a useful member, it would not be considered that I as an individual had failed, but that all women had failed, and there would be little chance for others to serve in the near future.'[333] Walking 'on eggs' was an interesting turn of phrase, for the complete absence of fresh eggs, even at Claridge's, and the revolting powdered substitute, drove some of the American delegation to distraction. Mrs Roosevelt was overcome by a gift of fresh eggs, perhaps brought from Devon by Dorothy, who played her part in a gathering of American friends to cheer her visit.[334]

It had been Christopher Martin's friendship with Benjamin Britten and Peter Pears, as well as Imogen Holst, that had enabled Dartington's music making that now worked so well. Six months earlier in June of 1945, Dorothy and Leonard, Cicely Martin and Peter Cox had been at Sadler's Wells for the first night of Britten's *Peter Grimes* with Peter Pears singing the part of Grimes and Joan Cross as Ellen Orford. They had experienced the uncanny silence when the music died, which erupted into cheering and fourteen curtain calls. The opera was voted 'thrilling' and marking 'the reinstatement of opera in the musical life of this country'.[335] Ben and Peter (as even Dorothy called them) were easily persuaded to give a concert in Christopher Martin's memory at Dartington in the July, and during their visit the talk naturally veered towards Ben's hope for an English Opera Group. There had been difficulties at Sadler's Wells, and – at least in July of 1945 – Covent Garden and Glyndebourne seemed a long way from reopening. It was agreed 'to give Benjamin Britten's opera company a start at Dartington next April'. Dorothy promised £2,000, about one third of the estimated cost of the first production. Britten was diverted by his song cycle of Donne's *Holy Sonnets*, a quartet for strings and a 'small film' which turned out to be *The Young Person's Guide to the Orchestra*. He began working on the new opera, *The Rape of Lucretia*, at the end of January 1946, with the April deadline slipping.[336]

For some reason, possibly bad weather, she was unable to reach London for Maynard and Lydia Keynes's Gala for the Arts Council which reopened Covent Garden on 20th February, all its red plush and gilt restored through superhuman efforts on behalf of the staff and volunteers. Though she saw a later performance of the sublime *Sleeping Beauty* with Fonteyn and Helpmann, Dorothy missed the gala night speculation about Glyndebourne's reopening and of Ben's new *Lucretia*, or she might have asked some questions. Lord Keynes died at Easter, on 21st April, and she mourned a friend as well as an ally who believed, as she did, in a liberal arts policy of 'arts for all' which had been expressed in his Arts Council's motto, 'The Best for the Most'. By this time she knew that Ben's friend and producer Eric Crozier had made a visit to Glyndebourne and become so enraptured with John Christie's plans for reopening on the grand scale that he had to stay overnight (borrowing a pair of Christie's capacious green silk pyjamas); the next morning saw the birth of the English Opera Group, with directors Crozier, Christie and Britten. The opening production was to be *The Rape of Lucretia* and, in an extra slight, it was to be managed by Rudolf Bing, to whom Dartington had given refuge with Frederick Ashton and the Vic-Wells Ballet at the start of the war.

In public she withdrew gracefully – 'Glyndebourne can obviously provide greater facilities and considerably more prestige' (which sounded like Leonard) – but privately Dorothy had never missed Chris

Martin more. Eric Crozier came to see Cicely Martin, and Peter Cox took him over to Leonard and Dorothy who 'listened graciously and seemed on the surface to accept the situation'. Next morning Dorothy summoned Peter Cox, saying, 'Please tell Ben that I am withdrawing my offer for this scheme but will be happy to discuss with him any alternative project he likes to propose.' Cox saw Ben and Peter in London, and was met with 'implacable hostility'.[337]

The affair of *Lucretia* (another maltreated woman) found Dorothy in a quandary: should she not have given way? Long ago, before Glyndebourne's first season, she and John and Audrey Christie had agreed that they were doing very different things, but had the territories become confused? She invited the Christies to Upper Brook Street, perhaps to apologise for the 'muddle', perhaps to tell them how much she loved Glyndebourne and to wish them the very best for their reopening. She went to some lengths, and had to steel herself, to see Anne Wood, the former BBC singer who was managing English Opera, and found her 'very understanding of the difficulties created by these emotionally erratic and unpredictable artists'. She relented and agreed that her 'original pledge would hold good, under the present circumstances' so that *Lucretia* would get her backing, but she could not consent to join the Opera Board (just as she had declined the Arts Council). She was pleased that English Opera had a promise of £3,000 from the Arts Council and 'that a number of eminent people are obviously deeply impressed' but of course she could not give Dartington's money to the lavish and elitist Glyndebourne in future.[338]

Her puzzlement went beyond the opera. She had visited Toynbee Hall and her old friend Albert Mansbridge, pleased to find an increase in government funding for his WEA, but disappointed at the talk of post-war apathy, that people were 'glad to sit at home' rather than pursue outside interests. The Arts Council's first motto 'The Best for the Most' had to be scrapped as it quickly became clear that the heirs of the new Socialist landslide Britain did not want 'high culture', opera and ballet at any price.[339] As she sat surrounded by the red plush and gilt of Covent Garden, did the voice of Jane Addams whisper in her ear that there was 'a crucial distinction between doing good *to or for* people and doing good *with* them'? She wrote to Peter Cox who had borne the brunt of all the ill tempers, thanking heaven for his moral courage: 'I love to see the way you face things out and tell people the truth and never shirk the unpleasant things that have to be said – it's a grand quality.'

Michael Straight had managed to get passages home for Miss Jefferies, Ruth, Dorcas and Eloise and they all arrived on 3rd May, a Friday. Driving across the New Forest and through Dorset to Exeter and Dartington was an emotional journeying according to Michael, seeing 'England green and beautiful and come through'. Dorothy had arranged for Miss Jefferies to have a house of her own, where Dorcas Edwards and Eloise Elmhirst would live in her care while finishing their schooling. It was Ruth Elmhirst who had the most difficult homecoming. She was now twenty and had spent her seven most formative years in America; she was very musical, and at Sarah Lawrence College she had studied with the composer William Schuman, a brilliant beginner in the world of Copland and Barber, and something of an idol to the college girls. Ruth's holidays were mostly spent with Biddy at Ridgefield among Biddy's Actors Studio familiars including Lee Strasberg, Marilyn Monroe and Marlon Brando, and Ruth had been romancing with the still hirsute Yul Brynner. Devon, Dorothy feared, would seem very tame.[340]

After seeing Glyndebourne's opening *Lucretia*, redeemed for Dorothy by the singing of the young Kathleen Ferrier, and going on to Leeds Castle, where Olive Baillie's daughter and Dorothy's great-niece Susan Winn married Geoffrey Russell, the summer melted into pleasantries. In late July she went to London to try a new travel experience, leaving on the 26th from the Victoria Terminal on a swish coach for the new Heathrow Airport. She was with Biddy for her 2nd August birthday, her thirty-second, and spent most of her time getting to know her grandson Willard Dolivet, whom she quickly came to adore. Louis Dolivet was working for the United Nations in New York, and had just published a *Handbook on the New World Organization*, describing the structures and purposes of the leviathan body of fifty-one states.

She was relieved to see that the book demonstrated his considerable ingenuity and charm in earning the confidence of the highest officials, and carrying him behind the scenes of the Secretariat, the Security Council and the International Court of Justice.[341] Unfortunately the handbook no sooner appeared than the 'New World Organization' found itself wrestling with the fragmenting Middle East and the 'iron curtain' coming down across eastern Europe. Louis now wanted his mother-in-law's backing for his *United Nations World magazine*, his presentation of UN current affairs to a still mystified public.

As soon as she finished talking with Louis she moved to Old Westbury and a day with 'Mike and I alone', undoubtedly talking politics for part of the time. Some of her concerns at the loss of FDR must have been grounded in the unknown abilities of the 'failed haberdasher' now President Truman as the leader of the free world. Truman's work on civil rights legislation, a cause she had supported for more than thirty years, encouraged her and now she heard from Michael that their friend Henry Wallace was to lead the Progressive challenge in the 1948 campaign. Some light relief came with Leonard's arrival for a short holiday, and then a concert at Tanglewood, tea at Willard Straight Hall, a meeting with Bruce Bliven and Irving Berlin's *Annie Get Your Gun* on Broadway were fitted in before their flight home.

Mary 'Mamma' Elmhirst died on Sunday 6th October and they went north for the funeral on the Tuesday. In the afternoon Dorothy noted 'a ploughing match', undoubtedly long planned but not unsympathetic as a tribute gathering in the memory of a countrywoman. Back at Dartington Peter Cox introduced Dorothy to Clifford Ellis of Bath School of Art, who along with Elmslie Philip, the director of Education for Devon, offered their approval of the mix of artistic practice and teaching that she and Peter hoped to continue at Dartington. Dorothy had asked Frances Hodgkin and Sven Berlin to become resident artists but they had declined. Once again when things were not quite as she hoped she turned to 'a new beginning' at something she could control, becoming increasingly engrossed in preparations for her Thursday evening Shakespeare classes. These were originally started to give the music students the context for many of their song settings, but they grew in popular appeal and were now open to all. The musician John Wellingham remembers how highly organised she was at allotting roles and plotting the scenes. The students read their parts with strict observance to Shakespeare's texts, and acted out the movements, much as in theatrical rehearsals though without any costumes or an end performance. These were intense two-hour sessions held in her house, with Thomas serving tea to the exhausted players afterwards, while Dorothy conducted the debriefing discussions. She was adapting things she had learned from Mischa Chekhov, that the words, phrasings, intonations and meanings were paramount, they were the keys to the characters and events, whereas the scenery and stagecraft were optional overlays. She read the newspaper critics, looked out for interesting productions and her timing was perfect, for she caught Peter Brooke's *Love's Labour's Lost* at the Memorial Theatre at Stratford-upon-Avon, and discovered a lasting joy.[342] The extravagant pre-war film *Mutiny on the Bounty*, starring Clark Gable and Charles Laughton, and Tom Eliot's play *The Family Reunion* gave her pleasurable autumn evenings, then it was time for the Christmas tree, carol singing and the other festivities of 'our Christmas' at home.

Dorothy had seen little of Whitney, but she had had lots of quiet talks with Daphne. He had come out of the RAF garlanded with medals for a brilliant flyer's war, one of the surviving heroic 'Few', and a stranger to the grim greyness of austerity London. He decided to study for his Commercial Pilot's B Licence, an arduous business, and finding that his friend, the Spitfire flyer and ferry pilot Diana Barnato Walker, had the same ambition they agreed to share an instructor. As Diana later wrote, because of the bitterly cold weather they also shared her mother's house in Tite Street, Chelsea, where there was prized central heating, which inevitably led to what Diana called their 'wonderful friendship'.[343]

The Chalet at Portwrinkle had been returned from the Ministry of Defence, and so the family were there again for the New Year, of

1947, with a new face in the party, Ruth's beau Maurice Ash, a friend of Michael Young's from the LSE. William Elmhirst, who had been learning letterpress printing and bookbinding under Charles Inman at Dartington, was due for his National Service but decided that he would rather be a 'Bevin Boy' and go down the mines; he was to work at Betteshanger Colliery in Kent, and live in lodgings at Deal. Dorothy's sixtieth birthday was approaching, and by then that notorious winter had set in, recorded in her *Garden Notebook*:

> January – returned from London at 2 a.m. in the midst of an American blizzard. Today in walking about the snow came above my Wellingtons. And yet the air is warm – that devastating east wind has ceased to blow. Papers say this is the coldest spell for 60 years or so. We've been feeding the birds – would we could do the same for our tender trees and shrubs.

Percy Cane managed his January visit, and on 6th February the Princess Royal and Lord Harewood, undaunted, arrived for tea. 'February – four days of deep snow – food brought up by sledge – no cars, no buses, only Joe Maitland's van to do the essentials. Floods in the house at 3 a.m.'

Dorothy was closeted with her typewriter, reporting to Peter Cox, who was in America. They were planning a memorial to Christopher Martin and the previous autumn Dorothy had seen and bought Henry Moore's bronze maquette *Reclining Figure* from the Leicester Galleries, and Peter had arranged with Moore for the large figure to be installed. They had chosen the site at the top of Cane's steps, though at a discreet distance, and in dappled shade. 'I've had a good talk, by the way, with Henry Moore, and everything is going ahead rapidly,' Dorothy now told Peter. 'Bill Foote is making the concrete foundation and Mr Miller in the sawmill is producing the wooden pedestal – and soon, very soon, we shall be ready to receive the figure – but actually we should wait, I think, till you return.' She continued:

Have you been reading about our difficulties here?...
there's a sense of crisis not unlike certain periods of the
war – and we all rush to the wireless for the latest news...
At present [15th February] though the snow is gone, there
is a kind of paralysing blight of cold lying on the land,
that dead grey stillness that penetrates everything and
reduces activity to a low ebb. And all these poor people,
with dwindling fuel supplies, with blackouts and shut-
downs, with two million out of work and possibly more
drastic measures to come are enduring hardships that one
imagined could not recur once the war was over – but
once again Dartington is favoured beyond all deserving,
for, being outside the main current of life, we escape the
cruellest blows of fortune.[344]

The winter clung on, but immediately before Easter, on the first
weekend in April she was diverted as 'Mike arrives'. On Easter Day after
church she was at her typewriter because Michael wanted schedules
and notes typed for Henry Wallace's imminent arrival on a speaking
tour. Together they caught the London train on Easter Monday, and
saw Carol Reed's film *Odd Man Out*, starring James Mason. Wallace
arrived the next day, she gave a lunch for him on the Wednesday, they
all went to a reception at the Savoy on Thursday, and Wallace spoke
at Central Hall in Westminster on the Friday. On Saturday Michael
and Wallace headed north for Manchester, and Dorothy escaped to
Stratford-upon-Avon.

Michael was so like his father, with all Willard's vivacity and
kindness to others which made him so endearing, and also Willard's
impetuosity and flow of ideas which she now found exhausting. Henry
Wallace, an amiable farmer at heart, pacifist, radical and somewhat
mystical, qualities which meant he had been ousted from the vice-
presidency in favour of Harry Truman just in case FDR died, now
found himself at odds with Truman in office, and sacked by him.

TWELVE: 'THE HASTING DAY'

Michael had played some part in persuading Wallace that he might revive a Progressive Party, with an idea that *The New Republic* – also in need of a revival – should be his vehicle. Wallace was to be installed as puppet editor, with Dorothy coaxing agreement from the mild-mannered Bruce Bliven, and Michael as his ghost-writer. Later Bliven revealed that Michael – putting Wallace's face, or half of it, on the cover – wanted to make *The New Republic* into a liberal version of the semi-glossy *Time* magazine, but it soon became clear that the readers wanted to keep their old highbrow version printed on 'butcher paper' and written by journalists they knew. Notwithstanding, the candidate and his backer, with his mother's money, were sounding out views on Progressivism in Europe to relay to Americans at home.[345]

In late spring Henry Moore's *Reclining Figure* arrived – 'in a tatty old lorry with an old man and a boy' – and Peter Cox watched with some amazement as they levered the giant figure into place using old railways sleepers. 'She' seemed immediately at home and everyone was pleased. Moore wrote:

> I tried to make a figure which could rightly be called a memorial figure. I wanted the figure to have a quiet stillness and a sense of permanence as though it could stay there for ever to have strength and seriousness in its effect and yet be serene and happy and resolved, as though it had come to terms with the world, and could get over the largest cares and losses.[346]

With the Third Programme restored to life Dorothy finds new radio joys. *Love's Labour's Lost* is broadcast in April, and *Macbeth* on 1st May, and then as if to recompense for that dreadful winter, the summer's pleasures: the Chelsea Flower Show, her grand-daughter Camilla for the holidays, Rodgers and Hammerstein's *Oklahoma!*, a trip to Glyndebourne and on to Sissinghurst, then to see William at Deal and explore Walmer and Sandwich. Another magical tour takes her to Stratford via Hidcote Manor garden, coming home via Westonbirt, which she finds it impossible to pass by. In late June she makes a diary note, 'Biddy must not finance *United Nations World*', and when Biddy arrives there is a harrowing trip to the London lawyers where they are told that Louis Dolivet is not Louis at all, his real name is Ludovic Brecher and he was already married before he met Biddy. Dorothy does not record her reaction – they cheer themselves with Flanagan and Allen and The Crazy Gang at the Victoria Palace Theatre immediately after the news, and as little Willard is her chief concern she hopes Biddy will not do anything in a hurry.

Family affairs take over her life. The young people come and go through August at the Chalet or at home where Leonard is preparing for his International Conference of Agricultural Economists, a biennial affair which he now regards as his most important venture, and which runs from late August into early September. They go with Ruth to meet Maurice's parents, Mr and Mrs Gilbert Ash, for lunch in London, seeing Donagh MacDonagh's *Happy as Larry* afterwards. On 6th November they have a family lunch for Whitney's thirty-fifth birthday, and Ruth and Maurice are married the following day, with dinner at the Connaught in the evening. About a week later Dorothy leaves for New York and Old Westbury where they celebrate little Willard's third birthday on 25th November and she has 'a talk with Louis and Biddy at midnight'. For Thanksgiving on the 27th Michael and Belinda and their children arrive, and they 'rescue hemlocks' in the now sad and declining garden. She has to give a lunch at *The New Republic* where Henry Wallace is still the figurehead but disaster looms as the American Communist Party are giving him 'bear hugs' for his pro-Russian opinions, which even the Progressives won't like. A session with Miss Evison, Anna Bogue's successor at the William Collins Whitney Foundation, is her last duty; the Foundation's work continues but now the annual distribution is about $55,000 a year. She has adopted a policy of always leaving on a high note, and this time it is the young Marlon Brando in Elia Kazan's *A Streetcar Named Desire* who is the toast of Broadway, then seeing Ethel Derby and the Delanos before 'a wonderful flight' home, to be met by Whitney and

Daphne who take her out to dinner. Their daughter Camilla loves to be with her grandmother for the holidays, so it is a united 'our Christmas' that ends the year.

For the New Year of 1948 the Chalet sports a new telephone, but Dorothy spends a great deal of time in bed. Biddy arrives in mid-January, presumably to disentangle herself from Louis/Ludovic with her mother's help. Three days later William comes home from the coalmine at Betteshanger, released because months underground have badly affected his lungs; he will work on one of the Dartington farms. He is nineteen at the end of February – the age at which Dorothy made her debut – so she arranges a significant 'Birthday Cake'. Arthur Waley and Beryl de Zoete are her most frequent visitors; some of their Bloomsbury friends dubbed them professional weekenders, but Dorothy is so different, loyally uncritical, and she unearths her memories of China for Arthur (who has never been there) and loves Beryl's tales of the dance. It is the coming of spring that really cheers her, her garden is the best medicine: 'April – a dream of beauty – the 8 Tai Hakus on the White Hart lawn. They really are something quite apart – even more wonderful than [*Prunus x*] yedoensis.'

The 'Tai Haku', the Japanese Great White Cherry is the newest and best for English gardens, and these had been planted on the advice of her gardening friend, the painter Will Arnold-Forster.[347] Dorothy also sees the more subtle effects:

> I realized yesterday that it is shadows which add so much
> to the beauty of everything. Now that the beech leaves are
> out the trees are beginning to cast shadows – and it gives
> immediately a kind of variety and subtlety and mystery to
> the whole scene. I think this must be the perfect moment
> – just when the beeches burst into leaf.

Percy Cane, still a regular as her garden guru, would have been pleased with that. After the beech and cherry blossom, the rhododendrons were her joy. She and Leonard (or was it Will Arnold-Forster?) snatched an April weekend in Cornwall to see them in their glory at Penjerrick and Carclew and other gardens. On 1st May a jaunt the other way, to see the Stevensons' collection of rhododendron species at Tower Court, Ascot, and on to Wisley, where many of the Hooker hybrids have come to rest. Garden open day at Dartington was 15th May, which became a regular fixture. At the end of May she flies to New York, where Biddy is waiting to take her to see her Broadway play *The Heiress* and meet the new man in her life, Peter Cookson who is playing the romantic lead, the part played in the film by Montgomery Clift. Daisy Harriman comes to tea – they must have much to talk about as they cannot have met for years. Daisy was America's heroic Minister in Norway at the start of the war and now – at seventy-eight – she has a high profile as a Democratic campaigner. Or perhaps it is Dorothy campaigning on behalf of Michael, as Henry Wallace is leading the nominations as the Progressive on the Democratic Party ticket and some months of expensive campaigning loom. Michael's wife Belinda is ill with tuberculosis and in hospital and so Dorothy plays grandmother-in-chief to their sons David and Mikey as well. With Belinda recovering she leaves at the end of June, with hardly time to draw breath before a crowded musical month at Dartington, with Imogen Holst's production of Britten's *Rejoice in the Lamb* and the summer school for string players. Dorothy sees Donald Sinden as Hamlet in London, making no comment, and David Lean's film of *Oliver Twist*. The Bristol Old Vic Theatre School's performance of J.B. Priestley's *Time and the Conways* appears in her diary, perhaps as a treat after Dorcas Edwards's interview at medical school, or possibly because William has expressed an interest in drama school? In America, Henry Wallace is acclaimed in Philadelphia as the Progressive Democratic candidate – is Michael Straight in line for political office at last?

After an August trip to Paris she comes home exhausted and retires to the Chalet. Leonard's father Papa Elmhirst 'died this a.m.' on 6th September, so they go north for the funeral on Wednesday 8th. The following week Ruth and Maurice leave Heathrow; they are to spend a year in America while Maurice studies at Yale; Ruth is expecting her first child so Dorothy makes a mental note that she will have to fly over early next year. With all, or most, of her children occupied elsewhere she gives herself over to William Shakespeare, seeing in quick succession *Othello*, *The Winter's Tale*, *Hamlet* and *The Merchant of Venice*. This is Sir Barry Jackson's second and last year as director at Stratford and they are lively productions, Robert Helpmann's gaunt if not emaciated Hamlet lounging against Ophelia's enormous crinoline, and Anthony Quayle and Paul Scofield vying for mastery in *Othello* with the young Claire Bloom as Desdemona. This season confirms Dorothy's preference for seeing her Shakespeare in Stratford, where she is well attuned to Elizabeth Scott's modern Memorial Theatre and she enjoys variations in sets and costumes as long as the language is given the priority.

Britain cheered up a little in 1948 with the Wembley Olympic Games, which do not feature in Dorothy's diary, and the trumpeting, or perhaps modest piping, for the Festival of Britain planned for three years hence. This rising mood among the young and younger meant that the life of many a sixty-something, grey-haired grandmother became subsumed into her family's desires and activities and Dorothy was no exception. Her days become filled with pleasing one or another of those closest to her: it is a more subtle sort of sacrifice than in earlier years but it is unending, and even insidious as she is deluded by love and duty – or convenience – into squandering her naturally fading energies.

Shakespeare and her garden, rare moments of luxury at Elizabeth Arden's salon in Mayfair and more frequent sessions with Irene Champernowne at the Withymead Centre are about all she has for herself. Her motherly loyalty to Dorcas Edwards and Eloise Elmhirst is unfailing; Dorcas begins her medical studies at Bristol in September, Dorothy will be there whenever a mother is required and Dorcas always comes home for her holidays; Eloise, known as 'El', well and truly abandoned by her father Richard Elmhirst, who found it necessary to become an American citizen and serve in the Pacific war, is studying agriculture at Moulton College at Northampton. Dorothy drives to and fro in all weathers to Northampton, and then to remote farms in Lincolnshire and Yorkshire where Eloise is working. Richard, 'Richie', has come home (with a citation for bravery at the Battle of Iwo Jima) and settled in deepest Scotland to run farm holidays for city children with his new wife Morna Haggard. Later in that September Leonard arrives home most probably from India, as his return is closely followed by visits from Dr Mukherjee, director of the Indian Agricultural Research Institute and his son Santos, and a few days later the dancer Uday Shankar, the brother of the sitar-playing Ravi.[348] Leonard, who is fifty-five now, has been away a great deal and busier than ever as the current president of the Royal Forestry Society along with all his other duties, which now include a place on the organising committee for the Festival of Britain. On 10th October Dorothy notes 'a quiet Sunday with Jerry' as a rarity.

When Sir Miles Thomas had joined BOAC earlier in that year he had written of finding that the chief executive at Stratton House in Piccadilly was 'a dynamic, well-nourished enthusiast' named Whitney Straight.[349] Whitney's trajectory in the airline and aero-engine business was only ever upwards from now on; his gallant war and his skill at driving very fast cars, along with his bonhomie made him immensely popular in international business and political circles, circles which held no charms for his mother. Dorothy's policy over his affair with Diana Barnato Walker was to listen sympathetically when she was needed; Whitney and Diana's son Barney Walker had been born in the spring of 1947 and when she met him as a toddler he was immediately enfolded into her affections.

In November President Truman achieved a miraculous re-election, overcoming all his rivals, and the beaten Henry Wallace retired to his farm in South Salem to work on poultry genetics. Michael and Belinda are busy restoring their Green Spring Farm in Virginia, Michael plans to write novels, and he is moving *The New Republic* and its profitable stable-mate *Antiques* to new homes in Washington, and disposing of his father's *Asia* magazine and one called *Theatre Arts* in the process.

Dorothy's year ends quietly with 'Jerry', as she notes in her *Garden Notebook* for December:

> J and I saw, in the light of the moon, the cherry *[Prunus] subhirtella autumnalis* in its fragile delicate bloom. These moonlight nights have been quite unearthly – absolute stillness. Mild softness in the air – and the white roof of the Barn Theatre glistening like snow.

Leonard, now her adored 'Jerry', speaking at
The Withymead Centre

Dartington at least is in 'such a state of harmony' as she has never known; is it the load slipping from her shoulders? Dr Bill Slater, their original managing director, has retired and Peter Sutcliffe has succeeded him, 'a great success'. Her pet Estates Committee, made up of representatives from all departments of Dartington life, is taking over executive responsibilities, 'all pointing in the direction of decentralizing controls'. The whole is becoming a federation of individual departments, a miniature of the United States of America.[350]

THIRTEEN: THE TIME
OF FEW FLOWERS

We die
As your hours do, and dry
Away
Like to the summer's rain;
Or as the pearls of morning's dew;
Ne'er to be found again.[351]

February of 1949 found her in chilly New York to meet Michael, who whisked her off to Jamaica in a rather touching attempt to entertain her by visiting his and Whitney's friend from the 1930s, Ian Fleming, and Fleming's new neighbour Noël Coward. They had St Valentine's Day drinks at Coward's newly built villa Blue Harbour; he and Graham Payn were only ten days into their first visit to the completed house and were still in raptures over the view from their veranda, Coward admitting to almost bursting 'into tears of sheer pleasure'. They all went rafting on the Rio Grande, with Fleming and his lover Ann Rothermere, gliding downstream between hills 'befeathered with bamboo and bright with flowers' (the description is Fleming's) on the narrow wooden rafts made for carrying bananas down to Port Antonio. The trip took several hours, stopping for fishing and swimming, an 'enchantingly languid... elegant and delicately romantic adventure' (Fleming again).[352] Dorothy enjoyed the rafting, and a cycle ride the next day, and she just made it back to New York in time for the birth of Ruth's daughter, Kathryn, on 20th February. She remained till the end of March, helping Ruth, seeing little Willard Dolivet to his first school – Biddy was in Baltimore with *The Heiress* – and seeing for herself Arthur Miller's *Death of a Salesman*, just opened on Broadway.

All the programmes for the 1949 Stratford Shakespeare Festival are in her collection – it is a satisfying 'company' year with Quayle, Gielgud, Godfrey Tearle and Tyrone Guthrie boxing and coxing at directing and acting – *Macbeth, Much Ado, A Midsummer Night's Dream, Cymbeline, Othello* and the little known *Henry VIII* – with the younger Jill Bennett, Robert Hardy and Harry Andrews. She manages to see them all during the summer before the big event of the year, when she and Leonard and William set out in their pre-war big black Ford V8 – lunching at Lyme Regis, dining at Petworth – for Newhaven and the car ferry to France. They make purposeful progress via Chartres and Dijon, arriving in Stresa on Lake Maggiore for Leonard to make his opening speech to his International Conference of Agricultural Economists on 20th August. The conference drones on for eight days, too much for Dorothy and in a mood to clash with her romantic memories of the lake and Isola Bella, though she says nothing of this, and so she and William divert to looking at her favourite churches in Verona, Padua and Venice. Dorothy encounters the Spenders, Stephen and Natasha, briefly in Venice.[353] The long drive back through France evokes more memories than she cares to dwell on, nor speak of, and ends in a rough Channel crossing. More memories surface with the news of the death of Almeric Paget, her much-loved brother-in-law, and to avoid the jealousies between her two families which arise in these situations she goes to stay with Whitney and Daphne for the funeral.

Ruth, Maurice and the infant Kathryn had come home from America in the summer, staying for a while at Dartington before they decided to buy a farm in north Essex. It was no secret that Ruth wanted to be well away from the influence of Dartington, but now the journey from Devon to Essex and back again all along tiresome A-roads becomes part of Dorothy's life. She is deeply aware that Ruth feels the least valued in her mother's affections and so perhaps the journeying is a kind of penance, as Dorothy takes charge of Kathryn for long stays while Ruth is engrossed in the restoration of her house. The rewards are that little Kathryn and her grandmother become the best of friends, and Ruth has a beautiful home. Maurice too is discreet, as witnessed in the architect of Harlow New Town, Sir Frederick Gibberd's gleeful account of the birth of the Harlow Art Trust:

> A stranger called, asked to see the General Manager, and in the course of their conversation suggested that he might show him and his wife round the town. It turned out that the stranger was Maurice Ash – at that time living close to Harlow and having business interests in the town – [and he] suggested that a substantial sum might be provided by the Elmgrant Trust to launch a scheme for providing art for the town.[354]

Maurice had also suggested Sir Philip Hendy, director of the National Gallery and now married to Cicely Martin, as the chairman, and Henry Moore, who lived at nearby Much Hadham, as a supporter of the Harlow scheme, connections that Maurice had acquired directly from Dorothy. Maurice's 'business interests' were connected to his father, the contractor Gilbert Ash, who was to build Gibberd's butterfly-shaped, nine-storey 'tower' block, The Lawn, cleverly set in the midst of seven great oak trees on the edge of Mark Hall North neighbourhood housing in Harlow.

On a chilly Tuesday in mid-January, 1950, Whitney sees Dorothy off from Heathrow – is this purely chivalry or is there an edge to their talk as he ushers her through his company's VIP lounge? Whitney is concerned about the amount of family money that Michael has spent on the Wallace campaign and on moving *The New Republic* operation to Washington and he wants the American family trust broken so that Michael is no longer in control. Dorothy's trip is mostly taken up with her first visit to Michael and Belinda's Green Spring Farm in Fairfax County, northern Virginia. The farm dates from the settling of Tidewater Virginia in good King George III's golden days, a pretty colonial house with a smallholding, where Beatrix Farrand had been working on the garden.[355] Leonard joins her for a week and together they break the news to editor Bruce Bliven that they intend to find a buyer for *The New Republic*, and then they visit the family's attorney Milton Rose for advice about trusts for Dorothy's grandchildren. She has to face up to losing the last remnants of her American life, but she says nothing, and finds comfort in looking after Willard Dolivet while Biddy is engrossed in rehearsals.

They are home in time for the General Election on Thursday 23rd February, a dispiriting affair. Labour won with 315 seats to 298 for the Conservatives, resulting in the narrowest of working majorities, and prompting Harold Nicolson to comment ruefully of his former colleagues that 'they cannot carry on with a Socialist policy when it is now clear that the country dislikes it'. It was Labour's obsession with the nationalisation of steel and other industries and utilities that 'the country' was wary of, an obsession that seemed to elevate dogma above simple human needs. Dorothy's only notes on her feelings about the politics of this time are in an orange-covered notebook, made as she sat at the back of a seminar chaired by Sir Stafford Cripps (with whom Leonard had been to India): 'young people don't know the Labour Party', 'a tension exists between the trades unions and the Party', 'Labour has no principles, only tactics and no future' and the shop floor had no use for the Trades Unions Council where 'only activists and communists had voices'.[356] These were needle-pricks to the heart of one who had supported and believed in trade unions for forty years, since she had marched down Fifth Avenue with their demands for improvements to factory working conditions. Her precious ideal of unions seemed hijacked by vandals in mid-twentieth-century Britain. Labour's lack of principles – and worse, 'a void where there are no morals or faiths or loves' – was bound up in Aneurin Bevan's mantra that 'steel represented the culmination of phase one of Labour Rule' and that if they blenched or held back on nationalisation 'Labour would lose its very soul'.[357]

The orange-covered notebook suggests that Labour is losing Dorothy, and though she says no more, her disillusion can be plotted through Michael Young's actions. Young, no longer her 'Youngster' but in his mid-thirties and author of this, his second election-winning manifesto for Labour, had 'slipped in' one piece of creative thinking concerning another of her favourite causes, 'a commitment to introduce a consumer advisory service' and he added that 'no one on the National Executive Committee made anything of it'. A month after the election Young spoke to the Fabians of the Socialist way of life as a 'brotherhood', with the basis in family life, a family supported against disruption 'under the impact of modern forces', and of restoring 'a sense of community' for those living in cities.[358] This surely reflected his upbringing at Dartington, drawn into Dorothy's fold, and he remained close to her; he was a Dartington trustee, and the name of his political friend the 'rising star' Anthony Crosland appears in her diary. Young became disillusioned, nothing was done about consumer rights and the testing of products, he left the research office in the summer and later in the year he set off on a world tour. Dorothy's sympathies for Socialism in Britain seemed to leave with him.

On the Sunday after the election there had been a celebration for William's twenty-first birthday. He was still undecided about a career and although none of Dorothy's children had any need to work idleness was not an option. William had grown up in the shadows of his dynamic half-brothers, let alone the brilliant 'Youngster', and undoubtedly his months at Betteshanger Colliery had left their mark on this privileged but neither academic nor overly confident young man. He was in London and undergoing Freudian analysis, this at the suggestion of Michael's wife Belinda who was in analysis herself as a process in her qualification as a child psychologist. Dorothy admired Belinda's work, and she felt equally proud of William's courage in his search for self-knowledge, but she did not tell them of her own talks with her Jungian therapist Irene Champernowne at Withymead, which were carried on quietly beneath the financial patronage that she and Leonard gave to the work of the clinic and its staff.[359]

Early in May, on a Monday, she went for tea to Diana Walker's house in Chelsea for her first meeting with her grandson Barney Walker. Stephen and Natasha Spender's daughter Lizzie was born later in the month, and as something of a surprise – their meeting in Venice had marked (almost) the moment of Lizzie's conception – Dorothy was added to the list of Lizzie's godparents, with Elizabeth Bowen, Laurens van der Post, Muriel Gardiner Buttinger and Lucille Curzon.[360] For Leonard's birthday on 6th June, Imogen Holst and her students gave a first performance of Britten's setting of *Five Flower Songs*, singing on the lawn outside the open windows. The *Songs* were commissioned by Ruth as a Silver Wedding present to her parents – Maurice Ash had been at Gresham's at Holt at the same time as Britten (and Donald Maclean).[361]

In America at the end of June President Truman ordered his troops to defend South Korea from attack from the north, the consequences unimagined, but neither disturbing Dorothy's summer. Michael arrived with his son David sporting a complete cowboy outfit, with Stetson and studded boots, which astonished everyone; the cowboy went to the Chalet with his grandmother while Michael spent a week in London. For the second year running he attended the Apostles' dinner to meet his old Cambridge friends, the usual purpose of old boy dinners. It would have been in character for him to want to tell them how he had stood up to the House Un-American Activities Committee's questioning about his well-known liberal views and connections to Henry Wallace. The HUAC did not count Cambridge in the 1930s, nor had he enlightened them. Dorothy was completely sympathetic over the hated HUAC.

Dartington's busy summer was dominated by the *Made in Devon* exhibition for which Peter Cox and his colleagues collected from over seventy lenders, objects ranging from Plymouth porcelain to traditional edging-tools; the more unusual being violins by Arthur Richardson of

Crediton, cow blankets intended for New Zealand farms, each farm with its own design, the botanical drawings (as yet unpublished) of the Rev. William Keble Martin's Devon wild flowers, and books from Charles McNally's Dartington bindery.[362] *Made in Devon* ran for five weeks attracting eleven thousand visitors; as it was a local foretaste of the national 1951 Festival of Britain Leonard gave Herbert Morrison a conducted tour, and it was opened by Dorothy's friend of thirty years, Albert Mansbridge.

Their August holiday was a tour – via Stratford (*Julius Caesar*, *Measure for Measure* and *King Lear*), Southwell Minster, Eloise at her farm in Lincolnshire, the Hull ferry and Durham – to Edinburgh where they were the guests of Gerald Barry, director-general of the Festival of Britain. They heard Elisabeth Schwarzkopf's recital on her first appearance in Edinburgh, saw Thomas Beecham conducting *Ariadne auf Naxos* and lunched with Hans and Cissy Oppenheim, who now lived in Scotland. They arrived home in time for the start of 'Johnny' Johnson's Gardening Course, now an annual feature in her diary, followed by the PEP Executive and the Harvest Festival – then a few days in bed, which she now needed after every spell of intense activity. Her autumn was quiet, lots of Kathryn Ash, Barney Walker to tea in London, two days in November devoted to Whitney, and in early December she gave lunch to Ben Britten – a peace-making, and she had given him money for his opera *Albert Herring*. All was sweetness and light there now, but not elsewhere; she had dreaded the day when, as her own brothers' conflicting opinions had torn her family in half, Whitney and Michael would disagree, bitterly, and she feared that day had come, or would come in April when a family conference had been arranged. She had held at the back of her diary a tiny printed cutting of the words of John Donne:

> No man is an Island, entire of itself; every man is a piece
> of the Continent, a part of the main.

On 4th February 1951 Dartington gave a farewell concert for Imogen

Holst. Imogen's music making had more than fulfilled Dorothy's dream of enriching community life, the shyest of people had found a confident joy in singing under her direction and their harmonies had thrilled the old stones. But after eight years Imogen was exhausted. 'You will realise,' she confessed, 'that when one is always teaching amateurs and future professionals who are still immature, one needs to be constantly criticized on one's own music by someone who one knows is a better musician than oneself.' She had come to feel isolated, as for 'all the blessings of South Devon' there were not 'many musicians better than me at that time'. She moved to Aldeburgh as Britten's musical assistant, which was her idea of heaven.[363]

The spring conference was devoted to Victor Bonham-Carter and his book *The English Village*; he was appointed Dartington's official historian.[364] Immediately afterwards, in early April, the family conference convened, with Whitney, Biddy, Michael and their lawyer Milton Rose; both Leonard and William were in the house. Dorothy's presence was Lear-like, her court was held in her elm-panelled sitting room, vases of scented narcissi and blossom placed beside each comfortable chair, with her offspring making their entrances and exits in varying shades of temper. Whitney had forewarned her of his case and now he stated it forcefully; he was horrified at the huge sum given to Louis/Ludovic – whom he had met once, if that – for his United Nations magazine, he insisted that *The New Republic*'s drain on the family resources must cease, and he complained that the lawyers drawing up the new trust for Dorothy's grandchildren had not been fair to his daughter Camilla, who was the eldest.[365] His lawyers had suggested a figure to compensate him and to meet this it was inevitable that *The New Republic* had to be sold to Gilbert Harrison, and – as the real shock – Dorothy's home at Old Westbury, her home for all of her life and her father's legacy, had also to be sold. William Elmhirst, who was twenty-two at the time, remembers that he and his half-sister Biddy really wanted to save Old Westbury for their mother and themselves, but it was impossible.[366]

The meeting broke up, Whitney leaving immediately. There was an irony that her children's demands had really caused Dorothy's neglect of *The New Republic*; Bruce Bliven had written tactfully that her support had become 'impracticable' after Michael's Henry Wallace hiatus, that he was unwell himself and wished to retire, and that Michael was not equipped to be the editor.[367] Gilbert Harrison, impeccably liberal and a fighter for veterans' causes, was an excellent prospect; his wife-to-be Anita McCormick Blaine even more so, as she had financed the successor to Dewey's Laboratory School in Chicago and other educational causes that matched Dorothy's own. There was a small hitch in that they had to marry so that Anita's McCormick fortune could be used by Gilbert Harrison to buy the paper – shades of Dartington's history repeating.[368]

The business done, Dorothy set out to mend the rifts and hurt feelings; she met her grand-daughter Camilla, just home from school in Switzerland, for lunch in London, and then Daphne for tea. In a quiet moment, out of Camilla's hearing, Daphne may have told her mother-in-law that she was pregnant (after a gap of fifteen years), the confirmation of her and Whitney's mended marriage. Dorothy knew from her visits to Diana's house in Tite Street that Whitney's was a presence there, but she said nothing. Biddy had gone to Essex to see Ruth, who was not at the conference, and then home to America. For the rest, Michael, Leonard, Maurice Ash and Dorothy had their attentions diverted to the imminent opening of the Festival of Britain, and Leonard took them around the South Bank site.

On that misty and cold but thankfully dry Ascension Day morning Leonard and Dorothy were in their seats in St Paul's Cathedral by ten for the Festival Service. Dorothy does not say what she thought of the ceremonial gloriously restored, the aisles glittering with gold braid and mayoral chains, the well-polished Scouts and Guides, and the Royal Procession of Gentlemen-at-Arms, Yeomen Warders, Trumpeters and Heralds costumed as if on their way to the Red Queen's garden. Gerald Barry found it all 'richly moving'; they finished by singing 'Jerusalem' and then the National Anthem, but he and others quickly realised that this was not for ordinary mortals as the choir and the State

Trumpeters soared into the descant 'that seemed to shiver the fabric of the building'.[369] King George VI stood on the cathedral steps with Prime Minister Attlee, Winston Churchill and 'Lord Festival' Herbert Morrison, to declare the Festival open to a vast crowd that stretched as far as the eye could see. Then the glistening, jingling Household Cavalry reformed into the Royal Procession back to Buckingham Palace. In the evening Dorothy and Leonard were in the Festival Hall for the opening concert, another outburst of patriotism, 'Zadok the Priest', Arne's 'Rule Britannia', Elgar's 'Pomp and Circumstance No. 1', Vaughan Williams's 'Serenade to Music' and the 'Hallelujah Chorus'. The BBC commentator Audrey Russell thought it 'an evening of elation and exhilaration', and 'the quality of sound was astonishing' from the players of five symphony orchestras and the massed choirs, their words 'actually intelligible'.[370]

The next morning they were all out again for the King's opening of the South Bank Exhibition and the Pleasure Gardens; Dorothy found works by 'her' artists, Ben Nicholson, Barbara Hepworth and Henry Moore, taking centre-stage, and the sleek modern interior design that she had championed twenty years earlier had come into its own. The Festival earned no notebook, nor even comments in her diary, it was Leonard's stage as a council member, and she settled into her role as his consort.

A distant happy memory from forty-seven years before, if she was counting, surfaced at the end of term in July when Michael, Belinda and Camilla joined them for a motor tour to Paris, Évreux and Angers and Pyrénées-Atlantique; she noted cathedrals, crusader castles and Basque ballets. Back at home Dartington gave a party for the British Council, Stratford was in patriotic mode with the trilogy of *Henry IV, Parts 1 and 2* and *Henry V*, with noble performances from Harry Andrews and Michael Redgrave upstaged by the debut of Richard Burton as Prince Hal and Henry V. Dorothy visited Compton Wynyates and Charlecote with the Liddell Harts as Leonard was off to Chicago to prepare for his agricultural economists' conference. Winston Churchill was returned as Prime Minister on 26th October, and Dorothy left for New York the following day – purely a coincidence, though she was never a Churchill fan. At Old Westbury she spent days 'going through old trunks', this depressing task lightened by the presence of her grandson Willard Dolivet, whom she took to the Natural History Museum and on a visit to Cornell. Leonard joined them for Thanksgiving and Willard's birthday, his eighth, on 25th November.

Little can be said about the beginning of 1952 except to chronicle the events: Daphne gave birth to a daughter Amanda at the end of January, King George died at Sandringham a week later, Eloise Elmhirst was married to John Sharman on 9th February and they made their home in Northumberland; on the 15th the streets of London were draped in black for the King's funeral, the shuffling, slow-marching procession passing silent crowds in great contrast to the Festival opening of only ten months before; people were saddened by the loss of their wartime King, and fearful for the young woman who had to succeed him; Dorothy was no royal watcher but she was deeply sympathetic. And all the time she was dealing with the laborious transatlantic business of selling *The New Republic* and Old Westbury – endless letters, phone calls and trips to her London lawyers. The toll this was taking is partly revealed in a Good Friday letter she wrote to Irene Champernowne at Withymead, whom she had been seeing regularly throughout the winter: 'I realize with great joy that new life has come to me, and it has come from you – Easter will be for me a day of infinite gratitude for knowing you – and for being able, here and there, through my contact with you, to glimpse something of the Holy Spirit.'[371]

Easter was spent at the Chalet, and Amanda Straight was christened a few days later. Is Dorothy's 'new life' in part her acceptance, her faith, for she has become a regular at church, often at Rattery with the Bridgettine community at Syon Abbey? At Dartington the summer is musical, Leonard goes off to his Chicago conference in mid-August, Dorothy is left with *Coriolanus*, *Macbeth* and *The Tempest* at Stratford.[372] Then the blow falls, two words in her diary on Sunday, 7th September: 'Willard died'. Two words that opened the oldest of wounds, but struck anew with the sharpest sorrow; this time it was her darling grandson, whom she so loved, eight years old and drowned in a boating accident.[373] She flies off to New York to comfort Biddy, eventually coming home to her garden:

> December – Tremendous rain here – the English oaks still have their copper foliage and are wonderful with the sun shining through; a disaster has befallen Ghond [the mature Monterey pine] – two days ago Mr Johnson noticed a crack in the trunk, then last night on Christmas Eve, about 11 p.m. – Jerry and I, from the study, heard the fatal sound of its fall. Despite the rain Jerry went out with a lantern and found half the tree gone – no harm done to any other trees – these trees seem to know how to fall – but oh, it is crushing to lose so much of our noble Ghond.

In February she was airborne again, for the apparent completion of *The New Republic* and Old Westbury sales. Back home she religiously notes 'our Wedding' now on every 3rd April, but she seems to spend a great deal of time in bed, including at Easter. She is in London for the Queen's Coronation (in the crowd) and for Britten's *Gloriana* (in the audience) and a week later they show the film *A Queen is Crowned* at Dartington. Another week and it is Foundation Day, and then on 23rd June she notes the birth of Biddy's baby, a first son for her and Peter Cookson. A 'very dull' *Taming of the Shrew* at Stratford, a visit to Compton Verney, Peggy Cripps's wedding to her African lawyer Joe Appiah, Christopher Fry's *Ring Round the Moon*, Mr Cane in the garden, and visitors Robert and Mildred Woods Bliss from Dumbarton Oaks – this a first and last echo of Beatrix Farrand's hope that the Oaks and Dartington think of themselves as transatlantic fellows.[374] Gregory Peck and Audrey Hepburn in *Roman Holiday* begin her autumn delights, followed by Tom Eliot's *The Confidential Clerk* in London, *Antony and Cleopatra* and Redgrave's *King Lear* at Stratford, and the autumn colours at Westonbirt Arboretum on the way home. She made a special note of listening to the carols from King's College, Cambridge on Christmas Eve. Little Kathryn Ash and

Dorcas Edwards – the latter now triumphantly 'Dorcas, M.B., Ch.B.', as Dorothy notes – are there for the holiday.

Dorothy is sixty-seven in January 1954, and she needs her Dextrosol energy pills and more frequent rest days. Beside her favourite chair is a memorial volume of photographs of Biddy's beautiful little Willard. With *The New Republic* safely in Gilbert Harrison's hands, and Old Westbury gone, she hardly murmurs when the Park Avenue apartment is sold and she is reduced to being a guest in America. As Leonard usually goes to India in January she is free to visit Michael and Belinda in Virginia and catch up on the Washington political gossip, as she loved to do when she was young.

> May 1954 – Two really warm days – tea out of doors – cotton dress on – joyful! – this is the peak of the year when each day brings a deeper realization of beauty. The beeches – a maze of quivering green – as we sit on the Loggia and look through these screens of beech, one behind the other, as far as the eye can see.

1955 began with three weeks at Michael and Belinda's Green Spring Farm; she was back home when a month later, on Friday 18th February, her diary noted 'first attack', followed by a second two days later. Leonard was away, it had snowed and she forbade any fuss. Fortunately Peter Cox disobeyed and phoned William in London, who sped down to Devon bringing their friend Molly Underwood – and Dorothy later admitted that Molly's nursing her through her 'worst attack' on 28th February saved her life. Dorothy's diary did not fail – with her youthful enthusiasm she filled in her Line-A-Day 'as if her life depended on it', which it now probably did – as she kept herself aware of comings and goings. She attempted to get out of bed and promptly fainted, and on 14th March she was in Torbay Hospital under the care of the cardiologist Sir John Parkinson. Leonard who had come home, Michael who had flown over and Ruth and William were her only visitors.

From then on the small landmarks counted; 'up in chair' on 28th, 'up for lunch' on 31st, and 'first walk' on 1st April. A week later she was home for Easter, rejoicing in the 'first real spring day'. Her slow steps to recovery are reminiscent of 1924 and that earlier breakdown. Baths, three on consecutive days because they were an unbelievable luxury, were followed by 'dress today' on 21st April.[375] William, home from drama school, had been in constant attendance but now he had to leave. In her *Garden Notebook* for May she wrote: 'After three months of illness I am back in the garden sitting – with Jerry – everything so late this year that even today the beeches are only just in leaf, and as always they seem to be the great experience of Spring.'

For long weeks she was denied her own bedroom, which was up two flights of stairs, and she remained in her sick room beside the Courtyard, a revelation of Dartington's daily life, as she described to Peter Cox:

> I have come to feel the pulse of the Centre in quite a new
> way – watching people come and go all day long – hearing
> voices from my window, seeing the shadows on my ceiling
> of figures passing to and fro, waiting for the comforting
> sound of the old bell striking seven in the morning, and
> enjoying all the community services that start early in the
> day and continue till nightfall. It is wonderful to feel such
> a throbbing life in the Courtyard and, though inactive, to
> be able to take some part in it all.[376]

On Sunday, 22nd May, she walked to the summerhouse, but William had to bring her back in the wheelchair. She was recalled to life; she noted the election on 26th May, the Conservatives returned to power with Anthony Eden as Prime Minister, without comment; she made a brief appearance on a wet and cold Foundation Day on 11th June, and was able to return to her own bedroom at the end of July, her Courtyard life over. The Summer School of Music played beneath her windows in August, and on Mr Cane's visit she was able to catch up with the modifications to the Open Air Theatre; in mid-September Leonard gallantly escorted her to Stratford for *Twelfth Night*, *The Merry Wives of Windsor*, *Macbeth* and

All's Well That Ends Well, they came home via Oxford, seeing Daphne du Maurier's *September Tide* at the Playhouse, then a gentle drive through the Cotswolds. Mrs Nancy Lancaster came to lunch, a feather in the garden's cap, and then – in early October – 'I drove for the first time to meet Jerry, and worked in the garden'.[377] In a rather shaky hand she wrote at the back of her 1955 diary, 'In reverence and gratitude I should like to testify to all the loveliness that life has given me.'

Her doctors advised her to avoid the worst of the English winter and so in early 1956 she and Leonard made their first trip to Harbour Island in the Bahamas: 'this must be the loveliest of all coral islands in the world – a jade sea, a long white beach, hundreds of birds, perpetual sunshine and clear, warm starlight nights and peace – almost beyond understanding,' she wrote to Peter Cox. She was caught in the spell of their 'sweet little cottage', Alma their gentle maid, 'so much time to read', time to observe and time together; their chief sport was tempting the humming birds with pieces of fruit – 'we have such a good time'.[378] She had come to the end of a long series of partings and losses, and now here was Leonard, staying with her till the end. She learned to smile patiently through his slow-burning stories and oft-repeated jokes, even to love the repetitions. Of her many notebooks the most poignant is one marked 'For Jerry, something of what I have learned in this year of grace 1955'.

She wrote to William in good time for his twenty-seventh birthday at the end of February:

> It is strange how often you appear in my dreams as the person who saves me from some dire predicament. So often the situations are foolish and trivial – but always caused by anxiety – and almost always you are, somehow, there to pull me through. In my unconscious you must represent some sustaining and saving power – even as you do in my conscious mind. For it is always some kind of a miracle to me that Jerry and I should have a son who is so completely what we would want him to be – so perceptive

in feeling, and so wise and mature in thought – and so deeply true to himself.[379]

At Dartington the Foundation Day of 1957 was a day to remember – 'unbelievably warm, no wind but with soft airs' – and the medieval pageant which filled the new Open Air Theatre and the tiltyard was full of colour with lively caparisoned horses (their protruding legs revealing trousers and socks). 'Tremendous success,' noted Dorothy, adding with a touch of gardener's pride that her Sunny Border 'looks nice'.

William had graduated from LAMDA and joined the company at Stratford, playing his first part as Peter of Pomfret, the ill-fated harbinger of bad tidings in *King John*. That September Dorothy spent 'three heavenly days' staying at the Arden Hotel and meeting William when he was free; one afternoon they drove out of town and found a sunny place to sit while William read from *As You Like It*. She wrote to Leonard:

> I had never realised the startling beauty of certain lines and speeches until he brought them to life for me. He himself so completely absorbs Shakespeare's thought and meaning that it is like seeing something for the first time to hear him read and expound. It was a wonderful experience for me, full of revelation.[380]

William's acting was a surprise joy to his mother, a more delicate blooming than Biddy's unstoppable flowering in whatever role she played; William's father was perhaps less enthusiastic as he patiently endured the latest of the theatrical surprises that had erupted in their years of marriage ever since *Journey's End*.

For Dorothy her intense and knowledgeable relationship with Shakespeare was the last stand of her independence. The programmes from her Stratford seasons are all covered with her comments, scrawled in the low light of the intervals: Ralph Richardson's *Macbeth* made 'every word clear but he lacks distinction of speech', Anthony Quayle's Caius Martius was 'sincere but so lacking in style – his voice harsh, limited in range and unrhythmical'; that *Coriolanus* had 'too much shouting' and at least one member of the audience had her hands over her ears. That said, she enjoyed the scenery and costumes and came very near to being an ardent fan of the Motley threesome, theatrical designers Margaret and Sophie Harris and Elizabeth Montgomery.

She followed William through the 1958 season: he was the Sexton in the High Victorian *Much Ado About Nothing* and in the chorus for Peter Hall's Jacobean – all ruffs and satin breeches – *Twelfth Night*. He went to Russia with the company and remembers the smart young KGB agent with impeccable English who came to their Leningrad hotel, and how Guy Burgess came to see a rehearsal.[381] On their return there was talk of strike action among the spear carriers, which prompted William to leave for Scarborough and theatre in the round with Stephen Joseph and Alan Ayckbourn, where Dorothy saw some performances. She continued to seek out her Shakespeare; one of the last performances she saw was of Douglas Seale's Old Vic *King Lear*, 'which didn't seem like *Lear* at all' but was redeemed by Paul Daneman as the Fool – 'I could never watch anyone else while he was on the stage – he has a wonderful face – a kind of tragic mask that reflects every tiny shade of thought and feeling – and his movements and gestures have a kind of internal beauty and expressiveness that just wrings the heart.'[382]

To their friends, Leonard and Dorothy were still the 'kind, warm-hearted' Elmhirsts; they had known the Huxleys, Julian and Juliette, at least since the early 1930s and the founding of PEP. He was the same age as Dorothy, seventy-two, and had been knighted for his work with UNESCO, but now suffered bad bouts of depression. Juliette, who was Swiss and still very pretty, had bravely accomplished forty years of an adventurous marriage, but was now utterly miserable, and they came to Dartington, to a lodging in the Courtyard, for a month of peace. It was the late autumn of 1959 and Juliette's distress had clearly found a sympathetic listener in Leonard, who wrote:

My dear Juliette, I have, since you were here, been wanting to write to you about my own experience of living alongside persons with a strong sense of world-unity and mission, and so driven and confused by their imaginative tensions: these sometimes eliminate, almost entirely, from their field of consciousness the needs, hungers and feelings of those who, often at close quarters, try to serve and love – worship even; and yet, just at these moments when, like a faithful dog, they need a pat or a gesture, either draw an absolute blank or worse. In my own experience, and I have lived at close quarters with two world-conscious people in my time 'they know not what they do' – wrapped up in the world of their own imagination, locked-up in their contemplation of the universe; they can seem at moments as if they wanted to bite the helping hand they most need and even commit murder on the most sensitive part of one's devoted care and respect for them. They don't really mean it, and can be absolutely devastated when they discover of just what heinous crime they have been guilty – but it has somehow to be borne.

He ends by saying that in the world 'there simply are not more than a few of these far-reaching people at a time, and they are immensely precious'. (In 1924 when Dorothy was recovering from her breakdown he had told her 'that the world can't afford to lose you again and you know it'.) He sums up his own 'martyrdom': 'they need all we can give and be, to give of their best; and so through bitterness we learn, if possible without becoming bitter in return'.

Juliette Huxley was modestly conscious of her own effort, 'often a poor job, with nothing to boast about; only a sense that there was a next day and a new hope for halcyon times between the clouds'. She and her husband had fifteen more years together and with her support he wrote two volumes of distinguished memoirs.[383] Dorothy could never have known of Leonard's letter for it would surely have rocked the foundations of all that they had done. Juliette published the text as an epilogue to her own *Leaves of the Tulip Tree* memoir in 1986.[384]

In early 1960 Dorothy stayed with Michael and Belinda, as was now her habit, before she went on to Harbour Island; in her birthday letter to William she wrote of the 'happy days' with her grandchildren, the youngest her namesake Dorothy Straight aged two 'who has a way of bending down her head to be kissed which completely melted my heart'.[385] Michael's first novel *Carrington* was about to be published and he was politically on the inside track once more as a friend of the Kennedys and of the still influential Walter Lippmann. Lippmann gave a dinner party for Dorothy and invited 'about ten interesting people' that he thought she would like to meet, among them Senator Hubert Humphrey. In her report to William she wrote:

> After dinner we all gathered in a group and put questions
> to him, and I must say, I was very impressed by his sincerity
> and true liberal attitude. He is Michael's – and Walter's
> favourite candidate, but I'm afraid that Kennedy – being
> such a shrewd politician, will win out in the primaries.[386]

Leonard arrived from India in time for them to go to Harbour Island together, to Pink Sands Lodge for main meals but otherwise on their own in their 'cottage', taking long walks on the 'whitest, finest beach in all the world – and of course welcoming in all its aspects this brilliant turquoise sea'. They read a great deal, Leonard reading Dante's *Il Purgatorio* aloud, until Dorothy had had enough and resorted to her Proust or W.B. Yeats. Michael had given her some volumes of Yeats whom she had adopted as 'the most important poet of our age – I study him for at least four hours a day while Jerry works at his recorder – and plays sweet little tunes nearby.'[387]

Home at Dartington her Arts Department was now the Arts Centre, and evolving into the Dartington College of Arts, with the trustees and Peter Cox working to resign their core values of teaching and practice, of professional performance and community entertainments, to the demands of Ministry accreditation. March brought the debut of the Dartington String Quartet – Colin Sauer, Keith Lovell, Alexander 'Bobby' Kok and Peter Carter – with their concert in Exeter Cathedral. Whether in celebration of this landmark, or in appreciation of the complex demands made upon him, Dorothy wanted to give Peter Cox and his wife Bobbie a present. For the second time in her life (the first at Hull-House more than fifty years ago) her bounty was declined, or perhaps it was politely suggested that it could be put to another use? Dorothy's hand-written confession is dated 21st March 1960:

> Dearest Peter... of course I couldn't take it back – because you see, it helps me so much to be able to give something away. I suppose I have always had a sense of guilt about my privileged position – and at one time in my early life I came very close to dispossessing myself completely of my wealth – I resolved then to try never to use my money in order to exert power – and though I realise this is not possible in any ultimate sense I have tried – perhaps unwisely – to withdraw from positions of authority that were too strongly buttressed by the all too obvious financial power behind. However, this is a long story and a devious way of saying that you must allow me to make such a very small gift – I could then feel less guilty if I bought myself a whole collection of new hats! Blessings on you, Dorothy.[388]

Her 'long story' riffles back through the pages of this book and her 'confession' explains some of her enigmas: how, in 1925, Leonard's long absences from England and his very detachment from English life seemed as virtues, allowing them to settle in a remote place where she was unknown; how her, and their, disdain for English coteries and nepotism led them to reject the progressive school pioneers and the legacy of the Arts and Crafts Movement so richly deposited in the countryside of south-west England; and why she accepted the role of mere dinner-party giver to PEP when her political experience matched the best of them, and then ran in almost indecent haste from the Arts Council, the English Opera Board and any committee of the great and the good.

The following year when the College of Arts was being established and Peter Cox was thinking of leaving, her valedictory letter to him from far-away Pink Sands explains even more:

> When I stop to realize what you have created for us I feel quite overwhelmed; at the end of the war when you took over from Chris [Martin] there was virtually no Arts Department left – the buildings were dilapidated, the artists themselves scattered to the winds – and the possibility of reviving any kind of activity in the field of the arts looked a hopeless undertaking. But you did it – and not only did you build again a centre for the arts but you gave direction and purpose to the whole undertaking making it essentially an educational enterprise.

Her affection for Peter bolstered her regard for the truth as she acknowledged 'the indifference or hostility on the part of the outside world' which he 'gradually changed to one of respect and admiration for the work carried on at Dartington', and 'within the organisation you managed to create an atmosphere of generosity, goodwill and kindly humanism that has affected hundreds of students – not to speak of visitors, staff, and everyone who comes into contact with you – so that the influence you exert, even indirectly, extends far afield'. She warmed to her ending, 'And just think of the opportunities you have brought to the whole of Devon to participate in the concerts, the plays, the ballets, the exhibitions, the Christmas Festivals, the short courses – in fact all the rich and varied aspects of life you have brought to us – there is just no end to the contribution you have made.'[389]

She found it extremely hard to let him go, and fortunately he did not leave, but that is another story.[390]

In May 1962, in her *Garden Notebook*:

> Bluebells a thick mass – lovely. Returning from London
> after 4 days absence the whole scene has changed –
> everything has come at once. I think this is the most
> utterly moving and beautiful moment I have ever known
> here. Oaks, beeches, even the chestnuts and planes are
> coming now – and the great beech at the top of the
> steps – from the terrace looking down I wondered how
> everything could be so overwhelming yet real. Davidia
> and Eleagnus wonderful – and the Dell – oh – what
> richness. I am amazed at the success of the colour – I
> can't find anything to change!

Walter Thomas her tall butler, and 'Tommy' to everyone but Dorothy,
died that year – he was an irreplaceable loss. She was still surrounded,
cocooned in the devotion of her household staff and her secretaries,
Kathleen Hull-Brown who shuttled between Devon and New York,
and the young Mary Bride Nicholson, who would become the loyal
guardian of her legacy. She had given up her Dartington trusteeship
in favour of Ruth – people said their voices were indistinguishable
when heard across the garden – and Maurice Ash was also a trustee.
He and Ruth had 'come home' from Essex and were settling into the
most outrageously elegant Palladian villa called Sharpham House sited
on a 'too heavenly' bluff above the Dart at Ashprington.[391] Maurice
shared Leonard's experimental streak where stewardship of the land
was concerned – he believed that 'the paradigm has shifted' from
the traditions of the West 'now running into the sands' towards the
philosophy of the East, and Sharpham was to be part of that shift.

In 1963 Michael Straight's friendship with the Kennedys resulted
in his being offered the chairmanship of the National Endowment for
the Arts, the best job he could possibly dream of, matching his own
Camelot-style interests (his second novel was shortly to be published)
and vindicating his father's failed ambitions. He thought carefully,

and declined, fearing 'something in his background' that the necessary security clearance would uncover. His friends who knew were amazed, the president was mystified and reported as raising his eyebrows and asking bluntly, 'Is he a queer?'[392]

It seems unlikely that Michael mentioned this to his mother, though Dorothy could have heard from others, even perhaps Daisy Harriman, now over ninety and a favourite of the president. Michael was reputedly most upset when the bright young agent from the FBI sent to interview him turned out to be the son of their Old Westbury gardener – shades of his embarrassment as a boy in the chauffeur-driven limousine deposited at the Lincoln School and told to mix with 'ordinary' children.[393] Soon, however, this mattered not a jot as the attentions of the FBI and the rest of the world were consumed by the events on Dealey Plaza in Dallas on that 22nd November.

There was a small postscript later when Michael agreed to travel to England to meet Sir Anthony Blunt, now director of the Courtauld Institute and Surveyor of the Queen's Pictures, in the presence of secret service observers. It was all very undramatic, Michael's formal unmasking of Blunt as a 'talent spotter' for the Russians at Cambridge in the 1930s. Blunt's biographer Miranda Carter has revealed that the 'upper section' of Courtauld students, and their parents, gossiped about their mysterious director being the Fourth Man to Donald Maclean, Guy Burgess and Kim Philby long before Michael's 'unmasking'.[394] Dorothy had other friends – Sir Philip Hendy, director of the National Gallery, and his wife Cicely, and Stephen and Natasha Spender – who would have calmed her fears. Nothing transpired, Michael returned to his Green Spring Farm and his novel writing, the Queen was apparently informed but Sir Anthony retained his positions. The matter would not be aired in public again in Dorothy's lifetime.

There was, though, a slight connection to the last mystery of her life, the fate of her collection of paintings, once her treasures. On that distant sunny Sunday before the war the young Anthony Blunt had encouraged her to buy her Picasso, the small square oil of the face of *Girl with Head on Table* with rosebud mouth and pink dot cheeks on a green check ground – people always remarked how 'it lit up the room'. On that even more distant day when Mark Tobey had introduced her to the work of Ben Nicholson as 'the real thing', she had bought two paintings, as she reported to Leonard, 'for us and for Dartington'. Nicholson's and Kit Wood's works fired her ambition that Dartington's old grey walls should wear a modern face, that students and visitors would be aware of youth and creativity, their minds stretched and conditioned to new forms and new ways of seeing their world. Her collection had grown throughout the 1930s, she had more than a dozen (known to be the best) works by Kit Wood, including his pencil sketch of Jean Cocteau, almost as many by Winifred Nicholson, and some by Ben, who courted her as a sympathetic collector on behalf of his friends. She was buying the elixir of youth, as befitted the Dartington ethos, but she was also supporting artists making their way without any public subsidies; she bought works by Edward Bawden, William Roberts, Jacob Epstein, David Jones, Roger Fry, Eric Gill, Clare Leighton, Alfred Wallis, the Dartington residents Mark Tobey and Cecil Collins, and another favourite Frances Hodgkin, all the 'Modern British' flowering. She was a wonder to the gallery world, someone who bought for her belief in the transformative qualities of the paintings and drawings, rather than for an investment. From Jim Ede, then a curator at the Tate Gallery, in whose judgement she had faith, she acquired two small pieces by Henri Gaudier-Brzeska, a little naked *Alabaster Boy* and a small bronze torso, both treasures she kept near her. Augmented by Leonard's collection of studio pots from Bernard Leach and Lucie Rie, and juxtaposed with her Chinese prints, some botanical studies, a landscape by Peter De Wint that had been her father's, and the flamboyant paintings of Ignacio Zuloaga y Zabaleta (a favourite of Willard's), her collection had drawn gasps of wonder and delight from so many of Dartington's visitors. Graham Sutherland had come, having heard the gossip, and found what he called 'a myth come to life'.[395]

Music and drama dominated Dartington's arts after the war; many of the paintings were lent to exhibitions and public galleries, but Dorothy was no longer the dealers' delight and her purchase of the Henry Moore maquette from the Leicester Galleries for Chris Martin's memorial commission in 1947 was exceptional. Her favourite pieces were still hanging in her London flat and on her house walls at Dartington but many more were stored away. Why was there no Dartington Gallery to radiate the spirit of the place? A gallery had been mooted, most probably by Jim Ede, but he was absent abroad for twenty years; when he returned to Cambridge in the mid-1950s to create his 'poor man's' Dumbarton Oaks he wrote to Dorothy wondering 'if you were only a dream?' He heard nothing, presumably because of her illness. Ede's Kettle's Yard open house afternoons in term time, where undergraduates could enjoy his collection of contemporary art, soon acquired admiration and fame. He did reach Dorothy in 1964, asking her to lend her *Alabaster Boy* for a Gaudier-Brzeska exhibition in Paris; she refused to part with him but agreed to lend the small bronze torso, which was exhibited. Sporadic correspondence ensued but when Ede did visit Dartington he only glimpsed her in passing and they seemed as strangers; was he black-listed with other importuning dealers? Did her frailty keep her from the realisation that Kettle's Yard, Ede's *living place*, his 'continuing way of life' from the times they had both lived through, was both a homage to and a celebration of her own embrace of the modern?[396]

Now in 1965 she was divesting herself of her most beloved paintings – Ben Nicholson's *Charbon*, Cecil Collins's *Fools*, Winifred Nicholson's flowers, many by Kit Wood, John Piper's *Old Church Tower* – even the little *Alabaster Boy* are all made over to the Dartington Hall Trust, except for Wood's *Pony and Trap, Ploare, Brittany*, which was given to Ruth.[397]

In her Garden Diary for March she wrote:

> Hundreds of people in the garden on this first perfect day of Spring. Warm sun and no wind. The stillness brings such peace. And now people wander down to the stream – in fact everywhere you look the place is thick inlaid with humans – and dogs and prams and cameras and all the happy paraphernalia of a Sunday out – and into the Spring.

Leonard and Dorothy Elmhirst, Founders' Day 1967

Their winter weeks in paradise continued to benefit her physical frailties, but to prevent Pink Sands feeling too much like the ante-room to eternity – the utter peace was no longer quite such a miracle – she invited her young. Michael and his family were the nearest and most frequent visitors, and in February 1967 Biddy came all the way from Los Angeles; over forty years had gone by since, in 1925, Dorothy had taken her star-struck daughter to Hollywood, and now Biddy was living and working there. 'I wish you could have seen her,' she wrote in William's birthday letter, 'telling ghost stories to the two girls who were stretched on a bed at her feet and almost in a trance... I was overcome myself by the extraordinary power that Biddy has to radiate light and warmth and the glory of being alive. It is as if she reflected light directly from the sun – and the warmth affects everyone around her – and a kind of spiritual joyousness is born.'[398]

On the following Founders' Day, 10th June 1967, Dorothy addressed the gathering, a unique event which surprised everyone; it was more than forty years since the beginning of their project and now Dartington was filled with professional newcomers with careers to pursue, people she had never spoken to, and who took little notice of the rather frail grey-haired lady crossing the Courtyard; who was she? A hushed 'Dorothy' came the reply, as if she was already a haunting ghost. Now she was standing before them in the Great Hall, still tall, still slim and expensively but unobtrusively dressed. At first her voice sounded English, but gradually her clipped a's and long o's became more evident, and the slightest of American lilts ended her sentences. She was short of breath but determined in her message, 'take the present day, but don't take it too easily' for it was the outcome of a long, long struggle. She meant them to hear of the 'selfishness, hostility and misrepresentation' that had beset their efforts, but to know that 'the quality of dynamic life' was here from the start.

Her soft, clear voice was mesmerising and she warmed to her purpose to recall five distinct periods of Dartington's development, inspired by Leonard's ideas. She gave him sole credit. The beginnings and the restoration of the Great Hall by the 'genius' William Weir taught reverence for the old and joy in the new. We had a 'sense of life, working together, doing things together, life, life, life, with the school for our own children and others as part of our house'. Then came the American phase, Leonard's friends from Cornell who 'set the pattern for work on the land', the teachers from Columbia, and Mark Tobey, Nellie Van, the Barn Theatre, the dancers and Beatrix Farrand, so very distinguished and christened 'Queen Elizabeth'. The 1930s were depressing times, t-i-m-e-s, she drawled as if painfully remembering, with their open door to the refugee artistes from Europe, all those lost souls with their talents and their dark memories. In wartime Dartington's doors opened ever wider to hundreds of evacuees, for whom they managed to carry on their education. There was 'music in every corner' thanks to Imogen Holst and her gift 'of bringing everyone into a life of music'. Frederick Ashton and the Sadler's Wells Company were here, the Estates Committee was started and the First Founders' Day was celebrated in 1943.

She spoke of a 'kind of miracle' in the way the challenges of the post-war world were being met; it becomes clear that her history lesson is meant to bolster Dartington's essential values against the inevitable expansion, and 'the danger of losing contact with the individual'. Her audience might have feared she was flagging, not realising what a well-trained actor she was, and she modulated her voice for her finale.

'I wonder sometimes if we take too much for granted – that England gives us freedom – Freedom. Thank God England is free, never, never, never take that for granted. Beauty – too many people are condemned to live without beauty, and "some urban living was cruelty". Beauty and Peace must be treasured here and are found especially in the garden. And new life, always! Not change and decay in all around I see but change and new life all around I see, we need never despair. I never thought anyone could have been as happy as I have been for forty-two years, it is almost too much for one person to be given. Carry on! Carry on, always, please.'[399]

In early 1968 their flights to Harbour Island were cancelled – 'plans changed overnight because of my (psychosomatic) liver pain' – and she was laid low once again. Her *Garden Notebook* for March noted:

> Sunday morning with Jerry in the garden – the first time I have been able to get out and enjoy what I see. For weeks now we have been under the blight of east wind that can darken our days – And now, suddenly, today the wind has changed into the north bringing sun and strong blue sky, and hopefulness back into the heart.

'Our Wedding Day', 3rd April, was spent at the Chalet with 'my two so dearly-beloveds' Leonard and William, reading poetry and listening to the sea. Later in the month, she wrote in her *Garden Notebook*, 'A pleasant day for Mr Cane's visit. The slope with white star-like daffodils at its best and the magnolias glorious and Tai Hakus at their peak – he was delighted – but there were still adjustments to be made, the fine tuning – such an endearing proceeding.'

August too was spent at the Chalet, which she had decided to leave to William, who was now married to Heather Williams, a former student of Imogen's and oboe teacher. For her thoughts Dorothy is using a green flower-covered notebook from Mr McNally's bindery, a gift 'from the Children of your Christmas Parties'. Inside she kept a card from Gladys Szechenyi, her oldest friend, who had died in 1965.

Her September *Garden Notebook* says:

> Coming back after 3 weeks at the Chalet I am struck by the growth – the tremendous growth of everything – all the shrubs and trees look gloriously full of life and rich in development. I've never felt it so strongly before and never have I been so conscious of the perfect shape of it all. The form is so clear and strong – so exciting in every part of the garden – what a revelation is here – of beauty, of variety, of interest that never ceases to draw me deeper into the mystery of this wonderful place. And this is the time of few flowers.

Her diary is full of dates for shopping, carol concerts and parties; Saturday 14th December was the night of the school party at Foxhole to which Leonard went with William and Michael Young. Dorothy felt she needed to go to bed early, and there she died quietly at some time before midnight.

The quiet of her passing touched people most; she had been seen crossing the Courtyard and going indoors as usual, and it was impossible to believe it was for the last time. The silence of the Sunday morning was deep; William remembered that they were all stunned, not knowing what to do. In the evening the Great Hall was crowded for carol singing, all eyes drawn – many with tears – to the sight of her empty chair. Memorial services were held at Dartington and in the Grosvenor Chapel in Mayfair in January; the service at St Thomas's Episcopal church on Madison Avenue was on 23rd January, which would have been her eighty-second birthday. Her body had been cremated and her ashes placed in her garden.

The Times of 24th February 1969 noted that she had left £77,000 with £65,000 paid in duty. Clearly her fortune was still elsewhere, her children and grandchildren being provided with separate trusts; a note in Whitney Straight's papers shows that he received something over $800,000 from the Morgan Guaranty Trust later that year. Dorothy's will had been made in 1965, leaving all her personal belongings to Leonard, Ruth and William, and making generous bequests to everyone at Dartington who had looked after her so well; there was an annuity to Mrs Emily Thomas 'in the hope that' she would continue to look after Leonard.

Of his father-in-law, now in his mid-seventies, Maurice Ash wrote perceptively of his 'remarkable energies' which were now concentrated on his work to unite two Oxford institutes, Agrarian Affairs and Agricultural Economics, to ensure a future for his own International Conference of Agricultural Economists. Oxford University awarded him an honorary degree which he added to four others, from Durham, Exeter, Freiburg and Visva Bharati; he stalwartly refused any honours from the British government. He spent some time going through Dorothy's papers and notebooks, annotating and editing in smudgy blue pen, and thinking to protect her he probably destroyed a great deal. Her diaries, the testaments to her addiction to activity which was inherited from her mother Flora, the major sources for this book, remained untouched.

At Dartington the younger generation of Ruth and Maurice Ash and Michael Young were eager for progress. William Elmhirst, also a trustee, had a difference with them, which led to his resignation, leaving Dartington in the autumn of 1972, never to see his father again. In December that year Leonard married Susanna Isaacs, a doctor and psychologist and a school contemporary of Michael Young at Dartington. They spent time in Italy before leaving for California where Susanna taught at the University of Southern California's Los Angeles campus. Leonard died there on 16th April 1974, a few weeks short of his eighty-first birthday. Susanna brought his ashes back to Dartington.

SOURCES AND FURTHER READING

As befits her two lives there are major collections of papers in America and England, all now with online catalogues. The *Dorothy Whitney Straight Elmhirst papers, collection number 3725 (prefix DWS)* in the Division of Rare and Manuscript Collections in the Carl A. Kroch Library, Cornell University, have a small amount of material relating to her childhood, and the complete correspondence between her and Willard Straight throughout their relationship and marriage from 1909–1918, as well the letters of sympathy after his death.

A related and larger *Collection number 1260 (prefix WDS), the Willard Dickerman Straight Papers 1880–1918* have his juvenilia, his diaries, notebooks, drawings, paintings and photographs especially from his time in the Far East and from his official career. These papers, edited by Dorothy, formed the basis of Herbert Croly's *Willard Straight*, published in 1924; they were kept at Old Westbury, some selected by George Bennett for an exhibition on the 25th anniversary of Willard Straight Hall at Cornell in 1950, then subsequently sent to the Division of Rare & Manuscript Collections, formally donated in 1953 by Beatrice and Michael Straight.

In the year 2000 I sought and obtained the permissions of the Dartington Hall Trust and the Elmgrant Trust to use their archives, then held at Dartington, though subsequently moved to the Devon

Record Office, Great Moor House, Bittern Road, Sowton, Exeter EX2 7NL – devrec@devon.gov.uk.

Dartington's *Papers of Dorothy Whitney Elmhirst 1914–1968 (prefix DWE)* have the early diaries and notebooks she brought with her when she came to England in 1925, and the collection appears complete until her final year, 1968. These small and fragile diaries, the key to her life of activity, have formed the bedrock of this book. The Dorothy Whitney Elmhirst (DWE) and related Leonard Knight Elmhirst (LKE) Collections have the correspondence between them, and in addition DWE/Arts and DWE/General Correspondence contain materials relating to contemporary celebrities. There is apparently no correspondence with any of her children and I understand there is a closed family collection, but then Dorothy's actions clearly demonstrate her feelings towards each of them, and I don't imagine they wrote many letters, especially after the telephone was installed at Dartington in the early 1930s.

Published sources are as follows:

Addams, Jane. *Twenty Years at Hull-House*. New York: Macmillan, 1910.

Auchincloss, Louis. *The Book Class*. London: Weidenfeld & Nicolson, 1984.

Auchincloss, Louis. *A Voice from Old New York*. Boston: Houghton Mifflin Harcourt, 2010.

Banham, Mary, and Bevis Hillier, eds. *A Tonic to the Nation: The Festival of Britain 1951*. London: Thames & Hudson, 1976.

Bartlett, Mary. *Inky Rags: Letterpress Printing and Bookbinding on the Dartington Hall Estate 1935–2010*. Buckfastleigh: Itinerant Press, 2010.

Benton, Charlotte. *A Different World: Emigre Architects in Britain: 1928–1958*. RIBA Heinz Gallery, 1995.

Berkeley, Ellen P., and Matilda McQuaid, eds. *Architecture: A Place for Women*. Washington: The Smithsonian Institution Press, 1989.

Biddle, Flora M. *The Whitney Women and the Museum They Made*. New York: Arcade Publishing, 1999.

Bliven, Bruce. *Five Million Words Later*. New York: J. Day Co, 1970.

Boller, Paul F. *Presidential Wives: An Anecdotal History*. New York: Oxford University Press, 1988.

Bonham-Carter, Victor, and William B. Curry. *Dartington Hall: The History of an Experiment*. New York: Cornell University Press, 1958.

Boydell, Christine. *The Architect of Floors: Modernism, Art and Marion Dorn Designs*. Coggeshall: Schoeser, 1996.

Brown, Jane. *Beatrix: The Gardening Life of Beatrix Jones Farrand 1872–1959*. New York: Viking, 1995.

Brown, Jane. *Eminent Gardeners*. London: Viking, 1990.

Brown, Jane. *The Modern Garden*. Thames & Hudson, 2000.

Carpenter, Humphrey. *Benjamin Britten*. London: Faber and Faber, 1992.

Carter, Miranda. *Anthony Blunt: His Lives*. London: Macmillan, 2001.

Cherry, Bridget, and Nikolaus Pevsner. *The Buildings of England: Devon*. Penguin UK, 1999.

Cochran, Molly, ed. *The Cambridge Companion to Dewey*. United Kingdom: Cambridge University Press, 2008.

Cox, Peter. *The Arts at Dartington*. United Kingdom: Peter Cox, 2005.

Croly, Herbert. *Willard Straight*. New York: Macmillan, 1924.

Cross, Tom. *The Shining Sands: Artists in Newlyn and St Ives 1880–1930*. Cambridge: Westcountry Books, 1994.

Cross, Tom. *Painting the Warmth of the Sun, St Ives Artists 1939–1975*. New York: Lutterworth/Parkwest Press, 1995.

Dangerfield, George. *The Strange Death of Liberal England*. London: Serif, reprint 2012.

Darley, Gillian. *Octavia Hill: A Life*. Constable: 1990.

De Tocqueville, Alexis. *Democracy in America*. London: Penguin Group, reprint 2000.

Dudley, Roger, and Ted Johnson. *Weston-super-Mare and the Aeroplane 1910–2010*. United Kingdom: Amberley Publishing, 2010.

Ebrey, Patricia B. *The Cambridge Illustrated History of China*. New York: Cambridge University Press, 1999.

Elmhirst, Paul B., ed. *The Family Budget 1914–1919*. The Elmhyrste Press, 2011.

Emery, Anthony. *Dartington Hall*. Oxford: Clarendon P., 1970.

Eyre, Richard, and Nicholas Wright. *Changing Stages, A view of British and American Theatre in the Twentieth Century.* New York: Alfred A. Knopf, 2001.

Forster, E.M. *A Passage to India.* London: Penguin Books, 1924.

Friedman, B.H. *Gertrude Vanderbilt Whitney.* Garden City: Doubleday, 1978.

George, Alexander L., and Juliette George. *Woodrow Wilson and Colonel House: A Personality Study.* Dover Publications, 1956.

Grotelueschen, Mark E. *The AEF Way of War: The American Army and Combat in WWI.* New York: Cambridge University Press, 2007.

Gwynn, Stephen, ed. *The Letters and Friendships of Sir Cecil Spring Rice, 2 vols.* London: Constable & Co., 1929.

Hirsch, Mark D. *William C. Whitney: Modern Warwick.* Hamden: Archon Books, 1948.

Howarth, T.E.B. *Cambridge Between Two Wars.* London: Collins, 1978.

Hoyt, Edwin P. *The Whitneys: An Informal Portrait 1635–1975.* New York: Weybright & Talley, 1976.

Huxley, Juliette. *Leaves of the Tulip Tree.* London: J. Murray, 1986.

Jaffe, Patricia. *Women Engravers.* London: Virago, 1988.

James, Henry. *The Ambassadors.* The North American Review, 1903.

Klein, Maury. *The Life & Legend of E.H. Harriman.* Chapel Hill: University of North Carolina Press, 2000.

Kynaston, David. *Austerity Britain 1945–51.* London: Bloomsbury, 2007.

Levy, David W. *Herbert Croly and The New Republic: The Life & Thought of an American Progressive.* Princton: Princeton University Press, 1985.

Mackrell, Judith. *Bloomsbury Ballerina.* London: Weidenfeld & Nicolson, 2008.

MacMillan, Margaret. *Peacemakers: Six Months that Changed the World.* London: John Murray, 2001.

Manheim, Michael, ed. *The Cambridge Companion to Eugene O'Neill.* Cambridge: Cambridge University Press, 1998.

Marshall, Gail, and Judith Haber. *Shakespeare and Victorian Women.* Cambridge: Cambridge University Press, 2009.

Marx, Leo. *The Machine in the Garden.* United Kingdom: Oxford University Press, 1964.

Mellor, David, ed. *Cecil Beaton: Exhibition Catalogue*. London: Barbican Art Gallery, 1986.

Moore, Lucy. *Anything Goes: A biography of the Roaring Twenties*. London: Atlantic Books, 2008.

Nevins, Allan. *Cleveland: A Study in Courage*. American Political Biography Press, 1952.

Nicholson, Jovan. *Ben Nicholson, Winifred Nicholson, Christopher Wood, Alfred Wallis, William Staite Murray: Art and Life 1920–1931*. United Kingdom: Philip Wilson Publishers, 2013.

Parker, Matthew. *Goldeneye: Where Bond was Born: Ian Fleming's Jamaica*. United Kingdom: Hutchinson, 2014.

Perry, Roland. *Last of the Cold War Spies: The Life of Michael Straight*. Cambridge: Da Capo Press, 2005.

Phillips, Sarah T. *This Land, This Nation, Conservation, Rural America and the New Deal*. New York: Cambridge University Press, 2007.

Pinder, John, ed. *Fifty Years of Political & Economic Planning, 1931–1981*. London: Heinemann, 1981.

Preston-Dunlop, Valerie. *Rudolf Laban: An Extraordinary Life*. United Kingdom: Princeton Book Co Pub, 1998.

Rauchway, Eric. 'A Gentleman's Club in a Woman's Sphere, How Dorothy Whitney Straight created *The New Republic, Journal of Women's History*, vol. 11, no. 2, Summer 1999.

Reynolds, David. *Rich Relations: The American Occupation of Britain 1942–1945*. London: HarperCollins Publishers, 1995.

Roosevelt, Eleanor. *On My Own*. London: Hutchinson, 1959.

Roosevelt, Theodore. *An Autobiography*. London: Macmillan, 1913.

Rothschild, Miriam, Kate Garton, and Lionel De Rothschild. *The Rothschild Gardens*. London: Gala Books, 1996.

Seymour-Jones, Carol. *Beatrice Webb: Woman of Conflict*. Chicago: Dee, Ivan R. Publisher, 1992.

Snell, Reginald. *From the Bare Stem: Making Dorothy Elmhirst's Garden at Dartington Hall*. Devon Books, 1989.

Steel, Ronald. *Walter Lippmann and the American Century*. Boston: Little Brown and Company, 1980.

Stevens, Anthony. *Withymead Centre: A Jungian Community for the Healing Arts*. Sigo Press, 2004.

Straight, Michael. *After Long Silence*. New York: W.W. Norton, 1980.

Sutherland, John. *Stephen Spender: The Authorized Biography*. Penguin Books, 2004.

Swanberg, William A. *Whitney Father, Whitney Heiress, Two Generations of One of America's Richest Families*. New York: Scribner, 1980.

Tindall, George B., and David E. Shi. *America: A Narrative History*, [1984]. New York: W.W. Norton, 1999.

Valder, Peter. *Gardens in China*. Portland: Timber Press, 2002.

Vidal, Gore. *Palimpsest: A Memoir*. Random House, 1995.

Walker, Diana B. *Spreading My Wings*. Sparkford: Patrick Stephens, 1994.

Weidman and Martin, eds. *Nassau County Long Island in Early Photographs 1869–1940*. New York: Dover Publications, 1981.

Whybrow, Marion. *The Leach Legacy: St Ives Pottery and Its Influence*. United Kingdom: Sansom & Company, 1996.

Young, Michael. *The Elmhirsts of Dartington*. London: Routledge & Kegan Paul, 1982.

ENDNOTES

1   De Tocqueville, 'How Aristocracy Could Issue from Industry', p. 531.

2   The Newport News Shipbuilding Hull no. 1, the tugboat *Dorothy*, was launched in 1891 and restored and returned to Newport News in 1976.

3   Gwynn ed., vol. 1, 22nd April 1887. For Dorothy's godmother Frances Cleveland, see Nevins pp. 304–11, Boller Chapter 21.

4   De Tocqueville, 'How the Girl is Found beneath the Features of the Wife', p. 565.

5   Flora Payne Whitney born 25th January 1842, William Collins Whitney born 5th July 1841. For their courtship and marriage see Hirsch pp. 36 ff., Hoyt pp. 124 ff, Swanberg, Chapter 2.

6   Dorothy's siblings: Leonora Payne Whitney born and died 1870; Henry (Harry) Payne Whitney born 28th April 1872; Pauline Payne Whitney born 21st March 1874; (William) Payne Whitney born 21st March 1876; Olive Payne Whitney born 22nd January 1878, died 1883.

7   Dorothy's memoir *Inagua South*, dated 2nd February 1959 (DWE) and Mary Bride Nicholson's typescript of the hand-written original (DWE), is the main evidence for 'the somewhat hidden story' of her early life.

8   Swanberg p. 50. See also Mark Hirsch, 'A Gallant Lady', *New York History* April 1946; Hirsch wrote a manuscript of over 100,000 words on Flora's life, DWS 3725 Series II, Box 5, folder 8, unpublished.

9   Dorothy's own memories from *Inagua South* 1959 (DWE).

10 Almeric Hugh Paget born 14th March 1861, 6th son of General Lord Alfred Paget, died 1886, and his wife Cecilia Wyndham. For Harry and Gertrude's wedding in Newport, see Friedman pp. 144–7.

11 Her father's passion for horse racing was lost on Dorothy, though it passed to Harry Whitney and Pauline's daughter Miss Dorothy Paget. Volodyvoski won the 1901 Derby.

12 Mrs George Keppel (1868–1947), Edward VII's discreet and kind mistress, escaped to New York when she thought it tactful.

13 Addie Randolph's coming-out, Swanberg pp. 195–7.

14 Flora Payne wrote 'Summering Amongst the Catskills' signed 'Clevelander', published in the *Cleveland Daily Herald*, 15th September 1870.

15 Washington Irving's *Sketch Book* (1819), which included 'The Legend of Sleepy Hollow', gave Americans their own folk tales, hence Nathaniel Hawthorne's image of the steam locomotive violating the Catskill mountain country became the metaphor for the industrialisation of America. See Marx, 1964.

16 October Mountain is now an 11,000-acre State Forest; at Aiken in South Carolina, Whitney Park, including the much enlarged Joye Cottage on Whiskey Road and Easey Street where Dorothy stayed, has extensive recreational facilities.

17 Friedman p. 270 on the interior of 871 Fifth Avenue, where Gertrude Whitney lived until her death in 1942, when most of the contents were sold and the house was subsequently demolished. For Harriman's appendicitis and survival, see Klein, pp. 294–7. Dorothy could never write of her father's death, which is sensitively covered in Swanberg pp. 215–21; Gwynn ed., p. 598, notes the funeral in the (Episcopal) Grace Church, on 6th February 1904, with a 'great congregation' and a wreath of lilies placed on his empty pew. Woodlawn Cemetery in the Bronx is now a National Historic Landmark and the Whitney graves are prominent.

18 WCW's legacy to Dorothy, Swanberg pp. 221, 227.

19 Beatrice Bend was the daughter of George Bend, late president of the New York Stock Exchange, whose widow Marraine became their regular travelling companion and Dorothy's adoptive 'mother'.

20   An audit of Whitney's once-reviled developments can now include the elevated railway that is Manhattan's High Line Park.

21   Swanberg p. 226 on her approach, 'I like you and hope you will like me'.

22   'Greek mythology' from a letter, Leonard Elmhirst to Joseph P. Lash, 18th October 1968, Papers of Joseph P. Lash, Box 44 Library, Hyde Park, NY, kindly found for me by David Michaelis researching his biography of Eleanor Roosevelt, email 28th September 2011. Dorothy's school work notebooks DWS 3725 Series II, Box 5, folders 1–7. 'Books I have read' notebook came to England, DWE/G/S7/F.

23   For her jottings on this first trip to Europe, Line-A-Day diary, DWE/G/S7/A/001.

24   For Gertrude Whitney's dilemma see Friedman, 'Wedlock', pp. 213–14, also Biddle, 1999.

25   Robert Bacon (1860–1919), Assistant Secretary of State 1905, Ambassador to France 1909–12, during WW1. Robert Law Bacon his son (1884–1938), Harvard 1907, US Treasury 1910–11, then Kissel, Kinnicutt & Company, married Virginia Murray 1913, Republican Congressman 1923–38. Elihu Root (1845–1937), Secretary of State 1905–9, Senator for New York, Nobel Peace Prize 1912; his mother was Nancy Whitney Buttrick.

26   Florence Jaffray Hurst 'Daisy' Harriman (1870–1967), vivacious favourite in political circles, married to J. Borden Harriman. She was an active suffragist and Democrat interested in social welfare, Minister to Norway in 1937 and awarded the Citation of Merit by President Kennedy in 1963.

27   Roosevelt's First United States Volunteer Cavalry were called Rough Riders; they were a mix of cowboys and college men of legendary exploits, if only for four months in 1898 in the Cuban Campaign.

28   Roslyn etc., see Weidman and Martin eds., 1981.

29   Her style was the now familiar Colonial Revival, which 'continues to influence interiors across the US and has become known as the quintessential American aesthetic', Victoria Maw reporting on an exhibition at the Museum of the City of New York, *Financial Times*, 18/19th February 2012.

30 Klein p. 290.

31 Unlike the Whitneys and their many homes, Harriman had only Arden, his much-loved country place, the former Greenwood Iron Works estate in the Ramapo Highlands, about forty miles north of Jersey City, see Klein pp. 68–9.

32 Mary Harriman (1881–1934), 'Harriman expected no less of his daughters than of his sons', Klein p. 299. Mary was well educated, finishing at Barnard College, and well travelled as her father's companion; she is the acknowledged founder of the Junior League for the Promotion of Settlement Movements across North America and internationally.

33 Ruth Morgan (1870–1934) became Dorothy's most valued counsellor and friend; sometime president of the Colony Club, a leader in civil rights and social welfare activism, a commissioner for the Red Cross in WW1 and on the National Committee on the Causes and Cure of War; see DWE/G/8A for surviving correspondence. Dorothy's daughter Ruth Elmhirst born in 1926 was named after her.

34 Swanberg p. 250.

35 Lillian D. Wald (1867–1940), a native of Cincinnati, had come to train as a nurse at New York City Hospital and, finding so many immigrants living in terrible conditions, opened a house for nurses to work in the community, which evolved into the Henry Street Settlement, which still exists as a lively welfare centre; correspondence survives from 1909, DWS 3725, Box 2, folder 48.

36 Lillian Wald to Dorothy, 16th June 1909.

37 Henry James, *The Ambassadors*, 1903 codifies Dorothy's society and its pitfalls, for which Paris offered both escape and retribution; her Book Class was devastatingly lampooned by Louis Auchincloss, *The Book Class*, 1984, which was set in 1908.

38 Swanberg pp. 244–5 has the full text, undated, but 1907.

39 Grosvenor Atterbury had by now expressed his interest in social housing, hospitals etc., which interested Dorothy; she would have found it impossible to acquire architectural training (even if she could draw) and marriage was not the solution. See my *Beatrix*, 1995, for Farrand's training, and Ellen Perry Berkeley ed., *Architecture, A Place for Women*, 1989, for other pioneers.

40   These 'horrid feelings' which she does not explain would seem to come from meeting too many 'clothes-horse' and 'trophy' wives in Russia; at home she had carved out a useful life because of her desire to work and help the needful, but now her comedy of manners lifestyle threatened to overwhelm her again.

41   Her text trails off after this; Swanberg p. 245 suggests she meant Sheldon Whitehouse or Bob Bacon, but related events taken from other sources – Alice Roosevelt Longworth, Klein etc. – confirm she is thinking of Willard Straight whom she believes is 'spoken for'.

42   On her return to America Dorothy found a press cutting that she kept (and somehow it arrived into her Dartington papers) about Harriman's fury at Mary's 'engagement', also Klein pp. 300–1. Mary was to marry Charles Cary Rumsey in 1910.

43   Toynbee Hall in Commercial Street, Aldgate, was founded in 1884 as the pioneering University Settlement House where Oxbridge undergraduates lived and served the people of London's East End.

44   Jane Addams (1860–1935) explained her philosophy and experiences in *Twenty Years at Hull-House*, 1910; Chapter 12 'Tolstoyism' tells of her visit to Tolstoy. She won the Nobel Peace Prize in 1931 and the website Nobelprize.org has a contemporary biography and bibliography.

45   Addams, Chapter 6 'Subjective necessary for Social Settlements'.

46   John Dewey (1859–1952) and his book *The School and Society* were to be the sources of Dorothy's beliefs about education for her own children and for her later syllabus for the school at Dartington; see Cochran ed., *The Cambridge Companion to Dewey*, p. 27, and Noddings, 'Dewey's philosophy of education', pp. 265–87.

47   Sheldon Whitehouse (1883–1965), Eton and Yale, diplomatic postings in South America, Athens, Russia, Stockholm and Paris for the 1919 Peace Conference; he married Mary Alexander in 1920.

48   WSPU branches from all over the country sent their members to march through the streets of London to Hyde Park on Sunday 21st June 1908; photographs show the park 'a sea of faces' – 'an extraordinary scene' never witnessed before, *Daily Chronicle, 25th June*.

49   Atterbury married Dorothy Johnstone in 1923.

50 Sylvia Pankhurst (1882–1960), after this meeting with Dorothy, became increasingly at odds with Christabel and the 'middle-class' WSPU; she worked with the Labour Party and with working women.

51 Details of Willard's early life are taken from Dorothy's edited versions in Croly's *Willard Straight*, 1924; his diaries from his schooldays and earliest writings were included in his papers left at Old Westbury, now the Willard Dickerman Straight Archive 1825–1925 at Cornell, WDS 1260; his notebooks, photographs and drawings of his time in China are also in WDS 1260.

52 Senator Root's letter 17th June 1909, DWS 3725 Series I, Box 2, folder 27.

53 Katie Hickman, *Daughters of Britannia*, 1999, pp. 38–43.

54 Willard from Peking, 4th September 1909, this letter begins Series I of the Cornell Archive DWS 3725 (*not* WDS 1260), Box 1, sixty letters from Willard to Dorothy 1909–18; her letters to him are in DWS 3725 Series I, Box 4, 36 folders.

55 Swanberg pp. 278–80 records their diary notes of their days in Peking.

56 Tony Scotland, *The Empty Throne*, 1993, explains these names and relationships.

57 Valder pp. 172–8; Willard's Yu Chuan San is Yuquan Shan, Jade Spring Hill; Mrs Little says 'it is quite a place to spend a happy day in' and visitors rave about it; clearly the most serious destruction was yet to come.

58 Rudyard Kipling, 'Recessional', 1897, 'The White Man's Burden', 1899.

59 Valder pp. 190–91 quoting Mrs Little.

60 'Oh Wise Man of the East' 17th November 1909 on China Navigation Company notepaper is the first letter in the Dorothy to Willard sequence, DWS 3725 Series I, Box 4, folder 4.

61 'Dear Guardian of Borderland' 26th November 1909 on Palace Hotel Shanghai notepaper, refers to 'Borderland', their code for their future happy life together. 'Borderland' was a dream place, a happiness afar off, much used by architects of ideal housing for young married couples.

62 Dorothy to Kate Barnes, DWS 3725 Series I, Box 4, folders 42/3.

63 Swanberg pp. 285–6 describes her time in Cairo.

64 Robert Bacon, now Ambassador in Paris, seems the key to her taking cover 'in our little American family group here', see Hermione Lee, *Edith Wharton*, 2007, p. 272.

65 King Edward VII had died on 6th May 1910 and was buried at Windsor on 20th May; his people were stunned and political circles were embroiled in a constitutional conference that kept them at their desks until late July. Almeric Paget was the newly elected MP for Cambridge. The Deepdene, ripe for gothic romance, was Thomas Hope's Greek Revival treasure house. See David Watkin, *Thomas Hope and the Neo-Classical Idea*, 1968.

66 Professor Morse Stephens's letter, 8th July 1910 from 7 Lansdowne Road, Holland Park, was tucked into Dorothy's diary or notebook and came to England, DWE/G/9/Box R–V.

67 'real lasting American influence', Klein p. 343; Klein p. 440 notes the tale of the house-painter working at Arden, the Harrimans' house, who 'happened to look down at the loggia below' and saw the frail Harriman sitting with 'a heavy-set visitor who wielded an enormous black cigar' – the painter had worked for J.P. Morgan and recognised him and thus became the only witness to this last meeting between 'the two most powerful men in America'. Harriman had died on 9th September 1909. Swanberg p. 291 comments that it was Willard's 'misfortune' to be so romantically involved while his career was on the line; he was the specialist who understood the Chinese whereas his American masters did not; they needed him but he was not one of them. J.P. Morgan (1837–1913) was the doyen of western bankers, well known to Dorothy's father; Harry Pomeroy Davison, aged forty-six, had worked his way from the teller's desk to the partners' room at Morgan's and had his own prospects to consider.

68 Klein p. 300 on Willard's increasing contact with the elite: 'he was not only poor, he was an artist, with an artist's temperament and sensitivity. His character was made of porcelain, theirs of marble – dense, polished and solid'.

69 Roosevelt family correspondence DWS 3725 Series I, Box 2, folder 43 and Box 3, folder 10.

70 Swanberg p. 309.

71 Ibid.

72 Ethel Roosevelt Derby (1891–1977) was Theodore Roosevelt's only daughter with his second wife Edith and she became Dorothy's closest friend at this time; correspondence as note 69 above.

73 Swanberg p. 321 notes Harry's announcement in New York, press clippings DWS 3725 Series II, Box 5, folder 14; the headlines aside, Swanberg p. 319 adds: '[Dorothy] had become increasingly maternal towards Straight. She had babied him and he seemed to enjoy babying more than his normal hearty masculinity would make one expect'. I might add that with the loss of his great god Harriman he had anointed Dorothy the goddess of his fate.

74 Dorothy had confided in Lillian Wald; they discussed her indecision over Willard, and they had both visited Henry Street before leaving for Europe and their marriage.

75 DWS 3725 Series I, Box 4, folder 18 has this sequence of letters and cables from leaving the *Olympic* to their wedding day, 7th September, ending with Willard's note of that morning. Dorothy disliked having her photograph taken; the few wedding photographs that survive are in DWS 3725 Series II, Boxes 6, 7 and 9.

76 Klein p. 300, see note 68 above.

77 'My Wonder of the World' letter is undated on Hôtel Vendôme, Paris notepaper but headed 'at Erquelinnes' on the Belgian border not far from Mons; Dorothy's from Versailles is dated 23rd September; letters of congratulations on their engagement and marriage, DWS 3725 Series I, Box 3, folders 1–14. Right up to and beyond their marriage it seems Beatrice Bend maintained her opposition, though there is no other written evidence of this.

78 Ebrey 1996, pp. 265–6 for the bomb incident etc. Their time in the Philippines was not wasted: an agricultural school was founded in Willard's name and still being supported by Dorothy thirty years later. Swanberg p. 329 for New York headlines.

79 Willard's papers, notebooks, press cuttings, articles and photographs recording his life in China are a major part of his archive, WDS 1260 at Cornell.

80   Details of the 'lovely Chinese things' from the sale catalogue for the property of Westbury Holdings Corporation at Gimbel Brothers, 33rd Street and Broadway, 19th to 21st February 1942, private collection.

81   Nancy Langhorne Astor (1879–1964), Viscountess Astor, was the first woman to take her seat in the House of Commons, as Member for the Plymouth Sutton constituency in 1919. In personality Nancy was fearless, outspoken and at times abrasive and so unlike Dorothy, but they were sisters beneath the skin.

82   The International Exhibition of Modern Art, mid-February to mid-March 1912, held at the National Guard's Armory at Lexington Avenue and 26th Street, was sensational for its introduction of European Cubism and Impressionism as well as contemporary American Realism. Photographs show the stark Armory interiors wreathed and swagged in luxuriant evergreens, and Gertrude and Dorothy each gave $1,000 'for decorations', Friedman pp. 324–6.

83   The date of the loan was 18th June 1912, between the Hongkong & Shanghai Banking Corporation in London, Deutsche-Asiatiche in Berlin, Banque de L'Indochine in Paris, J.P. Morgan, Kuhn Loeb, First National and National City Banks, these latter of New York (the American Group), and was to be administered by Morgan Grenfell, 22 Old Broad Street, London, M.M. Warburg of Hamburg, Morgan Harjes of Paris, the Russo-Asiatic Bank of St Petersburg and the Yokohama Bank of Japan, all bearing equal costs, rights and shares. The Wilson administration's cancellation of the loan 'with the hose of presidential rhetoric', Croly p. 460, was especially galling as – Croly insists – the Washington Conference 1921–2 would reinstate the benevolent protectorate over China that the Group had attempted. See Jerry Israel, *Progressivism and the Open Door: America and China 1904–21*, 1971; Michael H. Hunt, *The Making of a Special Relationship: the U.S. and China to 1914*, 1983.

84   Beatrix Jones Farrand (1872–1959), an enterprising and largely self-taught garden designer and landscape architect with several clients on Long Island, was the natural choice for their garden. For her connections see my *Beatrix*, 1995, Chapter 6 'Aunt Pussy [Edith Wharton] Miss

Nimrod [Beatrix] and Old Celimare [Henry James]'. She designed a children's playhouse and garden and a kitchen garden for the Straights. Their Chinese garden has gone but a similar pink-walled version by Farrand for the Rockefellers' Eyrie at Seal Harbor, Maine, survives; the original plans are in Farrand's Reef Point Gardens Collection, Library of the College of Environmental Design, University of California, Berkeley.

85 'blow of his disappointments', Croly pp. 461–2. Swanberg pp. 334–5 made a 'judicious estimate' of Willard's earnings: $2,000 per year as consul at Mukden, $3,000 in the State Department, $10,000 in Peking, doubled as his success with the loan was imminent, but this would not go far in Manhattan even in 1913. Dorothy gave $50,000 to Smith College, Northampton, Ma., for its Million Dollar Appeal that summer, acknowledged on 21st June 1913.

86 'big job for Willard', DWS 3725 Series I, Box 2, folder 43; Roosevelt's *Autobiography*, 1913, tells his story up until his 1912 defeat by President Wilson, and explains his policies, ostensibly setting the scene for his 1916 campaign. Chapter XIII 'Social and Industrial Justice' and Roosevelt's words, 'because of things I have done on behalf of justice to the workingman, I have often been called a Socialist', pp. 523 ff, confirmed Dorothy's political loyalties.

87 Eric Rauchway, *A Gentleman's Club in a Woman's Sphere: How Dorothy Whitney Straight Created the New Republic*, pp.60–85, *Journal of Women's History*, Vol. 11, No. 2 Summer 1999, a copy sent to the author by Michael Straight; Herbert David Croly (1869–1930) was the son of David Goodman Croly, editor of *New York World*, and Jane Cunningham Croly, 'Jenny June', a nationally syndicated columnist. David Croly was strongly humanist, and his son 'was presented to the goddess of Humanity' confirming the belief that private life was subordinate to public service. Herbert spent two years at Harvard but returned home to assist his ailing father in editing *The Real Estate Record & Builders' Guide*, which became *Architectural Record* after his father's death in 1889. In 1892 he had married Louise Emory, a Radcliffe student and artist, his perfect partner; 'it is not too much to say [both the Crolys] loved Dorothy as a daughter', Levy, p. 277.

88   Alvin Johnson recounting this story in *Pioneer's Progress*, p. 233, added, 'I doubt the accuracy of the reporting. Nobody has ever recorded a miracle accurately... how could it have happened that Fate should have placed an immense fortune in the hands of a woman so brave, so true, so beautiful as Dorothy Straight? A real angel.'

89   Rauchway pp. 73–5; Levy pp. 186 ff on Croly and his vision.

90   From a surviving menu it seems the lunches were very healthy: appetisers of olives, radish, celery and grapefruit, followed by consommé, shad, roast chicken with redcurrant jelly, asparagus, rice croquettes and tomato-jelly salad, finished with strawberry shortcake and coffee.

91   The 14th November issue carried war reports from Frank Simonds and Noel Brailsford.

92   The raids were on 16th December, Liddell Hart, *The First World War*, 1970, p. 105.

93   Swanberg p. 348.

94   Willard's letters to the infant Whitney Straight, Swanberg p. 350.

95   Edward Mandell House (1858–1938), honorary colonel, 'small, pale, self-effacing and frail', appeared sympathetic and friendly, 'an intimate man – even when cutting your throat'; President Wilson was dependent on him as 'the only person... with whom he could discuss everything', Macmillan p. 25; 'a small, dapper tetchy Texan, wealthy – whom Wilson called "my alter ego" – soft-voiced, enigmatic, and sent around Europe touting for peace', George and George, 1964.

96   Pauline Payne Whitney Paget is buried in the churchyard of St Mary's, Hertingfordbury in Hertfordshire, her monument sculpted by Gertrude Whitney in 1920.

97   Walter Lippmann (1889–1974) was cutting his teeth on *The New Republic* on his way to becoming 'the greatest journalist of his age'; Steel, 1980, Chapter 9 'Electing a War President', portrays Lippmann's brilliant cajoling of Croly and his colleagues to make *The New Republic* indispensable to its readership and to President Wilson.

98   It was Lippmann who conjured the reasons 'to lead this great peaceful people into war', and he flattered Wilson (in an editorial), writing 'only a statesman who will be called great could have made American

intervention mean so much to the generous forces of the world', Steel pp. 112–13.

99 Dorothy gave no indication that she suspected Colonel House of speaking with forked tongue, but this becomes clear in Steel pp. 116–17. Much to Croly's displeasure, in June 1917 Lippmann 'severed his connection with the editorial board' to join the War Department; Lippmann applied himself to 'studying and speculating on the approaches to peace and the reaction from the peace' – surely Willard could have done something like this? Even the chosen Lippmann was criticised for his friendships with John Dewey, Charles Beard and John Reed, all radicals whom Dorothy knew well – was it Dorothy's politics that baulked Willard's progress?

100 19th November 1917 at City Hall, Swanberg pp. 371–2.

101 Major Murphy wrote to Dorothy ostensibly to thank her for befriending his wife Maud, but he added, 'it is hard to have made the great sacrifice to serve – and then serve in a way comparatively small and seemingly inconsequential – but that is all many of us can do – and we must be content in doing as well as we may what comes to our hands – so do keep Willard from the line, where it would be wrong and in the ultimate analysis rather selfish for him to go', 5th August 1918, WDS Microfilm reel 6, 52/3/322.

102 For the 2nd Division's engagement at Belleau Wood and Vaux, June–July 1918, Grotelueschen, 2006, pp. 206 ff.

103 The magazines were *Asia* and *Antiques* as well as *The New Republic*, and Willard had ambitions to start a newspaper. A letter dated 9th August 1918, from Harry Davison now at Red Cross headquarters in Washington and returned from France, tells Dorothy, 'As you know there is no one who is so loved by as many people as Willard Straight, and on every side "over there" I was told of the fine work he had done and predictions of the work he would accomplish.' WDS 1260 Microfilm reel 6, 54/322.

104 Twain's 1889 satire was sinister reading for Willard's state of mind: the time-travelling Hank Morgan makes his cynical way through medieval England, his future-knowledge masked as wizardry to wreak havoc,

the last battle being an attack on a post defended by wire and machine guns.

105 When Colonel House was still promising Willard a job 'one day' he was setting up a secret War Data Investigation Bureau, called the Inquiry, with Walter Lippmann co-ordinating the work of over a hundred experts in all fields – no job for Willard there either? It was an Inquiry Memorandum that framed the president's 'Fourteen Points for Peace' speech, towards which Lippmann 'felt a sense of paternity', Steel pp. 128–34.

106 DWS 3725 Box 1, folder 60 and Box 4, folders 38–41 have their last uncensored letters and cables; Daisy Harriman's letters telling of Willard's death, WDS 1260 Microfilm reel 7, 166/167/247. Mrs Harriman arranged the return of his belongings and papers and consequently letters, press clippings, medical records are in WDS 1260 Series V, mainly Boxes 22 and 23. Walter Lippmann wrote to Dorothy, 'in the last eight weeks I was closer to Willard than ever before – we talked far into the night, hoping, planning, sometimes doubting, but in the end renewed – in that personal loneliness which is the background of so many of us here there was mixed also a fear that what we had meant, and what alone could justify it all, was not the meaning and justification of those who will decide,' Steel p. 151.

107 The cards from the funeral flowers, DWS 3725 Series I, Box 2, folder 26; additional papers, copies of cables, photographs of Suresnes cemetery, DWS 3725 Series III, Box 8, folders 13, 14 and 15.

108 George Bennett's letters from France, WDS 1260 Series VII, Box 39.

109 DWS 3725 Series I, Box 2, folders 25, 27 and 51 have some eight hundred letters of condolence from 12th December 1918 through the first six months of 1919.

110 This letter from Mrs Herman Kinnicutt, formerly May Tuckerman, makes its presence felt; the simple entry 'May' is often in Dorothy's diary. Their correspondence is in DWS 3725 Series I, Box 2, folders 47–49, dated 1904–22.

111 Louisa Weinstein to George Bennett, Swanberg p. 449. Bennett returned to work at Old Westbury, and eventually accompanied Dorothy to Dartington.

112   'Between two worlds', a play by Adrian Bean and David Hendy, BBC
      Radio 3, 24th July 2011, drew my attention to the story of Raymond; the
      desperation of the bereaved was so widespread that every esoteric belief
      – Christian Science, Theosophy, Spiritualism and early Scientology –
      became important. Dorothy collected into her Commonplace Book
      Rupert Brooke's Sonnet 'Not With Vain Tears' as well as 'The Soldier'
      and 'Safety'.

113   Moreton Frewen of Brede in Sussex, a larger than life knight errant,
      maker and loser of fortunes in the Wild West, aged seventy-one, was
      considering Spiritualism, '[it] brings me a nice humble simple note
      which satisfies me that I am going to see my old friends again. This
      is rather what one wants', Anita Leslie, *Mr Frewen*, England, 1966,
      p. 201.

114   'DWS The Argosy of Grace', the text in Dartington archives
      DWE/G/5 General Correspondence, filed alphabetically under Mrs
      Paul Hammond (the former Susan R. Sedgwick, widow of Arthur W.
      Swann.

115   Bertrand Russell, *A History of Western Philosophy*, 1946, 2004, p. 731.
      Russell expressed his admiration for John Dewey who was 'very liberal'
      but never a Marxist, 'having emancipated himself with some difficulty
      from the traditional orthodox theology, he was not going to shackle
      himself with another'.

116   'to commit suicide', Richard Eyre and Nicholas Wright, *Changing
      Stages*, 2001, p. 146; also O'Neill's plays at this time, Stephen A. Black,
      'Celebrant of Loss', pp. 4–17 in Manheim ed., 1998.

117   Eyre and Wright p. 146.

118   Major Grotelueschen gives separate figures for each action, and that
      (Dorothy's) 77th Division suffered fewer than nine hundred casualties
      1st–11th November, but they were trained for trench warfare, p. 339.
      There are impressive websites: AEF Facts gives 116,708 killed of which
      53,513 were battlefield deaths, and the rest died in the US, many of the
      effects of Spanish influenza on gas-damaged lungs, but the total killed
      and wounded is well over 300,000; westernfrontassociation.com gives
      compatible figures.

119 The fate of Sacco and Vanzetti is widely documented. *The New Republic* covered it regularly, marking 'The murder of Sacco and Vanzetti' 10th August 1927, but Dorothy's name is never mentioned.

120 Rose Schneiderman (*c.*1882–1972) worked in garment factories as the breadwinner for her family before she was twenty; she organised trade unions and came to prominence speaking out against the maiming of her sister workers amidst unguarded machinery, and the spate of deaths from fires behind the locked doors of factories, these reforms now the challenges to WTUL.

121 Whitman's words are from the final stanzas of 'Passage to India', 1871–81, *Leaves of Grass and Selected Prose*, Crasnow and Bigsby eds., 1993, pp. 356–64; Dorothy's Whitman notebook in DWE/G/S7/E/002.

122 This copy is in WDS 1260 Series IV, Box 20, folder 17.

123 Levy's biography of Croly, sub-titled *The Life and Thought of an American Progressive*, especially 'The Years of Despair 1919–1930', pp. 295 ff.

124 John Rothschild was their tutor for part of every summer until 1926 aside from his work for the Student Forum of New York hosting Youth Movement exchange students. A report for *The Harvard Crimson* dated 22nd November 1922 (available online) describes his connection to this pre-Hitler German Youth Movement as leading the youthful in spirit 'and not necessarily the youth of years' away from the defeated militarism to a liberal culture based on philosophy, literature and religious beliefs.

125 Benjamin Seebohm Rowntree (1871–1954), son of Joseph Rowntree the great Quaker philanthropist and chocolate maker of York, had interests closely allied to Dorothy's; he had studied poverty, gambling and labour conditions, and published *The Human Needs of Labour*, 1919, and *The Human Factor in Business*, 1921. He became chairman of Rowntree in 1923 (until 1941) and remained a friend to Dorothy.

126 Albert Mansbridge (1876–1952), a native of Gloucester, was educated at evening classes and devoted to the cause of adult education, setting up the Workers' Educational Association in 1903.

127 Rev. Phillip 'Tubby' Clayton (1885–1972) was the Vicar of All Hallows by the Tower 1922–62. Dorothy supported Toc H but when he extended

his work to leprosy relief in Africa his appeal came at the moment of her deepest despair, making her feel inadequate for not going to Africa herself.

128   Kenneth Lindsay (1897–1991) was to be a founder of PEP, then Independent National MP for a Kilmarnock seat 1933–45, his career strongly influenced by this visit to America. He describes 1130 Fifth Avenue as 'a kind of conference centre for her causes – there could be three different meetings in progress simultaneously, on three different floors', Young p. 72. He also gave Michael Young the oft-repeated phrase describing Dorothy's society at this time, as 'made up of men and women who walked down Fifth Avenue with serious tread, intellectuals most of them with uphill work to do in a sad world', Young p. 71.

129   The genesis of Willard Straight Hall at Cornell is to be found among the hundreds of letters of condolence that Dorothy received in December 1918 and early 1919. The poignancy of his words and the date on Dorothy's birthday alerted me to Professor Brauner's letter on the WDS 1260 Microfilm reel 8; his 'ideas' letter of 31st October 1919 and President Schurman's of 28th October are also here.

130   Press cutting with photographs 'In Beautiful Ceremony at Suresnes Thousands Pay Tribute to Heroes', 31st May 1923, WDS 1260 Microfilm 173/180 with additional material in Series V, Boxes 22 and 24.

131   Research into the virulence of the 1918 virus continues, and the University of Arizona released results on 28th April 2014 showing that those born 1880–1900 (Willard was born 1881) were most vulnerable to the H1N1 strain because they did not possess antibodies from previous exposure. Willard's case is complicated presumably by his time in China (where he complained of flu in 1909) and also by the fact that the gas damage to his lungs was unrecognised.

132   The British diplomat Sir Mark Sykes, born 1879, died from similar causes a few weeks later, on 16th February 1919 in the Hôtel Lotti near the Tuileries Gardens. *The Independent*, 17th September 2008, reported that Sir Mark's lead-lined coffin had been exhumed to gain DNA of the H1N1 virus for further research into present-day pandemics.

133 Ophelia's Song, Shakespeare, *Hamlet*, Act IV Scene 5.

134 Anna Bogue's note on the contents of the casket, DWE/C/1923–4.

135 The chapter title is from John Masefield (1878–1967), 'The Passing Strange', *Collected Poems*, 1923, and from Dorothy's Commonplace Book:

> For all things change, the darkness changes,
> The wandering spirits change their ranges,
> The corn is gathered to the granges.
> The corn is sown again, it grows:
> The stars burn out, the darkness goes;
> The rhythms change, they do not close.

She typed the whole long poem out for Leonard, because it meant so much to her.

136 'glad you've come', 25ᵗʰ July 1924, Dartington Archive LKE/DWE Box E. Leonard Knight Elmhirst (1893–1974) was the second of nine children of the Rev. William Elmhirst and his wife Mary, a family well rooted in Yorkshire country society. He had an MA from Cambridge in 1915; his priestly vocation and being certified 'unfit' kept him from the war, in which two of his brothers were killed. Leonard worked for the YMCA with British soldiers in remote parts of India and the Middle East, observing that 'the Indians' as well as 'the Turks' left deserts wherever they went; he lost his convictions, telling his father that he 'could not honestly put my name to most of the things the Church demands', Young p. 27. Sam Higginbottom, a missionary in Allahabad who had started an agricultural institute and taught the leper colony to make gardens, inspired Leonard, exhorting him to go to an American university for a 'down-to-earth' education in practical agriculture. For a fuller biography, see Young, Chapter 2 'The Englishman'.

137 Young, Chapter 4 'Together' begins with Leonard Elmhirst's diary entry for 'a Friday' in September 1920, p. 61, for when he had first seen Dorothy in New York. Although written in hindsight this is misleading, as they were not 'together' (at least not outside of Leonard's fantasy) nor would they be for more than four years; archivists distort timings, and the Dartington arrangement of LKE/DWE Personal Letters

misleadingly begins in 1920, when she was not DWE until 1925, but then the Cornell archives call her DWS well before she married Willard Straight.

138 Dartington DWE/LKE Personal Letters 1920/21. These letters make dispiriting reading: Dorothy's maternal attitude is reminiscent of her 'babying' of Willard in 1911 but now babying without love, only a kind of patrician flattery; Leonard is protesting adoration and at the same time demeaning her sensibilities and intelligence with lugubrious tales.

139 'for the benefit of India', DWE/LKE 28th June 1921.

140 18th August 1921.

141 Leonard from Calcutta, 10th January 1922; he ends, 'whatever the answer I'll be for ever, ever your own loving friend', DWE/LKE.

142 The eldest Elmhirst brother William was killed at Serre on the Somme on 13th November 1916, aged twenty-four; then came Leonard; Christopher was killed in the Dardanelles in 1915, aged twenty; Thomas was brilliant at Dartmouth, a balloon pilot hunting U-boats and in 1920 in command of the RAF Flying Boat Base at Malta; Victor, Marlborough, Sandhurst, Royal Flying Corps; Richard, Rugby, Household Brigade, 2nd Lieutenant in the Coldstream Guards; Alfred 'Pom', Winchester, Bisley Prizewinner and outstanding cricketer destined to become a family solicitor. See Paul B. Elmhirst ed., 2011.

143 Dorothy's 1923 diary, 11th August, notes Leonard 'too critical' of Willard Straight ms, and Herbert Croly as 'hurt'.

144 'a Jerusalem', Leonard from 1130 Fifth Avenue to Dorothy at Woods Hole, 25th July 1924 continuing to 5th August. Euphoric notes fly – 'in spirit and in absence' is linked to Leonard's 'If I can only see you every year for a few weeks or even a few days I shall be content' – and yet the nucleus of their school is here; in retrospect this is the denouement of Leonard's struggle (not revealed to Dorothy) to choose between her and Tagore, as was now forced upon him. Rabindranath Tagore (1861–1941), Nobel Laureate, was a figure of world status, beloved, of crucial influence in India. The Institute for Rural Reconstruction that he and Leonard had achieved at Surul fulfilled Leonard's dreams; his love for Tagore's 'beauty and stature' transforms Leonard so that he

could write, 'one touch of your magic wand and my imagination… finds the windows of the cage open and its wings free'. Even Michael Young, closer to Leonard than anybody else, knew little of Leonard's emotional life in India. Tagore's play *Red Oleanders* about an old man, a younger man and a beautiful girl was dedicated to Leonard, Young pp. 86–8.

145 Verdict on *A Passage to India* 3rd September 1924, DWE/LKE.

146 Leonard's proposal from London 18th September reached Dorothy on 25th September and her reply is dated 28th – 'Do you really and truly want me to join you in April?', Dartington DWE/LKE.

147 Her enthusiasm seems prompted by two *New Republic* pieces: Frank H. Simonds, 'The British Revolution', 2nd April 1924 (on Ramsay MacDonald's Labour government) and H.M. Tomlinson, 'The England of Hardy', 12th January 1921, included in Conklin ed., *The New Republic Anthology 1915–35*, 1936.

148 Hasan Zillur Rahim, 'Tagore and Victoria Ocampo', bdnews24.com (Bangladesh) 19th June 2011.

149 Michael Straight wrote of his eight year old's passion for birds and wild animals from his reading of Ernest Thompson Seton's *Biography of a Grizzly*, *How to Play Indian*, etc. Seton's 'rather tough, call of the wild morality' affected him, 'thanks to Seton the tragic sense of life was imprinted on my own for good. I sensed, perhaps, the reason for my mother's sadness, and so, for me, Seton's stories had the ring of truth', Straight p. 29.

150 Young pp. 103–5 tells of Leonard's search for Dartington, informed by Leonard himself; additionally Dartington Hall Estate before 1945, T/EST/1/A3 Particulars of Sale etc., T/EST/1/A5.

151 Irene Rachel Elmhirst (1902–78) seems to have been accomplished indoors and out – and Dorothy found a friend in her. She married George Barker in 1935 and they had two daughters, but he was killed in a riding accident in 1945.

152 Young p. 104.

153 Louise Croly from 255 East 71st Street, NYC to Dorothy, 23rd February 1925; Herbert Croly to Dorothy 10th and 27th February 1924, typed transcripts DWE/G/2.

154 Dorothy does not say, but 'much of it I don't care for at all' could have referred to the extremes of prosperity and the poverty of the migrant labourers, for she was travelling in Steinbeck country – he was educated at Salinas High School and Stanford – which formed the background for so many of his stories.

155 Anna Bogue's role as the perfect amanuensis, relayer of messages, organiser of the children's welfare, buyer of presents and arranger of everyone's travelling comes into focus in DWE/US/Office series. Mrs Bend from Rome to Mr Elmhirst 19th February 1925, to 'My precious Dorothy' 21st March, to 'dear Leonard' 18th April; 28th April records Whitney's arrival in Rome, all DWE/G/1.

156 'nice crank', Friedman pp. 468–9.

157 Dartington Hall Estate before 1945, T/Est/1/A5.

158 As note 157 above.

159 My essay 'The Henry James Americans' in *Eminent Gardeners*, 1990, describes this coterie of Americans who preferred to live in England.

160 Young p. 97 quotes Susie Hammond's reflection on Dorothy's second marriage from her letter to him of May 1977.

161 Masefield, as note 135.

162 Oundle School, presumably on H.G. Wells's recommendation – his *Story of a Great Headmaster*, 1923, paid tribute to the progressive methods of Frederick William Sanderson of Oundle, who had died in 1922. The visit to Stratford and Clifford Chambers is from Dorothy's 1925 diary; my investigation of this on a bursary from the Hosking Houses Trust at Clifford Chambers resulted in 'Dorothy: A biographical essay', 2011, which plots her life's echoes of Shakespearean heroines.

163 Dartington DWE/C/1, 23rd November 1925, President Farrand on the opening of Willard Straight Hall.

164 'learning by doing': Leonard was keen that the whole estate was 'to be the school's common workshop', an attitude to strike horror into the hearts of his farming neighbours. Dorothy led nature walks, and gardening, beekeeping and botanical projects were available. Michael Young joined the school in 1929 largely because his Australian grandfather would pay for him to learn about fruit farming. These four

principles from the *Outline* prospectus are in Young pp. 136–9. See also Cochran ed., Chapter 12 'Dewey's philosophy of education', pp. 265 ff.

165 Presumably when Whitney, Beatrice and Michael arrived in England there was no going back. Dorothy's notebook DWE/G/S7/E/007, Friday 24th September 1926, 'Wyatt Rawson arrived from Totnes at four bringing five children, Keith and Mary Ponsford, Michael Preston, Lorna Nixon, Louis Heidinger'; Whitney, Beatrice and Michael met them for tea and games.

166 Dorothy to Susie Hammond 15th March 1927, DWE/G/5.

167 This work was not completed until February 1938.

168 Henry Avray Tipping (1855–1933), architectural editor of *Country Life*, is likely to have been Lord Sandwich's introduction; there is now a biography, Helena Gerrish, *Edwardian Country Life: The Story of H. Avray Tipping*, 2011.

169 Jane [Sylvia] Fox-Strangways taught for about two years and became Dorothy's first close friend in Devon; her letters begin in 1928, DWE/G/4. Her poems edited by Dorothy were published in 1949 and later in special editions from the Dartington Bindery. Dorothy paid her medical fees and left her a legacy to pay for her nursing home; she died in 1975 aged eighty-three.

170 King James Version, John 3:8.

171 Young pp. 151–2.

172 As note 166 above.

173 1130 Fifth Avenue, now a New York City Landmark and for some years the International Center for Photography, is at the time of writing a private house again.

174 'clothed in dollar bills', an alienation confirmed from an interesting source: Agatha Christie, Mrs Max Mallowan, their neighbour down the Dart valley, gives her heroine Mary Ann the words, 'I have connections with that large part of the European world which is still heavily snobbish as far as birth is concerned. A poor and shabby countess sits down first at the table whilst a rich American with a fabulous fortune in dollars at the bank is kept waiting', *Passenger to Frankfurt: An Extravaganza*, 1970, 1993, p. 94.

175   Dorothy to Leonard about Fincham 8th October 1925, Young p. 112. Albert Fincham had been Sir Edwin Lutyens's foreman and clerk (and he knew how to charm Dorothy) and his Arts and Crafts style cottages are most fitting.

176   Snell, 1989, pp. 23–4.

177   DWE/US/Office folders have the Committee on Commitments papers through the 1920s.

178   The purchase of the Chalet is covered in LKE/4/G. It was made over by Deed of Gift to William Elmhirst in 1952.

179   Maurice Browne (1881–1955) wrote long autobiographical articles for *Nash's Pall Mall* in January/February 1933 and 'Milestones toward Journey's End', *c*.1932, and these and the correspondence are in folders LKE/BR/1–6. As with the Chalet above this archival assignment is because Leonard signed the letters, but there would have been no Chalet and no *Journey's End* but for Dorothy's intuition and inspiration. Browne returned to live at Dartington and wrote his autobiography, *Too Late to Lament*, which was published the year he died; he is buried in St Mary's graveyard at the end of the drive.

180   Ellen Van Volkenburg, 'Nellie Van' as she became known, came to Dartington from considerable success in America with the Chicago Little Theatre and serious classic roles. She remained teaching at Dartington, particularly encouraging Beatrice Straight; they went together to the Cornish School of Arts in Seattle, then Nellie returned to Dartington where she took part in the Chekhov classes, playing Dorothy's role in *The Possessed* in New York in 1939. She returned to Devon after the war, when Dorothy helped her to buy a cottage, then she went back to America, leaving the cottage to Maurice Browne.

181   Additional information on *Journey's End* from the 2005 revival at the Playhouse Theatre, London, and director David Grindley's programme notes. Laurence Olivier's commitment elsewhere was with Noël Coward in America.

182   It was his mother's privilege to call him 'Bill' but he preferred William in later life, as he will be called here.

183 And for his father who was Leonard Knight Elmhirst, with William for Dorothy's father and for the eldest Elmhirst, 'Willie', killed in 1916.

184 This must have been Leonard's first meeting with Tagore since they had parted in early 1925, and it was his first return to the ashram since 1924.

185 Michael's discomfort was linked to his mother's misery, Straight p. 41. Dorothy never went to India again and Leonard resumed his trips alone or with colleagues, just as she so often went to America alone.

186 Their apparent assumption that they had nothing to learn from established progressive schools, Badley's Bedales (1893) and A.S. Neill's Summerhill (1921), did not endear them to educational circles. Young p. 175 tells how Dorothy bought Swedish crockery and furniture at Heal's for the juniors, all broken in a short while, 'Neill could have saved Dorothy the money if only he had been asked. He knew better than she how destructive children can be'. Neill became jealous of Dartington's resources, which marred their relationship. Dorothy visited Bedales in 1935 after Headmaster Curry had invited Bedales' staff and pupils to Devon. They had nothing to do with Dora Russell's Beacon Hill (1927) until the Russells' marriage ended in 1934 and their children Kate and John arrived at Dartington.

187 Young p. 156 for his own arrival at Dartington; it was not the least of the school's successes that it transformed the would-be fruit farmer into the 'dream maker', *Observer* Profile, 27th May 2001; also, a shaman 'who sowed dragon's teeth' (Noel Annan), founder of the Consumers' Association, Which, the Open University, the School for Social Entrepreneurs, etc., Asa Briggs, *Michael Young: Social Entrepreneur*, 2001.

188 Whitney Straight's early flying career is from Dudley and Johnson, 2010.

189 See Victor Bonham-Carter, 'The Story of Dartington' part 2 in *The Countryman*, Summer 1953.

190 Leonard to Curry, 29th April 1930, quoted in Young p. 162.

191 Maggie Giraud ed., *House for Mr Curry*, a delightful miscellany designed by Sue Snell, to mark the restoration of High Cross House in 1995.

192 Curry quoted in *Country Life*, the article and photographs of 11th February 1933 reproduced in *House for Mr Curry*.

193 Young pp. 163–4 on Curry's personality.

194   The phrase is Gerald Heard's, see note 214 below, in 'The Dartington Experiment', 1934.

195   Emery, 1970, for 'The Owners and History', especially Chapter 3 'The Later Holands and their Successors 1400–1559'.

196   Paul Robeson (1898–1976) was playing in O'Neill's *The Emperor Jones* when Dorothy saw him in late 1925. Press cuttings and reviews for *Othello*, LKE/BR/1–6. Robeson went to Hollywood to play in *Showboat*, the film of *The Emperor Jones* and *Sanders of the River*, he was too much the 'star' for Dorothy to call a friend but she watched his career and he next appears supporting Henry Wallace's campaign in 1948 with Michael Straight.

197   Maurice Browne quotes from cuttings in LKE/BR/1–6.

198   Edmund Wilson to Stanley Dell, quoted in Steel p. 175; Wilson to Lionel Trilling 3rd May 1957 gives the story of his time at *The New Republic* in Castronovo and Groth eds., *Edmund Wilson: The Man in Letters*, 2001, pp. 71–71.

199   Herbert Croly to Dorothy undated but 1923/4, DWE/G/2.

200   Major Murphy to Dorothy, 5th August 1918, WDS 1260 Microfilm reel 6, 52/3/322.

201   Mark Tobey (1890–1976) was a teacher and a lively creative presence for most of the 1930s; he helped Dorothy to realise the possibilities of a community of artists.

202   Jovan Nicholson, 2013, especially p. 31 ff. for Ben and Winifred Nicholson and their friendship with Kit Wood.

203   J. Nicholson p. 35 ff., also Tom Cross, 1994, especially Chapter 12 'A Meeting in St Ives' (Wallis, Wood and Ben Nicholson).

204   Ibid.

205   DWE/Arts/1 opens on 3rd November 1930 with a catalogue of paintings by the late Christopher Wood and contains letters etc., detailing Dorothy's early collecting.

206   Ellen Van Volkenburg and Edward N. Beck eds., *Miss Aunt Nellie: The Autobiography of Nellie C. Cornish*, 1964, p. 128 quoted in Young note 9 p. 367.

207   *Married Love or Love in Marriage* by Dr Marie Stopes (1880–1958) first appeared in 1918, followed by books varying the themes of birth control,

sexual health, marriage counselling and children's welfare. Contraceptive advice was sought by Dorothy in New York and her choice of the most eminent gynaecologist in London presumably ensured this continued. Dr Stopes's first Birth Control Clinic in London had opened by the time Dorothy arrived; soon after William's birth the National Birth Control Council (later the Family Planning Association) was opening clinics all over the country, one of the first in Plymouth as a result of Lady Astor's influence.

208   Straight p. 40.

209   Young pp. 221–3. Bernard Leach (1887–1958) had established his studio in St Ives in 1920 and Dorothy had asked him to come to Dartington in 1927, when he brought Jane Fox-Strangways. Leach continued to advise at Dartington but never relinquished his base in St Ives; Dorothy's importance in forwarding his career is rarely recognised.

210   [Henry] Noel Brailsford (1873–1958) wrote for *The New Republic* and shared Dorothy's interest in arms limitation and studying the causes of war, which had led him to 1130 Fifth Avenue. In his 1928 lectures he covered the League of Nations, 'Naval Compromise and Disarmament', 'Debts, Danes and Rhineland' and 'Social Rationalization' in Germany and America. He was trapped in a difficult marriage to the WSPU activist Jane Brailsford who died in 1937; in 1944 he married Eva Maria Perlmann. F.M. Leventhal's *The Last Dissenter*, 1985, and Spartacus Educational online essay by John Simkin.

211   Clare Leighton (1899–1989) is described by her fellow engraver Patricia Jaffe 'to have designed and engraved with her whole being, and in her writings too, the enormous physicality of her response to visual and emotional experiences comes over so strongly that she must have taught many women how to unleash a hitherto unacknowledged power in themselves', *Women Engravers*, 1988, pp. 35–7.

212   Young p. 207. [Henry FitzGerald] Gerald Heard (1889–1971) was an intellectually and morally adventurous man of faiths, homosexual, and Dorothy's most prolific correspondent and a regular visitor until he left for America in 1939.

213 Their surviving correspondence DWE/G[eneral correspondence]/filed alphabetically H.

214 Gerald Heard, 'The Dartington Experiment', in *The Architectural Review*, April 1934.

215 *The Architectural Review* was in its heyday under the direction of Hubert de Cronin Hastings and J.M. Richards.

216 Gertrude Jekyll's *Flower Decoration for the House*, 1907, with deceptively simple arrangements of flowers, leaves and berries in glass, pewter or china jugs or vases, became the Dartington style, passed from Jane Fox-Strangways to Emily Thomas and still honoured today.

217 For the *Circle* philosophy and Moore, Nicholson, Hepworth and Chermayeff, see my *The Modern Garden*, 2000, Chapter 2 'Britain in the 30s'.

218 Boydell, 1996; plate 51 (from *The Architectural Review*) shows 'a remodelled flat by modernist architect Serge Chermayeff with rugs by Marion Dorn, 1935', which is Dorothy's Upper Brook Street flat.

219 The building spree of the 1930s is concisely covered in Bridget Cherry's revision of Pevsner's *The Buildings of England: Devon*, 1999, pp. 314–19.

220 Benton, 1995, essay by David Elliott, 'Gropius in England: A documentation 1934–1937', pp. 107–24.

221 Impington Village College by Gropius and Fry, 'one of the best buildings of its date in England, if not the best', Pevsner, *The Buildings of England: Cambridgeshire*, 2nd ed., 1970, pp. 412–13.

222 Henry Morris (1889–1961) was intended for the priesthood but his experiences on the Western Front made that impossible for him, and he turned to education; from 1922 until 1954 he was Education Officer for Cambridgeshire. He believed that schools needed to be 'remade' to embrace the millions 'who learn by practice and action', and that 'a consciousness and involvement with all the arts was vital to the moral character and emotional development of future generations'. See Lottie Hoare, 'The ideas and influence of Henry Morris' in *Crafts* magazine, 1999.

223 John Maynard Keynes's letters to Dorothy with comments from Lydia Keynes DWE/G/6.

224 Lydia Lopokova (1885–1981) was an Imperially schooled ballerina who began creating roles in St Petersburg before she was twenty, touring to Berlin and Paris, where she danced *The Firebird*, then to New York in 1911. She came to London in 1918 with Diaghilev's company where 'her grace and pathos and entrancing cleverness' and 'true comic genius' captivated critics and balletomanes, including Keynes, whom she married in August 1925. See Mackrell, 2008.

225 Arthur Waley (1889–1966) mastered oriental languages while working at the British Museum, his translation of *The Tale of Genji* was published 1925–33, and the intimate secrets of the Lady Murasaki's court etiquette fuelled the craze for all things Japanese. He was a prolific translator, absorbed in his work and a soothing presence. For fifty years he was the partner of Beryl de Zoete (1879–1962), the dancer and expert on Balinese and Indian traditions as well as eurythmics; she was Dorothy's most well-informed adviser; DWE/G/11.

226 See note 106 above, Lippmann quoted by Steel, p. 151.

227 Kurt Jooss (1901–79) was admired all over Europe for his dance theatre, though he was a difficult genius as his subjects were emotionally harrowing for both dancers and audiences. Once again Dorothy's judgement led her into a realm of pioneering excellence that was foreign in every way to rural Devon; her quiet rescue of the Jooss Company was extraordinary and accomplished without fuss or publicity. Jooss remained in England until 1949 when he returned to Essen.

228 DWE/Gardens is a sequence of eight boxes, DWE/GN/1 has the correspondence from 1927 and with these drawings, articles and photographs Dorothy's becomes one of the best-documented gardens in England. Beatrix Farrand's papers are in her Reef Point Gardens Collection, Library of the College of Environmental Design, University of California, Berkeley, ref. 871 Dartington Hall 1933–1938. See also Snell, 1989, and my *Beatrix*, 1995, Chapter 10 'Transatlantic Fellows, Dumbarton Oaks and Dartington Hall'.

229 Farrand correspondence in date order in DWE/GN/1–8.

230 Her Smythson diaries are complete from now until the end of her life, an impregnable and detailed record of her days; DWE/G/S7/A.

231 Young, Chapter 9 'A New Day for the Arts', especially pp. 227–9; also Cox, 2005, p. 10 ff. on the character and abilities of Christopher Martin.

232 Eli Whitney and Phineas Miller patented the cotton gin in 1794, and five years later Whitney developed machine tools to make parts for muskets with such precision that they were identical and could be assembled to a system.

233 See *Cecil Collins, A Retrospective Exhibition*, catalogue by Judith Collins, Tate Gallery 1989; also Cecil Collins, *The Dartington Years 1936–43*, 1997, ed. Diana Gower.

234 Dorothy's daughter-in-law to-be Daphne Finch-Hatton (1913–2003) and her brother Christopher (1911–50), later 15th Earl of Winchilsea and Nottingham, were the children of the 14th Earl and his American wife Margaretta Drexel.

235 *The Rock* was T.S. Eliot's latest work but soon eclipsed by *Four Quartets*, which Dorothy treasured; she called him Tom and lunched with him several times, though she cannot have found 'the most bank clerky of all bank clerks' (Aldous Huxley) nor the taciturn Faber editor to be forthcoming. This highlights Dorothy's rare ability, especially in the 1930s, to admire the poetry but refuse to 'gush' or lionise the poet, or any other artist.

236 Dorothy is the invisible tenant of the house; she had arranged everything with Captain Peter Cazalet, married to Wodehouses's stepdaughter Leonora, who appeared in her February diary.

237 Bliven, 1970, p. 168.

238 Coverage of Glyndebourne's eightieth anniversary in 2014 revealed that any differences with Dorothy must have been 'political'. Mrs Christie, the singer Audrey Mildmay (of Flete in Devon), influenced her husband 'to do the thing properly' and spend lavishly on the sumptuous festival 'welcoming ticketholders like guests at a garden party'; Rupert Christiansen, 'Aiming for the sky with their feet in the gardens', *Telegraph Saturday Review*, 7th June 2014.

239 See Alan Bignell, *Lady Baillie at Leeds Castle 1927–1974*, 2007.

240 John Cornford was the son of Francis M. Cornford, Lawrence Professor of Ancient Philosophy, and his wife the poetess Frances Cornford, who

was Charles Darwin's grand-daughter, so he could be as actively left wing as he liked and the heirs of Victorian Cambridge would simply smile benignly at the exuberance of youth. *Period Piece* by Gwen Raverat (also Darwin's grand-daughter), 1952, encapsulated the legends of 'the city of the Darwins'. Michael Straight was 'an innocent abroad' in Cambridge, amusing for his glamour, money and famous racing-driver brother; Howarth, 1978, p. 227.

241 George Barker was a huntsman of some note, joint master of the Badsworth; he served in the army in WW2 and was killed in a hunting accident in 1945. Irene Rachel and her two daughters moved to a farm in Berkshire, where she died in 1978.

242 *The Times* 18th July 1935, p. 19, 'Marriages, Mr Whitney Straight and Lady Daphne Finch-Hatton took place yesterday at St Margaret's Westminster.'

243 Dorothy's many notebooks in DWE/G/S7/D are sometimes difficult to date; 'the practice of religion' is clearly marked 'SS. Manhattan Sept. 13', a date which fits this trip and her only one on the *Manhattan*.

244 Howarth, Chapter 6 'Politics II' introduces the players in 'The Leftward movement of Cambridge politics in the thirties', quoting 'Sage' Bernal writing in *Cambridge Left*, 1933, pp. 209–10, and a rapturous review of Sidney and Beatrice Webb, *Soviet Communism: A New Civilization?*, 1935.

245 Howarth p. 212 describes Cornford as 'brilliant, fearless, farouche and monomaniac', able to write 'exquisitely tender lyric' poetry as well as 'savagely excoriate the bourgeois culture' of Cambridge.

246 Mikhail [Michael] Chekhov (1891–1955), born in St Petersburg, was the nephew of the playwright Anton Chekhov; there is an active Michael Chekhov Association online, which continues to arrange the teaching of his methods.

247 Dorothy had seen more of Walter Gropius during his three years in England than most people, and the elusiveness of 'the English Bauhaus' was a deep disappointment to her. She paid Gropius's fee for Impington Village College. He was soon spirited away from his Hampstead friends to a Harvard professorship. In his farewell speech in March 1937 he

said that he could not understand a nation that had expressed itself so perfectly in Georgian architecture but was now 'not so keen on taking the same chance with a new style that expressed the social structure and twentieth-century way of living', Benton p. 122.

248 The 'mother-son business', as she later called it, was the then contemporary reading of *Hamlet*, emphasising her acute concerns over Michael. After the war, in 1952 and a reading and 'really animated discussion' in her Shakespeare class, she 'threw out a new idea' derived from Irene Champernowne's recommendation of Professor Harold C. Goddard's *The Meaning of Shakespeare*, 1951, and his treatment of 'the father-son relationship [which] opens a new vista'; this perspective made the play even more important to her: letter 24th January 1952 to Leonard, quoted in Young p. 251.

249 *The Times* Tuesday 4th February 1936, p. 9, 'Notice is given that Mr Whitney Willard Straight of Woods Mews, Park Lane, W.1 is applying to the Home Secretary for naturalization'. Dorothy had applied to the American consul on 25th April 1935 to relinquish her American citizenship, but the process was not completed until 13th August 1947.

250 All the papers concerning Chekhov's time at Dartington are in DWE/Arts/15 beginning in 1935, continuing through Files 16–27.

251 Eyre and Wright p. 156.

252 Ibid. pp. 74–8 on Sean O'Casey (1880–1964), who 'had little to do with the English theatre' while he lived in Devon.

253 They were kept at home to attend the wedding of the school geography master Bill Hunter at Exeter Cathedral, to entertain the ageing Prince Serge Wolkonsky, one-time director of the Imperial Theatres in St Petersburg who hoped to move to England, and by Leonard's work for his first conference of agricultural economists.

254 The advent of Mischa Chekhov undoubtedly inspired Leonard's feelings about the wife he had worked so persistently to win just ten years earlier. He said he had lived with two such people – the other presumably Tagore – and 'they know not what they do' wrapped up in a world of their own imagination; letter to Juliette Huxley, November 1959, in Juliette Huxley, *Leaves of the Tulip Tree*, 1986, pp. 236–7.

255 From 'Chekhov Theatre Studio at Dartington Hall, England', seven-page typescript with Dorothy's hand-written amendments, DWE/A/15/Drama 6, 1935.

256 In her 1959 memoir *Inagua South* (DWE) she confesses her passion for the theatre as an art 'since the age of twenty', i.e. 1907, as the prelude to theatrical achievements at Dartington since 1926; she could edit her early interests, for no one at Dartington knew any different, and leave out her dalliance with the Provincetown Players and O'Neill, which was painful to remember. With this introduction to the Chekhov Studio she is writing for publication and looking forward; with *Inagua South* she is looking back from the age of seventy-two (also for publication) when her peace of mind had obscured her sometime need for O'Neill 'for whom dolefulness was a permanent condition'. See Eyre and Wright pp. 132–52.

257 Bloomsbury gossip said that Arthur Waley and Beryl de Zoete were 'professional weekenders' but Dorothy was not so censorious; H[arold] S[tanley] 'Jim' Ede (1895–1990), his early correspondence DWE/A/2; letters from Ben Nicholson are also in this file, offering her paintings and also telling her of the birth of his and Barbara Hepworth's triplets for whom she eventually arranged places at the school.

258 *Michael Chekhov, the Dartington Years*, a film produced and directed by Martin Sharp, introduced by Simon Callow, The Michael Chekhov Centre UK in association with the Dorothy Whitney Elmhirst Trust and Palomino Films, 2002.

259 Noel Brailsford's letter from 37 Belsize Park Gardens, NW3, is dated 11th December 1936.

260 Dorothy's reply 21st December, DWE/G/1.

261 Frances Cornford, John's mother, had fallen into 'one of her worst depressions' in 1934, which lasted for six years, hence the need for Michael's help; see 'Frances Cornford, 1886–1960' by Helen Fowler in Shils and Blacker eds., *Cambridge Women: Twelve Portraits*, 1996, pp. 137–58. Frances, whose recovery was sudden, grew increasingly friendly with Dorothy on her visits to James at Dartington, but she took James away from the school when he was eight because she discovered he

had not learned to read. After a good education and a distinguished career James Cornford, who thought of Dartington as his 'lost paradise', eventually became chairman of the Dartington Hall Trust; he died in 2011.

262　'At a memorial meeting for John Cornford, Aneurin Bevan evoked loud applause when he declared "John Cornford was a Communist and I am a member of the Labour Party. I believe that the sacrifice of Cornford, [E.C.B.] Maclaurin and the International Brigade will weld these two parties into one" – it was the age of the Popular Front and "no enemies to the Left"'; also 'there was much talk of fraternity and solidarity', Howarth p. 216; this suggests that Michael's fears were in his own imagination.

263　Goronwy Rees quoted in Carter, 2001, pp. 171–2; Rosamund Lehmann, told by Goronwy Rees in 1937 that Burgess had asked him to work for anti-Fascism, replied that 'she didn't think it was such a shocking announcement. All the young men were going off to fight in Spain and I thought this was just Guy's way of helping'.

264　Carter p. 130 on Rozika Rothschild's 'dressed-up subsidy to her son's clever young friend'.

265　Blunt was twenty-nine, ten years older than Michael Straight, a fledgling art historian who joined the Warburg Institute later in 1937; in the August he went to the Paris Exhibition where the 'true star' was the small Spanish pavilion displaying Picasso's *Guernica* and his etchings *The Dream and Lie of Franco*. Blunt's conflicting responses, that the artist's 'heart was in the right place' but 'where is his brain? Where are his eyes?', formed the basis of his 'problem' with Picasso for the rest of his career. At his death in 1983 a set of limited edition prints of *The Dream and Lie of Franco* were found in his belongings, treasured to his end; Carter pp. 204–5, 208. It is tempting to suppose that Blunt, finding Dorothy's heart to be in the right place when they talked in the garden, suggested she buy her Picasso, *Girl with Head on Table*, painted in 1932, from Rosenberg and Helft in Bruton Street; the gallery was shortly to leave London at the outbreak of war. The painting was in the 1960 Tate Gallery Picasso exhibition, No. 128 *Girl with Head on Table* lent by Mrs L.K. Elmhirst; it was sold at Sotheby's on 16th April 1975 for £27,000.

266　William Collins Whitney Foundation papers April–May 1937, DWE/ US/9 explain the conversion of her annual charitable giving into this formal Foundation now organised into six categories identified by Ed Lindeman's research as: The Arts (modern architecture, experimental theatre, indigenous American cultures); Education (experimental teaching and projects, public education); Social and Economic Planning; Peace and Freedom (international relations, cultural understanding, civil liberties, minority groups); Social Problems (housing, child labour, labour laws, consumer protection, birth control); and Research (fellowships and scholarships). The current list of grants was as usual a long one, to adult and workers' education, the Committee on Race Relations, school leavers' welfare and the rehabilitation of miners among the more unusual. A grant was given to a drama project in Provincetown and to the 'holistic' and self-sufficient Black Mountain College in North Carolina – Gropius had designed radical buildings on pilotis (not built) and the design school was created on Bauhaus lines under Josef Albers and his textile designer wife, Anni Fleischmann Albers.

267　The surviving correspondence with Eleanor Roosevelt is in DWE/G/9 General correspondence R–V.

268　25th March 1937, quoted by Young p. 234, who asserts 'She loved him, without any of the eroticism that Mischa was not keen on'; p. 368, note 33 quotes Chekhov on love: 'its highest aspects we refer to as platonic love and romanticism; the baser, lowest end is just animal gratification', Michael Chekhov, *Michael Chekhov's To the Director and Playwright*, ed. Charles Leonard, 1963, p. 19.

269　From 'Chekhov Theatre Studio at Dartington Hall, England', as note 255 above.

270　Young p. 233 quoting from Eileen O'Casey, *Sean*, 1971, p. 206; also Eyre and Wright p. 78.

271　Dorothy's and Dartington's role in rescuing Laban is documented in Valerie Preston-Dunlop, *Rudolf Laban: An Extraordinary Life*, 1998; from his refuge in Wales Laban and his protégée Jean Newlove contributed to the war effort by teaching workers to move effectively and with economy of energy, popularised as 'Time and Motion' study. Later, with Lisa Ullman he set up his Art of Movement Studio in Surrey, where he died in 1958. His work is carried on at the Trinity Laban Conservatoire in Deptford, London, in the striking and colourful new building by architects Herzog & de Meuron and Michael Craig-Martin.

272 Leonard is quoted in Young p. 236.

273 On 23rd February following [1938] Eleanor Roosevelt wrote to Dorothy about a meeting of Rural Women of the World, and in her reply on 4th March Dorothy wrote, 'Michael is very happy to be in the State Department and he is deeply grateful to you for the help you gave him... I only hope that he may be of some real use', DWE/G/9.

274 Perry, 2005, p.84 for Michael's meeting with Blunt; for his losing his half of the paper, p. 94.

275 Steel p. 369 for the talk Dorothy would have heard, if not at the White House.

276 The 'green diamonds' notebook DWE/G/S7/E/019 begins at Woods Hole on 7th August; also a previous notebook with 'red starry' cover, 'what I might have done in Ship's Hospital' i.e. concentrate upon objects in view – the electric light bulb, the case of her travelling clock, a book binding, her glove – all realised as 'the outer shell of protection for some fragile inner thing'; she realised 'the need for relief from static surroundings' so she watched the clouds through the high porthole. Mrs Eloise Sharman, 3rd August 2010, said she had never forgotten how Dorothy stayed with her in the Ship's Hospital, and contracted mumps herself. Walter Lippmann to Bruce Bliven and to Harold Nicolson, Steel p. 374; also Bliven pp. 197 ff., on *The New Republic*'s editorials.

277 Beatrix Farrand to Dorothy and Leonard, my *Beatrix*, p.167. Her final account covered the Great Court, Forecourt, Garden front, Wilderness, Azaleas, Open Air Theatre, Rock Garden, Heath Garden, Kitchen Garden, Greenhouse, Flowers for cutting, Loggia etc., plans and paperwork $1,000 and expenses another $1,000. For a detailed description of her work see Chapter IV 'From the New World' in Snell, 1989.

278   Young p.234.

279   Alice Crowther was leaving for Australia where she became well known as a voice coach and speech therapist teaching at Waldorf International Schools.

280   Dorothy from the Chalet to Anna Bogue 3rd January 1939, DWE/US/10.

281   Victor, 3rd Lord Rothschild (1910–90), had inherited the ancient and beautiful Tring Park in 1935, lived there for a while but then offered the manor, park and woodlands and Walter Rothschild's museum collection of natural history and ornithology to the British Museum as a gift; the gift was declined.

282   Her *Statendam* notebook is in the collection DWE/G/S7.

283   Ibid.

284   Young pp. 237–8.

285   Tagore was increasingly frail and would die in 1941.

286   The author was M.L. Haskins (1875–1957), poet, social reformer and social worker; she studied and taught at the LSE. LSE History website has a biography by Sue Donnelly, LSE Archivist.

287   See Dudley and Johnson, as Chapter 7, note 25.

288   The complete list is: household wages £67; pensions £5; £25 for eating in the White Hart; £1. 10s for other food; £1. 4s. for milk; newspapers £1. 10s; laundry £5; telephone £3. 10s; fuel/coal £3 [wood free from estate]; electricity £10; maintenance and repairs £10; wine £4; window cleaning £2. 5s.

289   Tennyson's *The Ancient Sage* was first published in *Tiresias and Other Poems*, 1885, but reached a wider readership in Nicholson and Leeds eds., *The Oxford Book of Mystical Verse*, 1917.

290   Political and Economic Planning adds another layer to Dorothy's life. It had been founded in 1931 under the chairmanship of Sir Basil Blackett of the Bank of England, where early meetings were held, with Max Nicholson, Gerald Barry (later director-general of the Festival of Britain), Lawrence Neal of the school outfitters Daniel Neal & Sons, Kenneth Lindsay, Julian Huxley and Leonard Elmhirst. Weekend gatherings were held at Dartington and from 1933 to 1963

the office was at 16 Queen Anne's Gate, SW1; see John Pinder ed., 1981.

291 Israel Sieff, *The Memoirs of Israel Sieff*, 1970, p. 192.

292 Nicholson, 'PEP through the 1930s: Growth, Thinking, Performance' in Pinder ed., pp. 32–53.

293 Kenneth Lindsay, 'PEP through the 1930s: Organisation, Structure, People' in Pinder ed., pp. 9–31, especially 'Origin and Birth' and 'The Contribution of Dartington'.

294 Liddell Hart quoted in Cox, Chapter 2 'Dartington as I found it', p. 20.

295 Young pp. 308–9.

296 The statue of Flora, 'a later 17th century figure cast in lead', was given to Leonard and Dorothy by the Dartington community on Foundation Day 1967, Snell p. 68.

297 Quoted in Young pp. 283–4 and comes from her lecture notes for her talks in America, which were typed out after her death, DWE/Lectures/1; LKE/USA/10.

298 Letter from Michael Chekhov in America, 25th October 1940, DWE/Arts/23.

299 *Dante Sonata* was first performed in London on 23rd January 1940.

300 Typescript 'My American Talk' from Noel Brailsford, DWE/G/1.

301 Lord Lothian died 'in post' on 12th December 1940.

302 That dinner was more influential than has been recognised for with presidential approval it gained for Britain – in the known, trusted and non-political Elmhirsts – the confidence of the Department of Agriculture. Wilson's influential career in the Department (USDA) is covered in some detail in Phillips, 2007.

303 The 'Food for Defense program', Phillips, pp. 215 ff. Nancy Astor wrote to Eleanor Roosevelt asking to make a speaking tour on Britain's behalf, but because of her strong political allegiance she was politely refused.

304 Natasha Litvin, aged twenty-one, married Stephen Spender on 9th April 1941 and after a fortnight in Cornwall they arrived at Dartington where she relished the rare opportunity to play on a concert grand piano.

305 All their schedules, stops and comments come from Dorothy's 1941 diary; notes for her talks are filed with LKE/USA/10.

306 Dorothy carefully noted that Leonard was to see Sir Owen Chalkley, British consul, and Sir Arthur Salter, chief of the Shipping Mission and his colleague in PEP, and consequently it has been suggested that Leonard's meetings had something to do with America's decision to give the Royal Navy the infamous 'Fifty Ships' as a symbol of good intent; his brother, now Air Commodore Thomas Elmhirst, may have been influential. Leonard's war work, rather secret, via USDA and PEP, let alone his influence in India, has never been explained, but post-war governments made repeated offers of a title as a reward, which he consistently refused.

307 Bliven p. 197.

308 Beatrice Straight was now twenty-seven, a successful actor with much of her mother's independence of mind. Louis Dolivet was extremely handsome but came as a surprise to Dorothy, i.e. a complete stranger; he was possibly a friend of Michael Straight's.

309 The Veterans Patriotic Hall has now been renamed in honour of Bob Hope, who did so much for military morale during the war.

310 Stewart Lynch, who had been appointed by Beatrix Farrand, was now unwell, and so David Calthorpe was the Hall's gardener; Snell p. 49.

311 Todd Gray, *Exeter in the 1940s: War, Destruction and Rebirth*, 2004, p. 70 ff.

312 Snell p. 49.

313 Reynolds, 1996, p. 161.

314 The Ministry of Information correspondence is in DWE/Lectures 1942–1945/1/A.

315 For WEA talks, DWE/L/1/B; for Women's Institutes and Townswomen's Guilds, DWE/L/1/C.

316 Frances Spalding, *John Piper, Mfanwy Piper: Lives in Art*, 2009, p. 228.

317 Margaret Mead was well known for her early researches in the South Seas: *Coming of Age in Samoa, Growing Up in New Guinea, Sex and Temperament in Three Primitive Societies*.

318 Cecil Collins, as in Chapter 9, note 4, and Naomi Rowe, *In Celebration: Cecil Collins*, 2008.

319 DWE/A/2; *Procession of Fools*, *The Happy Hour*, two of Dorothy's 'treasures' and three other paintings by Collins, with works by Alfred

Wallis, Winifred Nicholson, Christopher Wood, Ben Nicholson, John Piper, David Jones, Bernard Leach and Lucie Rie were sent to Sotheby's/Dartington Hall Trust sales 15th/16th November 2011 'sold to support the Trust's work in the Arts, Social Justice and Sustainability'.

320   Reynolds, particularly pp. 354 ff on D-Day.

321   Christopher Martin's work at Dartington is described by Michael Young in *The Elmhirsts of Dartington*, and with generosity and affection in the early pages of Cox, *The Arts at Dartington 1940–1983*; in a letter to the author 7th October 2012 Peter Cox wrote more of his relationship with the Martins.

322   Robert Herrick (1591–1674), 'To Daffodils', one of the *Five Flower Songs* set to music by Benjamin Britten and dedicated to 'Leonard and Dorothy Elmhirst on the occasion of their twenty-fifth Wedding Anniversary'. Herrick was a favourite poet of Dorothy's; he was given the living of Dean Prior just to the west of Dartington in 1630, lost it between 1647 and 1660, but spent the last fourteen years of his life in the village. See also Boris Ford ed., *Benjamin Britten's Poets: An anthology of the poems he set to music*, 1994, rev., 1996, p. 157.

323   Peter Cox and Jack Dobbs eds., *Imogen Holst at Dartington*, 1988, Imogen's candid interview with Jack Dobbs, pp. 9–27.

324   Cox and Dobbs p. 30; also Cox, Chapter 4 'Working with Imogen'.

325   From Dorothy's long hand-written eulogy, DWE/G/Roosevelt.

326   Ibid.

327   Cox p. 131.

328   Dorothy to Leonard in Bengal, 14th August 1944, quoted in Young p. 313.

329   The quotations from her *Garden Notebooks* are from Snell, Chapter 7, pp. 72 ff.

330   Percy Cane (1881–1976); his work is described in detail by Snell, Chapter 5 'Garden into Landscape'.

331   *The Gardens at Dartington Hall*, p. 7; Dorothy wrote this guide in 1965.

332   In the critical conversations I had prior to writing this book, with Lord Young who died in 2002, Michael Straight who died in 2004 and James Cornford who died in 2011, I gained a single strong impression that

I had to 'rescue' Dorothy from the powerful, perhaps overbearing men who surrounded her.

333   Eleanor Roosevelt, *On My Own*, 1959, Chapter 5 'With the U.N. in London', p. 69.

334   'a lady who lived on a farm' brought the eggs, ibid. p. 68.

335   Carpenter, 1992, pp. 221–4.

336   Ibid. pp. 226, 236.

337   Cox, Chapter 5 'Looking After Visiting Musicians', especially p. 40; also Carpenter, pp. 236–7.

338   Cox pp. 28–42 quoting Dorothy's letter of 28th January 1947 about her meeting with Anne Wood.

339   Kynaston, 2007, Chapter 7 'Glad to Sit at Home', p. 176.

340   *Letters Across the Atlantic, correspondence between Leonard and Dorothy and their daughter Ruth, 1939–46*, letters found after Ruth's death in 1986 and edited by her daughter Kate (Kathryn) Caddy for private circulation. The letters are affectionate but in reality, when she was back in England, 'Ruth fought a losing battle to be close to her mother' and after unsatisfactory relationships at Dartington she met and became engaged to Maurice Ash.

341   Louis Dolivet, *The United Nations: A Handbook on the New World Organization*, 1946, preface by Trygve Lie (First Secretary-General). This book and his marriage confirmed Dorothy's faith in Louis enough to give him a significant sum for his magazine, supposedly $250,000.

342   John Wellingham in conversation with the author, 2013. His interest in Shakespeare was allied to his expertise in Baroque and Early Music, especially for the organ, which he continued to teach.

343   Diana Barnato Walker, *Spreading My Wings*, 1994, pp. 197–9. Whitney Straight died on 5th April 1979; Diana died in 2008.

344   Dorothy to Peter Cox in America, 15th February 1947.

345   Bliven, Chapter 13, pp. 266–71. Paul Robeson and the folk singer Pete Seeger both joined Michael on the Wallace campaign.

346   Henry Moore quoted in *The Gardens at Dartington Hall*, p. 16.

347   Will Arnold-Forster, the marine painter, lived at Eagle's Nest at Zennor on the Cornish coast; he was the widower of Katharine 'Ka'

Cox, Rupert Brooke's 'the best I can do in the way of a widow'; he died in 1951.

348 Uday Shankar was already well known in Europe as an Indian dancer, but the younger Ravi (1920–2012) became internationally famous for his sitar playing, eventually living in America.

349 Sir Miles Thomas, *Out on a Wing*, 1964.

350 Young p. 316.

351 Robert Herrick, 'To Daffodils'.

352 Parker, 2014, pp. 11–12.

353 Sutherland, p. 345.

354 Frederick Gibberd, Ben Hyde Harvey, Len White et al., *Harlow: The Story of a New Town*, 1980, p. 244. The Elmgrant Trust had been set up in 1936 by the Elmhirsts and Beatrice Straight to give grants beyond the immediate Dartington spheres; initial funds were given to the Harlow Art Trust, chairman Sir Philip Hendy, and Henry Moore was commissioned for his majestic *Family Group* completed in 1956.

355 Michael Straight, *On Green Spring Farm*, 2004, his last book. See also Ross Netherton and Nan Netherton, *Green Spring Farm*, 1970, a history resulting from interviews with Michael and Belinda Straight, including Appendix G 'A Visit from Mr Polevoy', *The New Republic* 16th July 1956, a Project Gutenberg eBook online.

356 Harold Nicolson had been the Labour MP for West Leicester for ten years until 1945. He and Dorothy having politics and gardening in common were easy acquaintances and met at the RHS Vincent Square shows; orange notebook DWE/G/S7/E.

357 Kynaston pp. 391, 535.

358 Ibid. pp. 539–41 on Young's disenchantment.

359 William Elmhirst has written of this part of his life, *William & The Solar Quest*, 2010, see thesolarquest-theonlyway.com.

360 Sutherland p. 354.

361 *Five Flower Songs*, Op. 47 (1950), see Ford ed. The poems are Herrick's 'To Daffodils', 'The Succession of the Four Sweet Months', George Crabbe's 'Marsh Flowers', 'The Poor and their Dwellings', 'The Lover's

Journey', John Clare's 'The Evening Primrose' and 'The Ballad of Green Broom' (anon).

362 Mary Bartlett, *Inky Rags*, 2010, tells the story of the bindery.

363 Imogen Holst (1907–84), quoted from Cox and Dobbs; also Cox, Chapter 4; Carpenter pp. 310–12.

364 Victor Bonham-Carter and W.B. Curry, *Dartington Hall: The History of an Experiment*, 1958.

365 A possible reason for some of Whitney's bitterness was revealed by Diana Barnato Walker talking to Roland Perry in August 1999. She recalled Whitney being so upset that he had asked 'for a second Scotch' having heard that 'Michael is a Russian spy'; see Perry pp. 231–2.

366 The author in conversation with William Elmhirst.

367 Bruce Bliven, at the end of *Five Million Words Later*, writes of the sale of the paper, of his heart attack and retirement to California, where he died in 1977; his papers are in Stanford University Library.

368 Gilbert Harrison (1915–2008), publisher and editor-in-chief for twenty years from 1953, had a successful reign; he was pro-Civil Rights, against the Vietnam War and indulgent of the paper's losses; he raised the circulation to around a hundred thousand.

369 Gerald Barry, 'The Opening Ceremony' in Mary Banham and Bevis Hillier eds., *A Tonic to the Nation*, 1976, pp. 21–3.

370 Ibid., Audrey Russell, 'A broadcasting marathon', pp. 166–8; also 1951 South Bank Festival Guide, author's collection.

371 Dorothy to Irene Champernowne, quoted in Young p. 211, from sight of Dr Anthony Stevens's book on Withymead, prior to publication in 1986.

372 Her pencilled notes cover the programmes: Anthony Quayle is redeemed for his final humility, she finds Rosalind Atkinson's Volumnia 'holds the stage' though saying nothing, the witches are poor – should not be indoors – the production too dark, but 'the stage sinks for them', DWE/Arts/S1, programmes 1935–67.

373 7th September had been her wedding day, Willard Straight's lucky seven. The boy's father Louis Dolivet/Ludovic Brecher had by this time been exposed as a Comintern agent and banned from America

but he attended the funeral before returning to France where he was a successful film producer.

374 Beatrix Farrand was living quietly in Maine, though kept up her correspondence asking about the garden. Her last letter in early 1959 asked Leonard for photographs but by the time he sent them she had died, on 27ᵗʰ February 1959.

375 Her notes on her illness are from her 1955 diary.

376 Letter to Peter Cox, 5ᵗʰ July 1955.

377 Mrs Nancy Lancaster (1897–1994), a Virginian and niece of Nancy Astor, 'spirited, glamorous, funny and self-willed', was a partner in Colefax & Fowler of 39 Brook Street, and a renowned gardener; there is a biography by Robert Becker, 1996.

378 Dorothy from Harbour Island to Peter Cox, 31ˢᵗ January 1956.

379 Dorothy from Harbour Island to William Elmhirst, 17ᵗʰ February 1956.

380 Dorothy from Stratford-upon-Avon to Leonard, 10ᵗʰ September 1957, quoted in Young p. 252

381 Alan Bennett's play *An Englishman Abroad*, 1983, was written from Coral Browne's memory of Guy Burgess visiting the company; William Elmhirst in conversation with the author, 12ᵗʰ January 2012.

382 Dorothy to William Elmhirst in Scarborough, n.d. but autumn 1958.

383 Julian Huxley, *Memories*, 1970, *Memories II*, 1973.

384 Juliette Huxley, Epilogue pp. 236–7 prints this letter from Leonard dated November 1959.

385 Dorothy to William Elmhirst, n.d. but his birthday letter for February 1960, written from East Indies Farm, Canaan, Connecticut.

386 Ibid.

387 Dorothy from Pink Sands to Peter Cox, 22ⁿᵈ February 1960.

388 Dorothy from Pink Sands to Peter Cox, 21ˢᵗ March 1960.

389 Dorothy from Pink Sands to Peter Cox, 8ᵗʰ February 1961.

390 See Cox, 2005, especially Parts 2 and 3 (1973–83).

391 Ruth and Maurice Ash had a second daughter Marian born 1956, and Claire born 1957, and a son Anthony who died in infancy. Ruth restored Sharpham House and made her garden, she taught spinning

and weaving, maintained her musical interests and had many friends; she developed motor neurone disease and died on 31ˢᵗ August 1986. See also Maurice Ash's essay in John Snelling ed., *Sharpham Miscellany*, 1992.

392   President Kennedy and Michael had moved in the same circles for years; in 1957 the then Senator was a groomsman with Michael at the wedding of Nina Gore Auchincloss and Newton Steers, while Mrs Kennedy the bride's stepsister, was matron of honour; a photograph is in Gore Vidal's *Palimpsest: A Memoir*, 1995. Michael Straight later married Nina Steers; he also wrote *Twigs for an Eagle's Nest: Government and the Arts 1965–78*, 1979. Michael died in 2004.

393   The memory retained from the age of five (1921) until his confessional *After Long Silence*, along with the name of the gardener's boy, I think 'Jimmy'.

394   Carter, Chapter 17 'Penitent Impenitent' examines the operational misfortunes that beset British Intelligence during the 1960s, which perhaps protected Dorothy from any serious concern.

395   Rachel Harrison, *Dorothy Elmhirst and the Visual Arts at Dartington Hall 1925–1945*, 2002, thesis for the University of Plymouth, catalogues the collection.

396   DWE/Arts/2/A1 has the 1935–36 correspondence with Jim Ede, then nothing until 15ᵗʰ March 1964, 'I think of you so often' from Ede, followed by the ungracious (un-Dorothy like) lending of the Gaudier torso. Kettle's Yard has correspondence with Leonard November/December 1968 agreeing to the casting of the *Alabaster Boy*, one bronze to be the gift of the Elmhirsts to the University of Cambridge, arranged a few days before Dorothy's death; the bronze boy still resides at Kettle's Yard.

397   Dorothy gave the Moore maquette to Peter and Bobbie Cox; her Picasso was sold in 1975, and many of the other works including the *Alabaster Boy* (original) and Wood's *Pony and Trap, Ploare, Brittany* were sent for sale at Sotheby's by the Dartington Hall Trust in November 2011.

398   Dorothy from Pink Sands to William Elmhirst, 16ᵗʰ February 1967

(her last visit). Beatrice Straight's acting career moved from the stage to a long list of film and television credits, including an Oscar, and she played Rose Kennedy in *Robert Kennedy and His Times*, 1985; she died in Los Angeles in 2001.

399 Recording of her 1967 Founders' Day address in the Dartington Hall Trust Archive.

ACKNOWLEDGEMENTS

The genesis of *Angel Dorothy* has been long, too long, and it is with deep regret as well as gratitude that I look back to the generous encouragement given to me many years ago by Lord Young and Dorothy's son, Michael Straight. My debt to her youngest son William Elmhirst is acknowledged in the introduction (and dedication) and the names of Maurice Ash (her son-in-law), James Cornford, Peter Cox and Charlotte Johnson must be added to those for whom my book and gratitude come too late. Charlotte wrote a brilliant study of Percy Cane's work for her Garden Conservation diploma at the Architectural Association and she was to edit Dorothy's garden diaries, but was not given time.

For original permissions to use the Dartington archives I would also like to thank Kate Caddy (Dorothy's grand-daughter Kathryn Ash) and Paul B. Elmhirst (both Trustees), Mary Bride Nicholson (for the Elmgrant Trust), Ivor Stolliday, Katy Hockings, Angie St John Palmer, Maggie Giraud, Heather McIntyre and Lucy Bartlett, most of whom I saw when the archives were kept at High Cross House. My visits to Mary Bartlett were always enlightening and delightful. Latterly my thanks go to the kind and efficient staff of the Devon Record Office at Sowton, Exeter, and the detailed catalogue references for their holdings are given in my Notes. Also at Dartington, my thanks go to the former CEO Vaughan Lindsay, as well as to the former financial advisor Christopher Zealley.

ACKNOWLEDGEMENTS

My first visits to the Rare and Manuscript Collections in the Carl A. Kroch Library at Cornell University were before the days of online catalogues and so the published guides to Dorothy's papers (Coll. No. 3725) and Willard Straight's (Coll. No. 1260) by Ingeborg Wald and Patricia H. Gaffney respectively have proved invaluable. My thanks go especially to Heather Furnas at Cornell for updating my research. These sources are also given in detail in my Notes. Paper collections such as Dorothy's and Willard's become ever more precious, and it is a sobering thought that soon there will be no additions of this kind. Collection No. 3725 conveys both sides of a complete and candid love story, a romance conducted around the world as it existed before 1919 and the Treaty of Versailles; Collection No. 1260 holds Willard's descriptions, drawings and photographs of the last years of Imperial China; both bestow the gift of time-travelling beyond imaginary realms and both collections are of inestimable value.

I acknowledge the published sources for my quotations and for illustrations, all I hope carefully noted in the preceding pages. Vera Brice and Leslie Robinson have once again blessed a book of mine with maps and plans, though we are sad that this time it is too late for 'Rob' to see the result. Rex Nicholls drew the galleon and white hart images. Yvonne Widger's patience has made it possible to use the illustrations credited to Dartington, and I am grateful for her long experience of that archive.

My thanks as ever to Caradoc King and to Mildred Yuan and Millie Hoskins; to my tolerant friends, most especially Patricia Reed for her art historian's wisdom and her sustaining hospitality in Devon, and to Ursula Buchan for her critical reading of an earlier version of *Angel Dorothy* and for our neighbourly writer-to-writer conversations. I am delighted to have been 'adopted' by Unbound and applaud the founders Dan, Justin and John for reasserting the importance of readers and writers to publishers, and for their beautiful books. Mathew Clayton and DeAndra Lupu have created *Angel Dorothy* as she is launched out into what DeAndra calls 'her universe'; blessings on them, Tamsin Shelton, Mark Ecob, Lauren Fulbright and everyone at Waterside, and to all the readers and supporters who sail with her.

LIST OF IMAGES

William Collins Whitney [Online, originally DWS Coll. 3725, Series II, Cornell]   9

Flora Payne Whitney [DWS Coll. 3725, Series II, Cornell]   9

Pauline and Payne Whitney [Private collection]   12

Dorothy's debut portrait [Private collection]   21

Harry and Gertrude Whitney [Private collection]   23

Dorothy's house at Old Westbury [Private collection]   26

Willard Straight c.1910 [DWS Coll. 3725, Series II, Cornell]   37

Dorothy and Willard on honeymoon [DWS Coll. 3725, Box 9, Cornell]   59

Old Westbury from the air showing Chinese garden [Private collection]   63

Willard, Dorothy and baby Whitney [Swanberg/ Dartington Hall Trust]   65

Willard and the family, 'soldiers three' [DWS Coll. 3725, Series II, Cornell]   72

Dorothy and Leonard at Dartington, 1925 [Dartington Hall Trust]   110

Willard Straight Hall [L.K. Elmhirst, 1925, Dartington Hall Trust]   113

Dorothy's five children [Dartington Hall Trust]   135

The Dartington Hall estate, 1930s [Vera Brice]   141

Dartington Hall and gardens, 1930s [Vera Brice]   144

Dorothy photographed by Cecil Beaton [Private collection]   157

'Windblown' Dorothy at Whitney's wedding [Private collection]   158

Michael Chekhov at Dartington [Dartington Hall Trust]   169

Louise Croly and Dorothy, Naushon, 1937 [Private collection]   174

William, Leonard and Ruth, Naushon, 1937 [Private collection]   175

William, Dorcas Edwards and Eloise Elmhirst [Private collection]   184

Dorothy and William, Chappaquiddick [Private collection]   198

Leonard and Dorothy's first tour, autumn 1941 [Vera Brice]   200, 201

Their second tour, winter 1941–42 [Vera Brice]   203

Dorothy the gardener [Private collection]   205

The gardens at Dartington, 1960s [Vera Brice]   221

Leonard speaking [Private collection]   237

Founders' Day 1967 [Dartington Hall Trust]   263

Images of the Galleon and the White Hart throughout [Vera Brice, drawn by Rex Nicholls]

INDEX OF PERSONS

Adams, Henry, 50
Addams, Jane, 29, 34, 71, 225
Agassiz, Elizabeth, 10
Agassiz, Louis, 10, 17, 37
Alcott, Louisa M., 20
Aldrich, Chester, 63, 82, 95, 140
Aldrich, Harriet, 81
Andrews, Harry, 239, 247
Appiah, Joe, 249
Arnold-Forster, Will, 233–4
Arvin, Newton, 153
Ash, Gilbert and Mrs, 232
Ash, Kathryn, 239–40, 244, 250
Ash, Maurice, 229, 232, 234–5, 239–40, 243, 246, 259, 267
Ash, Ruth (née Elmhirst), 114, 118, 120–1, 134, 149–51, 154, 156, 158, 165, 175, 178, 183, 197–8, 226, 262
    courtship and marriage, 229, 232, 234–5, 239
    and Dartington trusteeship, 259
    distanced from Dorothy, 239–40
    and Dorothy's illness, 250
    and Dorothy's will, 267
Ashcroft, Peggy, 2, 130
Ashton, Frederick, 143, 191, 194, 209, 264
Astor, Nancy, 61, 65, 71, 73, 85, 121, 138, 195, 207–8
Astor, Waldorf, 61, 65
Atterbury, Grosvenor, 25, 32, 35, 150
Attlee, Clement, 247
Auchincloss, Gordon, 79
Auchincloss, Joseph Howland, 26
Auden, W.H., 138, 153
Ayckbourn, Alan, 254

Bach, J.S., 154, 216
Bacon, Bob, 26, 30, 32–3
Bacon, Robert, 25, 30, 33, 50
Baillie, Sir Adrian, 154, 157
Baillie, Lady Olive (née Paget), 21, 35, 57, 154, 157, 226

Balfour, Arthur, 85
Banks, Leslie, 160
Barber, Samuel, 226
Barker, George, 156, 162
Barnes, Courtland, 26, 30, 62
Barnes, Kate (née Barney), 26, 30, 34, 45, 62
Barnett, Canon Samuel, 34
Barney, Charles, 33
Barney, Lilley, 25
Barr, Margaret, 143
Barry, Gerald, 244, 246
Bateson, Gregory, 211
Bawden, Edward, 261
Beaton, Cecil, 6, 156–7
Beecham, Thomas, 244
Bend, Beatrice, see Fletcher, Beatrice
Bend, Marraine, 21–2, 26, 30, 44, 47–8, 50, 56–7, 108, 121
Bennett, George, 73, 77–8, 82, 84, 97, 150, 182
Bennett, Jill, 239
Berenson, Bernard, 85
Berlin, Irving, 75, 227
Berlin, Sven, 227
Bernal, J.D., 161
Berry, Walter, 52
Betjeman, John, 210
Bevan, Aneurin, 189, 241
Beveridge, William, 209
Billings, Rev., 80
Bing, Rudolf, 224
Bland, J.O.P., 45
Blériot, Louis, 40
Bliss, Mildred Woods, 145, 249
Bliss, Robert Woods, 249
Bliven, Bruce, 153, 179, 202, 227, 231, 241, 246
Bloom, Claire, 235
Blunt, Anthony, 156, 173–4, 177, 182, 260
Blunt, Wilfrid, 156
Bogue, Anna, 70, 82, 97–8, 103, 108, 122, 152, 163, 181–2, 232

INDEX OF PERSONS

Bonham-Carter, Victor, 245
Bowen, Elizabeth, 243
Boyce, William, 216
Brailsford, Noel, 136, 153, 171–2, 191, 195–6, 200, 210
Brando, Marlon, 226, 232
Brauner, Olaf M., 94
Brent, Bishop, 82
Britten, Benjamin, 2, 211, 216, 223–5, 234, 243–5, 249
Brooke, Peter, 228
Brooke, Rupert, 123–4, 132, 172
Brown, Sir Arthur Whitten, 86
Browne, Maurice, 123–5, 130, 155, 168
Bryan, William Jennings, 62
Brynner, Yul, 226
Buchan, John, 173
Buchanan, James, 9
Bull, Dr William T., 18
Burgess, Guy, 173, 254, 260
Burr, Professor George Lincoln, 95, 114
Burton, Richard, 247
Bute, Marquess of, 134
Buttinger, Muriel Gardiner, 243

Calthorpe, David, 164, 204
Cane, Percy, 219–22, 229, 233, 249, 251, 265
Carter, Miranda, 260
Carter, Peter, 257
Catt, Carrie Chapman, 122
Chamberlain, Neville, 178, 180
Champernowne, Arthur, 110–11
Champernowne, David, 159
Champernowne, Gilbert, 155
Champernowne, Irene, 155, 159, 235, 243, 248
Chaucer, Geoffrey, 75
Chekhov, Anton, 31, 151
Chekhov, Michael, 152–3, 155, 161, 163–4, 166–9, 175–84, 186, 192, 194, 202, 204, 206, 219, 228
Chermayeff, Serge, 139–40
Childers, Erskine, 173
Christie, Audrey, 225
Christie, John, 224–5
Churchill, Winston, 190, 198, 247–8
Clayton, Rev. Phillip 'Tubby', 92
Clement, Colonel, 208
Cleveland, Frances 'Frankie' (née Folsom), 11, see also Preston, Frances Cleveland
Cleveland, President Grover, 8–9, 11–12, 20
Clift, Montgomery, 234
Clive, Colin, 124
Cocteau, Jean, 261
Colefax, Lady, 192
Collins, Cecil, 150, 211–12, 261–2
Collins, Elisabeth, 211–12
Conan Doyle, Arthur, 20
Conrad, Joseph, 173
Cookson, Peter, 234, 249
Copland, Aaron, 226
Cornell, Ezra, 94
Cornford, Professor F.M., 172, 192
Cornford, Frances, 172, 192

Cornford, James, 5
Cornford, John, 161, 156, 172
Cornish, Miss ('Miss Aunt Nellie'), 133–4
Coward, Noël, 238
Cox, Bobbie, 257
Cox, Peter, 2, 192, 195, 212, 215–16, 218, 223, 225–7, 229, 231, 243
 and Dartington College of Arts, 256–8
 and Dorothy's illness, 250–2
Cripps, Peggy, 249
Cripps, Sir Stafford, 241
Croly, Herbert, 65–7, 71, 73, 79–80, 83–4, 90–2, 96, 122, 143, 153
 disillusion and death, 130–1
 and Dorothy's second marriage, 102, 105, 112, 148
Croly, Louise, 66, 96, 105, 125, 152, 175
Crompton, Belinda, see Straight, Belinda
Crosland, Anthony, 242
Cross, Joan, 216, 223
Crozier, Eric, 224–5
Curry, Ena, 127, 150, 154, 170
Curry, William Burnlee, 127–8, 154, 156, 167, 170, 194
Curzon, Clifford, 216
Curzon, Lucille, 216, 243

Daneman, Paul, 254
Darwin, Charles, 172
Davidson, Jo, 85
Davis, Cecil, 77, 203
Davison, Henry Pomeroy, 36, 48, 54–5, 57, 62, 64, 67–8, 79
de Tocqueville, Alexis, 10, 148
De Wint, Peter, 261
de Zoete, Beryl, 143–4, 169, 191–2, 194, 233
Delano, William Adams, 24, 63, 79, 94, 114, 140, 202, 232
Deller, Alfred, 216
Derby, Ethel (née Roosevelt), 47, 54–6, 63, 68–9, 83, 232
Derby, Dr Richard, 54–5, 63, 68, 70
Dewey, John, 1, 35, 88–9
 educational theories, 115, 126–7, 164
Diaghilev, Sergei, 31, 143
Dobb, Maurice, 160–1, 174
Dodge, Mabel, 87
Dolivet, Louis, 202, 204, 226–7, 232–3, 245
Dolivet, Willard, 226, 239, 241
 death, 248–50
Donne, John, 224, 244
Dorn, Marion, 139–40
Dostoevsky, Fyodor, 31
 The Possessed, 175–7, 181–2, 186
Douty, Kathleen (née Wills), 111
D'Oyly Carte, Bridget, 206–7
D'Oyly Carte, Rupert, 140
Draper, Charles, 109
Drayton, Michael, 111
du Maurier, Daphne, 191, 252

Eddy, Mary Baker, 85

Ede, Jim, 133, 169–70, 204, 261–2
Eden, Anthony, 155, 251
Eden, Michael, 173
Edward VII, King, 16, 27
Edward VIII, King, 171
Edwards, Bridget, 134, 154
Edwards, Dorcas, 134, 149–50, 165, 178, 183, 197,
    226, 234–5, 250
Egan, Martin and Eleanor, 79
Einstein, Albert, 89
Eisenhower, Dwight D., 213
Eliot, Charles William, 17
Eliot, T.S., 151, 228, 249
Elkins, Katherine, 49, 51, 55
Ellis, Clifford, 227
Ellis, Havelock, 108
Elmhirst, Charles, 111
Elmhirst, Eloise, 134, 149–50, 165, 178, 183, 197,
    226, 235–6, 248
Elmhirst, Heather, 5
Elmhirst, Irene Rachel, 106, 109
Elmhirst, Leonard, 2–3, 5, 99–113
    acquires Dartington Hall, 106–7, 109–13
    and Baillies' visit, 154–5
    Dartington philosophy, 137–8
    and Dartington school, 115–17, 126
    death, 267
    devotion to Dorothy, 165–6, 185–6, 206
    and Dorothy's will, 267
    and Farrand's praise for Dartington, 146–7
    given credit for Dartington, 264
    and lost baby, 118, 120
    remarries, 267
    and Second World War, 187–214
    sympathy for Juliette Huxley, 254–6
Elmhirst, Mary Knight, 111, 125, 194, 198, 227
Elmhirst, Pom, 109, 111
Elmhirst, Richard, 109, 125, 132, 134, 235–6
Elmhirst, Ruth Whitney, see Ash, Ruth
Elmhirst, Tommy, 110
Elmhirst, Victor, 108, 116, 126
Elmhirst, Rev. William, 111, 194, 234
Elmhirst, William Knight ('Bill'), 5–7, 125, 134,
    149–50, 156, 158, 165, 175, 178, 183, 197–8,
    204, 213, 215, 229, 231, 239, 256
    and Dorothy's illness, 250–2
    and Dorothy's last days, 263, 265–6
    and Dorothy's will, 267
    and Freudian analysis, 242–3
    marriage, 265
    and Old Westbury sale, 245–6
    stage career, 253–4
Emerson, Ralph Waldo, 44
Epstein, Jacob, 261
Evison, Miss, 232

Fairbanks, Douglas, 106
Falconer, Lord, 27, 33, 35, 51
Farrand, Beatrix, 4, 63, 67, 83, 95, 121, 145–6, 152,
    155, 164, 177, 180, 204, 222, 249, 264
Farrand, Livingston, 95, 114
Farrand, Professor Max, 95, 146–7

Ferrier, Kathleen, 226
Fincham, Albert, 120
Finch-Hatton, Christopher, 156
Finch-Hatton, Daphne, see Straight, Daphne
Flanagan and Allen, 232
Fleming, Ian, 157, 238–9
Fletcher, Beatrice (née Bend), 67, 81, 108, 121
    courtship and marriage, 50, 61, 73
    death, 199
    Dorothy's companion, 19, 21–2, 26, 30–1, 33,
        39, 47, 50, 54, 56, 61–2
    and Dorothy's marriage, 48–9, 52, 57
Fletcher, Henry Prather, 41, 44–6, 57, 81, 199, 202
    courtship and marriage, 50, 61, 73
Flynn, Errol, 155
Foch, Marshal, 78, 82
Fonteyn, Margot, 224
Foote, Bill, 229
Ford, John, 203
Forster, E.M., 104
Fox-Strangways, Elinor, 188
Fox-Strangways, Jane, 117, 124, 133, 136, 139, 152,
    187–8
France, Anatole, 89
Frankfurter, Felix, 66
Fraser, James Earle, 93
Fraser, Mary, 40
Freud, Sigmund, 162
Frewen, Moreton, 86
Froelick, Louis, 84, 152
Fry, Christopher, 249
Fry, Maxwell, 142, 161
Fry, Roger, 138, 261
Fullerton, Morton, 52

Gable, Clark, 228
Garnett, Constance, 175
Gaudier-Brzeska, Henri, 169, 261–2
George III, King, 241
George V, King, 153, 162
George VI, King, 195, 247–8
George, Prince (Duke of Kent), 155, 187, 207
Gerard, Sumner, 27
Gershwin, George, 204
Gibberd, Sir Frederick, 240
Gibran, Khalil, 151
Gielgud, John, 149
Gill, Eric, 261
Gilliatt, William, 114, 117, 122, 124, 151
Gimson, Ernest, 158
Gogol, Nikolai, 152
Gordon, Hugh, 156, 161
Graham, Martha, 142, 204
Grant, Duncan, 138
Grey of Falloden, Viscount, 86
Gropius, Ise, 140, 154
Gropius, Walter, 140, 142, 144, 150–1, 154, 159,
    161, 219
Gwatkin, Fred, 152

Haggard, Morna, 236
Hall, Peter, 254

INDEX OF PERSONS

Hamada, Shoji, 136
Hamilton, Alexander, 93–4
Hammond, Susie, 111, 116–17, 197
Hand, Judge Learned, 66
Hardy, Robert, 239
Harewood, Lord, 229
Harriman, Daisy, 25, 69, 72, 75, 234, 260
    and Willard's death, 79–82, 84–5, 96–7
Harriman, E.H. 'Papa', 18, 28, 33, 38–9, 53, 83
Harriman, Mary, 28–9, 33, 49
Harris, Margaret and Sophie, 254
Harrison, Benjamin, 12
Harrison, Gilbert, 245–6, 250
Hart, Sir Robert, 37
Harvey, Patrick, 170
Haseltine, Herbert, 85
Hawthorne, Nathaniel, 17
Hay, Alice, 16
Hay, Helen, see Whitney, Helen Hay
Hay, John, 16
Hayward, Louis, 190
Healy, Lieutenant, 82
Heard, Gerald, 137–9, 149–52, 155, 159, 162, 178
Heckroth, Hein, 186, 211
Heinemann, Margot, 172
Helpmann, Robert, 194, 224, 235
Hendy, Cicely (née Martin), 149, 157, 188, 195, 212, 223, 225, 240, 260
Hendy, Sir Philip, 212, 240, 260
Hening, Robert, 140, 142
Hepburn, Audrey, 249
Hepworth, Barbara, 2, 139–40, 247
Herrick, Robert, 153
Heuser, Mr, 116
Hill, Octavia, 34
Hitchens, Ivon, 139
Hitler, Adolf, 178–80, 182–3, 190, 202, 205
Hodgkins, Frances, 133, 227, 261
Holand (or Holland), John, 129
Holst, Gustav, 216
Holst, Imogen, 2, 211, 216–17, 223, 234, 243–5, 265
Hopkinson, Tom, 190
Hosking, Sarah, 5
House, Colonel Edward, 70–3, 78–9, 81, 97
House, Mrs Edward, 83
Hsuan-T'ung, Emperor ('Last Emperor'), 42, 60
Hull, Charles H., 114
Hull-Brown, Kathleen, 259
Humphrey, Hubert, 256
Huxley, Aldous, 139
Huxley, Julian, 254
Huxley, Juliette, 254–6

Ibsen, Henrik, 168, 181
Inman, Charles, 229
Irving, Washington, 17
Isaacs, Dr Susanna, 2, 267

Jackson, Sir Barry, 235
James, Henry, 1, 20, 30, 62
James, William, 88
Jay, Delancey, 27

Jefferies, Edith 'Jeff', 115, 120, 134, 156, 165, 175, 183–4, 197, 226
Jekyll, Gertrude, 3–4, 139
John of Gaunt, 129–30
Johnson, Alvin, 66
Johnson, 'Johnny', 244
Johnston, Major Lawrence, 111
Johnson, Lyndon Baines, 202
Jones, David, 139, 169, 261
Jones, John Paul, 20
Jooss, Aino, 144, 149, 152
Jooss, Anna, 144
Jooss, Kurt, 143–4, 149, 152, 154, 156, 159, 165, 173, 176–7, 186, 214
Joseph, Stephen, 254

Kazan, Elia, 232
Keble Martin, Rev. William, 244
Kennedy, Joan, 155
Kennedy, John F., 259–60
Kennedy, Joseph P., 178
Keppel, Alice, 16
Kerr, Philip, 85
Keynes, John Maynard, 70, 96, 138, 143–4, 174, 188, 224
Keynes, Lydia, see Lopokova, Lydia
Kinnicutt, Herman, 30, 153
Kinnicutt, May (née Tuckerman), 20–2, 30, 83, 153
Kintore, Lady, 35
Kipling, Rudyard, 46, 64, 75
Kok, Alexander ('Bobby'), 257
Kreisler, Fritz, 18

Laban, Rudolph, 176, 186
Lambart, Adelaide ('Addie') (née Randolph), 15–16, 21, 26, 68, 96, 157
Lambart, Lionel, 26
Lancaster, Nancy, 252
Laughton, Charles, 228
Leach, Bernard, 2, 117, 135–6, 261
Lean, David, 234
Leighton, Clare, 136, 204, 261
Leonard, Mrs, 85
Lescaze, William, 127, 140, 142, 153
Liddell Hart, Basil, 191, 213, 247
Lindeman, Edouard, 122
Lindsay, Kenneth, 96, 114, 190, 193
Lippmann, Walter, 66, 71, 79–80, 83, 143, 179, 199, 256
Littell, Phil, 66
Llewellyn, Richard, 203
Lodge, Oliver, 85
Longworth, Nicholas, 25, 38
Lopokova, Lydia, 138, 143–4, 224
Lothian, Lord, 196
Lovell, Keith, 257
Lupino, Ida, 190
Lutyens, Edwin, 3

MacArthur, General Douglas, 75–6, 199
MacDonagh, Donagh, 232
McCormick Blaine, Anita, 246

McKenna, Pamela, 157
Maclean, Donald, 243, 260
McNally, Charles, 244, 266
Madison, Dolley, 8
Maitland, Joe, 229
Mansbridge, Albert, 92, 96, 208, 225, 244
Martin, Christopher, 149–50, 152–3, 157, 186–8, 192, 195, 212, 258
  death, 213–16, 224–5
  memorial, 229, 262
Martin, Rev, J.S., 149
Mary, Queen, 153
Masefield, John, 112
Mason, James, 230
Matisse, Henri, 222
Mead, Margaret, 211
Meyer, George von Lengerke, 36
Milburn, Devereux, 26
Miller, Arthur, 239
Miller, Edith Starr, 96, 101
Milne, Oswald P., 140, 143
Milton, John, 132, 168
Minto, 4th Earl of, 46
Mitchel, John Purroy, 73–4, 76
Mitchel, Olive, 76
Mitford, Nancy, 1
Monroe, Marilyn, 226
Montgomery, Elizabeth, 254
Moore, Henry, 139, 169, 229, 231, 240, 247, 261
Morgan, Edwin V., 37
Morgan, J.P., 48, 54–5, 60, 62
Morgan, Ruth, 29, 79, 88, 97, 105, 108, 114, 122
Morris, Henry, 142
Morrison, Herbert, 244, 247
Mosley, Oswald, 138
Mukherjee, Dr, 236
Murphy, Major Grayson, 75–6, 79, 131

Navarro, Mary Anderson de, 5, 111
Neill, A.S., 126
Newell, Professor Arthur, 208
Nicholson, Ben, 2, 132–3, 138, 140, 169, 247, 261–2
Nicholson, Jake, 133
Nicholson, Mary Bride, 259
Nicholson, Max, 189–90, 193
Nicholson, Winifred, 133, 140, 261–2
Nicolson, Harold, 137, 179, 208, 241
Niven, David, 155

O'Casey, Eileen, 165
O'Casey, Sean, 165, 176
Odlin, Richard, 132, 134, 136, 161, 168, 214
Olivier, Laurence, 123–4
Olmsted, Frederic Law, 4
O'Neill, Eugene, 87–8, 91, 130, 144
Oppenheim, Cissy, 244
Oppenheim, Hans, 181, 186, 244
Orage, Alfred, 130

P'u Lun, Prince, 41–2
Paderewski, Jan, 18

Paget, Almeric (Lord Queenborough), 14, 16, 21, 57, 86, 96, 101, 157, 239
Paget, Dorothy, 35, 57
Paget, Olive, see Baillie, Lady Olive
Paget, Pauline ('Polly') (née Whitney), 11, 13–14, 16, 19, 33, 35, 57, 120
  and Dorothy's marriage, 49–50
  illness and death, 47, 68, 71
Pankhurst, Christabel, 36
Pankhurst, Sylvia, 36
Parkhouse, William, 126
Parkinson, Sir John, 250
Payn, Graham, 238
Payne, Colonel Oliver Hazard, 10, 12, 14
Pears, Peter, 211, 216, 223, 225
Peck, Gregory, 249
Perry, Captain Oliver Hazard, 10
Perry, Commodore Matthew, 40
Pershing, General John, 82, 84–5
Peters, Ray, 172
Philby, Kim, 174, 260
Philip, Elmslie, 227
Phillips, William, 57, 77
Picasso, Pablo, 174, 222, 260
Piper, John, 189, 209–11, 262
Piper, Myfanwy, 210
Pole, Lady Beatrice Carew, 123
Porter, Cole, 75
Preston, Frances Cleveland, 81, see also Cleveland, Frances 'Frankie' (née Folsom)
Priestley, J.B., 234
Pritchard, Jack, 142, 161
Pritchard, Molly, 142
Proust, Marcel, 256

Quayle, Anthony, 235, 254

Ramsden, Elisabeth, 150
Randolph, Adelaide, see Lambart, Adelaide
Randolph, Arthur ('Bertie'), 15, 21, 68, 71
Randolph, Edith, 14–15, 37
Rawson, Wyatt, 116
Redgrave, Michael, 247, 249
Reed, Carol, 128, 230
Reed, John, 87
Rees-Mogg, Colonel, 111
Reid, Whitelaw, 35
Reinhardt, Max, 168
Richardson, Arthur, 243
Richardson, Ralph, 253
Rie, Lucie, 261
Rimsky-Korsakov, Nikolai, 31
Roberts, William, 261
Robeson, Paul, 2, 130, 160
Robinson, Corinne Roosevelt, 53, 84
Robinson, Mary ('Perdita'), 132
Rockefeller, John D., 8, 10
Roosevelt, Alice, 25, 28, 33, 38
Roosevelt, Archie, 83
Roosevelt, Eleanor, 90, 163, 175, 177–8, 194, 197, 217–18, 222–3
Roosevelt, Ethel, see Derby, Ethel

INDEX OF PERSONS

Roosevelt, Franklin D., 90, 153, 177, 190, 194, 196,
    198–9, 202, 206, 211
    death, 217–18, 227, 230
Roosevelt, Kermit, 47–8, 83
Roosevelt, Quentin, 70, 74, 76, 85–6
Roosevelt, Theodore, 16, 25, 47–8, 54, 62, 67, 71,
    76, 97
    death, 83–4
    Rough Riders, 27, 41
Roosevelt, Theodore junior, 70, 83
Root, Elihu, 25, 39, 46
Roper, Lanning, 4
Roper, Laura Wood, 4
Rosa, Carl, 110
Rose, Milton, 152, 241
Rothermere, Ann, 238
Rothschild, John, 92, 105, 122
Rothschild, Victor, 173, 182
Rowntree, Benjamin Seebohm, 92, 111
Rubinstein, Arturo, 150
Rudyard, Charlotte, 71
Rumsey, Charles Cary, 49
Russell, Audrey, 247
Russell, Bertrand, 87, 89, 137
Russell, Geoffrey, 226

Sacco and Vanzetti, 1, 89, 95
Sackville-West, Vita, 3, 138, 178–9
St Aubyn, Gwen, 178
Sanborn, Dorothy, 204
Sanderson, Frederick William, 113
Sauer, Colin, 257
Schiaparelli, Elsa, 148
Schneiderman, Rose, 90
Schofield, Paul, 235
Schuman, William, 226
Schwarzkopf, Elisabeth, 244
Scott, Elizabeth, 235
Seale, Douglas, 254
Seaman, Richard ('Dick'), 151–2, 157
Shakespeare, William, 5, 111, 132, 193, 212, 228,
    235, 239, 253
    All's Well that Ends Well, 252
    As You Like It, 253
    Coriolanus, 248, 254
    Cymbeline, 239
    Hamlet, 149, 162, 167, 235
    Henry IV, Parts 1 and 2, 247
    Henry V, 247
    Henry VIII, 239
    Julius Caesar, 244
    King John, 253
    King Lear, 168, 190, 244, 249
    Love's Labour's Lost, 228, 231
    Macbeth, 231, 239, 248, 251, 253
    Measure for Measure, 244
    The Merchant of Venice, 235
    The Merry Wives of Windsor, 251
    A Midsummer Night's Dream, 239
    Much Ado about Nothing, 239, 254
    Othello, 130, 235, 239
    Richard II, 129–30

The Taming of the Shrew, 168
    The Tempest, 248
    Twelfth Night, 167, 195, 199, 202, 204, 206,
    212, 251, 254
    The Winter's Tale, 235
Shankar, Ravi, 236
Shankar, Uday, 236
Sharman, John, 248
Shaw, George Bernard, 65, 96, 105
Sherriff, R.C., 123–4, 130
Sieff, Israel, 189–90, 193
Simon, Brian, 160–1
Simpson, Wallis, 171
Sinden, Donald, 234
Sitwell, Osbert, 210
Slater, Dr W.K. ('Bill'), 127, 237
Slattery, Rev., 82
Smith, James 'Silent', 54
Smythson, Frank, 148
Soelberg, Louise, 132, 134, 143
Soukop, Willi, 186
Soule, George, 66, 202
Sousa, John Philip, 11
Spalding, Frances, 210
Spence, Clara, 20
Spender, Lizzie, 243
Spender, Natasha, 197, 209–10, 239, 243, 260
Spender, Stephen, 197, 209–10, 239, 243, 260
Spring-Rice, Cecil, 9
Spry, Constance, 197, 219
Stanislavsky, Konstantin, 31, 163, 171
Steiner, Rudolf, 183
Stephens, Professor Henry Morse, 51, 98
Stevenson, Robert Louis, 20
Stewart, Murray, 45
Stokowski, Leopold, 127
Stone, Clara, 16
Straight, Amanda, 248
Straight, Beatrice Whitney ('Biddy'), 67, 71, 73, 75,
    86, 92
    in America, 152, 156, 158, 163–4, 169, 177,
    181–4, 187, 192, 194
    courtship and marriage, 202, 204, 232–4
    and Dorothy's last days, 263
    and Dorothy's second marriage, 102, 104–5,
    107–8, 114–16, 121, 135
    godmother to Bill, 125
    and Old Westbury sale, 245–6
    stage career, 132, 186, 195, 199, 202, 204, 206,
    226, 239, 241
    and Willard's death, 249–50
Straight, Belinda (née Crompton), 4, 167, 177, 179,
    183, 197, 204, 209, 232, 234, 241, 247, 250, 256
Straight, Camilla, 178, 181, 206, 231, 233, 245–7
Straight, Daphne (née Finch-Hatton), 150, 153,
    155–8, 162, 178, 181, 187, 233, 239, 246, 248
Straight, David Willard, 209, 234, 243
Straight, Dorothy, 256
Straight, Emma, 37
Straight, Hazel, 37, 50
Straight, Henry, 37
Straight, Laura, 50

Straight, Michael Whitney, 5, 71, 92, 96, 125, 132, 159, 179, 199, 209, 247
 in America, 175, 177–80, 182–4, 187, 197–9, 204, 209, 226, 238, 241, 250
 and Cambridge, 149, 151, 167, 172–5
 compared with Willard, 230
 courtship and marriage, 177, 179, 183
 and Dorothy's last days, 263
 and Dorothy's second marriage, 102, 104–5, 108, 114–16, 121, 134–5
 and family money, 240–1
 friendship with Kennedys, 259–60
 and Old Westbury sale, 245–6
 political ambitions, 230–1, 234, 240, 243, 246
 retains American citizenship, 162
 visits Russia, 160–1
 and Whitney, 126, 149, 151, 156, 162–3, 244
 writing career, 236, 256
Straight, Mikey, 234
Straight, Whitney Willard, 62, 69, 71, 73, 75–6, 86, 92, 162, 178, 181, 232, 239
 commercial flying career, 228, 236, 240
 and Dorothy's second marriage, 102–5, 107–8, 114–16, 121, 135
 finances, 267
 and flying, 126–7, 149, 151–2
 marriage and wedding, 150–1, 153, 155–9
 and Michael, 126, 149, 151, 156, 162–3, 244
 and Old Westbury sale, 245–6
 takes British citizenship, 162, 174
 war service, 187, 193, 195, 201, 204, 228
Straight, Willard, 1, 33, 36–8
 architectural pursuits, 63, 67
 and cancellation of Chinese loans, 62, 64, 97
 Chinese mementoes, 163
 compared with FDR, 218
 courtship and marriage, 40–57
 Croly's biography, 84, 93, 96, 98, 102, 131
 death, 80–6
 drawings and sketches, 182
 finances, 64
 and First World War, 67–79
 honeymoon, 58–61
 ill health, 77–80
 launches New Republic, 65–6, 90–1
 married life, 64
 memorials, 94–5, 98
 Professor Stephens' testimonial, 51–2
Strasberg, Lee, 163, 226
Stravinsky, Igor, 31
Sun Zhongshan, 60
Sutcliffe, Peter, 237
Sutherland, Graham, 261
Suttie, Dr Ian Dishart, 162
Swanberg, W.A., 3
Szechenyi, Gladys (née Vanderbilt), 13–14, 21, 34, 68, 86, 152, 156–7, 266
Szechenyi, Gladys (daughter), 86, 156
Szechenyi, Count Laszlo, 34

Taft, William Howard, 36

Tagore, Rabindranath, 100, 102, 105–6, 125, 154, 185
Tanner, Henry, 110
Tennyson, Alfred, 188
Thomas, Emily, 267
Thomas, Sir Miles, 236
Thomas, Walter, 134, 138, 218, 228, 259
Thompson, Francis, 151
Tipping, Henry Avray, 117, 121
Tobey, Mark, 132, 135–6, 150, 214, 261, 264
Tolstoy, Count Leo, 30, 31, 160
Tower, Roderick, 86
Truman, Harry S., 227, 230, 236, 243
Twain, Mark, 78

Ullman, Lisa, 177, 186
Underwood, Molly, 250

Van Allen, Commander James, 213
van der Post, Laurens, 243
van der Rohe, Mies, 128
Van Rensselaer, Martha, 94
Van Volkenburg, Ellen, 123–4, 132, 168, 186, 214, 264
Vanderbilt, Alfred, 70
Vanderbilt, Consuelo, 14, 34
Vanderbilt, Gertrude, see Whitney, Gertrude
Vanderbilt, Gladys, see Szechenyi, Gladys
Vaughan Williams, Ralph, 247

Wald, Lillian, 29–30, 56–7, 83
Wales, John, 126
Waley, Arthur, 143, 169, 191–2, 194, 233
Walker, Barney, 236, 243–4
Walker, Diana Barnato, 228, 236, 243
Wallace, Henry, 177, 196, 201, 227, 230–2, 234, 236, 240, 243, 246
Wallis, Alfred, 133, 261
Warren, Lloyd, 25
Webb, Beatrice, 34, 60, 65
Webb, Sidney, 60, 65
Weinstein, Louisa, 26, 39–40, 51, 56, 73, 84, 97, 114
Weir, William, 147, 264
Wellingham, John, 228
Wells, H. G., 71, 89, 113
Whale, James, 124
Wharton, Edith, 50, 52, 63, 180
Whitehouse, Sheldon, 35
Whitman, Walt, 90
Whitney, Barbara, 24, 108
Whitney, Dorothy
 acquires Dartington Hall, 106–7, 109–13
 affection for Peter Cox, 256–8
 architectural schemes, 63, 67
 art collection, 261–2
 buys Fool paintings, 212
 buys Picasso, 260–1
 childhood, 8–18
 coming-out ball, 25
 courtship, 40–51
 and Dartington College of Arts, 256–8
 and Dartington philosophy, 137–8

and Dartington school, 115–17, 120, 126
death, 266
disillusion with Labour Party, 241–2
early reading, 20
education, 20
and Farrand's praise for Dartington, 146–7
and Festival of Britain, 235–6, 244, 246
finances, 19–20, 64, 112, 240–1, 266–7
first visit to Europe, 20–3
and First World War, 67–79
and grandson's death, 248–9
harshness of temper, 218
honeymoon, 58–61
illness, 250–2
interest in gardens, 145–6
John Piper describes, 210
and Jungian therapy, 242–3
last letter to Willard, 88
launches *New Republic*, 65–6, 90–1
loneliness in England, 119–20
loses baby, 118, 120
love of theatre, 87–8, 123–4
married life, 64, 165–6, 185–6, 206
MoI talks, 208–9
and Old Westbury sale, 245–6, 248–50
retains American citizenship, 112
revives Dartington garden, 219–20
'Samaritan of all', 87, 96, 100
second marriage, 99–113
and Second World War, 180–1, 187–214
and social work, 28–30, 34–5
suffers breakdown, 96–8
suitors, 25–7, 32–5
support for the arts, 132–6, 139–40, 142–4,
    149–50, 154, 167–70
supports Glyndebourne, 224–6
and teacher training, 88
travels to the East, 39–46
typical charitable commitments, 122
and Whitney pedigree, 129–30
will, 267
and Willard's death, 80–6, 96–8
and women's suffrage, 35–6
Whitney, Eli, 8, 94, 150
Whitney, Elinor, 8
Whitney, Etta, 148
Whitney, Flora (mother), 8, 10–18, 20, 22, 37, 63 94
Whitney, Flora (niece), 24, 71, 74, 76, 83–4, 86, 108
Whitney, Gertrude (née Vanderbilt), 14–15,
    21–2, 24–5, 27, 49, 54, 68, 74, 81, 87, 148, 152,

182–4, 202
and Dorothy's second marriage, 108–9
Whitney, Harry, 11, 13–15, 18–19, 21–3, 27, 30, 61,
    74, 112
'Big Four' polo team, 26, 40
buys back father's house, 53–4
death, 131, 148
and Dorothy's marriage, 49, 51, 56–7
and Dorothy's second marriage, 108–9
and First World War, 68
legacy, 145
and Michael Straight, 174
Whitney, Helen Hay, 16, 25, 27, 36
Whitney, John, 8
Whitney, Leonora, 11
Whitney, Olive, 11–12, 18
Whitney, Pauline, *see* Paget, Pauline
Whitney, Payne, 11, 13–14, 16, 19, 27, 36, 81, 109
    death, 119, 148
Whitney, Robert de, 129–30
Whitney, Sonny, 24, 108, 183
Whitney, William Collins, 8–11, 14–20
Wilbur, Bishop, 109
Wilkie, Wendell L., 199–200
Williams, Heather, 265
Wilson, Edmund, 130
Wilson, Milburn L., 196, 199
Wilson, Woodrow, 62, 64, 67, 70–1, 78–9, 88, 97,
    199
Winchilsea and Nottingham, Countess of, 152, 156
Winchilsea and Nottingham, Earl of, 152
Winn, Pauline, 154
Winn, Susan, 154, 226
Winterbotham, Hiram, 192, 211
Wise, Marjorie, 116, 124, 127
Wodehouse, P. G., 151
Wood, Anne, 225
Wood, Christopher ('Kit') (painter), 132–3, 138,
    169, 261–2
Wood, Christopher (pianist), 137
Woolf, Virginia, 138
Wootton, Barbara, 191
Worth, Jean-Philippe, 22
Worth, Monsieur, 22

Yeats, W.B., 256
Young, Michael, 3, 5, 126, 130, 149, 156, 181, 185,
    222, 229, 242, 266–7
Yuan Shikai, General, 60 Supporters

SUPPORTERS

Unbound is a new kind of publishing house. Our books are funded directly by readers. This was a very popular idea during the late eighteenth and early nineteenth centuries. Now we have revived it for the internet age. It allows authors to write the books they really want to write and readers to support the books they would most like to see published.

The names listed below are of readers who have pledged their support and made this book happen. If you'd like to join them, visit www.unbound.com.

Libby Allen
Rafaele Appleby
Anne Arculus
Evelyn Balaam
Mary Bartlett
Cath Barton
Jeanne Battye
Lindsey Brodie
Julia Brown
Lesley Brown
Nicholas Brown
Philip Brown
Ursula Buchan

David Cadman
Jill Cansell
Georgina Churchlow
Dominic Cole
Harriet Cox
Suzanne Curtis
Rose Dejardin
Alvena Downing
Jon Edgar
Heather Elmhirst
William Elmhirst
Rick Faulkner
Keith Fielder